COLLEGE
WRITING
SKILLS

~~J. Mathison~~
~~Cindy Lapierre~~
~~L. Tremblay~~
~~L. Wormboldt~~
~~Brian Esprie~~
~~Jereda Adcock~~
~~Grant Boyington~~
Amanda Ferguson.

4910

COLLEGE
WRITING
SKILLS

THIRD EDITION

JOHN LANGAN
Atlantic Community College

McGraw-Hill, Inc.
New York St. Louis San Francisco Auckland Bogotá
Caracas Lisbon London Madrid Mexico City Milan
Montreal New Delhi San Juan Singapore
Sydney Tokyo Toronto

This book is printed on acid-free paper.

COLLEGE WRITING SKILLS

67890   DOC DOC   909876543

ISBN 0-07-036382-X

This book was set in Times Roman by Monotype Composition Company.
The editors were Lesley Denton and Susan Gamer.
The cover was designed by Rafael Hernandez.
R. R. Donnelley & Sons Company was printer and binder.

Library of Congress Cataloging-in-Publication Data

Langan, John, (date).
   College writing skills / John Langan. — 3rd ed.
      p.   cm.
   Includes index.
   ISBN 0-07-036382-X
   1. English language—Rhetoric.   2. English language—
Grammar—1950-   3. Essay.   I. Title.
PE1471.L34   1992
808'.042'0711—dc20   91-23765

ABOUT
THE AUTHOR

John Langan has taught reading and writing at Atlantic Community College near Atlantic City, New Jersey, for over twenty years. The author of a popular series of college textbooks on both subjects, he enjoys the challenge of developing materials that teach skills in an especially clear and lively way. Before teaching, he earned advanced degrees in writing at Rutgers University and in reading at Glassboro State College. He also spent a year writing fiction that, he says, "is now at the back of a drawer waiting to be discovered and acclaimed posthumously." While in school, he supported himself by working as a truck driver, machinist, battery assembler, hospital attendant, and apple packer. He presently lives with his wife, Judith Nadell, near Philadelphia. Among his everyday pleasures are running, working on his Macintosh computer, and watching Philadelphia sports teams or *L.A. Law* on TV. He also loves to read: newspapers at breakfast, magazines at lunch, and a chapter or two of a recent book ("preferably an autobiography") at night.

CONTENTS

PART FOUR
HANDBOOK OF SENTENCE SKILLS

TO THE INSTRUCTOR

College Writing Skills will help students master the traditional five-paragraph essay. It is a very practical book with a number of special features to aid teachers and their students.

KEY FEATURES

- ■ ***Four principles are presented as keys to effective writing.*** These four principles—unity, support, coherence, and sentence skills—are highlighted on the inside front cover and reinforced throughout the book. Part One focuses on the first three principles; Part Four serves as a concise handbook of sentence skills. The other parts of the book show how the four principles apply in different types of essay development (Part Two) and in specialized types of writing (Part Three).

- ■ ***Activities and assignments are numerous and varied.*** For example, in the opening two chapters there are over twenty activities to help students learn how to advance and support a thesis. There are over one hundred activities in the entire book. Such activities serve as an essential step between the explanation of a skill and a student's full understanding of that skill.

    A variety of writing assignments follows each of the types of essay development in Part Two. Some topics are highly structured, for students needing such support; others require more work on the part of the student. Instructors thus have the option of selecting those assignments most suited to the individual needs of their students.

■ ***Clear thinking is stressed throughout.*** This focus on logic starts with the section "To the Student" on page xvii. Then, in an early chapter (see page 34), students are introduced to the two principles that are the bedrock of clear thinking: *making a point* and *providing support to back up that point.* The focus on these principles continues throughout the book: a section on outlining in Part One offers practice in distinguishing between main and supporting ideas; writing assignments in Part Two provide direction in planning papers that support and develop a central point; many other activities in the book require students to develop basic thinking skills; a form that will help students prepare a well-thought-out essay appears on the inside back cover of the book. In short, students learn that clear writing is inseparable from clear thinking.

■ ***The traditional essay is emphasized.*** Students are asked to write formal essays with an introduction, three supporting paragraphs, and a conclusion. Anyone who has tried to write a solidly reasoned essay knows how much work is involved. A logical essay requires a great deal of mental discipline and close attention to a set of logical rules. Writing an essay in which there is an overall thesis statement and in which each of three supporting paragraphs begins with a topic sentence is more challenging than writing a free-form or expressive essay. The demands are significant, but the rewards are great.

Such a rigorous approach may seem limiting. But students discover quickly enough on their own that the rules can be broken. Indeed, in the general media they are exposed to daily, they see those rules being broken all the time (at times to the detriment of clear communication and sound thinking). First-year college students do not need to work on breaking or going beyond the rules; they need to learn the rules thoroughly and practice using them. Freedom to move beyond the rules effectively is possible only when they know what the rules are. Mastering the rules is, in fact, the cornerstone that students can build on to become powerful and versatile writers.

■ ***Writing is treated as a process.*** The second chapter, "Important Factors in Writing," discusses prewriting, rewriting, and editing. In addition, many writing assignments are accompanied by "Suggestions on How to Proceed" that give step-by-step directions in the process of writing a paper.

■ ***Lively models are provided.*** One (though by no means the only) way that students learn is by imitation. *College Writing Skills* thus provides several high-interest essays with each assignment. Students read and evaluate these essays in terms of the four standards: unity, support, coherence, and sentence skills. Student essays appear in place of professional ones, which typically run longer than five hundred words and vary widely from the regular five-paragraph format. The book assumes that students are especially interested in and challenged by the writing of their peers. After reading vigorous papers composed by other students and experiencing the power that good writing can have, students will be more encouraged to aim for similar honesty, realism, and detail in their own work.

■ ***The book is versatile.*** Since no two people use an English text in exactly the same way, the material has been organized in a highly accessible manner. Each of the five parts of the book deals with a distinct area of writing. Instructors can therefore turn quickly and easily to the skills they want to present.

■ ***Helpful learning aids accompany the book.*** Instructors will find useful the checklist of the four steps in essay writing on page 119 and the inside front cover. Also helpful will be the form for planning an essay on the inside back cover and the list of correction symbols on the last page. A thorough *Instructor's Manual* includes a model syllabus, suggestions for using the book, a detailed answer key, and mastery tests for a number of key skills in essay writing. In addition, a revised *set of thirty ditto master tests* is provided free to those adopting the text. These tests offer practice in a wide range of skills covered in the book, from generating and narrowing a thesis to outlining essays to editing papers for such common mistakes as fragments, verb problems, and run-ons. Both the Instructor's Manual and the ditto masters are available from the local McGraw-Hill representative or by writing to the College English Editor, McGraw-Hill, Inc., 1221 Avenue of the Americas, New York, New York 10020.

CHANGES IN THE THIRD EDITION

There are some significant changes in, and additions to, the new edition of *College Writing Skills*:

■ The chapter *"Important Factors in Writing"* has been revised and relocated; it is now the second chapter of the book. There are new sections on keeping a journal, writing as a process of discovery, prewriting in the form of diagramming or "mapping," and distinctions between editing and proofreading, as well as additional practice activities.

■ *"Introduction to Essay Development"*—the first chapter in Part Two—has been greatly expanded. Sections added are "Point of View in Writing,"

"Writing for a Specific Purpose and Audience," "Using Peer Review," and "Using a Personal Checklist."

- A new writing assignment is now included with each type of essay development in Part Two. This new assignment requires *writing with a specific purpose and for a specific audience.* (The student is asked, for example, to imagine himself or herself as an author of a campus newspaper column giving advice on romance.) This assignment helps round out a sequence of writing activities that progress from personal to objective topics.
- The chapter *"Using the Library"* has been substantially revised. It emphasizes the basic steps that students need to take in exploring possible topics for a research paper. It also describes the computerized search facilities that are a part of today's libraries.
- The chapter *"Writing a Research Paper"* has been expanded to include careful guidelines for MLA documentation and a complete model research paper.
- There are additions to many of the chapters in Part Four, "Sentence Skills." The chapter on *run-on sentences* now distinguishes clearly between fused sentences and comma splices and includes more activities. One of the chapters on verbs has been revised to include *standard and irregular verbs; wordiness* is now treated as part of a chapter on effective word use; a new chapter covers *adjectives and adverbs.* There are more practice materials for sentence fragments, subject-verb agreement, consistent verb tense, misplaced and dangling modifiers, parallelism, the comma, and commonly confused words.
- A newly designed Instructor's Manual includes, whenever possible, separate answer sheets for each skill. Teachers can easily copy the appropriate sheets and pass them out to students for self-teaching. And an expanded set of ditto masters provides more tests and activities than were previously available.

ACKNOWLEDGMENTS

Reviewers who have contributed to this edition through their helpful comments include Gale Alston, Roxbury Community College; Edna Boykin, Florida Agricultural and Mechanical University; John Covolo, Lakeland Community College; Linda Wheeler Donahue, Mattatuck Community College; Evelyn Etheridge, Paine College; Elaine Fitzpatrick, Massasoit Community College; Cara Fuchs, Fairleigh Dickinson University; Daniel B. Gallagher, Laredo Junior College; Cyril M. Leder, Mott Community College; Patricia Maida, University of the District of Columbia; Kathleen L. Pickard, Cuayahoga Community College;

Betty Slifer, College of Southern Idaho; and Linda Suddeth Smith, Midlands Technical College.

I wish to expecially acknowledge the review of June W. Siegel—the latest of many I have received over the years that have always been as lively as they are insightful. I also thank my McGraw-Hill editors, Lesley Denton and Sue Gamer, for their talented support. Finally, I am grateful to Janet M. Goldstein, Elaine J. Lessige, Carole Mohr, and my wife Judy Nadell, all writers and colleagues who provided ideas as I worked on the third edition.

JOHN LANGAN

TO
THE
STUDENT

The experience I had writing my first college essay has helped shape this book. I received a C− for the essay. Scrawled beside the grade was the comment, "Not badly written, but ill-conceived." I remember going to the instructor after class, asking about his comment as well as the word *Log* that he had added in the margin at various spots. "What are all these logs you put in my paper?" I asked, trying to make a joke of it. He looked at me a little wonderingly. "Logic, Mr. Langan," he answered, "logic." He went on to explain that I had not thought out my paper clearly. There were actually two ideas rather than one in my thesis, one supporting paragraph had nothing to do with either idea, another paragraph lacked a topic sentence, and so on. I've never forgotten his last words. "If you don't think clearly," he said, "you won't write clearly."

I was speechless, and I felt confused and angry. I didn't like being told that I didn't know how to think. I went back to my room and read over my paper several times. Eventually, I decided that my teacher was right. "No more logs," I said to myself. "I'm going to get these logs out of my papers."

My instructor's advice was invaluable. I learned that if you plan and think through an essay first, you'll have completed a major stage of the work. *College Writing Skills* develops this idea by breaking down the writing process into a series of easily followed steps.

Part One of the book presents the four basic steps or principles you'll need to write strong essays:

1   Begin with a clearly stated point or thesis.
2   Provide logical, detailed support for your thesis.
3   Organize your supporting material effectively.
4   Revise and edit carefully so that the material is presented in clear, error-free sentences.

Part Two describes a number of different ways you can organize and develop essays. Each chapter opens with a brief introduction followed by several essays written by students. Then comes a series of questions so that you can evaluate the essays in terms of the basic principles explained in Part One. Finally, a number of writing topics are presented, along with hints about prewriting to help you plan and write an effective paper.

Part Three helps with the many types of writing you will do in college: exam essays, summaries, reports, the résumé and job application letter, and the research paper. You will see that all these kinds of writing are variations of the essay form you have already learned.

Finally, Part Four offers review and practice in the skills needed to write sentences that are clear, error-free, and varied. Included is a series of selections to sharpen your proofreading and editing ability.

For your convenience, the book contains the following:

- On page 119 and the inside front cover, there is a checklist of the four basic steps in effective writing.
- On the inside back cover, there is an outline form to use when planning an essay.
- On the last page, there is a list of correction symbols.

Get into the habit of referring to these guides on a regular basis; they can help ensure that you'll produce clearly thought out, well-written essays.

College Writing Skills will help you learn, practice, and apply the thinking and writing skills you need to communicate effectively. But your starting point must be a determination to do the work needed to become a strong writer. The ability to express yourself clearly and logically can open doors for you, both in school and in your career. If you decide—and only you can decide—that you want this kind of power, this book will help you reach that goal.

JOHN LANGAN

COLLEGE
WRITING
SKILLS

PART ONE

BASIC
PRINCIPLES
OF ESSAY
WRITING

INTRODUCTION
TO THE
ESSAY FORM

This chapter will explain:

- **The importance of supporting a point in writing**
- **The difference between a paragraph and an essay**
- **The general structure of an essay**

AN IMPORTANT DIFFERENCE
BETWEEN WRITING AND TALKING

In your everyday conversation, you make all kinds of points or assertions. You say, for example, "It's not safe to walk in our neighborhood after dark"; "My boss is a hard person to work for"; or "Poor study habits keep getting me into trouble." The points that you make concern personal matters as well as, at times, outside issues: "That trade will be a disaster for the team"; "Lots of TV commercials are degrading to women"; "Students should have to work for a year before attending college."

The people you are talking with do not always challenge you to give reasons for your statements. They may know why you feel as you do, or they may already agree with you, or they simply may not want to put you on the spot; and so they do not always ask, "Why?" The people who read what you write, however, may not know you, agree with you, or feel in any way obliged to you. So if you want to communicate effectively with them, you must provide solid evidence for any point you make. An important difference, then, between writing and talking is this: *In writing, any idea that you advance must be supported with specific reasons or details.*

Think of your readers as reasonable persons. They will not take your views on faith, but they are willing to accept what you say as long as you support it. So remember to support with specific evidence any statement that you make.

POINT AND SUPPORT IN A PARAGRAPH

In conversation you might say to a friend who has suggested a movie, ''No thanks. Going to the movies is just too much of a hassle. Parking, people, everything.'' From shared past experiences, your friend may know what you are talking about, so that you will not have to explain your statement. But in writing, your point would have to be backed up with specific reasons and details.

Below is a paragraph on why moviegoing is a nuisance. A *paragraph* is a short paper of around 150 words. It usually consists of an opening point called a *topic sentence* followed by a series of sentences which support that point.

The Hazards of Moviegoing

Although I love movies, going to see them drives me slightly crazy. First of all, getting to the movie can take a lot of time. I have a thirty-five minute drive down a congested highway. Then, with a popular film, I usually have to wait in a long line at the ticket booth. Another problem is that the theater itself is seldom a pleasant place to be. A musty smell suggests that there has been no fresh air in the theater since it was built. Half the seats seem to be falling apart. And the floor often has a sticky coating that gets on your shoes. The worst problem of all is some of the other moviegoers. Kids run up and down the aisle. Teenagers laugh and shout at the screen. People of all ages loudly drop soda cups and popcorn tubs, cough and burp, and elbow you out of the armrest on either side of your seat. All in all, I would rather stay home and wait for the latest movie hits to appear on TV in the safety and comfort of my own living room.

Notice what the supporting evidence has done here. It has provided you, the reader, with a basis for understanding *why* the writer makes the point that is made. Through this specific evidence, the writer has explained and successfully communicated the idea that moviegoing can be a nuisance.

The evidence that supports the point in a paper often consists of a series of reasons followed by examples and details that support the reasons. That is true of the paragraph above: three reasons are provided, with examples and details that back up those reasons. Supporting evidence in a paper can also consist of anecdotes, personal experiences, facts, statistics, and the opinions of experts.

Activity

The paragraph on moviegoing, like almost any piece of effective writing, has two essential parts: (1) a point is advanced, and (2) that point is then supported. Taking a minute to outline the paragraph will help you understand these basic parts clearly. Write in the following space the point that has been advanced in the paragraph. Then add the words needed to complete the outline of the paragraph.

Point _____

_____

Support   1. *Time getting there* _____

      a. *Long drive* _____

      b. _____

   2. _____

      a. _____

      b. _____

      c. _____

   3. _____

      a. _____

      a. _____

      c. *People of all ages* _____

        (1) _____

        (2) *Cough and burp* _____

        (3) _____

POINT AND SUPPORT IN AN ESSAY

Much of your college writing will be in the form of five-hundred-word essays—papers of several paragraphs that support a single point. An *essay* typically consists of an introductory paragraph, three supporting paragraphs, and a concluding paragraph. The central idea, or point, developed in an essay is called a *thesis statement* rather than, as in a paragraph, a topic sentence. A thesis appears in the introductory paragraph, and the specific support for the thesis appears in the paragraphs that follow. The supporting paragraphs allow for a fuller treatment of the evidence that backs up the central point than would be possible in a single-paragraph paper.

Why Write Essays?

Mastering the essay form will help, first of all, on a practical level. For other courses, you will write specific forms of essays, such as the report and research paper. Many of your written tests will be in the form of essay exams. In addition, the basic structure of an essay will help in career-related writing, from a job application letter to the memos and reports that may become part of your work.

On a more abstract level, essay writing serves other valuable purposes. It will make you a better reader. You will become more aware of other writers' ideas and the evidence they provide (or fail to provide) to support those ideas. Most important, essay writing will make you a better thinker. Writing an essay forces you to sort out and organize your ideas and think them through clearly. You will learn to identify just what your ideas are and what support exists to back them up. Essay writing, in short, will give you practice in the process of clear and logical reasoning. Your ability to recognize ideas and to measure their validity will help you make sound decisions not just in school and career but in all phases of your everyday life.

A Model Essay

The following model should help you understand clearly the form of an essay. The writer of the paragraph on moviegoing later decided to develop her subject more fully. Here is the essay that resulted.

The Hazards of Moviegoing

Introductory paragraph

I am a movie fanatic. When friends want to know what picture won the Oscar in 1980 or who played the police chief in *Jaws,* they ask me. My friends, though, have stopped asking me if I want to go out to the movies. The problems in getting to the theater, the theater itself, and the behavior of some patrons are all reasons why I often wait for a movie to show up on TV.

First supporting paragraph

First of all, just getting to the theater presents difficulties. Leaving a home equipped with a TV and a video recorder isn't an attractive idea on a humid, cold, or rainy night. Even if the weather cooperates, there is still a thirty-minute drive to the theater down a congested highway, followed by the hassle of looking for a parking space. And then there are the lines. After hooking yourself to the end of a human chain, you worry about whether there will be enough tickets, whether you will get seats together, and whether many people will sneak into the line ahead of you.

Second supporting paragraph

Once you have made it to the box office and gotten your tickets, you are confronted with the problems of the theater itself. If you are in one of the run-down older theaters, you must adjust to the musty smell of seldom-cleaned carpets. Escaped springs lurk in the faded plush or cracked leather seats, and half the seats you sit in seem loose or tilted so that you sit at a strange angle. The newer twin and quad theaters offer their own problems. Sitting in an area only one-quarter the size of a regular theater, moviegoers often have to put up with the sound of the movie next door. This is especially jarring when the other movie involves racing cars or a karate war and you are trying to enjoy a quiet love story. And whether the theater is old or new, it will have floors that seem to be coated with rubber cement. By the end of a movie, shoes almost have to be pried off the floor because they have become sealed to a deadly compound of spilled soda, hardening bubble gum, and crushed Ju-Jubes.

Third
supporting
paragraph

Some of the patrons are even more of a problem than the theater itself. Little kids race up and down the aisles, usually in giggling packs. Teenagers try to impress their friends by talking back to the screen, whistling, and making what they consider to be hilarious noises. Adults act as if they were at home in their own living rooms and comment loudly on the ages of the stars or why movies aren't as good anymore. And people of all ages crinkle candy wrappers, stick gum on their seats, and drop popcorn tubs or cups of crushed ice and soda on the floor. They also cough and burp, squirm endlessly in their seats, file out for repeated trips to the rest rooms or concession stand, and elbow you out of the armrest on either side of your seat.

Concluding
paragraph

After arriving home from the movies one night, I decided that I was not going to be a moviegoer anymore. I was tired of the problems involved in getting to the movies and dealing with the theater itself and some of the patrons. The next day I arranged to have cable TV service installed in my home. I may now see movies a bit later than other people, but I'll be more relaxed watching box office hits in the comfort of my own living room.

GENERAL STRUCTURE OF AN ESSAY

The essay just presented—"The Hazards of Moviegoing"—is a good example of the standard short essay you will write in college English. It is a composition of slightly over five hundred words that consists of a one-paragraph introduction, a three-paragraph body, and a one-paragraph conclusion. The roles of these paragraphs are described and illustrated below.

Introductory Paragraph of an Essay

The introductory paragraph of an essay should start with several sentences that attract the reader's interest. It should then advance the central idea or thesis that will be developed in the essay. The thesis often includes a plan of development—a "preview" of the major points that will support the thesis. These supporting points should be listed in the order in which they will appear in the essay. In some cases, the plan of development is presented in a sentence separate from the thesis; in other cases, it is omitted.

Activity

1. In "The Hazards of Moviegoing," which sentences are used to attract the reader's interest?
   a.   First sentence
   b.   First two sentences
   c.   First three sentences

2. The thesis in "The Hazards of Moviegoing" is presented in which sentence?
   a. Third sentence
   b. Fourth sentence
3. The thesis contains a plan of development.
   a. Yes
   b. No
4. Write down the words in the thesis that announce the three major supporting points in the essay:

   a. _____

   b. _____

   c. _____

Supporting Paragraphs, or "Body," of an Essay

Most essays have three supporting points, developed at length over three separate paragraphs. (Some essays will have two supporting points, others four or more. For the purposes of this book, your goal will be three supporting points for most essays.) Each of the supporting paragraphs should begin with a *topic sentence* that states the point to be detailed in that paragraph. Just as the thesis provides a focus for the entire essay, the topic sentences provide a focus for each supporting paragraph.

Activity

1. What is the topic sentence for the first supporting paragraph of the essay?

   _____

   _____

2. The first topic sentence is then supported by details about (*fill in the missing words*):

   a. _____

   b. _____

   c. *Long ticket line* _____

3. What is the topic sentence for the second supporting paragraph of the essay?

    _____

    _____

4. The second topic sentence is then supported by details about (*fill in the missing words*):

    a. *Problems of old theaters (mustiness and* _____ *)*

    b. *Problems of new theaters (* _____ *and sound of adjoining movie)*

    c. *Problem of old and new theaters (* _____ *)*

5. What is the topic sentence for the third supporting paragraph of the essay?

    _____

    _____

6. The third topic sentence is then supported by details about (*fill in the missing words*):

    a. *Patrons (kids,* _____ *, and* _____ *)*

    b. *Distractions caused by people of all ages* _____

Concluding Paragraph of an Essay

The concluding paragraph often summarizes the essay by restating briefly the thesis and, at times, the main supporting points of the essay. In addition, the writer often presents a concluding thought about the subject of the paper.

Activity

1. Which two sentences in the concluding paragraph restate the thesis and supporting points of the essay?
    a. First and second
    b. Second and third
    c. Third and fourth
2. Which sentence contains the concluding thought of the essay?
    a. First
    b. Second
    c. Third
    d. Fourth

Diagram of an Essay

The following diagram shows you at a glance the different parts of a standard college essay.

Title of the Essay

Introduction

Opening remarks to catch reader's interest
Thesis
Plan of development (optional)

*Body
(supporting
paragraphs)*

Topic sentence (supporting point 1)
Specific evidence

Topic sentence (supporting point 2)
Specific evidence

Topic sentence (supporting point 3)
Specific evidence

Conclusion

Summary (optional)
General closing remarks

This diagram, along with the essay outline form that appears on the inside back cover of the book, will serve as a helpful guide when you are writing or evaluating essays.

IMPORTANT
FACTORS
IN WRITING

This chapter will discuss the importance of:

- **Your attitude about writing**
- **Knowing or discovering your subject**
- **Keeping a journal**
- **Prewriting**
- **Outlining**
- **Revising, editing, and proofreading**

The previous chapter introduced you to the essay form, and the chapters that follow will explain the basic steps in writing an essay and the basic standards for evaluating it. The purpose of this chapter is to describe a number of important general factors that will help you create good papers. These factors include (1) having the right attitude about writing, (2) knowing or discovering your subject, (3) keeping a journal, (4) prewriting, or having ways of getting started in writing, (5) outlining, and (6) revising, editing, and proofreading.

Your Attitude about Writing

One way to wreck your chances of learning how to write competently is to believe that writing is a "natural gift." People with this attitude think that they are the only ones for whom writing is an unbearably difficult activity. They feel that everyone else finds writing easy or at least tolerable. Such people typically say, "I'm not any good at writing" or "English was not one of my good subjects." They imply that they simply do not have a talent for writing, while others do. The result of this attitude is that people do not do their best when they write—or, even worse, that they hardly ever try to write. Their attitude becomes a self-fulfilling prophecy: their writing fails chiefly because they have brainwashed themselves into thinking that they don't have the "natural talent" needed to write. Unless their attitude changes, they probably will not learn how to write effectively.

A realistic attitude about writing—to replace the mistaken notion of writing as a "natural gift"—should build on the following two ideas.

1 ***Writing is hard work for almost everyone.*** It is difficult to do the intense and active thinking that clear writing demands. (Perhaps television has made us all so passive that the active thinking necessary in both writing and reading now seems harder than ever.) It is frightening to sit down before a blank sheet of paper and know that an hour later, nothing on it may be worth keeping. It is frustrating to discover how much of a challenge it is to transfer thoughts and feelings from one's head onto a sheet of paper. It is upsetting to find that an apparently simple writing subject often turns out to be complicated. But writing is not an automatic process: we will not get something for nothing—and we should not expect to. Competent writing results only from plain hard work—from determination, sweat, and head-on battle.

2 ***Writing is a skill.*** Writing is a skill like driving, typing, or preparing a good meal. Like any skill, it can be learned—if you decide that you are going to learn and then really work at it. This book will give you the extensive practice needed to develop your writing skills.

Activity

Answering these questions will help you evaluate your attitude about writing.

1. How much practice were you given writing compositions in high school?

_____Much   _____Some   _____Little

2. How much feedback (positive or negative comments) from teachers were you given on your compositions?

_____Much _____Some _____Little

3. How did your teachers seem to regard your writing?

_____Good _____Fair _____Poor

4. Do you feel that some people have a gift for writing and others do not?

_____Yes _____Sometimes _____No

5. When do you start writing a paper?

_____Several days before it is due

_____About a day before it is due

_____At the last possible minute

Many people who answer *Little* to questions 1 and 2 also answer *Poor, Yes,* and *At the last possible minute* to the other questions. On the other hand, people who answer *Much* or *Some* to questions 1 and 2 tend to have more favorable responses to the other questions. People with little *experience* in writing often have understandably negative feelings about their writing *ability*. But they should realize that writing is a skill they can learn with practice.

Knowing or Discovering Your Subject

Knowing Your Subject

Whenever possible, try to write on a subject which interests you. You will then find it easier to put the necessary time into your work. Even more important, try to write on a subject that you already know something about. If you do not have direct experience with a subject, you should at least have indirect experience— knowledge gained through thinking, prewriting (to be explained on pages 17–25), reading, or talking about the subject.

If you are asked to write on a topic about which you have no experience or knowledge, you should do whatever research is required to gain the information you need. The chapter "Using the Library" on pages 248–263 will show you how to use the library to look up relevant information. Without direct or indirect experience, or information gained through research, you will not be able to provide the specific evidence needed to develop the point you are trying to make. Your writing will be starved for specifics.

Discovering Your Subject

At times you will not know your subject when you begin to write. Instead, you will discover it in the *process* of writing. For example, when the author of the paper on moviegoing in the previous chapter first sat down to write her paper, her topic was going to be the drawbacks of old movie houses. As she began to accumulate details, she quickly realized that her topic was really the drawbacks of moviegoing in general. In other words, she only *thought* she knew her paper's focus when she began to write. In fact, she *discovered her subject in the course of writing*.

Another writer, without at first knowing his exact point, knew he wanted to write about a time when he had belonged to a gang and cruelly mugged someone. He began by getting down the grim details of the actual mugging. As he developed the details, he realized gradually what point he wanted to make. The paper that resulted, ''A Night of Violence,'' appears on page 197.

A third student author started with the idea that using computers in the classroom can be a real challenge. As she began getting details onto paper, her point became clearer, and she realized that she wanted to argue that computers in the classroom are a bad idea. Her paper, ''A Vote against Computers,'' is on page 205.

The moral of these examples is that sometimes you must write a bit in order to find out just what you want to write. Writing can help you think about and explore your topic and decide on the final direction of your paper. The techniques presented in the section on ''Prewriting'' starting on page 17 will suggest specific ways to discover and develop a subject.

One related feature of the writing process bears mention. Do not feel that you must proceed in a linear fashion when you write. That is, do not assume that the writing process must be a railroad track on which you go straight from your central point to ''supporting detail one'' to ''supporting detail two'' to ''supporting detail three'' to your concluding paragraph. Instead, proceed in whatever way seems most comfortable as you draft the paper. You may want to start by writing the closing section of your paper or by developing your third supporting detail.

Do whatever is easiest—and as you get material down on the page, it will make what you have left to do a bit easier. Sometimes, of course, as you work on one section, it may happen that another focal point for your paper will emerge. That's fine: if your writing tells you that it wants to be something else, then revise or start over as needed to take advantage of that discovery. Your goal is to wind up with a paper that makes a point and supports it solidly. Be ready to change direction and to make whatever adjustments are needed to reach your goal.

Activity 1

Answer the following questions.

1. What are three ways to get the knowledge you need to write on a subject?

   a. _____

   b. _____

   c. _____

2. A student begins to write a paper about the best job he ever had. After writing for about half an hour, he realizes that his details are all about what a wonderful person his boss was. What has happened in the process of writing?

   _____

3. Suppose you want to write a paper about problems that come with a holiday season. You think you can discuss family, personal, and financial problems. You feel you have the most details about financial problems. Should you start with that area, or with one of the other two areas?

   _____

Activity 2

Write for five minutes about the house, dormitory, or apartment where you live. Simply write down whatever details come to you. Don't worry about being neat; just pile up as many details as you can.

Afterwards, go through the material. Try to find a potential focus within all those details. Do the details suggest a simple point that you could make about the place where you live? If so, you've seen a small example of how writing about a topic can be an excellent way of discovering a point about that topic.

Keeping a Journal

Because writing is a skill, the more you practice it, the better you will become at it. One excellent way to get writing practice is to keep a daily (or "almost daily") journal.

At some point during the day—perhaps during a study period after your last class of the day, or right before dinner, or right before going to bed—spend fifteen minutes or so writing in your journal. Keep in mind that you do not have to plan what to write about or be in the mood or worry about making mistakes as you write; just write down whatever words come out. You should write at least one page in each session.

You may want to use a notebook that you can easily carry with you for on-the-spot writing. Or you may decide to write on loose-leaf paper that can be transferred later to a journal folder on your desk. No matter how you proceed, be sure to date all entries.

The content of your journal should be some of the specific happenings, thoughts, and feelings of the day. Your starting point may be a comment by a teacher, a classmate, or a family member; a gesture or action that has amused, angered, confused, or depressed you; something you have read or seen on television—anything, really, that has caught your attention and that you decide to explore a bit in writing. Some journal entries may focus on a single subject; others may wander from one topic to another.

Your instructor may ask you to make journal entries a specific number of times a week, for a specific number of weeks. He or she may require that you turn in your journal every so often for review and feedback. If you are keeping the journal on your own, try to make entries three to five times a week every week of the semester.

Keeping a journal will help you develop the habit of thinking on paper, and it can help you make writing a familiar part of your life. Your journal can also serve as a source of ideas for possible papers.

Following is an excerpt from one student's journal. As you read, look for a general point and supporting material that could be the basis for an interesting paper.

September 6

My first sociology class was tonight. The parking lot was jammed when I got there. I thought I was going to be late for class. A guard had us park on a field next to the regular lot. When I got to the room, it had the usual painted-cinder-block construction. Every school I have ever been in since first grade seems to be made of cinder block. Everybody sat there without saying anything, waiting for the teacher to arrive. I think they were all a bit nervous like me. I hoped there wasn't going to be a ton of work in the course. I think I was also afraid of looking foolish somehow. This goes back to grade school, when I wasn't a very good student and teachers sometimes embarrassed me in class. I didn't like grade school, and I hated high school. Now here I am six years later in college of all places. Who would have thought that I would end up here? The teacher appeared--a woman who I think was a bit nervous herself. I think I like her. Her name is Barbara Hanlin. She says we should call her Barbara. We got right into it, but it was interesting stuff. I like the fact that she asks questions, but then she lets you volunteer. I always hated it when teachers would call on you whether you wanted to answer or not. I also like the fact that she answers the questions and doesn't just leave you hanging. She takes the time to write important ideas on the board. I also like the way she laughs. This class may be OK.

Activity

1. If the writer of the journal entry above was looking for ideas for an essay, he could probably find several in this single entry. For example, he might write a narrative about the roundabout way he apparently wound up in college. See if you can find in the entry an idea that might be the basis for an interesting essay, and write your point in the space below.

    _____

2. Take fifteen minutes right now to write a journal entry on this day in your life. On a separate sheet of paper, just start writing about anything that you have seen, said, heard, thought, or felt today, and let your thoughts take you where they may.

Prewriting

If you are like many people, you may sometimes have trouble getting started with your writing. A mental block may develop when you sit down before a blank sheet of paper. You may not be able to think of a topic or an interesting slant on a topic. Or you may have trouble coming up with interesting and relevant details that you can use to support your topic. Even after starting a paper, you may hit snags or moments of wondering, ''Where to go next?''

The following pages describe five techniques that will help you think about and develop a topic and get words down on paper. These techniques, which are often called *prewriting techniques*, are a central part of the writing process. They are (1) brainstorming, (2) freewriting, (3) diagramming, (4) making a list, and (5) preparing a scratch outline.

TECHNIQUE 1: BRAINSTORMING

In *brainstorming*, you generate ideas and details by asking as many questions as you can think of about your subject. Such questions include *What? When? Why? How? Where?* and *Who?*

Following is an example of how one person, Tim, used brainstorming to generate material for a paper. Tim felt he could write about a depressing diner he had visited, but he was having trouble getting started. So he asked himself a series of questions about the experience and, as a result, accumulated a series of details that provided the basis for the paper he finally wrote.

Here are the questions Tim asked and the answers he wrote:

<u>Why</u> did I stop at the diner?   I was on the way home after driving all day, and I was tired. I decided to get a cup of coffee at the next diner.

<u>How</u> do I feel about diners?   I've always liked diners. I was looking forward to a friendly waitress and talk with the customers at the counter.

<u>What</u> was the diner like?   It was lonely. There were only a few people, and it was very quiet. Only one waitress was on duty. Even the parking lot looked lonely--trash was blowing around, and it was raining.

<u>Who</u> was in the diner?   Two workmen were sitting at the counter. There was also a young man sitting by himself at the far end of the counter. He looked depressed. There was a middle-aged couple in a booth. They weren't talking to each other--one was doodling, the other staring.

<u>What</u> happened at the diner?   I got out of there as fast as possible. I just wanted to get away from that lonely place and reach my home.

After brainstorming, Tim's next step was to prepare a scratch outline. He then prepared several drafts of the paper. The effective essay that eventually resulted from Tim's prewriting techniques appears on page 188.

Activity

To get a sense of the brainstorming process, use a sheet of paper to ask yourself a series of questions about a *pleasant* diner you have visited. See how many details you can accumulate about that diner in ten minutes.

TECHNIQUE 2: FREEWRITING

When you do not know what to write about a subject, or when you start to write but then become blocked, freewriting sometimes helps. In *freewriting*, you write without stopping for ten minutes or so. You do not worry about checking your spelling or punctuation, erasing mistakes, or finding exact words. If you get stuck, you write, ''I am looking for something to say,'' or repeat words until you get an idea. There is no need to feel inhibited, since mistakes do not count and you do not have to hand in your paper.

Freewriting will limber up your writing muscles and make you familiar with the act of writing. It is a way to break through mental blocks about writing and the fear of making errors. As you do not have to worry about making mistakes, you can concentrate on discovering what you want to say about a subject. Your initial ideas and impressions will often become clearer after you have gotten them down on paper. Through continued practice in freewriting, you will develop the habit of thinking as you write. And you will learn a technique that is a helpful way to get started on almost any paper.

Here is the freewriting that one student did to accumulate details for a paper on why she had decided to put her mother in a nursing home.

> I'm still upset about the whole thing, but seeing everything going downhill really forced the decision. Mom just needed so much help with all the pills and dressing and bathing. She needed more help than Daddy could handle by himself. Hospital bills in this country are outrageous, and Medicare doesn't pay for everything. Mom needed someone to work out her special diet because it was so complicated. The wheelchair rental was expensive. The hardest thing was the fact that she was breaking down emotionally, saying things like, "You don't care about me." We cared, but we worried about Dad. What an enormous strain he was under in all this. Mom really acted emotionally disturbed at times. She would call for an ambulance and tell them she was dying. Dad started to lose weight. The bills coming in started to fill an entire shopping bag. Some people think we were cruel, but we didn't have any other choice. My father doesn't drive, so he was walking all over town to get medicine and food.

The writer's next step was to use the freewriting as the basis for a scratch outline. The effective paper that eventually resulted from the author's freewriting, a scratch outline (see "Technique 5" below), and a good deal of rewriting appears on page 140.

Activity

To get a sense of the freewriting process, use a sheet of paper to freewrite about some of your own everyday worries. See how many ideas and details you can accumulate in ten minutes.

TECHNIQUE 3: DIAGRAMMING

Diagramming, also known as *mapping* or *clustering*, is another prewriting activity that can help you generate ideas and details about a topic. In diagramming, you use lines, boxes, arrows, and circles to show relationships between the ideas and details that come to you.

Diagramming is especially helpful to people who like to do their thinking in a very visual way. Whether you use a diagram, and just how you proceed with it, is up to you.

Here is the diagram that one student, Todd, prepared for a paper on differences between McDonald's and a fancy restaurant. This diagram, with its clear picture of relationships, was especially helpful for the comparison-contrast paper that Todd was doing. His final essay appears on page 152.

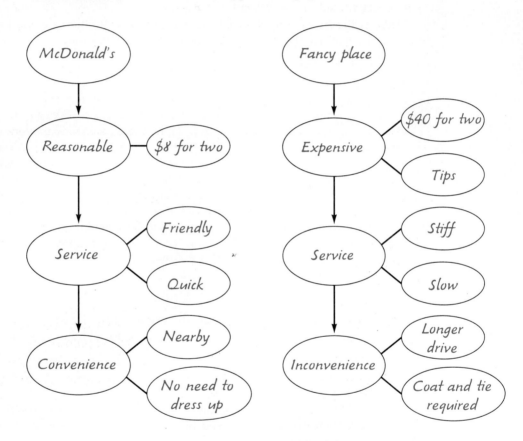

Activity

To get a sense of diagramming, use a sheet of paper to make a diagram of differences between two teachers or two jobs. See how many ideas and details you can accumulate in ten minutes.

TECHNIQUE 4: MAKING A LIST

Another prewriting technique is *making a list*. To get started on a paper, list as many different items as you can think of concerning your topic. Do not worry about repeating yourself, about sorting out major points from minor details, or about spelling or punctuating correctly. Simply make a list of everything about your subject that occurs to you. Your aim is to generate details and to accumulate as much raw material for writing as possible.

Following is a list prepared by one student, Jan, who was gathering details for an essay called "Benefits of Television." Her first step was simply to jot down thoughts and details that occurred to her.

Entertainment
Movies and sports events
Video games
Educational (important--save for last)
Relaxing after work
Covers major world events
Can be used with computers
Reduce stress (used for high-blood-pressure patients)
Rent videocassettes
Shows for children (Sesame Street)
Special cable services (sports, concerts)
College courses on TV

Notice that partway down her list Jan put in parentheses a note to herself that one thought (about the educational benefits of television) seems most important and should be saved for last. Very often, as you make a list, ideas about how to develop and organize a paper will occur to you. Jot them down.

Making a list is an excellent way to get started. Often, you then go on to make a scratch outline and write the first draft of your paper. (A scratch outline for Jan's list appears in the next section.)

Activity

To get a sense of making a list, use a sheet of paper to list specific problems you will face this semester. See how many ideas and details you can accumulate in ten minutes.

TECHNIQUE 5: PREPARING A SCRATCH OUTLINE

A scratch outline can often be the *single most helpful technique* for writing a good paper. It is an excellent complement to the prewriting techniques already mentioned. In a *scratch outline,* you think carefully about the exact point you are making, about the exact details you will use to support it, and about the exact order in which you will arrange them. The scratch outline is a plan or blueprint to help you achieve a unified, supported, and organized composition.

When you are planning an essay consisting of an introduction, three supporting paragraphs, and a conclusion (this is known as a *one-three-one* essay), a scratch outline is especially important. It may be only a few words, but it will be the bedrock upon which your whole essay will rest.

Here is the scratch outline Jan prepared for her general list on television:

Television can have real benefits.
1. Relaxation
2. Entertainment
3. Education

This brief outline made it clear to Jan that she could develop her essay on the basis of three distinct supporting points. While the outline appears simple, it represents a good deal of thinking on Jan's part. In the essays that you write, you should always try to develop such a basic outline.

With this outline, Jan knew she had a solid plan and a workable paper. As the next step in her writing process, she then felt comfortable about developing her scratch outline further by detailing the items that fit under each benefit:

1. Relaxation
   a. After work
   b. Reduce stress
2. Entertainment
   a. Network programming
   b. Cable programming
   c. Videocassettes and videodisks
   d. Video game
3. Education
   a. Children's shows
   b. College courses
   c. World events
   d. Computer capability

These scratch outlines enabled Jan to decide what to put into the paper, and in what order. Without having to write actual sentences, she took a giant step toward a paper that is unified (she left out items that are not related), supported (she added items that develop her point), and organized (she arranged the items in a logical way). These criteria for an effective essay are discussed on pages 87–110; and the essay that resulted from Jan's list and outlines is on page 95.

Activity

To get a sense of preparing a scratch outline, develop such an outline on reasons why you did or did not do well in high school. See how many ideas and details you can accumulate in ten minutes.

COMBINED USE OF THE FIVE PREWRITING TECHNIQUES

Very often a scratch outline follows brainstorming, freewriting, diagramming, and making a list. At other times, however, the scratch outline may substitute for the other four techniques. Also, you may use several techniques almost simultaneously when writing a paper. You may, for example, ask questions while making a list; you may diagram and outline a list as you write it; you may ask yourself questions and then freewrite answers to them. The five techniques are all ways to help you go about the process of writing a paper.

Activity 1

Answer the following questions.

1. Which of the prewriting techniques do you already practice?

    _____ Brainstorming

    _____ Freewriting

    _____ Diagramming

    _____ Making a list

    _____ Preparing a scratch outline

2. Which prewriting technique involves asking questions about your topic?

    _____

3. Which prewriting technique shows in a very visual way the relationship between ideas and details?

    _____

4. Which prewriting technique involves writing quickly about your topic without being concerned about grammar or spelling?

    _____

5. Which prewriting technique is almost always part of writing an essay?

    _____

6. Which prewriting techniques do you think will work best for you?

    _____

Activity 2

Below are examples of how the five prewriting techniques could be used to develop the topic "Problems of Combining Work and College." Identify each technique by writing B (for brainstorming), F (for freewriting), D (for the diagram), L (for the list), or SO (for the scratch outline) in the answer space.

_____

Never enough time
Miss campus parties
Had to study (only two free hours a night)
Give up activities with friends
No time to rewrite papers
Can't stay at school to play video games or talk to friends
Friends don't call me to go out anymore
Sunday no longer relaxed day--have to study
Missing sleep I should be getting
Grades aren't as good as they could be
Can't watch favorite TV shows
Really need the extra money
Tired when I sit down to study at nine o'clock

_____

What are some of the problems of combining work and school?

Schoolwork suffers because I don't have time to study or rewrite papers. I've had to give up things I enjoy, like sleep and touch football. I can't get into the social life at college, because I have to work right after class.

How have these problems changed my life?

My grades aren't as good as they were when I didn't work. Some of my friends have stopped calling me. My relationship with a girl I liked fell apart because I couldn't spend much time with her. I miss TV.

What do I do in a typical day?

I get up at 7 to make an 8 A.M. class. I have classes till 1:30, and then I drive to the supermarket where I work. I work till 7 P.M., and then I drive home and eat dinner. After I take a shower and relax for a half hour, it's about 9. This gives me only a couple of hours to study--read textbooks, do math exercises, write essays. My eyes start to close well before I go to bed at 11.

Why do I keep up this schedule?

I can't afford to go to school without working, and I need a degree to get the accounting job I want. If I invest my time now, I'll have a better future.

_____ Juggling a job and college has created major difficulties in my life.

1. Little time for studying
   a. Not reading textbooks
   b. Not rewriting papers
   c. Little studying for tests
2. Little time for enjoying social side of college
   a. During school
   b. After school
3. No time for personal pleasures
   a. Favorite TV shows
   b. Sunday football games
   c. Sleeping late

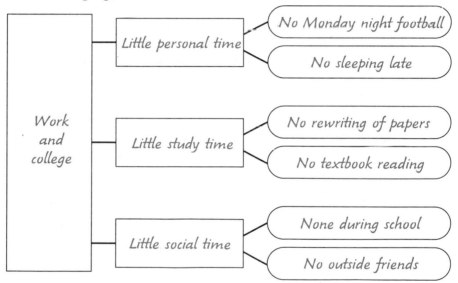

_____ It's hard working and going to school at the same time. I never realized how much I'd have to give up. I won't be quitting my job because I need the money and the people are friendly at the place where I work. I've had to give up a lot more than I thought. We used to play touch football games every Sunday. They were fun and we'd go out for drinks afterwards. Sundays now are for catch-up work with my courses. I have to catch up because I don't get home every day until 7, and I have to eat dinner first before studying. Sometimes I'm so hungry I just eat cookies or chips. Anyway, by the time I take a shower it's 9 P.M. or later and I'm already feeling tired. I've been up since 7 A.M. Sometimes I write an English paper in twenty minutes and don't even read it over. I feel that I'm missing out on a lot in college. The other day some people I like were sitting in the cafeteria listening to music and talking. I would have given anything to stay and not have to go to work. I almost called in sick. I used to get invited to parties but I don't much anymore. My friends know I'm not going to be able to make it, so they don't bother. I can't sleep late on weekends or watch TV during the week.

Outlining

As already mentioned, outlining is central to writing a good paper. An outline lets you see, and work on, the bare bones of a paper, without the distraction of a clutter of words and sentences. It develops your ability to think in a clear and logical manner. Outlining provides a quick check on whether your paper will be *unified*. It suggests right at the start whether your paper will be adequately *supported*. And it shows you how to plan a paper that is *well organized*.

The following series of exercises will help you develop the outlining skills so important to planning and writing a solid essay.

Activity 1

One key to effective outlining is the ability to distinguish between major ideas and details that fit under those ideas. The exercise below will develop your ability to generalize from a list of details and to determine a major thought.

Examples

Writing instruments

Pencil
Ball-point pen
Crayon
Felt-tip marker

Outer garments

Coat
Shawl
Jacket
Cape

1. _____

Spiderman
Superman
Wonder Woman
Batman

2. _____

Gas
Electricity
Water
Phone

3. _____

Boston Globe
The New York Times
Washington Post
Philadelphia Inquirer

4. _____

Tinsel
Mistletoe
Lights
Wreaths

5. _____

Chicken
Turkey
Cornish game hen
Duck

6. _____

Dictionary
Almanac
Encyclopedia
Atlas

7. _____   8. _____

   Chain   Loans
   Handlebars   Checking accounts
   Gearshift   Savings accounts
   Wheel spokes   Check cashing

9. _____   10. _____

   Wrinkles   Crutch
   Hearing loss   Cane
   Brittle bones   Metal walker
   Thinning hair   Artificial leg

Activity 2

Major and minor ideas are mixed together in the two lists below. Put the ideas
into logical order by filling in the outlines that follow.

1. Thesis: My high school had three problem areas.

   Involved with drugs   a. _____
   Leaky ceilings
   Students   (1) _____
   Unwilling to help after class   (2) _____
   Formed cliques
   Teachers   b. _____
   Buildings   (1) _____
   Ill-equipped gym   (2) _____
   Much too strict
                                  c. _____
                                     (1) _____
                                     (2) _____

2. Thesis: Working as a dishwasher in a restaurant was my worst job.

   Ten-hour shifts   a. _____
   Heat in kitchen
   Working conditions   (1) _____
   Minimum wage   (2) _____
   Hours changed every week
   No bonus for overtime   b. _____
   Hours   (1) _____
   Pay   (2) _____
   Noisy work area
                                  c. _____
                                     (1) _____
                                     (2) _____

Activity 3

Again, major and minor ideas are mixed together. In addition, in each outline one of the three major ideas is missing and must be added. Put the ideas into a logical order by filling in the outlines that follow and adding a third major idea.

1. Thesis: Joining an aerobics class has many benefits.

Make new friends   a. _____
Reduce mental stress
Social benefits   (1) _____
Strengthens heart   (2) _____
Improves self-image   b. _____
Mental benefits
Tones muscles   (1) _____
Meet interesting instructors (2) _____

   c. _____

(1) _____
(2) _____

2. Thesis: My favorite times in school were the days before holiday vacations.

Lighter workload   a. _____
Teachers more relaxed
Pep rallies   (1) _____
Less work in class   (2) _____
Friendlier atmosphere   b. _____
Less homework
Holiday concerts   (1) _____
Students happy about vacation (2) _____

   c. _____

(1) _____
(2) _____

Activity 4

Read the following essay and outline it in the spaces provided. Write out the central point and topic sentences and summarize in a few words the supporting material that fits under each topic sentence. One item is summarized for you as an example.

Losing Touch

Steve, a typical American, stays home on workdays. He plugs into his personal computer terminal in order to hook up with the office. After work, he puts on his stereo headphones, watches a movie on his home video recorder, or challenges himself to a game of electronic baseball. On many days, Steve doesn't talk to any other human beings, and he doesn't see any people except those on television. Steve is imaginary, but his lifestyle is very possible. The inventions of modern technology seem to be cutting us off from contact with our fellow human beings.

1

Thesis: _____

_____

The world of business is one area in which technology is isolating us. Many people now work alone at home. With access to a large central computer, employees such as secretaries, insurance agents, and accountants do their jobs at display terminals in their own homes. They no longer actually have to see the people they're dealing with. In addition, employees are often paid in an impersonal way. Workers' salaries are automatically credited to their bank accounts, eliminating the need for paychecks. Fewer people stand in line with their coworkers to receive their pay or cash their checks. Finally, personal banking is becoming a detached process. Customers interact with machines rather than people to deposit or withdraw money from their accounts. Even some bank loans are approved or rejected, not in an interview with a loan officer, but through a display on a computer screen.

2

First topic sentence: _____

_____

Support: 1. *Many people now work alone at home.* _____

2. _____

3. _____

a. _____

b. _____

Another area that technology is changing is entertainment. Music, for   3
instance, was once a group experience. People listened to music at concert
halls or in small social gatherings. For many people now, however, music is
a solitary experience. Walking along the street or sitting in their living
rooms, they wear headphones to build a wall of music around them. Movie
entertainment is changing, too. Movies used to be social events. Now, fewer
people are going out to see a movie. Many more are choosing to wait for a
film to appear on cable television. Instead of being involved with the
laughter, applause, or hisses of the audience, viewers watch movies in the
isolation of their own living rooms.

Second topic sentence: _____

_____

    Support: 1. _____

              2. _____

Education is a third important area in which technology is separating us   4
from others. From elementary schools to colleges, students spend more and
more time sitting by themselves in front of computers. The computers give
them feedback, while teachers spend more time tending the computers and
less time interacting with their classes. A similar problem occurs in homes.
As more families buy computers, increasing numbers of students practice
their math and reading skills with software programs instead of with their
friends, brothers and sisters, and parents. Last, alienation is occurring as a
result of another high-tech invention, videotapes. People are buying
videocassette tapes on subjects such as cooking, real estate investment,
speaking, and speed-reading. They then practice their skills at home rather
than by taking group classes in which a rich human interaction can occur.

Third topic sentence: _____

_____

    Support: 1. _____

              2. _____

              3. _____

Technology, then, seems to be driving human beings apart. Soon, we   5
may no longer need to communicate with other human beings in order to do
our work, entertain ourselves, or play the games we enjoy. Machines will be
the coworkers and companions of the future.

Revising, Editing, and Proofreading

An effective paper is almost never written all at once. Rather, it is written in a step-by-step process in which you take it through a series of stages—from prewriting to final draft.

In the first stage, described above, you *prewrite*, getting your initial ideas and impressions about the subject down on paper. You accumulate raw material through brainstorming, freewriting, diagramming, and making lists and scratch outlines.

In the second stage, you *write and revise several drafts* of your paper. You fill out and shape your paper, adding and subtracting as needed to move it as close as you can to its final form. You work to make clear the single point of your paper, to develop fully the specific evidence needed to support that point, and to organize and connect the specific evidence. For example, in the second draft you may concentrate on adding details that will further support the central point of your paper. At the same time, you may also eliminate details that, you now realize, do not truly back up your thesis. In the third draft, you may work on reorganizing details and adding connections between supporting paragraphs so that your material will hold together more tightly.

Ideally, you should now set your paper aside for a while, so that you can move into the editing and proofreading stage with a fresh, rested mind. In this last stage, you first *edit* the next-to-final draft; that is, you check it carefully for sentence skills—for correct grammar, mechanics, punctuation, and usage. Then you *proofread* the final copy of the paper for any typing or handwriting mistakes. Editing and proofreading are important steps that some people avoid, often because they have worked too hard (or too little) on the previous stages.

Remember that correcting mistakes in the next-to-final and final versions can turn an average paper into a better one and a good paper into an excellent one. A later section of this book will give you practice in editing and proofreading in the form of a series of editing tests (pages 457–467).

Activity 1

Answering the questions below will help you evaluate your attitude about revising, editing, and proofreading.

1. When do you typically start work on a paper?

    _____ Several nights before it's due

    _____ Night before it's due

    _____ Day it's due

2. How many drafts do you typically write when doing a paper?

   _____ One _____ Two _____ Three _____ Four or more

3. How would you describe your editing (checking the next-to-final draft for errors in grammar, punctuation, mechanics, and usage)?

   _____ Do little or no editing

   _____ Look quickly for and correct obvious errors

   _____ Consult a grammar handbook and a dictionary about all possible errors

4. How would you describe your proofreading (checking the final draft for typing or handwriting errors)?

   _____ Do not look at the paper again after the last word is written

   _____ May glance quickly through the paper

   _____ Read the paper over carefully to find mistakes

5. Do you ever get back papers marked for obvious errors?

   _____ Frequently _____ Sometimes _____ Almost never _____ Never

Activity 2

Following is a supporting paragraph from an essay called "Problems of Combining School and Work." The paragraph is shown in four different stages of development: (1) First full draft, (2) second draft, (3) next-to-final draft, (4) final draft. The four stages appear in scrambled order. Write the number 1 in the answer blank for the first full draft and number the remaining stages in sequence.

_____   I have also given up some special personal pleasures in my life. On Sundays, for example, I used to play softball or football, now I use the entire day to study. Another pleasure Ive had to give up is good old-fashioned sleep. I never get as much as I like because their just isnt time. Finally I miss having the chance to just sit in front of the TV, on weeknights. In order to watch the whole lineup of movies and sports that I used to watch regularly. These sound like small pleasures, but you realize how important they are when you have to give them up.

I've had to give up special personal pleasures in my life. I use to spend Sundays playing pick-up games, now I have to study. Im the sort of person who needs alot of sleep, but I dont have the time for that either. Sleeping nine or ten hours a night woul'dnt be unusual. Psychologists have shown that each individual need a different amount of sleep, some people as little as five hours, some as much as nine or ten. so I'm not unusual in that. But I've given up that pleasure too. The third thing is that I can't watch the TV shows I use to enjoy. This is another personal pleasure I've had to give up trying to balence work and school. These sound like small pleasures, but you realize how important they are when you have to give them up.

Besides missing the social side of college life, I've also had to give up some of my special personal pleasures. I used to spend Sunday afternoons, for example, playing lob-pitch softball or touch football, depending on the season. Now, I use Sunday as a catch-up day for my studies. Another pleasure I've lost is sleeping late on days off and weekends. I once loved mornings when I could check the clock, bury my head in the pillow, and drift off for another hour. These days I'm forced to crawl out of bed the minute the alarm lets out its piercing ring. Finally, I no longer have the chance to just sit, for three or four hours at a time, watching the movies and sports programs I enjoy. A leisurely night of <u>Monday Night Football</u> or a network premiere of a Clint Eastwood movie is a pleasure of the past for me now.

Besides missing the social side of college life, I've also had to give up some of my special personal pleasures. I used to spend Sunday afternoons, for example, playing lob-pitch softball or touch football, depending on the season. Now I use Sunday as a day for my studies. Another pleasure I've had to give up is sleeping late on days off and weekends. I once loved mornings when I could check the clock, bury my head in the pillow, and drifting off for another hour. These days I'm forced to get out of bed the minute the alarm lets out it's piercing ring. Finally, I no longer have the chance to just sit watching the movies and sports programs I enjoy. A liesurely night of <u>Monday Night Football</u> or a network premere of a Clint Eastwood movie is a pleasure of the past for me now.

THE FIRST AND SECOND STEPS IN ESSAY WRITING

This chapter will show you how to:

- **Start an essay with a point or thesis**
- **Support that point or thesis with specific evidence**

Now that you have a sense of the general structure of an essay, it is time to consider the basic steps involved in writing such a paper. The four steps are as follows:

1 Begin with a point or thesis.
2 Support the thesis with specific evidence.
3 Organize and connect the specific evidence.
4 Write clear, error-free sentences.

This chapter will describe the first two steps, and the chapter that follows (see page 62) will present the last two.

Step 1:
Begin with a Point or Thesis

Your first step in writing is to decide what point you want to make and to write out that point in a single sentence. Formulating your point or thesis right at the start will help in two ways. First, you will find out at once whether you have a clear and workable thesis. Second, you will be able to use the thesis as a guide while writing your essay. You will know what material to include by frequently asking yourself, "Does this support my thesis?" With the thesis as a guide, your chances of drifting away from the point of the essay are greatly reduced.

WRITING A GOOD THESIS

To write a good thesis, you must begin with a subject that is neither too broad nor too narrow. Suppose a teacher asks you to write a paper on some aspect of marriage. Such a topic is obviously too broad to cover in a five-hundred-word essay. You would have to write a book to support adequately any point you might make about the general subject of marriage. What you need to do, then, is to limit your subject. Narrow it down until you have a thesis that you can deal with specifically in four hundred to five hundred words. In the box that follows are examples of narrowed subjects.

General Subject	Limited Subject	Thesis
Marriage	Honeymoon	A honeymoon is perhaps the worst way to begin a marriage.
Family	Older sister	My older sister helped me overcome my shyness.
Television	TV preachers	TV evangelists use sales techniques to promote their messages.
Children	Disciplining of children	My husband and I have several effective ways of disciplining our children.
Sports	Players' salaries	High players' salaries are bad for the game, for the fans, and for the values our children are developing.

Activity

Sometimes a subject must go through several stages of limiting before it is narrow enough to write about. Below are four lists reflecting several stages that writers went through in moving from a general subject to a narrow thesis statement. Number the stages in each list from 1 to 5, with 1 marking the broadest stage and 5 marking the thesis.

List 1

_____ Teachers

_____ Education

_____ Math teacher

_____ My high school math teacher was incompetent.

_____ High school math teacher

List 2

_____ Bicycles

_____ Dangers of bike riding

_____ Recreation

_____ Recreational vehicles

_____ Bike riding in the city is a dangerous activity.

List 3

_____ Financial institutions

_____ Bank

_____ Dealing with customers

_____ Working in a bank

_____ I've learned how to handle unpleasant bank customers.

List 4

_____ Camping

_____ First camping trip

_____ Summer vacation

_____ My first camping trip was a disastrous experience.

_____ Vacations

Later in this chapter, you will get more practice in narrowing general subjects to thesis statements.

COMMON ERRORS IN WRITING A THESIS

When writing thesis statements, people often make one of several mistakes that undermine their chances of producing an effective essay. One mistake is to substitute an announcement of the subject for a true thesis idea. Other mistakes include writing theses that are too broad or too narrow, or theses that have more than one idea. Following are examples of all four errors.

1   Announcements Rather Than Statements

The subject of this paper will be my parents.
I want to talk about the crime wave in our country.
The "baby boom" generation is the concern of this essay.

2   Statements That Are Too Broad

My parents have been the most influential people in my life.
Crime is a major concern of everyone in our country.
The "baby boom" generation has changed history.

3   Statements That Are Too Narrow

My parents had only one child.

In the last year there have been over twenty robberies in our neighborhood.

The members of the post–World War II "baby boom" make up the largest single age group in America.

4   Statements That Contain More Than One Idea

My parents helped me grow in important ways, although in other respects I was limited.

The problem of America's overcrowded prisons must be solved, and judges must start handing out tougher sentences.

The "baby boom" generation has had many advantages, but it also faces many problems.

In the first group above, the sentences are not thesis statements but simple announcements of a topic idea. For instance, "The subject of this paper will be my parents" does not make a point but merely tells, in a rather weak and unimaginative way, the writer's general subject. A thesis statement must advance a point about a limited subject.

In the second group above, all the statements are too broad to be supported adequately. For example, "My parents have been the most influential people in my life" could not be supported with specific details in five hundred words or less. There are many autobiographies in which authors have devoted entire chapters to detailing the influence of their mothers or fathers on their lives.

In the third group above, there is no room in any of the three statements for support to be given. For instance, ''My parents had only one child'' is too narrow to be expanded into a paper. It is a simple fact that does not lend itself to much discussion. Such a statement is sometimes called a *dead-end statement*; there is no place to go with it. On the other hand, ''My parents helped me grow in three important ways'' is a point that you could go on to write about in an essay.

In the last group, each of the statements contains more than one idea. For instance, ''My parents helped me grow in important ways, although in other respects I was limited'' appears to have two separate ideas (''parents helped me grow'' *and* ''in other respects I was limited''). Thus the reader does not know what the real focus will be.

Activity

Part A: Write TN in the space next to each statement that is too narrow to be developed in an essay. Write TB beside each statement that is too broad to be covered in an essay.

_____   1.   The way our society treats its elderly people is unbelievable.

_____   2.   The first car that I owned was a Ford.

_____   3.   Computers have changed our society.

_____   4.   People who eat a lot of red meat are almost three times more likely to get colon cancer than people who eat mostly fish and chicken.

_____   5.   Action must be taken against drugs.

Part B: Write A beside each sentence that is an announcement rather than a thesis statement. Write 2 beside each statement that contains more than one idea.

_____   6.   My last car was dependable, but many American cars are poorly made.

_____   7.   The subject of this essay is daily prayer in our public schools.

_____   8.   Soap operas show many stereotyped characters, although they also portray real problems in American life.

_____   9.   I am going to write on my ideas concerning ''F'' grades.

_____   10.   The hardest teacher I ever had taught me a lesson I will never forget.

Step 2:
Support the Thesis
with Specific Evidence

The first essential step in writing a successful essay is to formulate a clearly stated thesis. The second basic step is to support the thesis with specific reasons or details.

To ensure that your essay will have adequate support, you may find an informal outline very helpful. Write down a brief version of your thesis idea and then work out and jot down the three points that will support that thesis.

Here is the informal outline that was prepared by the author of the essay on moviegoing:

```
Moviegoing is a problem.
1. Getting there
2. Theater itself
3. Patrons
```

An informal outline like this one looks simple, but achieving it often requires a great deal of careful thinking. The time spent, though, on developing a logical outline is invaluable. Once you have planned out the steps that logically support your thesis, you will be in an excellent position to go on to write an effective essay.

Activities in this chapter will give you practice in the crucial skill of clearly planning an essay.

Activity

Complete any five of the six informal outlines that follow, by adding a third logical supporting point (*c*) that will parallel the two already provided (*a* and *b*).

1. The first day on a new job can be nerve-wracking.
    a. Meeting new people
    b. Finding your way around a new place
    c. _____

2. My stepmother has three qualities I admire.
    a. Patience
    b. Thoughtfulness
    c. _____

3. At our school, the library is the worst place to study.
    a. Uncomfortable chairs and tables
    b. Little privacy
    c. _____

4. College students should live at home.
    a. Stay in touch with family
    b. Avoid distractions of dorm or apartment life
    c. _____

5. _____ is the worst job I've ever had.
    a. Difficult boss
    b. Poor pay
    c. _____

6. College is a stressful situation for many people.
    a. Worry about grades
    b. Worry about being accepted
    c. _____

THE IMPORTANCE OF SPECIFIC DETAILS

Just as a thesis must be developed with three supporting points, those supporting points must be developed with specific details. Specific details have two key values. First of all, details excite the reader's interest. They make writing a pleasure to read, for we all enjoy learning particulars about people, places, and things. Second, details serve to explain a writer's points. They give the evidence needed for us to see and understand general ideas.

All too often, the body paragraphs in essays contain vague generalities rather than the specific supporting details that are needed to engage and convince a reader. Here is what one of the paragraphs in "The Hazards of Moviegoing" would have looked like if the writer had not vividly detailed her supporting evidence.

> Some of the other patrons are even more of a problem than the theater itself. Many people in the theater often show themselves to be inconsiderate. They make noises and create disturbances at their seats. Included are people in every age group, from the young to the old. Some act as if they were at home in their own living rooms watching the TV set. And people are often messy, so that you're constantly aware of all the food they're eating. People are also always moving around near you, creating a disturbance and interrupting your enjoyment of the movie.

The box below contrasts the vague support in the preceding paragraph with the specific support in the essay.

Vague Support	*Specific Support*
1. Many people in the theater show themselves to be inconsiderate. They make noises and create disturbances at their seats. Included are people in every age group, from the young to the old. Some act as if they were at home in their own living rooms watching the TV set.	1. Little kids race up and down the aisles, usually in giggling packs. Teenagers try to impress their friends by talking back to the screen, whistling, and making what they consider to be hilarious noises. Adults act as if they were at home in their own living rooms and comment loudly on the ages of the stars or why movies aren't as good anymore.
2. And people are often messy, so that you're constantly aware of all the food they're eating.	2. And people of all ages crinkle candy wrappers, stick gum on their seats, and drop popcorn tubs or cups of crushed ice and soda on the floor.
3. People are also always moving around nearby, creating a disturbance and interrupting enjoyment of the movie.	3. They also cough and burp, squirm endlessly in their seats, file out for repeated trips to the rest rooms or concession stand, and elbow you out of the armrest on either side of your seat.

The effective paragraph from the essay provides details that make vividly clear the statement that the patrons are a problem in the theater. The writer specifies the exact age groups (little kids, teenagers, and adults) and the offenses of each (giggling, talking and whistling, and loud comments). She specifies the various food excesses (crinkled wrappers, gum on seats, dropped popcorn and soda containers). Finally, she provides concrete details that enable us to see and hear other disturbances (coughs and burps, squirming, constant trips to bathroom, jostling for elbow room). The ineffective paragraph asks us to guess about these details; in the effective paragraph, we vividly see and hear them.

In the strong paragraph, then, the sharp details capture our interest and enable us to share in the writer's experiences. They provide pictures that make each of us feel, "I am there." The particulars also enable us to understand clearly the writer's point that patrons are a problem. You should aim to make your own writing equally convincing by providing detailed support in your papers.

Activity

Write S in front of the two selections below that provide specific evidence to support their opening points. Write X in front of the two selections that follow their opening points with vague, general, and wordy sentences.

1. Building a wooden deck can be an enjoyable project only if you take certain precautions.

    Get a building permit before you start. If you don't have one, you may have to tear down everything you've built when the town's building inspector learns of your project. Also, purchase pressure-treated lumber for any posts that will be set into the ground. Ordinary wood, not treated with preservatives, will eventually rot from contact with soil and moisture.

2. My mother was a harsh disciplinarian.

    When I did something wrong, no matter how small, she would inflict serious punishment. She had expectations that I was to live up to, and she never changed her attitude. When I did not behave as I should, I was dealt with severely. There were no exceptions as far as my mother was concerned.

3. Some things are worse when they're "improved."

    A good cheesecake, for one thing, is perfect. It doesn't need pineapple, cherries, blueberries, or whipped cream smeared all over it. Plain old American blue jeans, the ones with five pockets and copper rivets, are perfect too. Manufacturers only made them worse when they added flared legs, took away the pockets, tightened the fit, and plastered white logos and designers' names all over them.

4. Pets can be more trouble than children.

    My dog, unlike my children, has never been completely housebroken. When he's excited or nervous, he still has an occasional problem. My dog, unlike my children, has never learned how to take care of himself when we're away, despite the fact that we've given him plenty of time to do so. We don't have to worry about our grown children anymore. However, we still have to hire a dog-sitter for him.

THE IMPORTANCE OF ADEQUATE DETAILS

One of the most common and serious problems in student writing is inadequate development. You must provide *enough* specific details to support fully the point in a body paragraph of an essay. You could not, for example, include a paragraph about a friend's unreliability and provide only a short example. You would have to add several other examples or provide an extended example showing your friend as an unreliable person. Without such additional support, your paragraph would be underdeveloped.

Students may try to disguise unsupported paragraphs through repetition and generalities. Do not to fall into this ''wordiness trap.'' Be prepared to do the plain hard work needed to ensure that each paragraph has solid support.

Activity 1

Both of the following body paragraphs were written on the same topic, and both have clear opening points. Which one is adequately developed? Which one, on the other hand, has only several particulars and uses mostly vague, general, wordy sentences to conceal the fact that it is starved for specific details?

Eternal Youth?--No Thanks

I wouldn't want to be a teenager again, first of all, because I wouldn't want to worry about talking to girls. I still remember how scary it was to call up a girl and ask her out. My heart would race, my pulse would pound, and perspiration would trickle down my face, adding to my acne by the second. I never knew whether my voice would come out deep and masculine, like Dan Rather's, or squeaky, like Pee Wee Herman's. Then there were the questions: Would she be at home? If she were, would she want to talk to me? And if she did, what would I say? The one time I did get up the nerve to take a girl in my homeroom to a movie, I was so tongue-tied that I stared silently at the box of popcorn in my lap until the feature finally started. Needless to say, I wasn't very interesting company.

Terrors of My Teenage Years

I wouldn't want to be a teenager again, first of all, because I wouldn't want to worry about talking to girls. Calling up a girl to ask her out was something that I completely dreaded. I didn't know what words to express or how to express them. I would have all the symptoms of nervousness when I got on the phone. I worried a great deal about how I would sound, and I had a lot of doubts about the girl's reaction. Once, I managed to call up a girl to go out, but the evening turned out to be a disaster. I was too unsure of myself to act in a confident way. I couldn't think of anything to say and just kept quiet. Now that I look back on it, I really made a fool of myself. Agonizing over my attempts at relationships with the opposite sex made adolescence a very uncomfortable time.

The first paragraph offers a series of well-detailed examples of the author's nerve-wracking experiences, as a teenager, with girls. The second paragraph, on the other hand, is underdeveloped. It speaks only of the "torture" of calling up a girl, whereas the first paragraph supplies such particulars as "My heart would race, my pulse would pound, and perspiration would trickle down my face." The second paragraph describes in a general way being "worried about my voice," whereas in the first paragraph, the author wonders if his voice will "come out deep and masculine, like Dan Rather's, or squeaky, like Pee Wee Herman's." And there is no specific description in the second paragraph of the evening that turned into a disaster. In summary, the second paragraph lacks the full detailed support needed to develop its opening point convincingly.

Activity 2

Take a few minutes to write a paragraph supporting the point that "My room is a mess." Afterwards, you and your classmates (or the other students in the small group you may be working within) should all read your paragraphs aloud. The most well-received paragraphs will be those with plenty of specific details.

Practice in Advancing and Supporting a Thesis

You now know the two most important steps in competent essay writing: (1) advancing a point or thesis and (2) supporting that thesis. The purpose of this section is to expand and strengthen your understanding of these two basic steps. You will first work through a series of activities on *developing* a thesis:

1   Identifying the different parts of an essay
2   Evaluating thesis statements
3   Completing thesis statements
4   Writing a thesis statement
5   Limiting a topic and writing a thesis

You will then sharpen your understanding of how to *support* a thesis effectively by working through the following activities:

6   Making words and phrases specific
7   Making sentences specific
8   Providing specific evidence
9   Identifying adequate supporting evidence
10   Adding details to complete an essay

1 IDENTIFYING THE DIFFERENT PARTS OF AN ESSAY

Activity

This activity will sharpen your sense of the different parts of an essay. An essay titled "Coping with Old Age" appears below with no indentations between paragraphs. Read the essay carefully, and then double-underline the thesis and single-underline the topic sentence for each of the three supporting paragraphs and the first sentence of the conclusion. Then write the numbers of those sentences in the spaces provided at the end.

Coping with Old Age

[1]I recently read about an area of the Soviet Union where many people live to be well over a hundred years old. [2]Being 115 or even 125 isn't considered unusual there, and these old people continue to do productive work right up until they die. [3]America, however, isn't such a healthy place for older people. [4]Since I retired from my job, I've had to cope with the physical, mental, and emotional stresses of being "old." [5]For one thing, I've had to adjust to physical changes. [6]Now that I'm over sixty, the trusty body that carried me around for years has turned traitor. [7]Aside from the deepening wrinkles on my face and neck, and the wiry gray hairs that have replaced my brown hair, I face more frightening changes. [8]I don't have the energy I used to. [9]My eyes get tired. [10]Once in a while, I miss something that's said to me. [11]My once-faithful feet seem to have lost their comfortable soles, and I sometimes feel I'm walking on marbles. [12]In order to fight against this slow decay, I exercise whenever I can. [13]I walk, I stretch, and I climb stairs. [14]I battle constantly to keep as fit as possible. [15]I'm also trying to cope with mental changes. [16]My mind was once as quick and sure as a champion gymnast. [17]I never found it difficult to memorize answers in school or to remember the names of people I met. [18]Now, I occasionally have to search my mind for the name of a close neighbor or favorite television show. [19]Because my mind needs exercise, too, I challenge it as much as I can. [20]Taking a college course like this English class, for example, forces me to concentrate. [21]The mental gymnast may be a little slow and out of shape, but he can still do a backflip or turn a somersault when he has to. [22]Finally, I must deal with the emotional impact of being old. [23]Our society typecasts old people. [24]We're supposed to be unattractive, senile, useless leftovers. [25]We're supposed to be the crazy drivers and the cranky customers. [26]At first, I was angry and frustrated that I was considered old at all. [27]And I knew that people were wrong to stereotype me. [28]Then I got depressed. [29]I even started to think that maybe I was a cast-off, one of those old animals that slow down the rest of the herd. [30]But I have now decided to rebel against these negative feelings. [31]I try to have friends of all ages and to keep up with what's going on in the world. [32]I try to remember that I'm still the same person who sat at a first-grade desk, who fell in love, who comforted a child,

who got a raise at work. [33]I'm not "just" an old person. [34]Coping with the changes of old age has become my latest full-time job. [35]Even though it's a job I never applied for, and one for which I had no experience, I'm trying to do the best I can.

Thesis statement: _____

Topic sentence of first supporting paragraph: _____

Topic sentence of second supporting paragraph: _____

Topic sentence of third supporting paragraph: _____

First sentence of the conclusion: _____

2   EVALUATING THESIS STATEMENTS

As was explained on pages 37–38, some writers substitute announcements of a subject for a true thesis idea. Others write statements that are too narrow to need support or development. Contrasting with such dead-end statements are ones that are wide open—too broad to be adequately supported in the limited space of a five-hundred-word essay. Finally, some thesis statements are vague, often containing more than one idea. They suggest that a writer has not thought out his or her main point sufficiently.

Activity 1

Write A beside the sentences that are announcements rather than thesis statements. Write OK beside the statement in each pair that is a clear, limited point that could be developed in an essay.

1. _____ a.   This essay will discuss the people you meet in exercise class.

   _____ b.   The kinds of workout clothes worn in my aerobics class identify the "jocks," "strugglers," and "princesses."

2. _____ a.   I made several mistakes in the process of trying to win the respect and affection of my teenage stepson.

   _____ b.   My thesis in this paper is relationships between stepparents and stepchildren.

3. _____ a.   A period of loneliness can teach you to use your creativity, sort out your values, and feel empathy for others.

   _____ b.   Loneliness is the subject of this paper.

4. _____ a.   This paper will be about sharing housework.

   _____ b.   Deciding who will perform certain unpleasant household chores can be the crisis that makes or breaks a marriage.

5. _____ a. My concern here is to discuss the "near-death" experiences reported by some patients.

   _____ b. There are several possible explanations for the similar "near-death" experiences reported by some patients.

Activity 2

Write TN beside statements that are too narrow to be developed in an essay. Write OK beside the statement in each pair that is a clear, limited point.

1. _____ a. I had squash, tomatoes, and corn in my garden last summer.

   _____ b. Vegetable gardening can be a frustrating hobby.

2. _____ a. The main road into our town is lined with billboards.

   _____ b. For several reasons, billboards should be abolished.

3. _____ a. There are more single-parent households in our country than ever.

   _____ b. Organization is the key to being a successful single parent.

4. _____ a. In my first job, I learned that I had several bad work habits.

   _____ b. Because I was late for work yesterday, I lost an hour's pay and was called in to see the boss.

5. _____ a. Americans abuse alcohol because liquor has become such an important part of our personal and public celebrations.

   _____ b. Consumption of wine, beer, and hard liquor increases in the United States every year.

Activity 3

Write TB beside statements that are too broad to be developed in an essay. Write OK beside the statement in each pair that is a clear, limited point.

1. _____ a. In many ways, sports are an important part of American life.

   _____ b. Widespread gambling has changed professional football for the worse.

2. _____ a. Modern life makes people suspicious and unfriendly.

   _____ b. A succession of frightening news stories has made me lose my trust in strangers.

3. _____ a. Toy ads on television teach children to be greedy, competitive, and snobbish.

   _____ b. Advertising has a bad influence on the values that children develop in life.

4. _____ a.   Learning new skills can be difficult and frustrating.

_____ b.   Learning a skill like writing takes work, patience, and a sense of humor.

5. _____ a.   I didn't get along with my family, so I did many foolish things.

_____ b.   Running away from home taught me that my parents weren't as terrible as I thought.

Activity 4

For each pair of statements, write 2 beside the one that contains more than one idea. Write OK beside the one in each pair that is a clear, limited point.

1. _____ a.   Working with old people changed my stereotyped ideas about the elderly.

_____ b.   My life has moved in new directions since the rewarding job I had working with older people last summer.

2. _____ a.   The new architecture on this campus is very unpleasant, although the expansion was desperately needed.

_____ b.   Our new college library building is ugly, intimidating, and inefficient.

3. _____ a.   Among the most entertaining ads on TV today are those for mail-order products.

_____ b.   Although ads on TV for mail-order products are often misleading, they can still be very entertaining.

4. _____ a.   My roommate and I are compatible in most ways, but we still have conflicts at times.

_____ b.   My roommate has his own unique systems for studying, writing term papers, and cleaning his room.

5. _____ a.   Although some good movies have come out lately, I prefer to watch old movies because they're more interesting.

_____ b.   Movies of the thirties and forties had better plots, sets, and actors than the ones made today.

3   COMPLETING THESIS STATEMENTS

Activity

Complete the following thesis statements by adding a third supporting point that will parallel the two already provided. You might want to check first the section on parallelism (pages 351–354) to make sure you understand parallel form.

1. Because I never took college preparatory courses in high school, I entered college deficient in mathematics, study skills, and _____.

2. A good salesperson needs to like people, to be aggressive, and _____ _____.

3. Rather than blame myself for failing the course, I blamed the professor, my adviser, and even _____.

4. Anyone who buys an old house planning to fix it up should be prepared to put in a lot of time, hard work, and _____.

5. Our old car eats gas, makes funny noises, and _____.

6. My mother, my boss, and my _____ are three people who are very important in my life right now.

7. Getting married too young was a mistake because we hadn't finished our education, we weren't ready for children, and _____ _____ _____.

8. Some restaurant patrons seem to leave their honesty, their cleanliness, and their _____ at home.

9. During my first semester at college, I had to learn how to manage my time, how to manage my diet, and _____.

10. Three experiences I wish I could forget are the time I fell off a ladder, the time I tried to fix my parents' lawn mower, and _____ _____ _____.

4   WRITING A THESIS STATEMENT

Activity

This activity will give you practice in writing an effective thesis—one that is neither too broad nor too narrow for the supporting points in an essay. An added value of the activity is that sometimes you will construct your thesis after you have decided what your supporting points will be. You will need to know, then, how to write a thesis that will match exactly the points that you have developed.

1. Thesis: _____
   a. My first car was a rebellious-looking one which matched the way I felt and acted as a teenager.
   b. My next car reflected my more mature and practical adult self.
   c. My latest car seems to tell me that I'm aging; it shows my growing concern with comfort and safety.

2. Thesis: _____
   a. Going to a two-year college can save up to $10,000 dollars in tuition.
   b. If the college is nearby, there are no room and board costs.
   c. All the course credits that are accumulated can be transferred to a four-year school.

3. Thesis: _____
   a. First, I tried simply avoiding the snacks aisle of the supermarket.
   b. Then I started limiting myself to only five units of any given snack.
   c. Finally, in desperation, I began keeping the cellophane bags of snacks in a padlocked cupboard.

4. Thesis: _____
   a. The holiday can be frightening for little children and can encourage vandalism in older ones.
   b. Children can be struck by cars while wearing vision-obstructing masks and dark costumes.
   c. More and more incidents of deadly treats filled with razor blades or contaminated with poisons are occurring.

5. Thesis: _____
   a. First of all, I was a typical "type A" personality: anxious, impatient, and hard-driving.
   b. I also had a family history of relatives with heart trouble.
   c. My unhealthy lifestyle, though, was probably the major factor.

5 LIMITING A TOPIC AND WRITING A THESIS

The following two activities will give you practice in distinguishing general from limited subjects and in writing a thesis.

Activity 1

Look carefully at the ten general and limited subjects below. Then see if you can write a thesis for any five of them.

Hint: To create a thesis for a limited subject, ask yourself, ''What point do I want to make about _____ (*my limited subject*)?''

General Subject	Limited Subject
1. Apartment	1. Sharing an apartment with a roommate
2. Self-improvement	2. Behavior toward others
3. Family	3. My mother
4. Eating out	4. Fast-food restaurants
5. Automobiles	5. Bad driving habits
6. Health	6. Regular exercise
7. Owning a house	7. Do-it-yourself repairs around the house
8. Baseball	8. Free-agent system
9. Parenthood	9. Being a single parent
10. Pollution	10. Noise pollution

Thesis statements for five of the limited subjects:

_____

_____

_____

_____

_____

_____

_____

_____

Activity 2

Here is a list of ten general subjects. Limit five of the subjects. Then write theses about those five limited subjects.

General Subject	*Limited Subject*
1. Pets	_____
2. Teenagers	_____
3. Television	_____
4. Work	_____
5. College	_____
6. Doctors	_____
7. Vacations	_____
8. Cooking	_____
9. Money	_____
10. Shopping	_____

Thesis statements for five of the limited subjects:

_____

_____

_____

_____

_____

_____

_____

_____

_____

6 MAKING WORDS AND PHRASES SPECIFIC

To be an effective writer, you must use specific rather than general words. Specific words create pictures in the reader's mind. They help capture interest and make your meaning clear.

Activity

This activity will give you practice at changing vague, indefinite words into sharp, specific ones. Add three or more specific words to replace the general word or words italicized in each sentence. Make changes in the wording of a sentence as necessary.

Example *Several of our appliances* broke down at the same time.
Our washer, refrigerator, and television broke down at the same time.

1. *Salty snacks* are my diet downfall.

_____

_____

_____

2. *Several sections* of the newspaper were missing.

_____

_____

_____

3. *Various gifts for men* were displayed in the department-store window.

_____

_____

_____

4. *Several items in my purse* had been crushed.

_____

_____

_____

5. I swept aside the *things* on my desk in order to spread out the road map.

    _____

    _____

    _____

6. The waitress told us we could have *several types of potatoes.*

    _____

    _____

    _____

7. The doctor examined *various parts of my body* before diagnosing my illness as bronchitis.

    _____

    _____

    _____

8. The *food choices* in the cafeteria were unappetizing.

    _____

    _____

    _____

9. Terry threw all the *junk* from the bottom of her closet into a large cardboard carton.

    _____

    _____

    _____

10. Our neighbor's family room has *a lot of electronic equipment.*

    _____

    _____

    _____

7   MAKING SENTENCES SPECIFIC

Again, you will practice changing vague, indefinite writing into lively, image-filled writing that helps capture your reader's interest and makes your meaning clear.

Compare the following sentences:

General	*Specific*
She walked down the street.	Anne wandered slowly along Rogers Lane.
Animals came into the space.	Hungry lions padded silently into the sawdust-covered arena.
The man signed the paper.	The biology teacher hastily scribbled his name on the course withdrawal slip.

The specific sentences create clear pictures in our minds. The details *show* us exactly what has happened. Here are four ways to make your sentences specific.

1   Use exact names.

He sold his *camper*.   *Vince* sold his *Winnebago*.

2   Use lively verbs.

The flag *moved* in the breeze.   The flag *fluttered* in the breeze.

3   Use descriptive words (modifiers) before nouns.

A man strained to lift the crate.
A *heavyset, perspiring* man strained to lift the *heavy wooden* crate.

4   Use words that relate to the senses—sight, hearing, taste, smell, touch.

That woman jogs five miles a day.
That *fragile-looking, gray-haired* woman jogs five miles a day.   (*sight*)
A noise told the crowd that there were two minutes left to play.
A *piercing whistle* told the *cheering* crowd that there were two minutes left to play.   (*hearing*)
When he returned, all he found in the refrigerator was bread and milk.
When he returned, all he found in the refrigerator was *stale* bread and *sour* milk.   (*taste*)
Neil stroked the kitten's fur until he felt its tiny claws on his hand.
Neil stroked the kitten's *velvety* fur until he felt its tiny, *needle-sharp* claws on his hand.   (*touch*)
Fran placed a sachet in her bureau drawer.
Fran placed a *lilac-scented* sachet in her bureau drawer.   (*smell*)

Activity

With the help of the methods described above, add specific details to any ten of the twelve sentences that follow. Use separate paper.

Examples   The person got off the bus.

The teenage boy bounded down the steps of the shiny yellow school bus.

She worked hard all summer.

All summer, Eva sorted peaches and blueberries in the hot, noisy canning factory.

1. The car would not start.
2. The test was difficult.
3. The boy was tired.
4. My room needs cleaning.
5. The student was bored.
6. The game was exciting.
7. A fire started.
8. A vehicle blocked traffic.
9. A large rock fell.
10. The salesperson was obnoxious.
11. The child started to cry.
12. The lounge area was busy.

8   PROVIDING SPECIFIC EVIDENCE

Activity

Provide three details that logically support each of the following points. Your details can be drawn from your direct experience or they can be invented. In each case, the details should show in a specific way what the point expresses in only a general way. State your details briefly in several words rather than in complete sentences.

Example   We quickly spruced up the apartment before our guest arrived.

1. Hide toys and newspapers in spare closet

2. Vacuum pet hairs off sofa

3. Spray air freshener around living room

1. The dinner was a disaster.

    _____

    _____

    _____

2. My seven-year-old nephew has some disgusting habits.

    _____

    _____

    _____

3. There are several reasons why I put off studying.

    _____

    _____

    _____

4. My parents never allowed me to think for myself.

    _____

    _____

    _____

5. I have several ways in which I can earn extra cash.

    _____

    _____

    _____

6. My car needs repairs.

    _____

    _____

    _____

7. Friday evening, I didn't sit still for a minute.

    _____

    _____

    _____

8. Mr. or Ms. _____ was the worst teacher I ever had.

    _____

    _____

    _____

9   IDENTIFYING ADEQUATE SUPPORTING EVIDENCE

Activity

The following body paragraphs were taken from student essays. Two of the paragraphs provide sufficient details to support their topic sentences convincingly. Write AD for *adequate development* beside those paragraphs. Three paragraphs use vague, wordy, general, or irrelevant sentences as an excuse for real supporting details. Write U for *underdeveloped* beside those paragraphs.

_____   1.   Another consideration in adopting a dog is the cost. Initial fees for shots and a license might add up to $40. Annual visits to the vet for heartworm pills, rabies or distemper shots, and general checkups could cost $50 or more. Then, there is the cost of food. A twenty-five-pound bag of dry food (the cheapest kind) costs around $10. A large dog can eat that much in a couple of weeks.

_____   2.   People can be cruel to pets simply by being thoughtless. They don't think about a pet's needs or simply ignore the needs. It never occurs to them that their pet can be experiencing a great deal of discomfort as a result of their failure to be sensitive. The cruelty is a result of the basic lack of attention and concern--qualities that should be there, but aren't.

_____   3.   If I were in charge of the nighttime programming on a TV network, I would make changes. I would completely eliminate some shows. In fact, all of the shows that proved of little interest would be canceled. Commercials would also change, so that it would be possible to watch them without wanting to turn off the TV set. I would expand the good shows so that people would come away with an even better experience. My ideal network would be a great improvement over the average lineup we see today on any of the major networks.

_____   4.   A friend's rudeness is much more damaging than a stranger's. When a friend says sharply, "I don't have time to talk to you just now," you feel hurt instead of angry. When a friend shows up late for lunch or a shopping trip, with no good reason, you feel that you're being taken for granted. Worst, though, is a friend who pretends to be listening to you but whose wandering eyes reveal a lack of attention. Then you feel betrayed. Friends, after all, are supposed to make up for the thoughtless cruelties of strangers.

_____   5.   Giving my first shampoo and set to a real person, after weeks of practicing on wigs, was a nerve-wracking experience. The customer was a woman who was very set in her ways. She tried to describe what she wanted, and I tried without much success to understand what she had in mind. Every time I did something, she seemed to be indicating in one way or another that it was not what she wanted. I got more and more nervous as I worked on her hair, and the nervousness showed. The worst part of the ordeal happened at the very end, when I added the final touches. Nothing, to this woman, had turned out right.

10   ADDING DETAILS TO COMPLETE AN ESSAY

Activity

The following essay needs specific details to back up the ideas in its supporting paragraphs. In the spaces provided, add a sentence or two of clear, convincing details for each idea. This activity will give you practice at supplying specific details and an initial feel for writing an essay.

Introduction

Life without Television

When my family's only television set went to the repair shop the other day, my parents, my sister, and I thought we would have a terrible week. How could we get through the long evenings in such a quiet house? What would it be like without all the shows to keep us company? We soon realized, though, that living without television for a while was a stroke of good fortune. It became easy for each of us to enjoy some activities alone, to complete some postponed chores, and to spend rewarding time with each other and friends.

First supporting paragraph

First of all, with no television to compete for our time, we found plenty of hours for personal interests. We all read more that week than we had read during the six months before. _____

_____

_____

We each also enjoyed some hobbies we had ignored for ages. _____

_____

_____

_____

In addition, my sister and I both stopped procrastinating with our homework. _____

_____

_____

_____

Second supporting paragraph

   Second, we did chores that had been hanging over our heads for too long. There were many jobs around the house that had needed attention for some time. _____

_____

_____

We also had a chance to do some long-postponed shopping. _____

_____

_____

And each of us also did some letter writing or other paperwork that was long overdue. _____

_____

_____

Third supporting paragraph

   Finally, and probably most important, we spent time with each other. Instead of being in the same room together while we stared at a screen, we actually talked for many pleasant hours. _____

_____

Moreover, for the first time in years my family played some games together. _____

_____

And because we didn't have to worry about missing this or that show, we had some family friends over a couple of evenings and spent an enjoyable time with them. _____

_____

_____

Conclusion

Once our television set returned, we were not prepared to put it in the attic. But we had a sense of how it can take over our lives if we are not careful. We are now more selective. We turn on the set for our favorite shows, certain sports events, and the news, but we don't leave it running all night. As a result, we find we can enjoy television and still have time left over for other activities and interests.

THE THIRD
AND FOURTH
STEPS
IN ESSAY
WRITING

This chapter will show you how to:

- Organize and connect the specific evidence in the body paragraphs of an essay
- Begin and end the essay with effective introductory and concluding paragraphs
- Write clear, error-free sentences

You know from the previous chapter that the first two steps in writing an effective essay are advancing a thesis and supporting it with specific evidence. The third step is to organize and connect the specific evidence, which appears in the supporting paragraphs of the essay. Most of this chapter will deal with the chief ways to organize and connect this supporting information in a paper. The chapter will also discuss how to start the essay smoothly with a suitable introductory paragraph and how to finish it effectively with a well-rounded concluding paragraph. Finally, the chapter will look briefly at the sentence skills that make up the fourth and final step in writing a successful paper.

Step 3:
Organize and Connect
the Specific Evidence

At the same time that you are generating the specific details needed to support a thesis, you should be thinking about ways to organize and connect those details. All the details in your essay must cohere, or stick together; in this way, your reader will be able to move smoothly and clearly from one bit of supporting information to the next. This section will discuss the following ways to organize and connect supporting details: (1) common methods of organization, (2) transitions, and (3) other connecting words.

COMMON METHODS OF ORGANIZATION

Time order and emphatic order are common methods used to organize the supporting material in an essay. (You will learn more specific methods of development in Part Two of this book.) *Time*, or *chronological, order* simply means that details are listed as they occur in time. *First* this is done; *next* this; *then* this; *after* that, this; and so on. Here is an outline of an essay in this book in which time order is used.

Thesis: However, for success in exercise, you should follow a simple plan consisting of arranging the time, making preparations, and following the sequence with care.

1. To begin with, set aside a regular hour for exercise.
2. Next, prepare for your exercise session.
3. If this is your first attempt at exercising, start slowly.

Fill in the missing word: The topic sentences in the essay use the words *To begin with* _____ and _____ to help show time order.

Here is one supporting paragraph from the essay:

Next, prepare for your exercise session. You do this, first, by not eating or drinking anything for an hour before the session. Why risk an upset stomach? Then, dress comfortably in something that allows you to move freely. Since you'll be in your own home, there's no need to invest in a high-fashion dance costume. A loose T shirt and shorts are good. A bathing suit is great in summer, and in winter a set of long underwear is warm and comfortable. If your hair tends to flop in your eyes, pin it back or wear a headband or scarf. After dressing, prepare the exercise area. Turn off the phone and lock the door to prevent interruptions. Shove the coffee table out of the way so you won't bruise yourself on it. Finally, get out the simple materials you'll need to exercise on.

Fill in the missing words: The paragraph uses the following words to help show time order: _____*Next*_____ , _____ , _____ , _____ , and _____ .

Emphatic order is sometimes described as "save-the-best-till-last" order. It means that the most interesting or important detail is placed in the last part of a paragraph or in the final supporting paragraph of an essay. (In cases where all the details seem equal in importance, the writer should impose a personal order that seems logical or appropriate to the details in question.) The last position in a paper is the most emphatic position because the reader is most likely to remember the last thing read. *Finally, last of all,* and *most important* are typical words showing emphasis. Here is an outline of an essay in the book that uses emphatic order:

Thesis: Celebrities lead very stressful lives; for, no matter how glamorous or powerful they are, they have too little privacy, too much pressure, and no safety.

   1. For one thing, celebrities don't have the privacy an ordinary person does.
   2. In addition, celebrities are under constant pressure.
   3. Most important, celebrities must deal with the stress of being in constant danger.

Fill in the missing words: The topic sentences in the essay use the words ___*For one thing*___ , _____ , and _____ to help show emphatic order.

Here is the third supporting paragraph from the essay:

   Most important, celebrities must deal with the stress of being in constant danger. The friendly grabs, hugs, and kisses of enthusiastic fans can quickly turn into uncontrolled assaults on a celebrity's hair, clothes, and car. Also, celebrities often get strange letters from people who become obsessed with their idols or from people who threaten to harm them. Worst of all, threats can turn into deeds. The attempt to kill Ronald Reagan and the murder of John Lennon came about because two unbalanced people tried to transfer the celebrity's fame to themselves. Famous people must live with the fact that they are always fair game--and never out of season.

Fill in the missing words: The words _____ are used to mark the most emphatic detail in the paragraph.

Some essays use a combination of time order and emphatic order. For example, the essay on moviegoing in the first chapter includes a time order: The writer first talks of getting to the theater, then of the theater itself, and finally of the behavior of patrons during the movie. At the same time, the writer uses an emphatic order, ending with the most important reason for her dislike of moviegoing: ''Some of the other patrons are even more of a problem than the theater itself.''

Activity

Part A: Read the essays referred to below and identify their method of organizing details—through time order, emphatic order, or a combination of both.

1.   ''My First Professional Performance'' (page 195)

     _____

2.   ''A Vote for McDonald's'' (page 152)

     _____

3.   ''Everyday Cruelty'' (page 121)

     _____

Part B: See if you can now complete the explanations that follow.

The essay titled ''My First Professional Performance'' uses (*add the missing word*) _____ order. The writer begins with the problems she experienced when she arrived at the carnival grounds, moves on to problems during the performance, and ends with the concert's rather abrupt finish. ''A Vote for McDonald's'' uses (*add the missing word*) _____ order. The writer presents three advantages of eating at McDonald's and ends with the most important one: reasonable prices. ''Everyday Cruelty'' uses a combination of (*add the missing words*) _____ order and _____ order. It moves from the beginning to the end of a particular workday. It also ends with the ''worst incident of mean-spiritedness'' that the writer witnessed that day.

TRANSITIONS

Transitions are signals that help readers follow the direction of the writer's thought. They are like signposts on the road that guide travelers. In the box that follows are some common transitional words and phrases, grouped according to the kind of signal they give to readers. Note that certain words provide more than one kind of signal.

Addition signals: one, first of all, second, the third reason, also, next, another, and, in addition, moreover, furthermore, finally, last of all

Time signals: first, then, next, after, as, before, while, meanwhile, soon, now, during, finally

Space signals: next to, across, on the opposite side, to the left, to the right, above, below, nearby

Change-of-direction signals: but, however, yet, in contrast, although, otherwise, still, on the contrary, on the other hand

Illustration signals: for example, for instance, specifically, as an illustration, once, such as

Conclusion signals: therefore, consequently, thus, then, as a result, in summary, to conclude, last of all, finally

---

Activity

1. Underline the four *addition* signals in the following selection:

> Another way that animals are abused is through their use in unnecessary lab and medical experiments. One instance is the use of rabbits in lab tests for cosmetic companies. The helpless animals are locked into neck restraints resembling the old-fashioned stocks used by the Puritans. Moreover, their eyes are pinned open with metal clamps. Solutions of experimental hair dye are dripped continuously into each rabbit's eyes to test the solution for possible irritation or cancer-causing effects. A second example of needless animal abuse involves the endless repetition of previously done experiments. Every year, science and medical students destroy thousands of monkeys, cats, dogs, and rabbits simply for practice. They repeat experiments whose results are well known and which they could learn from books and scientific reports. These are cases not of worthwhile advances in science but of the thoughtless destruction of life.

2.   Underline the three *time* signals in the following selection:

Once you've snagged the job of TV sports reporter, you have to begin working on the details of your image. First, invest in two or three truly loud sports jackets. Look for gigantic plaid patterns in odd color combinations like purple and green or orange and blue. These should become familiar enough to viewers so that they will associate that crazy jacket with that dynamic sportscaster. Next, try to cultivate a distinctive voice that will be just annoying enough to be memorable. A nasal whine or a gravelly growl will do it. Be sure to speak only in tough, punchy sentences that seem to be punctuated with imaginary exclamation points. Finally, you must share lots of pompous, obnoxious opinions with your viewers. Your tone of voice must convey the hidden message, "I dare anyone to disagree with me." When the home teams lose, call them bums. When players strike, talk sarcastically about the good old days. When a sports franchise leaves town, say, "Good riddance."

3.   Underline the three *space* signals in the following selection:

The vegetable bin of my refrigerator contained an assortment of weird-looking items. Next to a shriveled, white-coated lemon was a pair of oranges covered with blue fuzz. To the right of the oranges was a bunch of carrots that had begun to sprout points, spikes, knobs, and tendrils. The carrots drooped into U shapes as I picked them up with the tips of my fingers. Near the carrots was a net bag of onions; each onion had sent curling shoots through the net until the whole thing resembled a mass of green spaghetti. The most horrible item, though, was a head of lettuce that had turned into a pool of brown goo. It had seeped out of its bag and coated the bottom of the bin with a sticky, evil-smelling liquid.

4.   Underline the two *change-of-direction* signals in the following selection:

Taking small children on vacation, for instance, sounds like a wonderful experience for the entire family. But vacations can be scary or emotionally overwhelming times for children. When children are taken away from their usual routine and brought to an unfamiliar place, they can become very frightened. That strange bed in the motel room or the unusual noises in Grandma's spare bedroom may cause nightmares. On vacations, too, children usually clamor to do as many things in one day as they can and to stay up past their usual bedtime. And, since it is vacation time, parents may decide to give in to the children's demands. A parental attitude like this, however, can lead to problems. After a sixteen-hour day of touring the amusement park, eating in a restaurant, and seeing a movie, children can experience sensory and emotional overload. They become cranky, unhappy, or even rebellious and angry.

5. Underline the two *illustration* signals in the following selection:

> Supermarkets also use psychology to encourage you to buy. For example, in most supermarkets, the milk and the bread are either at opposite ends of the store or located far away from the first aisle. Even if you've stopped at the market only for staples like these, you must pass hundreds of items in order to reach them. The odds are that instead of leaving with a quart of milk, you'll leave with additional purchases as well. Special displays, such as a pyramid of canned green beans in an aisle or a large end display of cartons of paper towels, also increase sales. Because you assume that these items are a good buy, you may pick them up. However, they may not even be on sale! Store managers know that customers are automatically attracted to these displays, and they will use them to move an overstocked product.

6. Underline the two *conclusion* signals in the following selection:

> Finally, my grandmother was extremely thrifty. She was one of those people who hoard pieces of used aluminum foil after carefully scraping off the cake icing or beef gravy. She had a drawer full of old eyeglasses that dated back at least thirty years. The lens prescriptions were no longer accurate, but Gran couldn't bear to throw away "a good pair of glasses." She kept them "just in case," but we could never figure out what situation would involve a desperate need for a dozen pairs of old eyeglasses. We never realized the true extent of Gran's thriftiness, though, until after she died. Her house was to be sold, and therefore we cleaned out its dusty attic. In one corner was a cardboard box filled with two- and three-inch pieces of string. The box was labeled, in Gran's spidery hand, "String too short to be saved."

TRANSITIONAL SENTENCES

Transitions occur not only *within* the supporting paragraphs in an essay but also *between* the paragraphs. *Transitional,* or *linking, sentences* are used to help tie together the supporting paragraphs in an essay. They enable the reader to move smoothly and clearly from one idea and paragraph in an essay to the next idea and paragraph. Here are the two linking sentences in the essay on moviegoing:

> Once you have made it to the box office and gotten your tickets, you're confronted with the problems of the theater itself.

The words *made it to the box office* remind us of the point of the first supporting paragraph, while *confronted with the problems of the theater itself* presents the point to be developed in the second supporting paragraph.

> Some of the other patrons are even more of a problem than the theater itself.

The words *the theater itself* echo the point of the second supporting paragraph, while *some of the other patrons* announces the topic of the third supporting paragraph.

Activity

Given below is a brief sentence outline of an essay. In the outline, the second and third topic sentences serve as transitional or linking sentences. They both remind us of the point in the preceding paragraph and announce the point to be developed in the present paragraph. In the space provided, add the words needed to complete the second and third topic sentences.

Thesis

The most important values I learned from my parents are the importance of family support, of hard work, and of a good education.

First supporting paragraph

First, my parents taught me that family members should stick together, especially in times of trouble. . . .

Second supporting paragraph

In addition to teaching me about the importance of _____

_____,

my parents taught me the value of _____

_____. . . .

Third supporting paragraph

Along with the value of _____,

my parents emphasized the benefits of _____

_____. . . .

OTHER CONNECTING WORDS

In addition to transitions, there are three other kinds of connecting words that help tie together the specific evidence in a paper: repeated words, pronouns, and synonyms. Each will be discussed in turn.

Repeated Words

Many of us have been taught by English teachers—correctly so—not to repeat ourselves in our writing. On the other hand, repeating *key* words can help tie together the flow of thought in a paper. Below is a selection that uses repeated words to remind readers of the key idea on which the discussion is centered:

> One reason for studying psychology is to help you deal with your children. Perhaps your young daughter refuses to go to bed when you want her to and bursts into tears at the least mention of "lights out." A little knowledge of psychology comes in handy. Offer her a choice of staying up until 7:30 with you or going upstairs and playing until 8:00. Since she gets to make the choice, she does not feel so powerless and will not resist. Psychology is also useful in rewarding a child for a job well done. Instead of telling your ten-year-old son what a good boy he is when he makes his own bed, tell him how neat it looks, how happy you are to see it, and how proud of him you are for doing it by himself. The psychology books will tell you that being a good boy is much harder to live up to than doing one job well.

Pronouns

Pronouns (*he, she, it, you, they, this, that,* and others) are another way to connect ideas as you develop a paper. Using pronouns to take the place of other words or ideas can help you avoid needless repetition in a paper. (Note, however, that although pronouns are helpful, they should be used with care in order to avoid the unclear or inconsistent pronoun references described in this book on pages 355–367.) Here is a selection that makes use of pronouns:

> Another way for people to economize at an amusement park is to bring their own food. If they pack a nourishing, well-balanced lunch of cold chicken, carrot sticks, and fruit, they will avoid having to pay high prices for hamburgers and hot dogs. They will also save on calories. Also, instead of filling up on soft drinks, they should bring a thermos of iced tea. It is more refreshing than soda, and it is a great deal cheaper. Every dollar that is not spent at a refreshment stand is one that can be spent on another ride.

Synonyms

Using synonyms (that is, words that are alike in meaning) also can help move the reader clearly from one step in the thought of a paper to the next. In addition, the use of synonyms increases variety and interest by avoiding needless repetition of the same words.

Note the synonyms for *method* in the following selection:

There are several methods of fund-raising that work well with small organizations. One technique is to hold an auction, with everyone either contributing an item from home or obtaining a donation from a sympathetic local merchant. Because all the merchandise, including the services of the auctioneer, has been donated, the entire proceeds can be placed in the organization's treasury. A second fund-raising procedure is a car wash. Club members and their children get together on a Saturday and wash all the cars in the neighborhood for a few dollars apiece. A final, time-tested way to raise money is to give a bake sale, with each family contributing homemade cookies, brownies, layer cakes, or cupcakes. Sold by the piece or by the box, these baked goods will satisfyingly fill both the stomach and the pocketbook.

Activity

Read the selection below and then answer the questions about it that follow:

[1]When I think about my childhood in the 1930s, today's energy crisis and lowered thermostats don't seem so bad. [2]In our house, we had only a wood-burning cookstove in the kitchen to keep us warm. [3]In the morning, my father would get up in the icy cold, go downstairs, and light a fire in the black iron range. [4]When he called us, I would put off leaving my warm bed until the last possible minute and then quickly grab my school clothes. [5]The water pitcher and washing basin in my room would be layered with ice, and my breath would come out as white puffs as I ran downstairs. [6]My sisters and I would all dress--as quickly as possible--in the chilly but bearable air of the kitchen. [7]Our schoolroom, once we had arrived, didn't provide much relief from the cold. [8]Students wore woolen mitts which left their fingers free but covered their palms and wrists. [9]Even with these, we occasionally suffered chilblains. [10]The throbbing patches on our hands made writing a painful process. [11]When we returned home in the afternoon, we spent all our indoor hours in the warm kitchen. [12]We hated to leave it at bedtime in order to make the return trip to those cold bedrooms and frigid sheets. [13]My mother made up hot-water bottles and gave us hot bricks to tuck under the covers, but nothing could eliminate the agony of that penetrating cold when we first slid under the bedclothes.

1. How many times is the key word *cold* repeated? _____

2. Write here the pronoun that is used for *father* (sentence 4): _____;

    mitts (sentence 9): _____; *kitchen* (sentence 12): _____.

3. Write here the words that are used as a synonym for *cookstove* in sentence 3:

    _____; write in the words that are used as a synonym for

    chilblains in sentence 10: _____; write in the word that is

    used as a synonym for *cold* in sentence 12: _____.

INTRODUCTIONS, CONCLUSIONS, AND TITLES

So far, this chapter has been concerned with ways to organize the supporting paragraphs of an essay. A well-organized essay, however, should also have a strong introductory paragraph, an effective concluding paragraph, and a good title.

Introductory Paragraph

A well-written introductory paragraph will perform several important roles:

1   It will attract the reader's interest, encouraging him or her to go on and actually read the essay. Using one of the methods of introduction described below can help draw the reader into your paper.

2   It will supply any background information needed to understand the essay. Such information is sometimes needed so that the reader has a context in which to understand the ideas presented in the essay.

3   It will present a thesis statement. This clear, direct statement of the main idea to be developed in the paper usually occurs near the end of the introductory paragraph.

4   It will indicate a plan of development. In this "preview," the major points that will support the thesis are listed in the order in which they will be presented in the essay. In some cases, the thesis and plan of development may appear in the same sentence. In some cases, also, the plan of development may be omitted.

Common Methods of Introduction: Here are some common methods of introduction. Use any one method, or combination of methods, to introduce your subject in an interesting way to the reader.

1   ***Begin with a broad, general statement of your topic and narrow it down to your thesis statement.*** Broad, general statements ease the reader into your thesis statement by providing a background for it. In the example below, the writer talks generally about diets and then narrows down to comments on a specific diet.

> Bookstore shelves today are crammed with dozens of different diet books. The American public seems willing to try any sort of diet, especially the ones that promise instant, miraculous results. And authors are more than willing to invent new fad diets to cash in on this craze. Unfortunately, some of these fad diets are ineffective or even unsafe. One of the worst is the "Palm Beach diet." It is impractical, doesn't achieve the results it claims, and is a sure route to poor nutrition.

2 ***Start with an idea or situation that is the opposite of the one you will develop.*** This approach works because your readers will be surprised, and then intrigued, by the contrast between the opening idea and the thesis that follows it.

> When I decided to return to school at age thirty-five, I wasn't at all worried about my ability to do the work. After all, I was a grown woman who had raised a family, not a confused teenager fresh out of high school. But when I started classes, I realized that those "confused teenagers" sitting around me were in much better shape for college than I was. They still had all their classroom skills in bright, shiny condition, while mine had grown rusty from disuse. I had totally forgotten how to locate information in a library, how to write a report, and even how to speak up in class discussions.

3 ***Explain the importance of your topic to the reader.*** If you can convince your readers that the subject in some way applies to them, or is something they should know more about, they will want to keep reading.

> Diseases like scarlet fever and whooping cough used to kill more young children than any other cause. Today, however, child mortality due to disease has been almost completely eliminated by medical science. Instead, car accidents are the number one killer of our children. And most of the children fatally injured in car accidents were not protected by car seats, belts, or restraints of any kind. Several steps must be taken to remedy this serious problem.

4 ***Use an incident or brief story.*** Stories are naturally interesting. They appeal to a reader's curiosity. In your introduction, an anecdote will grab the reader's attention right away. The story should be brief and should be related to your main idea. The incident in the story can be something that happened to you, something you have heard about, or something you have read about in a newspaper or magazine.

> Early Sunday morning the young mother dressed her little girl warmly and gave her a candy bar, a picture book, and a well-worn stuffed rabbit. Together, they drove downtown to a Methodist church. There the mother told the little girl to wait on the stone steps until children began arriving for Sunday school. Then the young mother drove off, abandoning her five-year-old because she couldn't cope with being a parent anymore. This incident is one of thousands of cases of child neglect and abuse that occur annually. Perhaps the automatic right to become a parent should no longer exist. Would-be parents, instead, should be forced to apply for licenses granting them the privilege of raising children.

5 *Ask one or more questions.* But remember that questions need answers. You may simply want the reader to think about possible answers, or you may plan to answer the questions yourself later in the paper.

> What is love? How do we know that we are really in love? When we meet that special person, how can we tell that our feelings are genuine and not merely infatuation? And, if they are genuine, will these feelings last? Love, as we all know, is difficult to define. But most people agree that true and lasting love involves far more then mere physical attraction. It involves mutual respect, the desire to give rather than take, and the feeling of being wholly at ease.

6 *Use a quotation.* A quotation can be something you have read in a book or article. It can also be something that you have heard: a popular saying or proverb (''Never give advice to a friend''); a current or recent advertising slogan (''Reach out and touch someone''); a favorite expression used by friends or family (''My father always says . . .''). Using a quotation in your introductory paragraph lets you add someone else's voice to your own.

> "Fish and visitors," wrote Benjamin Franklin, "begin to smell after three days." Last summer, when my sister and her family came to spend their two-week vacation with us, I became convinced that Franklin was right. After only three days, I was thoroughly sick of my brother-in-law's corny jokes, my sister's endless complaints about her boss, and their children's constant invasions of our privacy.

Activity

The box below summarizes the six kinds of introduction. Read the introductions that follow and, in the space provided, write the number of the kind of introduction used in each case.

1. General to narrow	4. Incident or story
2. Starting with an opposite	5. Questions
3. Stating importance of topic	6. Quotation

_____

> The ad, in full color on a glossy magazine page, shows a beautiful kitchen with gleaming counters. In the foreground, on one of the counters, stands a shiny new food processor. Usually, a feminine hand is touching it lovingly. Around the main picture are other, smaller shots. They show mounds of perfectly sliced onion rings, thin rounds of juicy tomatoes, heaps of matchstick-sized potatoes, and piles of golden, evenly grated cheese. The ad copy tells you how wonderful, how easy, food preparation will be with a processor. Don't believe it. My processor turned out to be expensive, difficult to operate, and very limited in its use.

_____   People say, "You can't tell a book by its cover." Actually, you can. When you're browsing in the drugstore or supermarket and you see a paperback featuring an attractive young woman in a low-cut dress fleeing from a handsome dark figure in a shadowy castle, you know exactly what you're getting. Every romance novel has the same elements: an innocent heroine, an exotic setting, and a cruel but fascinating hero.

_____   We Americans are incredibly lazy. Instead of cooking a simple, nourishing meal, we pop a frozen dinner into the oven. Instead of studying a daily newspaper, we are contented with the capsule summaries on the network news. Worst of all, instead of walking even a few blocks to the local convenience store, we jump into our cars. This dependence on the automobile, even for short trips, has robbed us of a valuable experience-- walking. If we drove less and walked more, we would save money, become healthier, and discover fascinating things about our surroundings.

Concluding Paragraph

A concluding paragraph is your chance to remind the reader of your thesis idea. Also, the conclusion brings the paper to a natural and graceful end, sometimes leaving the reader with a final thought on the subject.

Common Methods of Conclusion: Any one of the methods below, or a combination of methods, may be used to round off your paper.

1 ***End with a summary and final thought.*** When Army instructors train new recruits, each of their lessons follows a three-step formula:
   a   Tell them what you're going to tell them.
   b   Tell them.
   c   Tell them what you've told them.

An essay that ends with a summary is not very different. After you have stated your thesis ("Tell them what you're going to tell them") and supported it ("Tell them"), you restate the thesis and supporting points ("Tell them what you've told them"). Don't, however, use the exact wording you used before. Here is a summary conclusion:

   Catalog shopping at home, then, has several advantages. Such shopping is convenient, saves you money, and saves you time. It is not surprising that growing numbers of devoted catalog shoppers are welcoming those full-color mail brochures that offer everything from turnip seeds to televisions.

Note that the summary is accompanied by a final comment that "rounds off" the paper and brings the discussion to a close. This combination of a summary and a final thought is the most common method of concluding an essay.

2 ***Include a thought-provoking question or short series of questions.*** A question grabs the reader's attention. It is a direct appeal to your reader to think further about what you have written. A question should follow logically from the points you have already made in the paper. A question must deal with one of these areas:

a Why the subject of your paper is important
b What might happen in the future
c What should be done about this subject
d Which choice should be made

You may provide an answer to your question in the conclusion. Be sure, though, that your question is closely related to your thesis. Here is an example:

> What, then, will happen in the twenty-first century when most of the population will be over sixty years old? Retirement policies could change dramatically, with the age-sixty-five testimonial dinner and gold watch postponed for five or ten years. Even television would change as the Geritol generation replaces the Pepsi generation. Glamorous gray-haired models would sell everything from toilet paper to televisions. New soap operas and situation comedies would reveal the secrets of the "sunset years." It will be a different world indeed when the young finally find themselves outnumbered.

3 ***End with a prediction or recommendation.*** Like questions, predictions and recommendations also involve your readers. A prediction states what will or may happen in the future:

> If people stopped to think before acquiring pets, there would be fewer instances of cruelty to animals. Many times, it is the people who adopt pets without considering the expense and responsibility involved who mistreat and neglect their animals. Pets are living creatures. They do not deserve to be acquired as carelessly as one would acquire a stuffed toy.

A recommendation suggests what should be done about a situation or problem:

> Stereotypes such as the helpless homemaker, harried executive, and dotty grandparent are insulting enough to begin with. Placed in magazine ads or television commercials, they become even more insulting. Now these unfortunate characters are not just being laughed at; they are being turned into hucksters to sell products to an unsuspecting public. Consumers should boycott companies whose advertising continues to use such stereotypes.

Activity

In the space provided, note whether each concluding paragraph ends with a summary and final thought (write S in the space), ends with a prediction or recommendation (write P/R), or ends with a question (write Q).

_____ 1.   Disappointments are unwelcome, but regular, visitors to everyone's life. We can feel depressed about them, or we can try to escape from them. The best thing, though, is to accept a disappointment and then try to use it somehow: step over the unwelcome visitor and then get on with life.

_____ 2.   Holidays, it is clear, are often not the fulfilling experiences they are supposed to be. They can, in fact, be nerve-wracking. How can one deal with the problem? Most experts agree that a person should schedule plenty of activities: more time with family, volunteer work, even overtime on the job. Staying active is preferable to the depressing time one might spend at home with only the hollow and flickering images on the TV for company.

_____ 3.   Some people dream of starring roles, their names in lights, and their pictures on the cover of People magazine. I'm not one of them, though. A famous person gives up private life, feels pressured all the time, and is never completely safe. So let someone else have that cover story. I'd rather lead an ordinary, but calm, life than a stress-filled one.

Titles

A title is usually a very brief summary of what your paper is about. It is often no more than several words. You may find it easy to write the title *after* you have completed your paper.

Following are the introductory paragraphs for two of the essays in this text, along with the titles of the essays.

Introductory Paragraph

I'm not just a consumer--I'm a victim. If I order a product, it is sure to arrive in the wrong color, size, or quantity. If I hire people to do repairs, they never arrive on the day scheduled. If I owe a bill, the computer is bound to overcharge me. Therefore, in self-defense, I have developed the following consumer's guide to complaining effectively.

Title: How to Complain

Introductory Paragraph

Schools divide people up into categories. From first grade on up, students are labeled "advanced" or "deprived" or "remedial" or "antisocial." Students pigeonhole their fellow students, too. We've all known the "brain," the "jock," the "dummy," and the "teacher's pet." In most cases, these narrow labels are misleading and inaccurate. But there is one label for a certain type of college student that says it all. That is, of course, "zombie."

Title: Student Zombies

Note that you should not underline the title. Nor should you put quotation marks around it. On the other hand, you should capitalize all but small connecting words in the title. Also, you should skip a space between the title and the first line of the text. (See "Manuscript Form," page 287.)

Activity

Write an appropriate title for each of the introductory paragraphs that follow.

1.   For my birthday this month, my wife has offered to treat me to dinner at the restaurant of my choice. I think she expects me to ask for a meal at the Chalet, the classiest, most expensive restaurant in town. However, I'm going to eat my birthday dinner at McDonald's. When I compare the two restaurants, the advantages of eating at McDonald's are clear.

   Title: _____

2.   I've been in lots of diners, and they've always seemed to be warm, busy, friendly, happy places. That's why, on a recent Monday night, I stopped in a diner for a cup of coffee. I was returning home after an all-day car trip and needed something to help me make the last forty-five miles. A diner at midnight, however, was not the place I had expected. It was different--and lonely.

   Title: _____

3.   If you see rock-concert audiences only on television or in newspaper photos, the people at these events may all seem to be excited teenagers. However, if you attended a few rock shows, you would see that several kinds of people make up the crowd. At any concert, you would find the typical fan, the out-of-place person, and the troublemaker.

   Title: _____

Step 4:
Write Clear, Error-Free Sentences

The fourth step in writing an effective paper is to follow the agreed-upon rules or conventions of written English. These conventions—or, as they are called in this book, *sentence skills*—must be followed if your sentences are to be clear and error-free.

Here are the most common of these conventions.

1 Write complete sentences rather than fragments.
2 Do not write run-on sentences.
3 Use verb forms correctly.
4 Make sure that subject, verbs, and pronouns agree.
5 Eliminate faulty parallelism and faulty modifiers.
6 Use pronoun forms correctly.
7 Use capital letters where needed.
8 Use correctly the following marks of punctuation: apostrophe, quotation marks, comma, semicolon, colon, hyphen, dash, parentheses.
9 Use correct paper format.
10 Eliminate wordiness.
11 Choose words carefully.
12 Check for possible spelling errors.
13 Eliminate careless errors.
14 Vary your sentences.

Space will not be taken here to explain and offer activities in all the sentence skills. Rather, they will be treated in detail in Part Four of this book, where they can be referred to easily as needed. Note that both the list of sentence skills on page 119 and the inside front cover (item 4) and the correction symbols on the last page of the book contain page references, so that you can turn quickly to those skills which give you problems.

Practice in Organizing and Connecting Specific Evidence

You now know the third step in effective writing: organizing the specific evidence used to support the thesis of a paper. You also know that the fourth step—writing clear, error-free sentences—will be treated in detail in Part Four. This closing section will expand and strengthen your understanding of the third step in writing. You will work through the following series of activities:

1 Organizing through time or emphatic order
2 Providing transitions
3 Identifying transitions and other connecting words
4 Completing transitional sentences
5 Identifying introductions and conclusions

1 ORGANIZING THROUGH TIME OR EMPHATIC ORDER

Activity 1

Use time order to organize the scrambled lists of supporting ideas below. Put 1 beside the supporting idea that should come first in time, 2 in front of the idea that logically follows, and 3 in front of the idea that comes last in time.

1. Thesis: When I was a child, Disney movies frightened me more than any other kind.

    _____ As a five-year-old, I found the story of *Pinocchio,* a boy transformed into a puppet, terrifying.

    _____ Although I saw *Bambi* when I was old enough to begin poking fun at ''baby movies,'' the scene during which Bambi's mother is killed has stayed with me to this day.

    _____ About a year after *Pinocchio,* I gripped my seat in fear as the witches and goblins of *Fantasia* flew across the screen.

2. Thesis: Beware of these pitfalls if you want to make the perfect cheesecake.

    _____ There's only one way to remove the cake cleanly and easily from its pan.

    _____ Plan in advance to have your equipment ready and the ingredients at room temperature.

    _____ Remember to time the baking process and regulate the oven temperature while the cake is baking.

3. Thesis: Applying for unemployment benefits was a confusing, frustrating experience.

    _____ It was difficult to find both the office and a place to park.

    _____ When I finally reached the head of the line after four hours of waiting, the clerk had problems processing my claim.

    _____ There was no one to direct or help me when I entered the large office, which was packed with people.

Activity 2

Use emphatic order (order of importance) to arrange the following scrambled lists of supporting ideas. For each thesis, write 1 in the blank next to the point that is perhaps less important or interesting than the other two, 2 beside the point that appears more important or interesting, and 3 beside the point that should be most emphasized.

1. Thesis: My after-school job has been an invaluable part of my life this year.

    _____   Better yet, it has taught me how to get along with many kinds of people.

    _____   Since it's in the morning, it usually keeps me from staying up too late.

    _____   Without it, I would have had to drop out of school.

2. Thesis: We received some odd gifts for our wedding.

    _____   The winner in the odd-gift category was a large wooden box with no apparent purpose or function.

    _____   Someone gave us a gift certificate for a massage.

    _____   Even stranger, my uncle gave me his favorite bowling ball.

3. Thesis: Donna is my most loyal friend.

    _____   She has even taken time off from work to do special favors for me.

    _____   She's always there in real emergencies or emotional crises.

    _____   She once lent me her favorite necklace to wear on a date.

2   PROVIDING TRANSITIONS

Activity

In the spaces provided, add appropriate transitions to tie together the sentences and ideas in the following essay. Draw from the words given in the boxes above the paragraphs. Use each word only once.

Annoying People

Former President Richard Nixon used to keep an "enemies list" of all the   1
people he didn't especially like. I'm ashamed to confess it, but I, too, have an
enemies list--a mental one. On this list are all the people I would gladly live
without, the ones who cause my blood pressure to rise to the boiling point.
The top three places on the list go to people with annoying nervous habits,
people who talk in movie theaters, and people who smoke in restaurants.

For example	First of all	Another	However

_____, there are the people with nervous habits.   2

_____, there are the ones who make faces. When in deep

thought, they twitch, squint, and frown, and they can be a real distraction

when I'm trying to concentrate during an exam. _____ type of nervous character makes useless designs. These people bend paper clips into abstract sculptures as they talk or string the clips into necklaces.

_____, neither of these groups is as bad as the people who make noises. These individuals, when they are feeling uncomfortable, bite their fingernails or crack their knuckles. If they have a pencil in their hands, they tap it rhythmically against whatever surface is handy--a desk, a book, a head. Lacking a pencil to play with, they jingle the loose change or keys in their pockets. These people make me wish I were hard of hearing.

On the contrary	Then	As a result	After	second

A _____ category of people I would gladly do away with is the ones who talk in movie theaters. These people are not content to sit   3

back, relax, and enjoy the film they have paid to see. _____, they feel compelled to comment loudly on everything from the hero's hairstyle to the appropriateness of the background music.

_____, no one hears a word of any dialog except theirs.

_____ they have been in the theater for a while, their interest

in the movie may fade. _____ they will start discussing other things, and the people around them will be treated to an instant replay of the last family scandal or soap opera episode. These stories may be entertaining, but they don't belong in a movie theater.

Otherwise	But	Last of all

_____, there are the restaurant smokers. If I have   4
ordered an expensive dinner, I don't appreciate having another diner's smelly cigar smoke compete with the aroma of my sirloin steak. Even the appetizing smell of a Big Mac or Whopper can be spoiled by the sharp fumes sent out by a nearby cigarette smoker. Often, I have to lean over to the next

table and ask the offender to stop smoking. _____, it is impossible for me to taste my food.

So long as murder remains illegal, the nervous twitchers, movie talkers,   5

and restaurant smokers of the world are safe from me. _____ if ever I am granted the power of life or death, these people had better think twice about annoying me. They might not have long to live.

3 IDENTIFYING TRANSITIONS AND OTHER CONNECTING WORDS

Activity

The following selections use connecting words to help tie ideas together. The connecting words you are to identify are set off in italics. In the space, write T for *transition*, RW for *repeated word*, S for *synonym*, or P for *pronoun*.

_____ 1. Kate wears a puffy, quilted, down-filled jacket. In this *garment*, she resembles a stack of inflated inner tubes.

_____ 2. Plants like poinsettias and mistletoe are pretty. *They* are also poisonous.

_____ 3. A strip of strong cloth can be used as an emergency fan-belt replacement. *In addition*, a roll of duct tape can be used to patch a leaky hose temporarily.

_____ 4. Newspapers may someday be brought to your home, not by paper carriers, but by computers. Subscribers will simply punch in a code, and the *machines* will display the desired pages.

_____ 5. I'm always losing my soft contact lenses, which resemble little circles of thick Saran Wrap. One day I dropped both of *them* into a cup of hot tea.

_____ 6. The molded plastic chairs in the classrooms are hard and uncomfortable. When I sit in one of these *chairs*, I feel as if I were sitting in a bucket.

_____ 7. One way to tell if your skin is aging is to pinch a fold of skin on the back of your hand. If *it* doesn't smooth out quickly, your skin is losing its youthful tone.

_____ 8. I never eat sloppy joes. *They* look as if they've already been eaten.

_____ 9. Clothing intended just for children seems to have vanished. *Instead*, children wear scaled-down versions of everything adults wear.

_____ 10. Some successful salespeople use voice tones and hand gestures that are almost hypnotic. Customers are not conscious of this *hypnotic* effect but merely feel the urge to buy.

_____ 11. The giant cockroaches in Florida are the subject of local legends. A visitor, according to one tale, saw one of the *insects*, thought it was a Volkswagen, and tried to drive it away.

_____ 12. Some thieves scour garbage cans for credit-card receipts. *Then*, they use the owner's name and card number to order merchandise by phone.

_____ 13. When the phone rang, I dropped the garden hose. *It* whipped around crazily and squirted water through the kitchen screen door.

_____ 14. There are many phobias other than the ones described in psychology textbooks. I have *phobias*, for instance, about toasters and lawn mowers.

_____ 15. My mother believes that food is love. *Therefore*, when she offers homemade cookies or cupcakes, I hate to hurt her feelings by refusing them.

4   COMPLETING TRANSITIONAL SENTENCES

Activity

Following are brief sentence outlines from two essays. In each outline, the second and third topic sentences serve as transitional, or linking, sentences. They both remind us of the point in the preceding paragraph and announce the point to be developed in the present paragraph. In the space provided, add the words needed to complete the second and third topic sentences.

Thesis 1

Cheaper cost, greater comfort, and superior electronic technology make watching football at home more enjoyable than attending a game at the stadium.

First supporting paragraph

> For one thing, watching the game on TV eliminates the cost of attending the game. . . .

Second supporting paragraph

> In addition to saving me money, watching the game at home is more _____ than sitting in a stadium. . . .

Third supporting paragraph

> Even more important than _____ and _____, though, is the _____ which makes a televised game better than the "real thing." . . .

Thesis 2

In order to set up a day-care center in your home, you must make sure your house will conform to state regulations, obtain the necessary legal permits, and advertise your service in the right places.

First supporting paragraph

> First of all, as a potential operator of a home day-care center, you must make sure your house will conform to state regulations. . . .

Second supporting paragraph

> After making certain that _____
> _____,
> you must obtain _____ . . . .

Third supporting paragraph

> Finally, once you have the necessary _____
> you can begin to _____ .

5   IDENTIFYING INTRODUCTIONS AND CONCLUSIONS

Activity

The box below lists six common kinds of introductions and three common kinds of conclusions. Read the three sets of introductory and concluding paragraphs that follow. Then, in the space provided, write the number of the kind of introduction or conclusion used in each case.

Introductions	Conclusions
1. General to narrow	1. Summary and final thought
2. Starting with an opposite	2. Question(s)
3. Stating importance of topic	3. Prediction or recommendation
4. Incident or story	
5. Question(s)	
6. Quotation	

_____

   Shortly before Easter, our local elementary school sponsored a fund-raising event at which classroom pets and their babies--hamsters, guinea pigs, and baby chicks--were available for adoption. Afterward, as I was driving home, I saw a hand drop a baby hamster out of the car ahead of me. I couldn't avoid running over the tiny creature. One of the parents had taken the pet, regretted the decision, and decided to get rid of it. Such people have never stopped to consider the real obligations involved in owning an animal. . . .

_____ A pet cannot be thrown onto a trash heap when it is no longer wanted or tossed into a closet if it begins to bore its owner. A pet, like us, is a living thing that needs physical care, affection, and respect. Would-be owners, therefore, should think seriously about their responsibilities before they acquire a pet.

_____ What would life be like if we could read each other's minds? Would communications be instantaneous and perfectly clear? These questions will never be answered unless mental telepathy becomes a fact of life. Until then, we will have to make do with less-perfect means of communication, such as letters, telephone calls, and face-to-face conversations. Each of these has its drawbacks. . . .

_____ Neither letters, phone calls, nor conversations guarantee perfect communication. With all our sophisticated skills, we human beings often communicate less effectively than howling wolves or chattering monkeys. Even if we <u>were</u> able to read each other's minds, we'd probably still find some way to foul up the message.

_____ "Few things are harder to put up with," said Mark Twain, "than the annoyance of a good example." Twain obviously knew the problems faced by siblings cursed with older brothers or sisters who are models of perfection. All our lives, my older sister Shelley and I have been compared. Unfortunately, my looks, talents, and accomplishments always ended up on the losing side. . . .

_____ Although our looks, talents, and accomplishments were constantly compared, Shelley and I have somehow managed not to turn into deadly enemies. Feeling like the Edsel of the family, in fact, helped me to develop a drive to succeed and a sense of humor. In our sibling rivalry, we both managed to win.

THE FOUR BASES FOR EVALUATING ESSAY WRITING

This chapter will show you how to evaluate an essay for:

- **Unity**
- **Support**
- **Organization**
- **Sentence skills**

In the preceding chapters, you learned the four essential steps in writing an effective paper. The box below shows how the steps lead to four standards, or bases, you can use in evaluating an essay.

Four Steps ⟶	*Four Bases*
1 If you advance a single point and stick to that point,	you will have *unity* in your paper.
2 If you support the point with specific evidence,	you will have *support* in your paper.
3 If you organize and connect the specific evidence,	you will have *coherence* in your paper.
4 If you write clear, error-free sentences,	you will have effective *sentence skills* in your paper.

This chapter will discuss the four bases of unity, support, coherence, and sentence skills and will show how these four bases can be used to evaluate a paper.

Base 1: Unity

Activity

The following student essays are on the topic ''Problems or Pleasures of My Teenage Years.'' Which one makes its point more clearly and effectively, and why?

Teenage Pranks

Looking back at some of the things I did as a teenager makes me break out in a sweat. The purpose of each adventure was fun, but occasionally things got out of hand. In my search for good times, I was involved in three notable pranks, ranging from fairly harmless to fairly serious.   **1**

The first prank proved that good, clean fun does not have to be dull. As a high school student, I was credited with making the world's largest dessert. With several friends, I spent an entire year collecting boxes of Jell-O. Entering our school's indoor pool one night, we turned the water temperature up as high as it would go and poured in box after box of the strawberry powder. The next morning, school officials arrived to find the pool filled with thirteen thousand gallons of the quivering, rubbery stuff. No one was hurt by the prank, but we did suffer through three days of a massive cleanup.   **2**

Not all my pranks were harmless, and one involved risking my life. As soon as I got my driver's license, I wanted to join the "Fliers' Club." Membership in this club was limited to those who could make their cars fly a distance of at least ten feet. The qualifying site was an old quarry field where friends and I had built a ramp made of dirt. I drove my battered Ford Pinto up this ramp as fast as it would go. The Pinto flew ten feet, but one of the tires exploded when I landed. The car rolled on its side, and I luckily escaped with only a bruised arm.   **3**

Risking my own life was bad enough, but there was another prank where other people could have been hurt, too. On this occasion, I accidentally set a valley on fire. Two of my friends and I were sitting on a hill sharing a few beers. It was a warm summer night, and there was absolutely nothing to do. The idea came like a thunderclap. We collected a supply of large plastic trash bags, emergency highway flares, and the half tank of helium left over from a science-fair experiment. Then we began to construct a fleet of UFOs. Filling the bags with helium, we tied them closed with wire and suspended several burning flares below each bag. Our UFOs leaped into the air like an army of invading Martians. Rising and darting in the blackness, they convinced even us. Our fun turned into horror, though, as we watched the balloons begin to drop onto the wooded valley of expensive homes below. Soon, a brush fire started and, quickly sobered, we hurried off to call the fire department anonymously.   **4**

Every so often, I think back on the things that I did as a teenager. I chuckle at the innocent pranks and feel lucky that I didn't harm myself or others with the not-so-innocent ones. Those years were filled with wild times. Today I'm older, wiser--and maybe just a little more boring.   **5**

Problems of My Adolescence

In the unreal world of television situation comedies, teenagers are   1
carefree, smart, funny, wisecracking, secure kids. In fact, most of them are
more "together" than the adults on the shows. This, however, isn't how I
recall my teenage years at all. As a teen, I suffered. Every day, I battled the
terrible physical, family, and social troubles of adolescence.

For one thing, I had to deal with a demoralizing physical problem--acne.   2
Some days, I would wake up in the morning with a red bump the size of a
taillight on my nose. Since I worried constantly about my appearance
anyway, acne outbreaks could turn me into a crying, screaming maniac.
Plastering on a layer of orange-colored Clearasil, which didn't fool anybody, I
would slink into school, hoping that the boy I had a crush on would be
absent that day. Within the last few years, however, treatments for acne
have improved. Now, skin doctors prescribe special drugs that clear up
pimples almost immediately. An acne attack could shatter whatever small
amount of self-esteem I had managed to build up.

In addition to fighting acne, I felt compelled to fight my family. As a   3
teenager, I needed to be independent. At that time, the most important thing
in life was to be close to my friends and to try out new, more adult
experiences. Unfortunately, my family seemed to get in the way. My little
brother, for instance, turned into my enemy. We're close now, though. In
fact, Eddie recently painted my new apartment for me. Eddie used to barge
into my room, listen to my phone conversations, and read my secret letters.
I would threaten to tie him up and leave him in a garbage dumpster. He
would scream, my mother would yell, and all hell would break loose. My
parents, too, were enemies. They wouldn't let me stay out late, wear the
clothes I wanted to wear, or hang around with the friends I liked. So I tried
to get revenge on them by being miserable, sulky, and sarcastic at home.

Worst of all, I had to face the social traumas of being a teenager. Things   4
that were supposed to be fun, like dates and dances, were actually horrible.
On the few occasions when I had a real date, I agonized over everything--my
hair, my weight, my pimples. After a date, I would come home, raid the
kitchen, and drown my insecurities in a sea of junk food. Dances were also
stressful events. My friends and I would sneak a couple of beers just to get
up the nerve to walk into the school gym. Now I realize that teenage
drinking is dangerous. I read recently that the number one killer of
teenagers is drunk driving. At dances, I never relaxed. It was too important
to look exactly right, to act really cool, and to pretend I was having fun.

I'm glad I'm not a teenager anymore. I wouldn't ever want to feel so   5
unattractive, so confused, and so insecure again. I'll gladly accept the crow's-
feet and stomach bulge of adulthood in exchange for a little peace of mind.

The _____ essay makes its point more clearly and effectively because

_____

_____

_____

UNDERSTANDING UNITY

The first essay is more effective because it is unified. All the details in the essay are on target; they support and develop each of the essay's three topic sentences ("The first prank proved that good, clean fun does not have to be dull"; "Not all my pranks were harmless, and one involved risking my life"; and, "Risking my own life was bad enough, but there was another prank where other people could have been hurt, too").

On the other hand, the second essay contains some details irrelevant to the essay's topic sentences. In the first supporting paragraph (paragraph 2), the sentences, "Within the last few years, however, treatments for acne have improved. Now, skin doctors prescribe special drugs that clear up pimples almost immediately," do not support the writer's topic statement that she had to deal with the physical problem of acne. Such details should be left out in the interest of unity. Go back to the second essay and cross out the two sentences in the second supporting paragraph (paragraph 3) and the two sentences in the third supporting paragraph (paragraph 4) that are off target and do not help support their topic sentences.

You should have crossed out the following two sentences: "We're close now . . . apartment for me" and "Now I realize . . . drunk driving."

The difference between the first two essays leads us to the first base or standard of effective writing: *unity*. To achieve unity is to have all the details in your paper related to your thesis and three supporting topic sentences. Each time you think of something to put into your paper, ask yourself whether it relates to your thesis and supporting points. If it does not, leave it out. For example, if you were writing a paper about the problems of being unemployed and then spent a couple of sentences talking about the pleasures of having a lot of free time, you would be missing the first and most essential base of good writing. The pages ahead will consider the other three bases that you must touch in order to succeed in your writing.

Base 2: Support

Activity

The following essays were written on the topic ''Dealing with Disappointment.'' Both are unified, but one communicates more clearly and effectively. Which one, and why?

Dealing with Disappointment

One way to look at life is as a series of disappointments. Life can certainly appear that way because disappointment crops up in the life of everyone more often, it seems, than satisfaction. How disappointments are handled can have a great bearing on how life is viewed. People can react negatively by sulking or by blaming others, or they can try to understand the reasons behind the disappointment.   1

Sulking is one way to deal with disappointment. This "Why does everything always happen to me?" attitude is common because it is an easy attitude to adopt, but it is not very productive. Everyone has had the experience of meeting people who specialize in feeling sorry for themselves. A sulky manner will often discourage others from wanting to lend support, and it prevents the sulker from making positive moves toward self-help. It becomes easier just to sit back and sulk. Unfortunately, feeling sorry for oneself does nothing to lessen the pain of disappointment. It may, in fact, increase the pain. It certainly does not make future disappointments easier to bear.   2

Blaming others is another negative and nonproductive way to cope with disappointment. This all-too-common response of pointing the finger at someone else doesn't help one's situation. This posture will lead only to anger, resentment, and, therefore, further unhappiness. Disappointment in another's performance does not necessarily indicate that the performer is at fault. Perhaps expectations were too high, or there could have been a misunderstanding as to what the performer actually intended to accomplish.   3

A positive way to handle disappointment is to try to understand the reasons behind the disappointment. An analysis of the causes for disappointment can have an excellent chance of producing desirable results. Often understanding alone can help alleviate the pain of disappointment and can help prevent future disappointments. Also, it is wise to try to remember that what would be ideal is not necessarily what is reasonable to expect in any given situation. The ability to look disappointment squarely in the face and then go on from there is the first step on the road back.   4

Continuous handling of disappointment in a negative manner can lead to a negative view of life itself. Chances for personal happiness in such a state of being are understandably slim. Learning not to expect perfection in an imperfect world and keeping in mind those times when expectations were actually surpassed are positive steps toward allowing the joys of life to prevail.   5

Reactions to Disappointment

Ben Franklin said that the only sure things in life are death and taxes.   1
He left something out, however: disappointment. No one gets through life
without experiencing many disappointments. Strangely, though, most people
seem unprepared for disappointment and react to it in negative ways. They
feel depressed or try to escape their troubles instead of using disappointment
as an opportunity for growth.

One negative reaction to disappointment is depression. A woman trying   2
to win a promotion, for example, works hard for over a year in her
department. Helen is so sure she will get the promotion, in fact, that she has
already picked out the car she will buy when her salary increase comes
through. However, the boss names one of Helen's coworkers to the spot.
The fact that all the other department employees tell Helen that she is the
one who really deserved the promotion doesn't help her deal with the
crushing disappointment. Deeply depressed, Helen decides that all her goals
are doomed to defeat. She loses her enthusiasm for her job and can barely
force herself to show up every day. Helen tells herself that she is a failure
and that doing a good job just isn't worth the work.

Another negative reaction to disappointment, and one that often follows   3
depression, is the desire to escape. Kevin fails to get into the college his
brother is attending, the college that was the focus of all his dreams, and
decides to escape his disappointment. Why worry about college at all?
Instead, he covers up his real feelings by giving up on his schoolwork and
getting completely involved with friends, parties, and "good times." Or Linda
doesn't make the varsity basketball team--something she wanted very badly--
and so refuses to play sports at all. She decides to hang around with a new
set of friends who get high every day; then she won't have to confront her
disappointment and learn to live with it.

The positive way to react to disappointment is to use it as a chance for   4
growth. This isn't easy, but it's the only useful way to deal with an inevitable
part of life. Helen, the woman who wasn't promoted, could have handled her
disappointment by looking at other options. If her boss doesn't recognize
talent and hard work, perhaps she could transfer to another department. Or
she could ask the boss how to improve her performance so that she would be
a shoo-in for the next promotion. Kevin, the boy who didn't get into the
college of his choice, should look into other schools.. Going to another college
may encourage him to be his own person, step out of his brother's shadow,
and realize that being turned down by one college isn't a final judgment on
his abilities or potential. Rather than escape into drugs, Linda could improve
her basketball skills for a year or pick up another sport--like swimming or
tennis--that would probably turn out to be more useful to her as an adult.

Disappointments are unwelcome, but regular, visitors to everyone's life.   5
We can feel depressed about them or we can try to escape from them. The
best thing, though, is to accept a disappointment and then try to use it
somehow: step over the unwelcome visitor on the doorstep and get on with
life.

The _____ essay makes its point more clearly and effectively because

_____

_____

_____

UNDERSTANDING SUPPORT

The second essay is more effective, for it offers specific examples of the ways people deal with disappointment. We see for ourselves the kinds of reactions people have to disappointment.

The first essay, on the other hand, gives us no specific evidence. The writer tells us repeatedly that sulking, blaming others, and trying to understand the reasons behind the disappointment are the reactions people have to a letdown. However, the writer never *shows* us any of these responses in action. Exactly what kinds of disappointments is the writer talking about? And how, for instance, does someone analyze the causes of disappointment? Would a person make up a list of causes on a piece of paper, or review the causes with a concerned friend, or speak to a professional therapist? In an essay like this, we would want to see *examples* of how sulking and blaming others are negative ways of dealing with disappointment.

Consideration of the two essays leads us to the second base of effective writing: *support*. After realizing the importance of specific supporting details, one student writer revised a paper she had done on being lost in the woods as the worst experience of her childhood. In the revised paper, instead of talking about "the terror of being separated from my parents," she referred to such specifics as "tears streamed down my cheeks as I pictured the faces I would never see again" and "I clutched the locket my parents had given me as if it were a lucky charm that could help me find my way back to the campsite." All your papers should include such vivid details!

Base 3: Coherence

Activity

The following two essays were written on the topic ''Positive or Negative Effects of Television.'' Both are unified, and both are supported. However, one communicates more clearly and effectively. Which one, and why?

Harmful Effects of Watching Television

In a recent cartoon, one character said to another, "When you think of the awesome power of television to educate, aren't you glad it doesn't?" It's true that television has the power to educate and to entertain, but unfortunately, these benefits are outweighed by the harm it does to dedicated viewers. Television is harmful because it creates passivity, discourages communication, and presents a false picture of reality.   1

Television makes viewers passive. Children who have an electronic baby-sitter spend most of their waking hours in a semiconscious state. Older viewers watch tennis matches and basketball games with none of the excitement of being in the stands. Even if children are watching <u>Sesame Street</u> or <u>The Electric Company</u>, they are being educated passively. The child actors are going on nature walks, building crafts projects, playing with animals, and participating in games, but the little viewers are simply watching. Older viewers watch a studio audience discuss issues with Phil Donahue, but no one will turn to the home viewers to ask their opinion.   2

Worst of all, TV presents a false picture of reality that leaves viewers frustrated because they don't have the beauty or wealth of characters on television. Viewers absorb the idea that everyone else in the United States owns a lavish apartment, suburban house, sleek car, and expensive wardrobe. Every detective, police officer, oil baron, and lawyer, male or female, is suitable for a pinup poster. The material possessions on TV shows and commercials contribute to the false image of reality. News anchors and reporters, with their perfect hair and makeup, must fit television's standard of beauty. From their modest homes or cramped apartments, many viewers tune in daily to the upper-middle-class world that TV glorifies.   3

Television discourages communication. Families watching television do very little talking except for brief exchanges during commercials. If Uncle Bernie or the next-door neighbors drop in for a visit, the most comfortable activity for everyone may be not conversation but watching <u>Wide World of Sports</u>. The family may not even be watching the same set; instead, in some households, all the family members head for their own rooms to watch their own sets. At dinner, plates are plopped on the coffee table in front of the set, and the meal is wolfed down during the <u>CBS Nightly News</u>. During commercials, the only communication a family has all night may consist of questions like "Do we have any popcorn?" and "Where's the <u>TV Guide</u>?"   4

Television, like cigarettes or saccharine, is harmful to our health. We are becoming isolated, passive, and frustrated. And, most frightening, the average viewer spends more time watching television than ever.   5

The Benefits of Television

We hear a lot about the negative effects of television on the viewer.   1
Obviously, television can be harmful if it is watched constantly to the
exclusion of other activities. It would be just as harmful to listen to records
or to eat constantly. However, when television is watched in moderation, it
is extremely valuable, as it provides relaxation, entertainment, and education.

First of all, watching TV has the value of sheer relaxation. Watching   2
television can be soothing and restful after an eight-hour day of pressure,
challenges, or concentration. After working hard all day, people look
forward to a new episode of a favorite show or yet another showing of
Casablanca or Red River. This period of relaxation leaves viewers refreshed
and ready to take on the world again. Watching TV also seems to reduce
stress in some people. This benefit of television is just beginning to be
recognized. One doctor, for example, advises his patients with high blood
pressure to relax in the evening with a few hours of television.

In addition to being relaxing, television is entertaining. Along with the   3
standard comedies, dramas, and game shows that provide enjoyment to
viewers, television offers a variety of movies and sports events. Moreover, in
many areas, viewers can pay a monthly fee and receive special cable
programming. With this service, viewers can watch first-run movies, rock
and classical music concerts, and specialized sports events, like European
soccer and Grand Prix racing. Viewers can also buy or rent movies to show
on their television sets through videodisk players or videocassette players.
Still another growing area of TV entertainment is video games. Cartridges
are available for everything from electronic baseball to Pac-man, allowing the
owner to have a video game arcade in the living room.

Most important, television is educational. Preschoolers learn colors,   4
numbers, and letters from public television programs, like Sesame Street, that
use animation and puppets to make learning fun. Science shows for older
children, like 1-2-3 Contact, go on location to analyze everything from
volcanoes to rocket launches. Adults, too, can get an education (college
credits included) from courses given on television. Also, television widens
our knowledge by covering important events and current news. Viewers can
see and hear presidents' speeches, state funerals, natural disasters, and
election results as they are happening. Finally, a television set hooked up to
a home computer can help its owner learn how to manage the household
budget, invest in the stock market, or master a foreign language.

Perhaps because television is such a powerful force, we like to criticize it   5
and search for its flaws. However, the benefits of television should not be
ignored. We can use television to relax, to have fun, and to make ourselves
smarter. This electronic wonder, then, is a servant, not a master.

The _____ essay makes its point more clearly and effectively because

_____

_____

_____

_____

UNDERSTANDING COHERENCE

The second essay is more effective because the material is organized clearly and logically. Using emphatic order, the writer develops three positive uses of television, ending with the most important use: television as an educational tool. The writer also includes transitional words that act as signposts, making movement from one idea to the next easy to follow. The major transitions include *First of all, In addition,* and *Most important;* transitions within paragraphs include such words as *Moreover, Still another, too, Also,* and *Finally.* And the writer of the second essay uses a linking sentence ("In addition to being relaxing, television is entertaining") to tie the first and second supporting paragraphs together clearly.

Although the first essay is unified and supported, the writer does not have any clear and consistent way of organizing the material. The most important idea to be developed (signaled by the phrase *Worst of all*) is discussed in the second supporting paragraph instead of being saved for last. None of the supporting paragraphs organizes its details in a logical fashion. The first supporting paragraph, for example, discusses older viewers, then younger viewers, then jumps back to older people again. The third supporting paragraph, like the first, leaps from an opening idea (families talking only during commercials), to several intervening ideas, back to the original idea (talking during commercials). In addition, this essay uses practically no transitional devices to guide the reader.

These two essays lead us to the third base of effective writing: *coherence.* All the supporting ideas and sentences in a paper must be organized so that they cohere, or "stick together." As has already been mentioned, key techniques for tying together the material in a paper include a clear method of organization (such as time order or emphatic order), transitions, and other connecting words.

Base 4: Sentence Skills

Activity

Following are two versions of an essay. Both are unified, supported, and organized, but one version communicates more clearly and effectively. Which one, and why?

"revenge"

[1]Revenge is one of those things that everyone enjoy. [2]People don't like to talk about it, though. [3]Just the same, there is nothing more tempting, more satisfying, or more rewarding than revenge. [4]The purpose is not to harm your victims. [5]But to let them know that I am upset about something they are doing. [6]Careful plotting can provide you with relief from bothersom coworkers, gossiping friends, or nagging family members.   1

[7]Coworkers who make comments about the fact that you are always fifteen minutes late for work can be taken care of very simply. [8]All you have to do is get up extra early one day. [9]Before the sun comes up, drive to each coworker's house, reach under the hood of his car, and disconnected the center wire that leads to the distrib. cap. [10]The car will be unharmed, but it will not start, and your friends at work will all be late for work on the same day. [11]If youre lucky, your boss might notice that you are the only one there and will give you a raise. [12]Later if you feel guilty about your actions you can call each person anonymously and tell them how to get the car running.   2

[13]Gossiping friends at school are also perfect targets for a simple act of revenge. [14]A way to trap either male or female friends are to leave phony messages on their lockers. [15]If the friend that you want to get is male, leave a message that a certain girl would like him to stop by her house later that day. [16]With any luck, her boyfriend will be there. [17]The girl won't know what's going on, and the victim will be so embarrassed that he probably won't leave his home for a month. [18]The plan works just as well for female friends, too.   3

[19]When Mom and Dad and your sisters and brothers really begin to annoy you, harmless revenge may be just the way to make them quite down for a while. [20]The dinner table, where most of the nagging probably happens, is a likely place. [21]Just before the meal begins, throw a handful of raisins into the food. [22]Wait about 5 minutes and, after everyone has began to eat, clamp your hand over your mouth and begin to make odd noises. [23]When they ask you what the matter is, point to a raisin and yell, Bugs. [24]Dumping the food in the disposal, the car will make a bee-line for mcdonald's. [25]That night, you'll have your first quiet, peaceful meal in a long time.   4

[26]A well-planned revenge does not have to hurt anyone. [27]The object is simply to let other people know that they are beginning to bother you. [28]You should remember, though, to stay on your guard after completing your revenge. [29]The reason for this is simple, coworkers, friends, and family can also plan revenge on you.   5

Revenge

Revenge is one of those things that everyone enjoys. People don't like to 1 talk about it, though. Just the same, there is nothing more tempting, more satisfying, or more rewarding than revenge. The purpose is not to harm your victims but to let them know that you are upset about something that they are doing to you. Careful plotting can provide you with relief from bothersome coworkers, gossiping friends, or nagging family members.

Coworkers who make comments about the fact that you are always 2 fifteen minutes late for work can be taken care of very simply. All you have to do is get up extra early one day. Before the sun comes up, drive to each coworker's house. Reach under the hood of your coworker's car and disconnect the center wire that leads to the distributor cap. The car will be unharmed, but it will not start, and your friends at work will all be late for work on the same day. If you're lucky, your boss might notice that you are the only one there and will give you a raise. Later, if you feel guilty about your actions, you can call your coworkers anonymously and tell them how to get their cars running again.

Gossiping friends at school are also perfect targets for a simple act of 3 revenge. A way to trap either male or female friends is to leave phony messages on their lockers. If the friend that you want to get is male, leave a message that a certain girl would like him to stop by her house later that day. With any luck, her boyfriend will be there. The girl won't know what's going on, and the victim will be so embarrassed that he probably won't leave his home for a month. The plan works just as well for female friends, too.

When Mom and Dad and your sisters and brothers really begin to annoy 4 you, harmless revenge may be just the way to make them quiet down for a while. The dinner table, where most of the nagging probably happens, is a likely place. Just before the meal begins, throw a handful of raisins into the food. Wait about five minutes and, after everyone has begun to eat, clamp your hand over your mouth and begin to make odd noises. When they ask you what the matter is, point to a raisin and yell, "Bugs!" They'll all dump their food in the disposal, jump into the car, and head for McDonald's. That night, you'll have your first quiet, peaceful meal in a long time.

A well-planned revenge does not have to hurt anyone. The object is 5 simply to let other people know that they are beginning to bother you. You should remember, though, to stay on your guard after completing your revenge. The reason for this is simple. Coworkers, friends, and family can also plan revenge on you.

The _____ essay makes its point more clearly and effectively because

_____

_____

_____

UNDERSTANDING SENTENCE SKILLS

The second essay is more effective because it uses *sentence skills*, the fourth base of competent writing. See if you can find and explain briefly the twenty sentence-skills mistakes made in the first essay. Use the space provided. The first mistake is described for you as an example. Note that comparing the first essay with the corrected essay will help you locate the mistakes.

1. *The title should not be set off with quotation marks.* _____

2. _____

3. _____

4. _____

5. _____

6. _____

7. _____

8. _____

9. _____

10. _____

11. _____

12. _____

13. _____

14. _____

15. _____

16. _____

17. _____

18. _____

19. _____

20. _____

Practice in Using the Four Bases

You are now familiar with the four standards, or bases, of effective writing: unity, support, coherence, and sentence skills. In this section you will expand and strengthen your understanding of the four bases as you:

1 Evaluate essays for unity
2 Evaluate essays for support
3 Evaluate essays for coherence
4 Evaluate essays for all four bases: unity, support, coherence, sentence skills

1 EVALUATING ESSAYS FOR UNITY

Activity

Both of the essays below contain irrelevant sentences that do not relate to the thesis of the essay or support the topic sentence of the paragraph in which they appear. Cross out the irrelevant sentences and put the numbers of those sentences in the spaces provided.

Playing on the Browns

¹For the past three summers, I have played first base on a softball team known as the Browns. ²We play a long schedule, including play-offs, and everybody takes the games pretty seriously. ³In that respect, we're no different from any other of the thousand or so teams in our city. ⁴But in one respect, we <u>are</u> different. ⁵In an all-male league, we have a woman on the team--me. ⁶Thus I've had a chance to observe something about human nature by seeing how the men have treated me. ⁷Some have been disbelieving; some have been patronizing; and fortunately, some have simply accepted me.

1

⁸One new team in the league was particularly flabbergasted to see me start the game at first base. ⁹Nobody on the Comets had commented one way or the other when they saw me warming up, but playing in the actual game was another story. ¹⁰The Comet first-base coach leaned over to me with a disbelieving grin and said, "You mean, you're starting, and those three guys are on the bench?" ¹¹I nodded and he shrugged, still amazed. ¹²He probably thought I was the manager's wife. ¹³When I came up to bat, the Comet pitcher smiled and called to his outfielders to move way in on me. ¹⁴Now, I don't have a lot of power, but I'm not exactly feeble. ¹⁵I used to work out on the exercise machines at a local health club until it closed, and now I lift weights at home a couple of times a week. ¹⁶I wiped the smirks off their faces with a line drive double over the left fielder's head.

2

The number of the irrelevant sentence: _____

[17] The next game, we played another new team, and this time their attitude was a patronizing one. [18] The Argyles had seen me take batting practice, so they didn't do anything so rash as to draw their outfield way in. [19] They had respect for my ability as a player. [20] However, they tried to annoy me with phony concern. [21] For example, a redheaded Argyle got on base in the first inning and said to me, "You'd better be careful, Hon. [22] When you have your foot on the bag somebody might step on it. [23] You can get hurt in this game." [24] I was mad, but I have worked out several mental techniques to control my anger because it interferes with my playing ability. [25] Well, this delicate little girl survived the season without injury, which is more than I can say for some of the "he-men" on the Argyles.

3

The number of the irrelevant sentence: _____

[26] Happily, most of the teams in the league have accepted me, just as the Browns did. [27] The men on the Browns coached and criticized me (and occasionally cursed me) just like anyone else. [28] Because I'm a religious person, I don't approve of cursing, but I don't say anything about it to my teammates. [29] They are not amazed when I get a hit or stretch for a wide throw. [30] My average this year was higher than the averages of several of my teammates, yet none of them acted resentful or threatened. [31] On several occasions I was taken out late in a game for a pinch runner, but other slow players on the team were also lifted at times for pinch runners. [32] Every woman should have a team like the Browns!

4

The number of the irrelevant sentence: _____

[33] Because I really had problems only with the new teams, I've concluded that it's when people are faced with an unfamiliar situation that they react defensively. [34] Once a rival team has gotten used to seeing me on the field, I'm no big deal. [35] Still, I suspect that the Browns secretly feel we're a little special. [36] After all, we won the championship with a woman on the team.

5

How to Con a Teacher

[1] Enter college, and you'll soon be reminded of an old saying: "The pen is mightier than the sword." [2] That person behind the teacher's desk holds your future in his or her ink-stained hands. [3] So your first important assignment in college has nothing to do with required readings, examinations, or even the hazards of registration. [4] It is, instead, how to con a teacher.

1

[5] The first step in conning a teacher is to use body language. [6] You may be able to convince your instructor you are special without even saying a word. [7] When you enter the classroom, be sure to sit in the front row. [8] That way, the instructor can't possibly miss you. [9] Then, as your teacher lectures, take notes frantically. [10] The teacher will be flattered that you think so much of his or her words that you want to write them all down. [11] Using a felt-tip pen

2

is superior to a pen or pencil; it will help you write faster and prevent aching wrists. [12]While you are writing, be sure to smile at the teacher's jokes and nod violently in agreement with every major point. [13]Most important of all, as class continues, sit with your body pitched forward and your eyes wide open, fixed firmly, as if hypnotized, on your teacher's face. [14]Make your whole body suggest that you are watching a star.

The number of the irrelevant sentence: _____

3

[15]Once you have mastered body language, it is time to move on to the second phase of teacher conning: class participation. [16]Everyone knows that the student who is most eager to learn is the one who responds to the questions that are asked and even comes up with a few more. [17]Therefore, be sure to be responsive. [18]Questions such as "How does this affect the future of the United States?" or "Don't you think that someday all of this will be done by computer?" can be used in any class without prior knowledge of the subject matter. [19]Many students, especially in large classes, get lost in the crowd and never do anything to make themselves stand out. [20]Another good participation technique is to wait until the instructor has said something that sounds profound and then ask him or her to repeat it slowly so you can get it down word for word in your notes. [21]No teacher can resist this kind of flattery.

The number of the irrelevant sentence: _____

4

[22]However, the most advanced form of teacher conning happens after class is over. [23]Don't be like the others who slap their notebooks closed, pick up their books, and rush out the door before the echoes of the final bell have died away. [24]Did you ever notice how students begin to get restless about five minutes before class ends, even if there's no clock on the wall? [25]Instead, be reluctant to leave. [26]Approach the instructor's desk hesitantly, almost reverently. [27]Say that you want to find out more about the topic. [28]Is there any extra reading you can do? [29]Even better, inquire if the instructor has written anything on the topic--and whether you could borrow it. [30]Finally, compliment your teacher by saying that this is the most interesting course you've ever taken. [31]Nothing beats the personal approach for making a teacher think you care.

The number of the irrelevant sentence: _____

5

[32]Body language, questions, after-class discussions--these are the secrets of teacher conning every college student should know. [33]These kinds of things go on in high school, too, and they're just as effective on that level. [34]Once you master these methods, you won't have to worry about a thing-- until the final exam.

The number of the irrelevant sentence: _____

2 EVALUATING ESSAYS FOR SUPPORT

Activity

Both of the essays below lack supporting details at certain key points. Identify the spots where details are needed in each essay.

Formula for Happiness

[1]Everyone has his or her own formula for happiness. [2]As we go through life, we discover the activities that make us feel best. [3]I've already discovered three keys for my happiness. [4]I depend on karate, music, and self-hypnosis.   1

[5]An activity which helps me to feel good physically is karate. [6]Before taking karate lessons, I was tired most of the time, my muscles felt like foam rubber, and I was also about twenty pounds overweight. [7]After about three months of these lessons, I began to notice an improvement in my physical condition. [8]I have also noticed that my endurance has increased. [9]At the end of my workday, I used to drag myself home to eat and watch television all night. [10]Now, I still have enough energy to play with my children, go shopping, or see a movie. [11]Karate has made me feel healthy, strong, and happy.   2

The spot where supporting details are needed occurs after sentence _____ .

[12]Singing with a choral group has helped me to achieve emotional well-being through the expression of my feelings. [13]In common situations where other people would reveal their feelings, I would remain quiet. [14]Since joining the chorus, however, I have had an outlet for my joy, anger, or sadness. [15]When I sing, I pour my emotions into the music and don't have to feel shy about expressing myself. [16]For this reason, I enjoy singing certain kinds of music the most, since they demand real depth of feeling.   3

The first spot where supporting details are needed occurs after sentence _____ .

The second spot occurs after sentence _____ .

[17]A very important activity which gives me peace of mind is self-hypnosis. [18]This is a total relaxation technique which I learned from a hypnotist several years ago. [19]Essentially I breathe deeply and concentrate on relaxing all the muscles of my body. [20]I then repeat a key suggestion to myself. [21]Because I practice self-hypnosis, I have gained control over several bad habits that have long been haunting me. [22]I have also learned to reduce the stress that goes along with my secretarial job. [23]Now I can handle the boss's demands or unexpected work without feeling tense.   4

The first spot where supporting details are needed occurs after sentence _____ .

The second spot occurs after sentence _____ .

[24]In short, my physical, emotional, and mental well-being have been greatly increased through karate, music, and self-hypnosis. [25]These activities have become important elements in my formula for happiness.   5

Problems of a Foreign Student

[1]About ten months ago I decided to leave my native country and come to   1
the United States to study. [2]When I got here, I suddenly turned into someone
labeled "foreign student." [3]A foreign student, I discovered, has problems.
[4]Whether from Japan, like me, or from some other country, a foreign student
has to work twice as hard as Americans do to succeed in college.

[5]First of all, there is the language problem. [6]American students have the   2
advantage of comprehending English without working at it. [7]But even they
complain that some professors talk too fast, mumble, or use big words. [8]As a
result, they can't take notes fast enough to keep up, or they misunderstand
what was said. [9]Now consider my situation. [10]I'm trying to cope with a
language that is probably one of the hardest in the world to learn. [11]Dozens
of English slang phrases--"mess around," "hassle," "get into"--were totally
new to me. [12]Other language problems gave me trouble, too.

The spot where supporting details are needed occurs after sentence _____ .

[13]Another problem I face has to do with being a stranger to American   3
culture. [14]For instance, the academic world is much different in Japan. [15]In
America, professors seem to treat students as equals. [16]Many classes are
informal, and the relationship between teacher and student is friendly; in
fact, students call some teachers by their first names. [17]In Japan, however,
the teacher-student relationship is different. [18]Lectures, too, are more formal,
and students show respect by listening quietly and paying attention at all
times. [19]This more casual atmosphere occasionally makes me feel
uncomfortable in class.

The spot where supporting details are needed occurs after sentence _____ .

[20]Perhaps the most difficult problem I face is a social one. [21]American   4
students may have some trouble making new friends or may feel lonely at
times. [22]However, they usually manage to find other people with the same
backgrounds, interests, or goals. [23]It is twice as hard to make friends,
though, if a person has trouble making the small talk that can lead to a
relationship. [24]I find it difficult to become friends with other students
because I don't understand some aspects of American life. [25]Students would
rather talk to someone who is familiar with these things.

The spot where supporting details are needed occurs after sentence _____ .

[26]Despite all the handicaps that I, as a foreign student, have to overcome,   5
I wouldn't give up this chance to go to school in the United States. [27]Each
day, the problems seem a little bit less overwhelming. [28]Like a little child
who is finally learning to read, write, and make sense of things, I am starting
to enjoy my experience of discovering a brand-new world.

3   EVALUATING ESSAYS FOR COHERENCE

Activity

Both of the essays that follow could be revised to improve their coherence. Answer the questions about coherence that come after each essay.

Noise Pollution

[1]Natural sounds--waves, wind, bird songs--are so soothing that companies sell tapes of them to anxious people seeking a relaxing atmosphere in their homes or cars. [2]One reason why "environmental sounds" are big business is the fact that ordinary citizens--especially city dwellers--are bombarded by noise pollution. [3]On the way to work, on the job, and on the way home, the typical urban resident must cope with a continuing barrage of unpleasant sounds.

[4]The noise level in an office can be unbearable. [5]From nine o'clock to five, phones ring, typewriters clack and clatter, intercoms buzz, and Xerox machines thump back and forth. [6]Every time the receptionists can't find people, they resort to a nerve-shattering public address system. [7]And because the managers worry about the employees' morale, they graciously provide the endless droning of canned music. [8]This effectively eliminates any possibility of a moment of blessed silence.

[9]Traveling home from work provides no relief from the noisiness of the office. [10]The ordinary sounds of blaring taxi horns and rumbling buses are occasionally punctuated by the ear-piercing screech of car brakes. [11]Taking a shortcut through the park will bring the weary worker face to face with chanting religious cults, free-lance musicians, screaming children, and barking dogs. [12]None of these sounds can compare with the large radios many park visitors carry. [13]Each radio blasts out something different, from heavy-metal rock to baseball, at decibel levels so strong that they make eardrums throb in pain. [14]If there are birds singing or wind in the trees, the harried commuter will never hear them.

[15]Even a trip to work at 6 or 7 A.M. isn't quiet. [16]No matter which route a worker takes, there is bound to be a noisy construction site somewhere along the way. [17]Hard hats will shout from third-story windows to warn their coworkers below before heaving debris out and sending it crashing to earth. [18]Huge front-end loaders will crunch into these piles of rubble and back up, their warning signals letting out loud, jarring beeps. [19]Air hammers begin an ear-splitting chorus of rat-a-tat-tat sounds guaranteed to shatter sanity as well as concrete. [20]Before reaching the office, the worker is already completely frazzled.

[21]Noise pollution is as dangerous as any other kind of pollution. [22]The endless pressure of noise probably triggers countless nervous breakdowns, vicious arguments, and bouts of depression. [23]And imagine the world problems we could solve, if only the noise stopped long enough to let us think.

1

2

3

4

5

1. In "Noise Pollution," what is the number of the sentence to which the transition word *Also* could be added in paragraph 2? _____
2. In the last sentence of paragraph 2, to what does the pronoun *This* refer? _____
3. What is the number of the sentence to which the transition word *But* could be added in paragraph 3? _____
4. What is the number of the sentence to which the transition word *Then* could be added in paragraph 4? _____
5. What is the number of the sentence to which the transition word *Meanwhile* could be added in paragraph 4? _____
6. What word is used as a synonym for *debris* in paragraph 4? _____
7. How many times is the key word *sounds* repeated in the essay? _____
8. The time order of the three supporting paragraphs is confused. Which supporting paragraph should come first? _____ Second? _____ Third? _____

Weight Loss

[1]The big fraternity party turned out to be the low point of my freshman year. [2]I was in heaven until I discovered that my date with handsome Greg, the fraternity vice president, was a hoax: he had used me to win the "ugliest date" contest. [3]I ran sobbing back to the dorm, wanting to resign from the human race. [4]Then I realized that it was time to stop kidding myself about my weight. [5]Within the next two years, I lost forty-two pounds and turned my life around. [6]Losing weight gave me self-confidence socially, emotionally, and professionally.

[7]I am more outgoing socially. [8]Just being able to abandon dark colors, overblouses, and tent dresses in favor of bright colors, T shirts, and designer jeans made me feel better in social situations. [9]I am able to do more things. [10]I once turned down an invitation for a great camping trip with my best friend's family, making up excuses about sun poisoning and allergies. [11]Really, I was too embarrassed to tell them that I couldn't fit in the bathroom in their Winnebago! [12]I made up for it last summer when I was one of the organizers of a college backpacking trip through the Rockies.

[13]Most important, losing weight helped me seek new professional goals. [14]When I was obese, I organized my whole life around my weight, as if it were a defect I could do nothing about. [15]With my good grades, I could have chosen almost any major the college offered, but I had limited my goal to

1

2

3

kindergarten teaching because I felt that little children wouldn't judge how I looked. [16]Once I was no longer fat, I realized that I love working with all sorts of people. [17]I became a campus guide and even had small parts in college theater productions. [18]As a result, last year I changed my major to public relations. [19]The area fascinates me, and I now have good job prospects there.

[20]I have also become more emotionally honest. [21]Rose, at the college counseling center, helped me see that my "fat and jolly" personality had been false. [22]I was afraid others would reject me if I didn't always go along with their suggestions. [23]I eventually put Rose's advice to the test. [24]My roommates were planning an evening at a Greek restaurant. [25]I loved the restaurant's atmosphere, but there wasn't much I liked on the menu. [26]Finally, in a shaky voice I said, "Actually, I'm not crazy about lamb. [27]How about Italian or Chinese food?" [28]They scolded me for not mentioning it before, and we had dinner at a Chinese restaurant and ended with coffee, dessert, and entertainment at the Greek restaurant. [29]We all agreed it was one of our best evenings out.

[30]Fortunately, the low point of my freshman year turned out to be the turning point leading to what promises to be an exciting senior year. [31]Greg's cruel joke became a strange sort of favor, and I've gone from wanting to resign from the human race to welcoming each day as a source of fresh adventure and self-discovery.

1. In "Weight Loss," what is the number of the sentence to which the transition words *For one thing* could be added in paragraph 2? _____

2. What is the number of the sentence to which the transition word *Also* could be added in paragraph 2? _____

3. What is the number of the sentence to which the transition word *But* could be added in paragraph 2? _____

4. In sentence 11, to what does the pronoun *them* refer? _____

5. What is the number of the sentence to which the transition word *However* could be added in paragraph 3? _____

6. What word is used as a synonym for *obese* in paragraph 4? _____

7. How many times is the key word *weight* repeated in the essay? _____

8. Which supporting paragraph should be placed in the emphatic final position? _____

4 EVALUATING ESSAYS FOR ALL FOUR BASES: UNITY, SUPPORT, COHERENCE, AND SENTENCE SKILLS

Activity

In this activity, you will evaluate two essays in terms of the four bases of unity, support, coherence, and sentence skills. Comments follow each supporting paragraph. Circle the letter of the *one* statement that applies in each case.

Chiggers

I had lived my whole life not knowing what chiggers are. I thought they were probably a type of insect Humphrey Bogart encountered in The African Queen. I never had any reason to really care, until one day last summer. Within twenty-four hours, I had vividly experienced what chigger bites are, learned how to treat them, and learned how to prevent them. 1

First of all, I learned that chiggers are the larvae of tiny mites found in the woods and that their bites are always multiple and cause intense itching. A beautiful summer day seemed perfect for a walk in the woods. I am definitely not a city person, for I couldn't stand to be surrounded by people, noise, and concrete. As I walked through the ferns and pines, I noticed what appeared to be a dusting of reddish seeds or pollen on my slacks. Looking more closely, I realized that each speck was a tiny insect. I casually brushed off a few and gave them no further thought. I woke up the next morning feeling like a settler staked to an ant hill by an Indian wise in the ways of torture. Most of my body was speckled with measlelike bumps that at the slightest touch burned and itched like a mosquito bite raised to the twentieth power. When antiseptics and calamine lotion failed to help, I raced to my doctor for emergency aid. 2

a. Paragraph 2 contains an irrelevant sentence.

b. Paragraph 2 lacks supporting details at one key spot.

c. Time order in paragraph 2 is confused.

d. Paragraph 2 contains two run-on sentences.

Healing the bites of chiggers, as the doctor diagnosed them to be, is not a simple procedure. It seems there is really no wonder drug or commercial product to help the cure. The victim must rely on a harsh and primitive home remedy and mostly wait out the course of the painful bites. First, the doctor explained, the skin must be bathed carefully in alcohol. An antihistamine spray applied several hours later will soothe the intense itching and help prevent infection. Before using the spray, I had to saturate each bite with gasoline or nail polish to kill any remaining chiggers. A few days after the treatment, the bites finally healed. Although I was still in pain, and desperate for relief, I followed the doctor's instructions. I carefully applied gasoline to the bites and walked around for an hour smelling like a filling station. 3

a. Paragraph 3 contains an irrelevant sentence.

b. Paragraph 3 lacks supporting details at one key spot.

c. Time order in paragraph 3 is confused.

d. Paragraph 3 contains one sentence fragment.

Most important of all, I learned what to do to prevent getting chigger bites in the future. Mainly, of course, stay out of the woods in the summertime. But if the temptation is too great on an especially beautiful day, I'll be sure to wear the right type of clothing, like a long-sleeved shirt, long pants, knee socks, and closed shoes. In addition, I'll cover myself with clouds of superstrength insect repellent. I will then shower thoroughly as soon as I get home, I also will probably burn all my clothes if I notice even one suspicious red speck.   4

a. Paragraph 4 contains an irrelevant sentence.

b. Paragraph 4 lacks supporting details at one key spot.

c. Paragraph 4 lacks transitional words.

d. Paragraph 4 contains a run-on and a fragment.

I will never forget my lessons on the cause, cure, and prevention of chigger bites. I'd gladly accept the challenge of rattlesnakes and scorpions in the wilds of the West but will never again confront a siege of chiggers in the pinewoods.   5

The Hazards of Being an Only Child

Many people who have grown up in multichild families think that being an only child is the best of all possible worlds. They point to such benefits as the only child's annual new wardrobe and lack of competition for parental love. But single-child status isn't as good as people say it is. Instead of having everything they want, only children are sometimes denied certain basic human needs.   1

Only children lack companionship. An only child can have trouble making friends, since he or she isn't used to being around other children. Often, the only child comes home to an empty house; both parents are working, and there are no brothers or sisters to play with or to talk to about the day. At dinner, the single child can't tell jokes, giggle, or throw food while the adults discuss boring adult subjects. An only child always has his or her own room but never has anyone to whisper to half the night when sleep doesn't come. Some only children thrive on this isolation and channel their energies into creative activities like writing or drawing. Owing to this lack of companionship, an only child sometimes lacks the social ease and self-confidence that come from being part of a closely knit group of contemporaries.   2

a. Paragraph 2 contains an irrelevant sentence.

b. Paragraph 2 lacks supporting details at one key spot.

c. Paragraph 2 lacks transitional words.

d. Paragraph 2 contains one fragment and one run-on.

> Second, only children lack privacy. An only child is automatically the   3
> center of parental concern. There's never any doubt about which child tried
> to sneak in after midnight on a weekday. And who will get the lecture the
> next morning. Also, whenever an only child gives in to a bad mood, runs
> into his or her room, and slams the door, the door will open thirty seconds
> later, revealing an anxious parent. Parents of only children sometimes don't
> even understand the child's <u>need</u> for privacy. For example, they may not
> understand why a teenager wants a lock on the door or a personal
> telephone. After all, the parents think, there are only the three of us, there's
> no need for secrets.

a. Paragraph 3 contains an irrelevant sentence.

b. Paragraph 3 lacks supporting details at one key spot.

c. Paragraph 3 lacks transitional words.

d. Paragraph 3 contains one fragment and one run-on.

> Most important, only children lack power. They get all the love; but if   4
> something goes wrong, they also get all the punishment. When a bottle of
> perfume is knocked to the floor or the television is left on all night, there's
> no little sister or brother to blame it on. Moreover, an only child has no
> recourse when asking for a privilege of some kind, such as permission to
> stay out to a late hour or to take an overnight trip with friends. There are
> no older siblings to point to and say, "You let them do it. Why won't you let
> me?" With no allies their own age, only children are always outnumbered,
> two to one. An only child hasn't a chance of influencing any major family
> decisions, either.

a. Paragraph 4 contains an irrelevant sentence.

b. Paragraph 4 lacks supporting details at one key spot.

c. Paragraph 4 lacks transitional words.

d. Paragraph 4 contains one fragment and one run-on.

> Being an only child isn't as special as some people think. It's no fun   5
> being without friends, without privacy, and without power in one's own
> home. But the child who can triumph over these hardships grows up self-
> reliant and strong. Perhaps for this reason alone, the hazards are worth it.

PART TWO

TYPES
OF
ESSAY
DEVELOPMENT

INTRODUCTION TO ESSAY DEVELOPMENT

This chapter will discuss

- **Nine patterns of essay development**
- **Point of view**
- **Writing for a specific purpose and audience**
- **Peer review of your papers**
- **The order of each chapter**
- **A personal checklist for your papers**

NINE PATTERNS OF ESSAY DEVELOPMENT

Traditionally, all writing has been divided into the following forms:

- Exposition

Examples	Comparison and contrast
Process	Definition
Cause and effect	Division and classification

- Description
- Narration
- Argumentation and persuasion

In *exposition,* the writer provides information about and explains a particular subject. The patterns of development in exposition include (1) giving examples, (2) detailing the process of doing or making something, (3) analyzing causes or effects, (4) comparing or contrasting, (5) defining a term or concept, (6) dividing something into parts or grouping it into categories. In this part of the book, each of the six patterns of exposition is presented in a separate chapter.

There are also individual chapters devoted to (7) description, (8) narration, and (9) argument. A *description* is a verbal picture of a person, place, or thing. In a *narration,* a writer tells the story of something that happened. *Argumentation* or *persuasion* is an attempt to prove a point or defend an opinion.

You will have a chance, then, to learn how nine different patterns can help organize material in your papers. Each of the nine patterns has its own internal logic and provides its own special strategies for imposing order on your ideas.

As you practice each pattern, you should keep two points in mind:

- While each essay that you write will involve one predominant pattern, very often one or more additional patterns may be involved as well. For example, consider the three model essays in the next chapter (''Examples''). The first essay, ''Everyday Cruelty,'' is developed through a series of examples. But there is also an element of narration, as the writer presents examples that occur as he proceeds through his day. In the second essay, ''Altered States,'' the use of examples is again the predominant pattern, but in a lesser way the author is also explaining the causes of altered states of mind. The third essay, ''Childhood Fears,'' also presents a series of examples but to a lesser degree also relies on narration and cause-and-effect.

- More important, an essay you write in almost any pattern will probably involve some form of argumentation. You will advance a point and then go on to support your point. To convince the reader that your thesis is valid, you may use a series of examples, or narration, or a description, or some other pattern of organization. In ''Everyday Cruelty,'' for instance, the author uses examples to support his point that people inflict little cruelties on each other. In an essay that appears later in Part Two, a writer supports the point that a certain diner is depressing by providing a number of descriptive details (see page 188). Another writer describes a certain experience in her life as embarrassing and then uses a narrative to persuade us of the truth of this statement (see page 195). And another writer advances the opinion that a fast-food restaurant can be preferable to a fancy one and then supplies comparative information about both to support his claim (see page 152). Much of your writing, in short, will have the purpose of persuading your reader that the idea you have advanced is valid.

POINT OF VIEW IN WRITING

When you write, you can take any of three approaches, or points of view: first-person, second-person, or third-person.

First-Person Approach

In the first-person approach—a strongly individualized point of view—you draw on your own experience, and speak to your audience in your own voice, using pronouns like *I, me, mine, we, our,* and *us.*

The first-person approach is most common in narrative essays based on personal experience. It also suits other essays where most of the evidence presented consists of personal observation.

Here is a first-person supporting paragraph from an essay on camping:

> First of all, I like comfort when I'm camping. My GMC motor home, with its completely equipped kitchen, shower stall, toilet, double bed, and color television, resembles a mobile motel room. I can sleep on a real mattress, clean sheets, and fluffy pillows. Next to my bed are devices that make me feel at home: a radio, an alarm clock, and a TV remote-control unit. Unlike the poor campers huddled in tents, I don't have to worry about cold, rain, heat, or annoying insects. After a hot shower, I can slide into my best nightgown, sit comfortably on my down-filled quilt, and read the latest best-seller while a thunderstorm booms outside.

Second-Person Approach

In the second-person approach, the writer speaks directly to the reader, using the pronoun *you*. The second-person approach is considered appropriate for giving direct instructions and explanations to the reader. That is why *you* is used throughout this book.

You should expect to use the second-person approach only when writing a process essay. Otherwise, as a general rule, *never* use the word *you* in writing. (If doing so has been a common mistake in your writing, you should review the rule about pronoun point of view on page 359.)

Third-Person Approach

The third-person approach is by far the most common point of view in academic writing. In the third person, the writer includes no direct references to the reader (*you*) or the self (*I, me*). Third person gets its name from the stance it suggests—that of an outsider or "third person," observing and reporting on matters of public rather than private importance. In this approach, you draw on information that you have gotten through observation, thinking, or reading.

Here is the paragraph on camping, recast in the third person. Note the third-person pronouns *their, them,* and *they,* which all refer to *campers* in the first sentence.

> First of all, modern campers bring complete bedrooms with them. Winnebagoes, GMC motor homes, and Airstream trailers lumber into America's campgrounds every summer like mobile motel rooms. All the comforts of home are provided inside. Campers sleep on real mattresses with clean sheets and fluffy pillows. Next to their beds are the same gadgets that litter their night tables at home--radios, alarm clocks, and TV remote-control units. It's not necessary for them to worry about annoyances like cold, heat, rain, or buzzing insects, either. They can sit comfortably in bed and read the latest best-sellers while a thunderstorm booms outside.

WRITING FOR A SPECIFIC PURPOSE AND AUDIENCE

The three most common purposes of writing are to *inform,* to *entertain,* and to *persuade*. As already said, most of the writing you will do in this book will involve some form of persuasion. You will advance a point or thesis and then support it in a variety of ways. To some extent, also, you will write papers that provide readers with information about a particular subject.

Your audience will be primarily your instructor, and sometimes other students as well. Your instructor is really a symbol of the larger audience you should see yourself as writing for—an educated, adult audience that expects you to present your ideas in a clear, direct, organized way. If you can learn to persuade or inform such an audience through your writing, you will have accomplished a great deal.

However, it will also be helpful for you to write some papers for a more specific audience. By so doing, you will develop an ability to choose words and adopt a tone of voice that is right for a given purpose and a given group of people.

In this part of the book, then, there is an assignment at or near the end of each chapter that asks you to write with a very specific purpose in mind and for a very specific audience. You will be asked, for example, to imagine yourself as a college sophomore making a presentation to incoming students about how to prepare for college life, as a client of a video dating service introducing himself or herself to potential dates, as a reader of a local newspaper writing a letter responding to a recent editorial, and as an author of a campus newspaper column giving advice on romance. Through these and other assignments, you will learn how to adjust your style and tone of voice to a given writing situation.

HOW TO PROCEED

Using Part Two:
The Progression in Each Chapter

After each type of essay development is explained, in the following chapters, student papers illustrating that type are presented, and then there are questions about the papers. The questions relate to unity, support, and coherence—the principles of effective writing explained earlier.

You are then asked to write your own essay. In most cases, the first assignment is fairly structured and provides a good deal of guidance for the writing process. The other assignments offer a wide and interesting choice of writing topics. In each case, the last or next-to-last assignment involves writing an essay with a specific purpose and for a specific audience. And in three instances (examples, cause-and-effect, and comparison or contrast), the final assignments require outside reading of literary works; a student model is provided for each of these assignments.

Using Peer Review

In addition to having your instructor as an audience for your writing, you will benefit by having another student in your class as an audience. On the day a paper is due, or on a day when you are writing papers in class, your teacher may ask you to pair up with another student. That student will read your paper, and you will read his or her paper.

Ideally, read the other paper aloud while your peer listens. If that is not practical, read it in a whisper while your peer looks on. As you read, both you and your peer should look and listen for spots where the paper does not read smoothly and clearly. Check or circle the trouble spots where your reading snags. Your peer should then read your paper, marking possible trouble spots.

Then, each of you should do three things.

1 Identification: On a separate sheet of paper, write at the top the title and author of the paper you have read. Under it, write your own name as the reader of the paper.

2 Outline: "X-ray" the paper for its inner logic by making up a scratch outline. The scratch outline need be no more than twenty words or so, but it should show clearly the logical foundation on which the essay is built. It should identify and summarize the overall point of the paper and the three areas of support for the point. Your outline can look as follows:

Point: _____

Support:

(1) _____

(2) _____

(3) _____

For example, here is a scratch outline of the essay on moviegoing on pages 6–7:

Point: *Going out to the movies presents too many problems.*
Support: *(1) Getting to the theater*
(2) Dealing with theater itself
(3) Putting up with other patrons

3 Comments: Under the outline, write the heading "Comments." Then make some useful comments.

Here is what you should comment on:

- Look at the spots where your reading of the paper snagged. Are words missing or misspelled? Is parallel structure lacking? Are there mistakes with punctuation? Is the meaning of a sentence confused? Try to figure out what the problems are and suggest ways of fixing them.
- Are there spots in the paper where you see problems with *unity, support,* or *organization?* If so, offer comments. For example, you might say, "More details are needed in the first supporting paragraph," or "Some of the details in the last supporting paragraph don't really back up your point."
- Finally, note something you really liked about the paper. You might, for instance, mention good use of transitions or a specific detail that is especially realistic or vivid.

After you have completed your evaluation of the paper, give it to your classmate. Your teacher may provide you with the option of rewriting a paper in light of the "peer feedback." Whether or not you rewrite, be sure to hand in the "peer evaluation form" with your paper.

Using a Personal Checklist

After you have completed a paper, there are three ways you should check it yourself. You should *always* do the first two checks, which take only a few minutes. Ideally, you should then take the time to do the detailed third check as well.

1 Read the paper *out loud.* If it does not sound right—if it does not read smoothly and clearly—then make the changes needed to ensure that it will be smooth and clear.

2 Make sure you can answer two basic questions clearly and concisely: "What is the point of my essay? What are the three distinct bits of support for my point?"

3 Last, evaluate your paper in terms of the detailed checklist that appears on the opposite page. (This checklist is repeated on the inside front cover of the book.) The numbers in parentheses refer to the pages of this book that discuss each skill.

Checklist of the Four Steps in Writing an Effective Essay

1 Unity

- Clearly stated thesis in the introductory paragraph of your paper (pages 7; 35–38; 46–52)
- All the supporting paragraphs on target in backing up your thesis (88–90; 100–102)

2 Support

- Three separate supporting points for the thesis (8–9; 22; 26–29; 39–40)
- *Specific* evidence for each of the three supporting points (39–42; 53–57; 91–93)
- *Plenty of* specific evidence for each supporting point (43–44; 58–61; 103–104)

3 Coherence

- Clear method of organization (63–65; 80–81; 94–96; 105–107)
- Transitions and other connecting words (66–71; 81–85)
- Effective introduction, conclusion, and title (7–9; 72–78)

4 Sentence Skills

- Fragments eliminated (294–307)
- Run-ons eliminated (308–319)
- Correct verb forms (320–328; 335–342)
- Subject and verb agreement (329–334)
- Faulty parallelism and faulty modifiers eliminated (343–354)
- Faulty pronouns eliminated (355–367)
- Adjectives and adverbs used correctly (368–373)
- Capital letters used correctly (374–381)
- Punctuation marks where needed:

a	Apostrophe (382–387)	d	Colon; Semicolon (405; 406)
b	Quotation marks (388–394)	e	Dash; Hyphen (406; 408)
c	Comma (395–404)	f	Parentheses (407)

- Correct paper format (287–288)
- Needless words eliminated (442–444)
- Correct word choices (437–442)
- Possible spelling errors checked (417–421)
- Careless errors eliminated through proofreading (31–33; 457–467)
- Sentences varied (447–456)

EXAMPLES

In our daily conversations, we often provide *examples*—that is, details, particulars, specific instances—to explain statements that we make. Here are several statements and supporting examples:

The first day of school was frustrating.	My sociology course was canceled. Then, I couldn't find the biology lab. And the lines at the bookstore were so long that I went home without buying my textbooks.
That washing machine is unreliable.	The water temperature can't be predicted; it stops in midcycle; and it sometimes shreds my clothing.
My grandfather is a thrifty person.	He washes and reuses aluminum foil. He wraps gifts in newspaper. And he's worn the same Sunday suit for twenty years.

In each case, the examples help us see for ourselves the truth of the statement that has been made. In essays, too, explanatory examples help your audience fully understand your point. Lively, specific examples also add interest to your paper.

In this section, you will be asked to provide a series of examples to support your thesis. First read the essays ahead; they all use examples to develop their points. Then answer the questions that follow.

ESSAYS TO CONSIDER

Everyday Cruelty

Last week, I found myself worrying less about problems of world politics   1
and national crime and more about smaller evils. I came home one day with
a bad taste in my mouth, the kind I get whenever I witness the little cruelties
that people inflict on each other. On this particular day, I had seen three
especially mean-spirited things happen.

I first thought about mean-spirited people as I walked from the bus stop   2
to the office where I work. I make this walk every day, and it's my first step
away from the comforts of home and into the tensions of the city. For me, a
landmark on the route is a tiny patch of ground that was once strewn with
rubbish and broken glass. The city is trying to make a "pocket park" out of it
by planting trees and flowers. Every day this spring, I watched the skinny
saplings put out tiny leaves. When I walked past, I always noted how big the
tulips were getting and made bets with myself on when they would bloom.
But last Wednesday, as I reached the park, I felt sick. Someone had knocked
the trees to the ground and trampled the budding tulips into the dirt.
Someone had destroyed a bit of beauty for no reason.

At lunchtime on Wednesday, I witnessed more meanness. Along with   3
dozens of other hungry, hurried people, I was waiting in line at McDonald's.
Also in line was a young mother with two tired, impatient children clinging
to her legs. The mother was trying to calm the children, but it was obvious
that their whining was about to give way to full-fledged tantrums. The lines
barely moved, and the lunchtime tension was building. Then, one of the
children began to cry and scream. The little boy's bloodcurdling yells
resounded through the restaurant, and people stared angrily at the helpless
mother. Finally, one man turned to her and said, "Lady, you shouldn't bring
your kids to a public place if you can't control them." The woman was
exhausted and hungry. Someone in line could have helped her with her
problem. Instead, even though many of the customers in the restaurant
were parents themselves, they treated her like a criminal.

The worst incident of mean-spiritedness that I saw that day happened   4
after I left work. As I walked to the bus stop, I approached an old woman
huddled in a doorway. She was wrapped in a dirty blanket and clutched a
cheap vinyl bag packed with her belongings. She was one of the "street
people" our society leaves to fend for themselves. The United States, the
richest country on earth, should not allow such suffering. Some of these
victims even live in cardboard boxes during the coldest winters.
Approaching the woman from the opposite direction were three teenagers
who were laughing and talking in loud voices. When they saw the old
woman, they began to shout crude remarks at her. One of them grabbed her
shopping bag and pretended to throw it out into the street. The woman
stared helplessly at them, like a wounded animal surrounded by hunters.
Then, having had their fun, the teenagers went on their way.

I had seen enough of the world's coldness that day and wanted to leave it   5
behind. At home, I huddled in the warmth of my family. I wondered why we
all contribute to the supply of petty cruelty. There's enough of it already.

Altered States

Most Americans are not alcoholics. Most of us do not smoke marijuana 1
to get high. LSD trips went out of style along with the flower children of the
sixties. Nevertheless, many Americans are walking and driving around with
their minds slightly out of kilter. In its attempt to cope with modern life, the
human mind seems to have evolved some defense strategies. Confronted with
inventions like the automobile, the television, and the shopping center, for
example, the mind will slip--all by itself--into an altered state.

First of all, the mind must now cope with the automobile. In the past, no 2
human being ever sat for hours at a time, in the same position, staring at
endless white lines and matched pairs of small red taillights. In order to
deal with this unnatural situation, the mind goes on automatic pilot. A
primitive, less-developed region of the brain takes over the actual driving. It
tells the foot when to apply pressure to the brake and gas pedal and directs
the eyes to stay open. Meanwhile, the rest of the brain continues on with
higher functions. It devises excuses for being late for work. It replays,
better than any video system, yesterday's Cowboys game. Or, it creates a
pleasant imaginary world where its owner wins all arguments, tells hilarious
jokes, and attracts the opposite sex like a magnet. By splitting into two
halves, the mind deals with the boredom of driving.

The mind has defenses not only against the auto but also against 3
television. Since too much staring at flickering images of police officers,
detectives, and talk-show hosts can be dangerous to human sanity, the mind
automatically goes into a TV hypnosis state. The eyes see the sitcom or the
dog food commercial, but the mind goes into a holding pattern. None of the
televised images or sounds actually enters the brain. This is why, when
questioned, people cannot remember commercials they have seen five seconds
before or why the TV cops are chasing a certain suspect. In this hypnotic,
trancelike state, the mind resembles an armored armadillo. It rolls up in
self-defense, letting the stream of televised information pass by harmlessly.

Perhaps the most dangerous threat to the mind, however, is the shopping 4
center. In the modern mall, dozens of stores, restaurants, and movie
theaters compete for the mind's attention. There are hundreds of questions
to be answered. Should I start with the upper or lower mall level? Which
stores should I look in? Should I bother with the sweater sale at J. C.
Penney? Should I eat fried chicken or a burger for lunch? Where is my car
parked? To combat this mental overload, the mind goes into a state
resembling the white-out experienced by mountain climbers trapped in a
blinding snowstorm. Suddenly, everything looks the same. The shopper is
unsure where to go next and cannot remember what he or she came for in
the first place. The mind enters this state deliberately, so that the shopper
has no choice but to leave.

Therefore, the next time you see drivers, TV viewers, or shoppers with 5
eyes as glazed and empty as polished doorknobs, you'll know these people are
in a protective altered state. Be gentle with them. They are merely trying to
cope with the mind-numbing inventions of modern life.

Childhood Fears

I remember my childhood as being generally happy and can recall   1
experiencing some of the most carefree times of my life. But I can also
remember, even more vividly, moments of being deeply frightened. As a
child, I was truly terrified of the dark and of getting lost; these fears were
very real and caused me some extremely uncomfortable moments.

Maybe it was the strange way things looked and sounded in my familiar   2
room at night that scared me so much. There was never total darkness, but
a streetlight or passing car lights made clothes hung over a chair take on the
shape of an unknown beast. Out of the corner of my eye, I saw curtains
seem to move when there was no breeze. A tiny creak in the floor would
sound a hundred times louder than in the daylight, and my imagination
would take over, creating burglars and monsters on the prowl. Darkness
always made me feel so helpless, too. My heart would pound, and I would lie
very still so that the "enemy" wouldn't discover me.

Another of my childhood fears was that I would get lost, especially on the   3
way home from school. Every morning I got on the school bus right near
my home--that was no problem. After school, though, when all the buses
were lined up along the curb, I was terrified that I'd get on the wrong one
and be taken to some unfamiliar neighborhood. I would scan the bus for the
faces of my friends, make sure the bus driver was the same one that had been
there in the morning, and even then ask the others over and over again to be
sure I was on the right bus. On school or family trips to an amusement park
or a museum, I wouldn't let the leaders out of my sight. And of course, I was
never very adventurous when it came to taking walks or hikes, because I
would go only where I was sure I could never get lost.

Perhaps one of the worst fears of all I had as a child was that of not   4
being liked or accepted by others. First of all, I was quite shy. Second, I
worried constantly about my looks, thinking people wouldn't like me because
I was too fat or wore braces. I tried to wear the "right" clothes and even had
intense arguments with my mother over the importance of wearing "flats"
instead of saddle shoes to school. I'm sorry that we had these arguments
now, especially since my mother is quite sickly and has spent the last year in
and out of the hospital. Being popular was so important to me then, and the
fear of not being liked was a powerful one.

One of the processes of evolving from a child to an adult is being able to   5
recognize and overcome or outgrow our fears. I've learned that darkness
does not have to take on a life of its own, that others can help me when I'm
lost, and that friendliness and sincerity will encourage people to like me.
Understanding the things that scared us as children helps us to cope with
our lives as adults.

■ Questions

About Unity

1. Which sentence in paragraph 4 of "Childhood Fears" should be omitted in the interest of paragraph unity? (*Fill in the first two or three words.*)

   _____

2. Which two sentences in paragraph 4 of "Everyday Cruelty" should be omitted in the interest of paragraph unity?

   _____   _____

3. Which thesis statement fails to mention all three of its supporting points in its plan of development?   _____

About Support

4. After which sentence in paragraph 4 of "Childhood Fears" are more supporting details needed?   _____

5. Which essay uses a single extended example in each of its supporting paragraphs?   _____

About Coherence

6. Which words in paragraph 4 of "Altered States" signal that the most important idea was saved for last?   _____

7. What are the two transition words in paragraph 4 of "Childhood Fears"?

   _____   _____

8. Which topic sentence in "Altered States" functions as a linking sentence between paragraphs?   _____

About the Introduction and Conclusion

9. Circle below the kind of introduction used in "Childhood Fears."
   a. Broad, general statement narrowing to thesis
   b. Idea that is the opposite of the one to be developed
   c. Quotation
   d. Anecdote
   e. Questions

10. Which transition word signals the conclusion of "Altered States"?

    _____

WRITING THE ESSAY

■ Writing Assignment 1

For this assignment, you will complete an unfinished essay by adding appropriate supporting examples. Here is the incomplete essay:

Problems with My Apartment

When I was younger, I fantasized about how wonderful life would be when I moved into my own apartment. Now I'm a bit older and wiser, and my fantasies have turned into nightmares. My apartment has given me nothing but headaches. From the day I signed the lease, I've had to deal with an uncooperative landlord, an incompetent janitor, and inconsiderate neighbors.

First of all, my landlord has been uncooperative. . . .

I've had a problem not only with my landlord but also with an incompetent janitor. . . .

Perhaps the worst problem has been with the inconsiderate neighbors who live in the apartment above me. . . .

Sometimes, my apartment seems like a small, friendly oasis surrounded by hostile enemies. I never know what side trouble is going to come from next: the landlord, the janitor, or the neighbors. Home may be where the heart is, but my sanity is thinking about moving out.

Note: If you do not have experience with an apartment, write instead on problems of living in a dormitory, or problems of living at home. Revise the introduction and conclusion so that they fit your topic. Problems in living in a dorm might include:

Restrictive dorm regulations
Inconsiderate students on your floor
A difficult roommate

Problems in living at home might include:

Lack of space
Inconsiderate brothers and sisters
Conflict with your parent or parents

How to Proceed

a   Brainstorm the assignment by making up answers to the following questions. Use separate paper.

How has the landlord been uncooperative?
In what ways have you been inconvenienced?
Has he been uncooperative more than once?
What has been your reaction?
What has been the landlord's reaction?
What kinds of things have you said to each other?

Who is the janitor?
What has he tried to fix in the apartment?
In what ways has he been incompetent?
How has he inconvenienced you?
Has the janitor's incompetence cost you money?
What is the worst example of the janitor's incompetence?

Who are the neighbors?
How long have they lived upstairs?
What kinds of hassles have you had?
Have these incidents happened several times?
If you have spoken to the neighbors, what did they say?
What is the worst problem with these neighbors?

The answers to these questions should serve as an excellent source of details for the essay.

b Keep in mind that you may use one extended example in each paragraph (as in the essay "Everyday Cruelty") or two or three short examples (as in "Childhood Fears").

c As you are writing drafts of your three supporting paragraphs, ask yourself repeatedly:

Do my examples truly show my landlord as *uncooperative*?
Do my examples truly show the janitor as *incompetent*?
Do my examples truly show my neighbors as *inconsiderate*?

Your aims in this assignment are twofold: (1) to provide *adequate* specific details for the three qualities in question and (2) to provide *enough* specific details so that you solidly support each quality.

d When you are satisfied that you have provided effective examples, proofread your paragraphs carefully for the sentence skills listed on page 119 and the inside front cover. Then write out the full essay on separate paper and submit it to your instructor.

■ Writing Assignment 2

Write an essay on the good or bad qualities (or habits) of a person you know well. The person might be a member of your family, a friend, a roommate, a boss or supervisor, a neighbor, a teacher, or someone else. Listed below are some descriptive words that can be applied to people. They are only suggestions; you can write about other qualities as well.

Honest	Persistent	Irresponsible	Spineless
Bad-tempered	Shy	Stingy	Good-humored
Ambitious	Sloppy	Trustworthy	Cooperative
Bigoted	Hardworking	Aggressive	Disciplined
Considerate	Supportive	Courageous	Sentimental
Argumentative	Suspicious	Compulsive	Defensive
Softhearted	Open-minded	Jealous	Dishonest
Energetic	Lazy	Modest	Insensitive
Patient	Independent	Sarcastic	Unpretentious
Reliable	Stubborn	Self-centered	Neat
Generous	Flirtatious		

You may want to write about three related qualities of one person (for example, "My brother is stubborn, bad-tempered, and suspicious") or about one quality that is apparent in different aspects of a person's life (for example, "My wife's sensitivity is apparent in her relationships with her friends at work, my parents, and our teenage son").

■ Writing Assignment 3

Write an essay that uses examples to develop one of the following statements or a related statement of your own.

> If you look hard enough, you can see complete strangers being kind to one another.
>
> The gossip tabloids sold at supermarket checkouts use several techniques to lure consumers into buying them.
>
> The Super Bowl is superhype, not supersport.
>
> The best things in life are definitely not free.
>
> Living with a roommate can help you learn honesty, tolerance, and consideration.
>
> There's more joy in simple pleasures than in life's great events.
>
> Looking for a job can be a stressful process.
>
> Pets in the United States are treated like surrogate children.
>
> Our lives would be improved without the automobile.
>
> American culture is infatuated with violence.

Be sure to choose examples that actually support your thesis. They should be relevant facts, statistics, personal experiences, or incidents you have heard or read about.

Organize each paragraph by grouping several examples that support a particular point. Or use one extended example—an incident or story that may take up a full paragraph.

Save the paragraph containing the most vivid, convincing, or important examples for last.

■ Writing Assignment 4

In this essay, you will write with a specific purpose and for a specific audience. Imagine that you have completed a year of college and have agreed to take part in your college's summer orientation program for incoming students. You will be meeting with a small group of new students to help them get ready for college life.

Prepare a brief presentation to the new students in which you make the point that they must be ready to take on more responsibility than they may have had to do in high school. Make vividly clear—using several hypothetical students as examples—just what the consequences of inappropriate behavior can be. To organize your presentation, you might want to focus on three of the following areas: teachers, class attendance, time control, class note-taking, textbook study, establishing regular times and places for study, and getting help when needed. Each area could be developed with detailed examples in a separate supporting paragraph.

■ **Writing Assignment 5**

Write an essay based on an outside reading. It might be a selection in one of the following books (most should be available in your college library) or another selection recommended by your instructor.

Dave Barry, *Greatest Hits**
John Chancellor, *Peril and Promise*
Ellen Goodman, *Making Sense**
Bob Greene, *Cheeseburgers**
Sue Hubbell, *A Country Year*
Maxine Hong Kingston, *The Woman Warrior*
Harold S. Kushner, *When All You've Ever Wanted Isn't Enough*
Anne Morrow Lindbergh, *Gift from the Sea*
William Least Heat Moon, *Blue Highways*
George Orwell, *Shooting an Elephant and Other Essays*
Richard Rodriguez, *The Hunger of Memory*
Andy Rooney, *Not That You Asked**
Al Santoli, *New Americans*
Phyllis Theroux, *Night Lights*
Calvin Trillin, *If You Can't Say Something Nice**
Alice Walker, *Living by the Word**
Marie Winn, *The Plug-in Drug*

Base your essay on some idea in the selection you have chosen and provide a series of examples to back up your idea. A student model is given on the following page.

*Or any other collection of essays by the same author.

In "A Hanging," George Orwell describes the execution of a condemned man in a Burmese prison. The prisoner, a Hindu, is marched from his cell, led onto a gallows, and killed when the drop opens and the noose tightens. The entire procedure takes eight minutes. As he depicts this brief incident, Orwell uses a series of details that make us sharply aware of the enormity of killing another human being. 1

The moments leading up to the hanging are filled with tension. Six tall guards, two of them armed with rifles, surround the prisoner, "a puny wisp of a man." To prevent his escape, the guards not only handcuff the man but also chain his handcuffs to their belts and lash his arms to his sides. The guards, nervous about fulfilling their duty, treat the Hindu like "a fish which is still alive and may jump back into the water." Meanwhile, the jail superintendent prods the head jailer to get on with the execution. The superintendent's irritability is a mask for his discomfort. Then, the procession toward the gallows is interrupted by the appearance of a friendly dog, "wagging its whole body, wild with glee at finding so many human beings together." This does not ease the tension but increases it. The contrast of the lively dog licking the doomed man's face momentarily stuns the guards and arouses in the superintendent a sense of angry urgency. 2

Next, in the gallows scene, Orwell uses vivid details that emphasize the life within the man who is about to die. The condemned prisoner, who has been walking steadily up to this point, moves "clumsily" up the ladder. And until now, he has been utterly silent. But, after the noose is placed around his neck, he begins "crying out to his god." The repeated cry of "Ram! Ram! Ram!" is "like the tolling of a bell," a death knell. The dog begins to whine at the sound, and the guards go "grey," their bayonets trembling. It is as if the hooded, faceless man on the wooden platform has suddenly become a human being, a soul seeking aid and comfort. The superintendent, who has been hiding his emotions behind a stern face, gives the execution order "fiercely." The living man of moments ago simply ceases to be. 3

After the hanging, Orwell underscores the relief people feel when the momentous event is over. The jail superintendent checks to be sure that the prisoner is dead and then blows out "a deep breath" and loses his "moody look." "One felt an impulse," Orwell says, "to sing, to break into a run, to snigger." Suddenly, people are talking and chattering, even laughing. The head jailer's story about a condemned prisoner who clung to the bars of his cell so tightly that it took six men to move him sets off a gale of laughter. On the road outside the prison, everyone who participated in the execution has a whiskey. The men, having been so close to death, need to reassure themselves of the fact that they are alive. They must laugh and drink, not because they are insensitive, but because they are shaken. They must try to forget that the dead man is only a hundred yards away. 4

"A Hanging" sets out to create a picture of death in the midst of life. Orwell tries to make us see, through the details he chooses, that killing a person results in "one mind less, one world less." Such an act--"cutting a life short when it is in full tide"--violates the laws of life and nature. 5

PROCESS

Every day we perform many activities that are *processes,* that is, series of steps carried out in a definite order. Many of these processes are familiar and automatic: for example, loading film in a camera, diapering a baby, or making an omelet. We are thus seldom aware of the sequence of steps that makes up each activity. In other cases, such as when a person asks us for directions to a particular place or when we try to read and follow the directions for a new table game that someone has given us, we may be painfully conscious of the whole series of steps involved in the process.

In this section, you will be asked to write a *process essay*—one that explains clearly how to do or make something. To prepare for this assignment, you should first read the student process papers that are presented and then respond to the questions that follow them.

ESSAYS TO CONSIDER

Successful Exercise

Regular exercise is something like the weather--we all talk about it, but   1
we tend not to do anything about it! Television exercise classes, records and
tapes, and new videocassettes and disks, as well as the instructions in books,
magazines, and pamphlets, now make it easy to have a personal, low-cost
exercise program without leaving home. However, for success in exercise,
you should follow a simple plan consisting of arranging the time, making
preparations, and following the sequence with care.

To begin with, set aside a regular time for exercise. If you have a heavy   2
schedule at work or school, this may be difficult, since you're rushed in the
morning and exhausted at night, and you have no time in between. However,
one solution is simply to get up half an hour earlier in the morning. Look at
it this way: If you're already getting up too early, what's an extra half hour?
Of course, that time could be cut to fifteen minutes earlier if you could lay out
your clothes, set the breakfast table, fill the coffee maker, and gather your
books and materials for the next day before you go to bed.

Next, prepare for your exercise session. To begin with, get yourself ready   3
by not eating or drinking anything before exercising. Why risk an upset
stomach? Then, dress comfortably in something that allows you to move
freely. Since you'll be in your own home, there's no need to invest in a high-
fashion dance costume. A loose T shirt and shorts are good. A bathing suit
is great in summer, and in winter a set of long underwear is warm and
comfortable. If your hair tends to flop in your eyes, pin it back or wear a
headband or scarf. Prepare the exercise area, too. Turn off the phone and
lock the door to prevent interruptions. Shove the coffee table out of the way
so you won't bruise yourself on it or other furniture. Finally, get out the
simple materials you'll need to exercise on.

If this is your first attempt at exercising, start slowly. You do not need   4
to do each movement the full number of times at first, but you should <u>try</u>
each one. After five or six sessions, you should be able to do each one the full
number of times. Try to move in a smooth, rhythmic way; doing so will help
prevent injuries and pulled muscles. Pretend you're a dancer and make each
move graceful, even if it's just climbing up off the floor. After the last exercise,
give yourself five minutes to relax and cool off--you have earned it. Finally,
put those sore muscles under a hot shower and get ready for a great day.

Establishing an exercise program isn't difficult, but it can't be achieved   5
by reading about it, talking about it, or watching models exercise on
television. To begin with, you're going to have to get up off that couch and do
something about it. Otherwise, as my doctor likes to say, "If you don't use it,
you'll lose it."

How to Complain

I'm not just a consumer--I'm a victim. If I order a product, it is sure to   1
arrive in the wrong color, size, or quantity. If I hire people to do repairs,
they never arrive on the day scheduled. If I owe a bill, the computer is bound
to overcharge me. Therefore, in self-defense, I have developed the following
consumer's guide to complaining effectively.

The first step is getting organized. I save all sales slips and original   2
boxes. Also, I keep a special file for warranty cards and appliance
guarantees. This file does not prevent a product from falling apart the day
after the guarantee runs out. One of the problems in our country is the
shoddy workmanship that goes into many products. However, these facts
give me the ammunition I need to make a complaint. I know the date of the
purchase, the correct price (or service charge), where the item was
purchased, and an exact description of the product, including model and
serial numbers. When I compose my letter of complaint, I find it is not
necessary to exaggerate. I just stick to the facts.

The next step is to send the complaint to the person who will get results   3
quickly. My experience has shown that the president of a company is the
best person to contact. I call the company to find out the president's name
and make sure I note the proper spelling. Then I write directly to that
person, and I usually get prompt action. For example, the head of AMF
arranged to replace my son's ten-speed "lemon" when it fell apart piece by
piece in less than a year. Another time, the president of a Philadelphia
department store finally had a twenty-dollar overcharge on my bill corrected
after three months of arguing with the computer had brought no results.

If I get no response to a written complaint within ten days, I follow   4
through with a personal telephone call. When I had a new bathtub installed
a few years ago, the plumber left a gritty black substance on the bottom of
the tub. No amount of scrubbing could remove it. I tried every cleanser on
the supermarket shelf, but I still had a dirty tub. The plumber shrugged off
my complaints and said to try Fantastik. The manufacturer never answered
my letter. Finally, I made a personal phone call to the president of the firm.
Within days a well-dressed executive showed up at my door. In a business
suit, white shirt, striped tie, and rubber gloves, he cleaned the tub. Before he
left, he scolded in an angry voice, "You didn't have to call the president." The
point is, I did have to call the president. No one else cared enough to solve
the problem.

Therefore, my advice to consumers is to keep accurate records, and when   5
you have to complain, go right to the top. It has always worked for me.

How to Pick the Perfect Class Schedule

As you look at the punch cards or computer printout that lists your 1
courses for next semester, do you experience a terrible sinking feeling in the
pit of your stomach? Have you gotten stuck with unwanted courses or a
depressing time schedule that cannot be changed? If so, you obviously don't
know how to select the perfect schedule. But by following a few simple
procedures, you can begin any semester with the right courses at the most
convenient times.

First, you must find the right courses. These are the ones that combine 2
the least amount of work with the fewest tests and the most lenient
professors. Ask your friends and acquaintances about courses in which they
received A's after attending only 25 percent of the classes. Ask around, too,
to see which professors have given the same tests for the last fifteen years.
Photocopies of these tests are usually cheap and widely available. Then, pick
up a copy of the master schedule and study it carefully. Find the telltale
course titles that signal an easy glide through a painless subject. Look for
titles like "History of the Animated Cartoon," "Arts and Crafts for
Beginners," and "Rock Music of the 1950s."

Next, when you have accumulated lists of easy instructors and subjects, 3
you can begin to block out time periods. The ideal schedule will vary
according to your individual needs. If you stay up late in order to watch old
movies or work the graveyard shift, you may want a daily schedule that
begins no sooner than noon. You should schedule only afternoon courses,
too, if you're one of those people who would rather be tortured than forced to
leave a warm, cozy bed in the morning. On the other hand, if you are a
"lark" who bounds out of bed at dawn, you may want to get your classes out
of the way as early as possible. That way you have the rest of the day free.
Morning classes are also necessary if you are a soap opera fanatic who can't
miss one day's events in Pine Valley or Port Charles.

Finally, you must outsmart the registration process. You want your 4
ideal schedule to pass through official channels untouched. The main way to
do this is to register early. Ignore things like registration by first letter of
last name or by number of accumulated credits. Desperate stories about
dying relatives or heartless employers will get you quickly through a
registration line. If a course does happen to be closed because you simply
couldn't register at 7:00 A.M., you may still be able to get in. Talk to the
professor and convince him or her that a serious, ambitious, hardworking
student like yourself would be a shining asset to the class. Be sure to carry a
list of backup courses to registration, though, just in case one of your chosen
classes switches professors or changes time periods. Be ready to fill in
vacant slots with courses that meet your strict requirements.

By following these suggestions, any student can pick the perfect class 5
schedule. College can thus become a nonirritating, almost pleasant activity
that disrupts your real life as little as possible. And you never know--you
might even learn something in "Creative TV Watching."

■ **Questions**

About Unity

1. Which supporting paragraph in "Successful Exercise" lacks a topic sentence? (*Write the paragraph number.*) _____

2. Which sentence in paragraph 2 of "How to Complain" should be omitted in the interest of paragraph unity? (*Fill in the first two or three words.*)

   _____

About Support

3. After which sentence in paragraph 3 in "Successful Exercise" are more specific details needed? _____

4. Which paragraph in "How to Complain" uses a single extended example to support its topic sentence? _____

5. What are the three key stages in the process of "How to Complain"?

   a. _____

   b. _____

   c. _____

6. What are the three key stages in the process of "Picking the Perfect Class Schedule"?

   a. _____

   b. _____

   c. _____

About Coherence

7. What are the four main transition words in paragraph 3 of "Successful Exercise"? _____   _____   _____   _____

8. Which topic sentence in "How to Pick the Perfect Class Schedule" functions as a linking sentence between paragraphs? _____

About the Introduction and Conclusion

9. Which method of introduction is used in "How to Pick the Perfect Class Schedule"?

   _____

10. Which essay ends with a recommendation?

   _____

WRITING THE ESSAY

■ Writing Assignment 1

Choose one of the ten topics below that you think you can write about in a process paper.

> How to do grocery shopping in a minimum of time
> How to select a car (new or used), apartment, or home
> How to do household cleaning efficiently
> How to drive defensively
> How to protect a home from burglars
> How to gain or lose weight
> How to relax
> How to study for an important exam
> How to play a position (third base, guard, goalie, etc.) in a team sport skillfully
> How to plan an event (party, wedding, garage sale, etc.)

How to Proceed

a   Now freewrite for ten minutes on the topic you have tentatively chosen. Do not worry about spelling, grammar, organization, or other matters of correct form. Just write whatever comes into your head regarding the topic. Keep writing for more than ten minutes if any additional details about the topic occur to you.

   This freewriting will give you a base of raw material that you can draw on in the next phase of your work on the essay. After freewriting for ten minutes, you should have a sense of whether there is enough material available for you to write a process essay about the topic. If so, continue as explained below. If not, choose another topic and freewrite about this new topic for ten minutes.

b   State your thesis in a single clear sentence. In your thesis, you can (1) say it is important that your audience know about this process (''Knowing how to register a complaint can save time and frustration'') or (2) state your opinion of this process (''Growing your own tomatoes is easier than you might think'').

c Make a list of all the steps that you are describing. Here, for example, is the list prepared by the author of "How to Complain":

Save sales slips and original boxes
Engrave items with ID number in case of burglary
Write letter of complaint
Make photocopy of letter
Create file of warranties and guarantees
Send complaint letter directly to president
Call company for president's name
Follow through with telephone call if no response
Make thank-you call after action is taken

d Number your items in time order; strike out items that do not fit in the list; add others you can think of. Thus:

1   Save sales slips and original boxes
    ~~Engrave items with ID number in case of burglary~~
4   Write letter of complaint
    ~~Make photocopy of letter~~
2   Create file of warranties and guarantees
5   Send complaint letter directly to president
3   Call company for president's name
6   Follow through with telephone call if no response
    ~~Make thank-you call after action is taken~~

e After making the list, decide how the items can be grouped into a minimum of three steps. For example, with "How to Complain," you might divide the process into (1) getting organized, (2) sending the complaint to the president, and (3) following up with further action. Or, with a topic like "How to Grow Tomatoes," you might divide the process into (1) soil preparation, (2) planting, and (3) care.

f Use your list as a guide to write the first rough draft of your paper. As you write, try to think of additional details that will develop your opening sentence. Do not expect to finish your paper in one draft. You should, in fact, be ready to write a series of lists and drafts as you work toward the goals of unity, support, and coherence.

g Be sure to use transitions such as *first, next, also, then, after, now, during,* and *finally* so that your paper moves smoothly and clearly from one step in the process to the next.

h While working on your paper, refer to the checklist on page 119 and the inside front cover to make sure you can answer *Yes* to the questions about unity, support, and coherence. Also, refer to the checklist when you proofread the next-to-final draft for sentence-skills mistakes, including spelling.

■ **Writing Assignment 2**

Any one of the topics below can be written as a process paper. Follow the steps suggested for the first essay.

> How to break a bad habit
> How to live with a two-year-old, a teenager, or a parent
> How to make someone like you
> How to make excuses
> How to fall out of love
> How to improve reading skills
> How to do well at a job interview
> How to care for an aging relative
> How to stay young
> How to improve a school or a place of work

■ **Writing Assignment 3**

Everyone is an expert at something. Write a process essay on some skill that you can perform very well. Write from the point of view that ''This is how _____ *should* be done.'' (Remember that a skill can be anything from ''starting a fire'' to ''setting up a new stereo system'' to ''dealing with unpleasant customers'' to ''using a personal computer.'')

■ **Writing Assignment 4**

In this essay, you will write with a specific purpose and for a specific audience. Imagine that you are ''Val Valentine,'' the author of a column in the campus newspaper that gives advice on romance. Someone has written to you asking how he can get to know a woman he has admired from afar (or how *she* can get to know a man she has admired from afar).

In your reply, suggest a process to the writer by which someone can meet and get to know another person on campus. You may describe a realistic process or a humorous one, in which you exaggerate the steps involved.

■ **Writing Assignment 5**

Write an essay in which you summarize, in your own words, the steps involved in doing a research paper or in preparing for and taking an essay exam. Both of these processes are explained in Part Three of this book. Before starting this paper, you should read ''Preparing a Summary'' on pages 227–236.

CAUSE
AND
EFFECT

Why did Janet decide to move out of her parents' house? What made you quit a well-paying job? Why are horror movies so popular? Why has Ben acted so depressed lately? Why did our team fail to make the league play-offs?

Every day we ask questions similar to those above and look for answers. We realize that many actions do not occur without causes, and we realize also that a given action can have a series of effects—for good or bad. By examining the causes or effects of an action, we seek to understand and explain things that happen in our lives.

You will be asked in this section to do some detective work by examining the cause of something or the effects of something. First read the three essays that follow and answer the questions about them. All three essays support their thesis statements by explaining a series of causes or a series of effects.

ESSAYS TO CONSIDER

A Necessary Decision

Have you ever seen a supermarket bag crammed full of medical bills for   1
just one person? Well, I have. I had known that my mother was sick as a
result of a failing kidney, but I had not realized how much trouble my
parents were having in dealing with that sickness. Only when I had saved
enough money to visit them in Florida did I discover just how critical the
situation had become. The problems were so serious, in fact, that I had to
make the decision to put my mother in a nursing home.

First, there were countless bills. Many were for drugs, since Mother was   2
taking about twenty-four pills a day along with receiving insulin injections.
Then there were hospital bills for the initial diagnosis, for batteries of tests,
and for the operation that prepared her for kidney dialysis. Next, there were
the ambulance bills for my mother's trips three times a week to the dialysis
clinic. And finally, there were clinic bills for $350 for each of the dozen or so
treatments she had already had. Unable to contend with the insurance
paperwork needed to pay for the bills, my father had stuffed all incoming
bills into a Winn-Dixie shopping bag in the closet.

She was confined to a wheelchair and needed help moving around. She   3
had to have assistance in getting dressed and undressed, going to the
bathroom, and getting into and out of bed. She also needed a very specialized
diet involving a combination of foods for renal, diabetic, and gallbladder
patients. In addition, she required emotional support. Sometimes she was
so depressed, she wouldn't eat unless she was urged to. "I'm going to die;
just let me die in peace," she would say, or "You don't love me anymore now
that I'm sick." These constant needs, I concluded, would benefit from
professional care.

Finally, I was concerned not only with my mother's needs but also with   4
my father's welfare. He assumed total responsibility for my mother. Since
he doesn't drive, he walked everywhere, including to the grocery store,
drugstore, laundromat, hospital, and clinic. Also, he did all the housework;
he fed, dressed, bathed, and medicated my mother; and he prepared her
special meals and snacks. In addition, her behavior was a strain on him.
She would wait until he was in the kitchen, and then she would call the
police or ambulance to say she was dying. Or she would wait until 3 A.M.
and telephone each of her children to say good-bye. Never robust, my father
dropped from 125 pounds to 98 pounds under the strain, caught a bad cold,
and finally telephoned me for help.

I conferred with a social worker, found a nursing home, and signed my   5
mother in. My father is able to get a bus that takes him, within twenty
minutes, right to the nursing home door. He has gained weight and has
gotten back in control of things to the point where he can handle the
paperwork again. Even my mother has recovered to the extent that she is
making my daughter a quilt. My decision was not easy, but it has turned out
to the best one for both my parents.

The Joys of an Old Car

Some of my friends can't believe my car still runs. Others laugh when   1
they see it parked outside the house and ask if it's an antique. But they
aren't being fair to my fourteen-year-old Datsun. In fact, my "antique" has
opened my eyes to the rewards of owning an old car.

One obvious reward is economy. Fourteen years ago, when my husband   2
and I were newly married and nearly broke, we bought the car--a shiny, red,
year-old leftover--for a mere $1800. Today it would cost five times as much.
We save money on insurance, since it's no longer worthwhile for us to have
collision coverage. Old age has even been kind to the Datsun's engine, which
required only three major repairs in the last several years. And it still
delivers twenty-six miles per gallon in the city and thirty-eight on the
highway--not bad for a senior citizen.

The second benefit is dependability. If a Datsun passes the twenty-   3
thousand-mile mark with no major problems, it will probably go on forever.
Our Datsun breezed past that mark many years ago and has run almost
perfectly ever since. Even on the coldest, snowiest mornings, I can count on
my car to sputter to life and roll surefootedly down the driveway. The only
time it didn't start, unfortunately, was the day I had a final exam. The
Datsun may have the body of an old car, but beneath its elderly hood hums
the engine of a teenager.

Last of all, there is the advantage of familiarity. When I open the door   4
and slide into the driver's seat, the soft vinyl envelops me like a well-worn
glove. I know to the millimeter exactly how much room I have when I turn
a corner or back into a streetside parking space. When my gas gauge is on
empty, I know that 1.3 gallons are still in reserve and I can plan
accordingly. The front wheels invariably begin to shake when I go more
than fifty-five miles an hour, reminding me that I am exceeding the speed
limit. With the Datsun, the only surprises I face are the ones from other
drivers.

I prize my fourteen-year-old Datsun's economy and dependability, and   5
most of all, its familiarity. It is faded, predictable, and comfortable, like a
well-worn pair of jeans. And, like a well-worn pair of jeans, it will be
difficult to throw away.

Stresses of Being a Celebrity

Last week, a woman signing herself "Want the Truth in Westport" wrote   1
to Ann Landers with a question she just had to have answered. "Please find
out for sure," she begged the columnist, "whether or not Oprah Winfrey has
had a face-lift." Fortunately for Ms. Winfrey's privacy, Ann Landers refused
to answer the question. But the incident disturbed me. How awful it would
be to be a celebrity, I thought, and always be in the public eye. Celebrities
lead very stressful lives, for no matter how glamorous or powerful they are,
they have too little privacy, too much pressure, and no safety.

For one thing, celebrities don't have the privacy an ordinary person has.   2
The most personal details of their lives are splashed all over the front pages
of the National Enquirer and the Globe so that bored supermarket shoppers
can read about "Cher and Her New Love" or "Arsenio's Deepest Fear." Even a
celebrity's family is hauled into the spotlight. A teenage son's arrest for pot
possession or a wife's drinking problem becomes the subject of glaring
headlines. Photographers hound celebrities at their homes, in restaurants,
and on the street, hoping to get a picture of a Jackie Onassis in curlers or a
Sean Penn in a fistfight. When celebrities try to do the things that normal
people do, like eat out or attend a football game, they run the risk of being
interrupted by thoughtless autograph hounds or mobbed by aggressive fans.

In addition, celebrities are under constant pressure. Their physical   3
appearance is always under observation. Famous women, especially, suffer
from the "she really looks old" or the "boy, has she put on weight" spotlight.
Unflattering pictures of celebrities are photographers' prizes to be sold to the
highest bidder; this increases the pressure on celebrities to look good at all
times. Famous people are also under pressure to act calm and collected
under any circumstances. There's no freedom to blow off steam or to do
something just a little crazy. Therefore, people who forget this must suffer
the consequences.

Most important, celebrities must deal with the stress of being in constant   4
danger. The friendly grabs, hugs, and kisses of enthusiastic fans can quickly
turn into uncontrolled assaults on a celebrity's hair, clothes, and car.
Celebrities often get strange letters from people who become obsessed with
their idols or from people who threaten to harm them. The attempt to kill
Ronald Reagan and the murder of John Lennon came about because two
unbalanced people tried to transfer the celebrity's fame to themselves.
Famous people must live with the fact that they are always fair game--and
never out of season.

Some people dream of starring roles, their names in lights, and their   5
pictures on the cover of People magazine. I'm not one of them, though. A
famous person gives up private life, feels pressured all the time, and is never
completely safe. So let someone else have that cover story. I'd rather lead
an ordinary, but calm, life than a stress-filled public one.

■ Questions

About Unity

1. Which supporting paragraph in ''A Necessary Decision'' lacks a topic sentence? (*Write the paragraph number.*) _____

2. Which sentence in paragraph 3 of ''The Joys of an Old Car'' should be omitted in the interest of paragraph unity? (*Write the first two or three words.*)

   _____

3. Rewrite the thesis statement of ''The Joys of an Old Car'' to include a plan of development.

   _____

   _____

About Support

4. How many effects are given to develop the thesis in ''Stresses of Being a Celebrity''? (*Check the right answer.*)

   _____ 1   _____ 2   _____ 3   _____ 4

   How many are given in ''The Joys of an Old Car''?

   _____ 1   _____ 2   _____ 3   _____ 4

5. After which sentence in paragraph 3 of ''Stresses of Being a Celebrity'' are more specific details needed? _____

6. How many examples are given to support the topic sentence ''One obvious reward is economy'' in ''The Joys of an Old Car''?

   _____

About Coherence

7. Which topic sentence in ''A Necessary Decision'' functions as a linking sentence between paragraphs? _____

8. What are the three main transition words in paragraph 3 of ''Stresses of Being a Celebrity''?

   _____   _____   _____

9. What are the three transition words in ''The Joys of an Old Car'' that signal the three major points of support for the thesis?

   _____   _____   _____

About the Introduction

10. Select from below the two methods of introduction that combine to form the first paragraph of "Stresses of Being a Celebrity."
    a. Broad, general statement narrowing to thesis
    b. Idea that is the opposite of the one to be developed
    c. Quotation
    d. Anecdote
    e. Questions

Activity 1

Complete the following outline of the essay titled "A Necessary Decision." The effect is the author's decision to put her mother in a nursing home; the causes of that decision are what make up each supporting paragraph. Summarize each cause in a few words. The first cause and one detail are given for you as an example.

Thesis: The problems were so serious, in fact, that I had to make the decision to put my mother in a nursing home.

1. *Countless bills* _____
   a. *Bills for drugs* _____
   b. _____
   c. _____
   d. _____
2. _____
   a. _____
   b. _____
   c. _____
3. _____
   a. _____
   b. _____
   c. _____

Activity 2

In scratch-outline form on separate paper, provide brief causes or effects for at least four of the ten statements below. Note the example. Make sure that you have three *separate* and *distinct* items for each statement. Also, indicate whether you have listed three causes or three effects.

Many youngsters are terrified of school.

1. *Afraid of not being liked by other students*

2. *Fearful of failing tests* } Causes

3. *Intimidated by teachers*

1. The availability of fast-food outlets has changed the eating habits of many Americans.

2. I would recommend (*or* not recommend) _____ (*name a certain course*) to other students.

3. The women's movement has had an enormous impact on women's lives.

4. There are several steps Congress should take to make automobile driving a safer matter.

5. Exercise has changed my life.

6. Students often have trouble adjusting to college for several reasons.

7. Videocassette recorders have changed the way we watch television.

8. _____ is a popular sport for several reasons.

9. Computers have begun to affect the lives of many families.

10. There are several advantages (*or* drawbacks) to living at home while going to school.

WRITING THE ESSAY

■ Writing Assignment 1

Decide, perhaps through discussion with your instructor or classmates, which of the outlines prepared above would be most promising to develop into an essay. Make sure that your supporting reasons are logical ones that actually back up your thesis statement. Ask yourself in each case, "Does this reason truly support my thesis idea?" See "How to Proceed" on the following page.

How to Proceed

a On separate paper, make a list of details that might go under each of the supporting points. Provide more details than you can possibly use. Here, for example, are the details generated by the writer of ''The Joys of an Old Car'' when she was working on her third supporting paragraph:

Car's familiarity:

Know how much space I have to park
Front wheels shake at fifty-five miles per hour
Know what's in glove compartment
Worn seat--comfortable
Know tire inflation (pounds of pressure)
Can turn corners expertly (space)
Gas tank has reserve
Radio push buttons are set for favorite stations
Know how hard to press brake
Know that reverse gear is over, <u>then</u> down

b Decide which details you will use to develop each of your supporting paragraphs. Also, number the details in the order in which you will present them. Here is how the writer of ''The Joys of an Old Car'' made decisions about the details in her final supporting paragraph:

2 Know how much space I have to park
4 Front wheels shake at fifty-five miles per hour
~~Know what's in glove compartment~~
1 Worn seat--comfortable
~~Know tire inflation (pounds of pressure)~~
2 Can turn corners expertly (space)
3 Gas tank has reserve
~~Radio push buttons are set for favorite stations~~
~~Know how hard to press brake~~
~~Know that reverse gear is over, then down~~

c As you are working on the drafts of your paper, refer to the checklist on page 119 and the inside front cover. Make sure that you can answer *Yes* to the questions about unity, support, and coherence.

d You may also want to refer to pages 72–77 for suggestions on writing an effective introduction and conclusion to your essay.

e Finally, use the checklist on page 119 and the inside front cover when you are proofreading the next-to-final draft of your paper for sentence-skills mistakes, including spelling.

■ Writing Assignment 2

Below are six thesis statements for a "cause" paper and six for an "effect" paper. In scratch-outline form, provide brief supporting points for four of the twelve.

List the Causes

1. Americans tend to get married later in life than they used to.
2. Childhood is the unhappiest time of life.
3. Being young is better than being old. (*Or vice versa.*)
4. _____ is the most difficult course I have ever taken.
5. My relationship with _____ (name a relative, employer, or friend) is better than ever.
6. It is easy to fall into an unhealthy diet in our society.

List the Effects

7. Punishment for certain crimes should take the form of community service.
8. Growing up in the family I have has influenced my life in important ways.
9. The average work week should be no more than thirty hours long.
10. A bad (*or* good) teacher can affect students in significant ways.
11. The drinking age should be raised to twenty-one in every state.
12. The fact that both parents often work has led to a number of changes in the typical family household.

■ Writing Assignment 3

If friendly aliens from a highly developed civilization decided to visit our planet, they would encounter a contradictory race of beings—us. We human beings would have reasons to feel both proud and ashamed of the kind of society the aliens would encounter. Write an essay explaining whether you would be proud or ashamed of the state of the human race today. Give reasons for your feeling.

■ Writing Assignment 4

In this essay, you will write with a specific purpose and for a specific audience. Imagine that a friend of yours is having a hard time learning anything in a class taught by Professor X. You volunteer to attend the class and see for yourself. You also get information from your friend about the course requirements.

Afterwards, you write a letter to Professor X, calling attention to what you see as causes of the learning problems that students are having in the class. To organize your essay, you might develop each of these causes in a separate supporting paragraph. In the second part of each supporting paragraph, you might suggest changes that Professor X could make to deal with each problem.

■ **Writing Assignment 5**

Write an essay in which you advance an idea about a poem, story, play, literary essay, or novel. The work you choose may be assigned by your instructor or require your instructor's approval. Use a series of two or more reasons and specific supporting evidence for each reason to develop your idea. A student model follows.

Paul's Suicide

Paul, the main character in Willa Cather's short story "Paul's Case," is a young man on a collision course with death. As Cather reveals Paul's story, we learn about elements of Paul's personality that inevitably come together and cause his suicide. Paul takes his own life as a result of his inability to conform to his society, his passive nature, and his emotional isolation.   1

First of all, Paul cannot conform to the standards of his own society. At school, Paul advertises his desire to be part of another, more glamorous world by wearing fancy clothes that set him apart from the other students. At home on Cordelia Street, Paul despises everything about his middle-class neighborhood. He hates the houses "permeated by kitchen odors," the "ugliness and commonness of his own home," and the respectable neighbors sitting on their front stoops every Sunday, "their stomachs comfortably protruding." Paul's father hopes that Paul will settle down and become like the young man next door, a nearsighted clerk who works for a corporate steel magnate. Paul, however, is repelled by the young man and all he represents. It seems inevitable, then, that Paul will not be able to cope with the office job his father obtains for him at the firm of Denny & Carson; and this inability to conform will, in turn, lead to Paul's theft of a thousand dollars.   2

Paul's suicide is also due, in part, to his passive nature. Throughout his life, Paul has been an observer and an onlooker. Paul's only escape from the prison of his daily life comes from his job as an usher at Pittsburgh's Carnegie Hall; he lives for the moments when he can watch the actors, singers, and musicians. However, Paul has no desire to be an actor or musician. As Cather says, "... What he wanted was to see, to be in the atmosphere, float on the wave of it, to be carried out ... away from everything." Although Paul steals the money and flees to New York, these uncharacteristic actions underscore the desperation he feels. Once at the Waldorf in New York, Paul is again content to observe the glamorous world he has craved for so long: "He had no especial desire to meet or to know any of these people; all he demanded was the right to look on and conjecture, to watch the pageant." During his brief stay in the city, Paul enjoys simply sitting in his luxurious rooms, glimpsing the show of city life through a magical curtain of snow. At the end, when the forces of ordinary life begin to close in again, Paul kills himself. But it is typical that he does not use the gun he has bought. Rather, more in keeping with his passive nature, Paul lets himself fall under the wheels of a train.   3

Finally, Paul ends his life because he is emotionally isolated. Throughout   4
the story, not one person makes any real contact with Paul. His teachers do
not understand him and merely resent the attitude of false bravado that he
uses as a defense. Paul's mother is dead; he cannot even remember her.
Paul is completely alienated from his father, who obviously cares for him but
who cannot feel close to his withdrawn, unhappy son. To Paul, his father is
only the man waiting at the top of the stairs, "his hairy legs sticking out of
his nightshirt," who will greet him with "inquiries and reproaches." When
Paul meets a college boy in New York, they share a night on the town. But
the "champagne friendship" ends with a "singularly cool" parting. Paul is
not the kind of person who can let himself go or confide in one of his peers.
For the most part, Paul's isolation is self-imposed. He has drifted so far into
his fantasy life that people in the "real" world are treated like invaders. As
he allows no one to enter his dream, there is no one Paul can turn to for
understanding.

The combination of these personality factors--inability to conform,   5
passivity, and emotional isolation--makes Paul's tragic suicide inevitable.
Before he jumps in front of the train, Paul scoops a hole in the snow and
buries the carnation that he has been wearing in his buttonhole. Like a
hothouse flower in the winter, Paul has a fragile nature that cannot survive
its hostile environment.

COMPARISON AND CONTRAST

Comparison and contrast are two thought processes we constantly perform in everyday life. When we *compare* two things, we show how they are similar; when we *contrast* two things, we show how they are different. We may compare or contrast two brand-name products (for example, Sony versus Zenith TV), or two television shows, or two cars, or two teachers, or two jobs, or two friends, or two courses of action we can take within a given situation. The purpose of comparing or contrasting is to understand each of the two things more clearly and, at times, to make judgments about them.

You will be asked in this section to write a paper of comparison or contrast. To help you prepare for this assignment, first read the three essays ahead. Then answer the questions and do the activities that follow the essays.

ESSAYS TO CONSIDER

Second Marriage

Married people live "happily ever after" in fairy tales, but they do so less   1
and less often in real life. I, like many of my friends, got married, divorced,
and remarried. I suppose, to some people, I'm a failure. After all, I broke my
first solemn promise to "love and cherish until death us do part." But I feel
that I'm finally a success. I learned from the mistakes I made in my first
marriage. This time around, the ways my husband and I share our free time,
make decisions, and deal with problems are very different.

I learned, first of all, not to be a clinging vine. In my first marriage, I   2
felt that every moment we spent apart was wasted. If Ray wanted to go out
to a bar with his friends to watch a football game, I felt rejected and talked
him into staying home. I wouldn't accept an offer to go to a movie or join an
exercise class if it meant that Ray would be home alone. I realize now that
we were often on edge or angry with each other just because we spent too
much time together. In contrast, my second husband and I spend some of
our free time apart and try to have interests of our own. I have started
playing racquetball at a health club, and David sometimes takes off to go to
the local auto races with his friends. When we are together, we aren't bored
with each other; our separate interests make us more interesting people.

I learned not only to be apart sometimes but also to work together when   3
it's time to make decisions. When Ray and I were married, I left all the
important decisions to him. He decided how we would spend money,
whether we should sell the car or fix it, and where to take a vacation. I
know now that I went along with this so that I wouldn't have to take the
responsibility when things went wrong. I could always end an argument by
saying, "It was your fault!" With my second marriage, I am trying to be a full
partner. We ask each other's opinions on major decisions and try to
compromise if we disagree. If we make the wrong choice, we're equally guilty.
When we rented an apartment, for example, we both had to take the blame
for not noticing the drafty windows and the "no pets" clause in our lease.

Maybe the most important thing I've learned is to be a grown-up about   4
facing problems. David and I have made a vow to face our troubles like
adults. If we're mad at each other or worried and upset, we say how we feel.
Rather than hide behind our own misery, we talk about the problem until we
discover how to fix it. Everybody argues or has to deal with the occasional
crisis, but Ray and I always reacted like children to these stormy times. I
would lock myself in the spare bedroom and pout. Ray would stalk out of the
house, slam the door, and race off in the car. Then I would cry and worry till
he returned.

I wish that my first marriage hadn't been the place where I learned how   5
to make a relationship work, but at least I did learn. I feel better now about
being an independent person, about making decisions, and about facing
problems. My second marriage isn't perfect, but it doesn't have the deep
flaws that made the first one fall apart.

A Vote for McDonald's

For my birthday this month, my wife has offered to treat me to dinner at the restaurant of my choice. I think she expects me to ask for a meal at the Chalet, the classiest, most expensive restaurant in town. However, I'm going to eat my birthday dinner at McDonald's. When I compare the two restaurants, the advantages of eating at McDonald's are clear.   1

For one thing, going to the Chalet is more difficult than going to McDonald's. The Chalet has a jacket-and-tie rule, which means I have to dig a sport coat and tie out of the back of my closet, make sure they're semiclean, and try to steam out the wrinkles somehow. The Chalet also requires advance reservations. Since it is downtown, I have to leave an hour early to give myself time to find a parking space within six blocks of the restaurant. The Chalet cancels reservations if a party is more than ten minutes late. Going to McDonald's, on the other hand, is easy. I can feel comfortable wearing jeans or a warm-up suit. I don't have to do any advance planning. I can leave my house whenever I'm ready and pull into a doorside parking space within fifteen minutes.   2

The Chalet is a dimly lit, formal place. While I'm struggling to see what's on my plate, I worry that I'll knock one of the fragile glass vases off the table. The waiters at the Chalet can be uncomfortably formal, too. As I awkwardly pronounce the French words on the menu, I get the feeling that I don't quite live up to their standards. Even though the food at the Chalet is gourmet, I prefer simpler meals. I don't like unfamiliar food swimming in dead-white sauce or covered with pie pastry. Eating at the Chalet is, to me, less enjoyable than eating at McDonald's. McDonald's is a pleasant place where I feel at ease. It is well lighted, and the bright-colored decor is informal. The employees serve with a smile, and the food is easy to pronounce and identify. I know what I'm going to get when I order a certain type of sandwich.   3

The most important difference between the Chalet and McDonald's, though, is the price difference. Dinner for two at the Chalet, even one without appetizers or desserts, would easily cost $40. And the $40 doesn't include the cost of parking the car and tipping the waiter, which can come to an additional $10. Once, I forgot to bring enough money. At McDonald's, a filling meal for two will cost around $8. With the extra $42, my wife and I can eat at McDonald's five more times, or go to the movies five times, or buy play-off tickets to a football game.   4

So, for my birthday dinner celebration, or any other time, I prefer to eat at McDonald's. It is convenient, friendly, and cheap. And with the money my wife saves by taking me to McDonald's, she can buy me what I really want for my birthday--a new Sears power saw.   5

Studying: Then and Now

One June day, I staggered into a high school classroom to take my final   1
exam in United States History IV. Bleary-eyed from an all-night study
session, I checked my "cheat sheets," which were taped inside the cuffs of my
long-sleeved shirt. I had made my usual desperate effort to cram the night
before, with the usual dismal results--I had made it only to page seventy-five
of a four-hundred-page textbook. My high school study habits, obviously,
were a mess. But, in college, I've made an attempt to reform my note-taking,
studying, and test-taking skills.

Taking notes is one thing I've learned to do better since high school   2
days. I used to lose interest in what I was doing and begin doodling, drawing
Martians, or seeing what my signature would look like if I married the cute
guy in the second row. Now, however, I try not to let my mind wander, and I
pull my thoughts back into focus when they begin to go fuzzy. In high
school, my notes often looked like something written in Arabic. In college,
I've learned to use a semiprint writing style that makes my notes
understandable. When I would look over my high school notes, I couldn't
understand them. There would be a word like "Reconstruction," then a big
blank, then the word "important." Weeks later, I had no idea what
Reconstruction was or why it was important. I've since learned to write
down connecting ideas, even if I have to take the time to do it after class.

Ordinary during-the-term studying is another area where I've made   3
changes. In high school, I let reading assignments go. I told myself that I'd
have no trouble catching up on two hundred pages during a fifteen-minute
bus ride to school. College courses have taught me to keep pace with the
work. Otherwise, I feel as though I'm sinking into a quicksand of unread
material. When I finally read the high school assignment, my eyes would
run over the words but my brain would be plotting how to get the car for
Saturday night. Now, I use several techniques that force me to really
concentrate on my reading.

In addition to learning how to cope with daily work, I've also learned to   4
handle study sessions for big tests. My all-night study sessions in high
school were experiments in self-torture. Around 2:00 A.M., my mind, like a
soaked sponge, simply stopped absorbing things. Now, I space out exam
study sessions over several days. That way, the night before can be devoted
to an overall review rather than raw memorizing. Most important, though,
I've changed my attitude toward tests. In high school, I thought tests were
mysterious things with completely unpredictable questions. Now, I ask
teachers about the kinds of questions that will be on the exam, and I try to
"psych out" which areas or facts teachers are likely to ask about. These
practices really work, and for me they've taken much of the fear and mystery
out of tests.

Since I've reformed, note-taking and studying are not as tough as they   5
once were. And there's been one benefit that makes the work worthwhile:
my college grade sheets look much different from the red-splotched ones of
high school days.

■ Questions

About Unity

1. In which supporting paragraph of ''A Vote for McDonald's'' is the topic sentence in the middle rather than, more appropriately, at the beginning?

    (*Write the paragraph number.*) _____

2. Which sentence in paragraph 4 of ''A Vote for McDonald's'' should be omitted in the interest of paragraph unity? (*Write the first two or three words.*)

    _____

About Support

3. After which sentence in paragraph 3 of ''Studying: Then and Now'' are more supporting details needed? _____

4. In which sentence in paragraph 3 of ''A Vote for McDonald's'' are more supporting details needed? _____

About Coherence

5. What transition signal is used in ''Second Marriage'' to indicate emphatic order? _____

6. What are the transition signals used in paragraph 2 of ''Second Marriage''?

    _____

7. What are the three points of contrast in paragraph 2 (''taking notes'') of ''Studying: Then and Now''?

    a. _____   b. _____

    c. _____

8. Which supporting paragraph in ''Second Marriage'' fails to follow the pattern of organization set by the other two? _____

About the Introduction and Conclusion

9. Circle the method of introduction used in ''Studying: Then and Now.''
    a. Broad, general statement narrowing to thesis
    b. Idea that is the opposite of the one to be developed
    c. Quotation
    d. Anecdote
    e. Questions

10. Circle the conclusion technique used in ''Second Marriage.''
    a. Summary   b. Prediction or recommendation   c. Question

METHODS OF DEVELOPMENT

There are two methods of development possible in a comparison or contrast essay. Details can be presented in a *one-side-at-a-time* format or in a *point-by-point* format. Each format is illustrated below.

One Side at a Time

Look at the following supporting paragraph from "A Vote for McDonald's":

> For one thing, going to the Chalet is more difficult than going to McDonald's. The Chalet has a jacket-and-tie rule, which means that I have to dig a sport coat and tie out of the back of my closet, make sure they're semiclean, and try to steam out the wrinkles somehow. The Chalet also requires advance reservations. Since it is downtown, I have to leave an hour early to give myself time to find a parking space within six blocks of the restaurant. The Chalet cancels reservations if a party is more than ten minutes late. Going to McDonald's, on the other hand, is easy. I can feel comfortable wearing jeans or a warm-up suit. I don't have to do any advance planning. I can leave my house whenever I'm ready and pull into a doorside parking space within fifteen minutes.

The first half of the paragraph explains fully one side of the contrast; the second half of the paragraph deals entirely with the other side. When you use this method, be sure to follow the same order of points of contrast (or comparison) for each side. An outline of the paragraph shows how the points for each side are developed in a consistent sequence.

Outline (One Side at a Time)

Going to the Chalet is more difficult than going to McDonald's.

1. Chalet
   a. Dress code
   b. Advance reservations
   c. Leave an hour early
   d. Find parking space
2. McDonald's
   a. Casual dress
   b. No reservations
   c. Leave only fifteen minutes ahead of time
   d. Plenty of free parking

Point by Point

Now look at the supporting paragraph below, which is from ''Studying: Then and Now'':

> Taking notes is one thing I've learned to do better since high school days. I used to lose interest in what I was doing and begin doodling, drawing Martians, or seeing what my signature would look like if I married the cute guy in the second row. Now, however, I try not to let my mind wander, and I pull my thoughts back into focus when they begin to go fuzzy. In high school, my notes often looked like something written in Arabic. In college, I've learned to use a semiprint writing style that makes my notes understandable. When I would look over my high school notes, I couldn't understand them. There would be a word like "Reconstruction," then a big blank, then the word "important." Weeks later, I had no idea what Reconstruction was or why it was important. I've since learned to write down connecting ideas, even if I have to take the time to do it after class.

The paragraph contrasts the two methods of note-taking point by point. The outline below illustrates the method.

Outline (Point by Point)

Taking notes is one thing I've learned to do better since high school days.

1. Level of attention in class
   a. High school
   b. College
2. Handwriting
   a. High school
   b. College
3. Completeness of notes
   a. High school
   b. College

When you begin a comparison or contrast paper, you should decide right away whether you are going to use the one-side-at-a-time format or the point-by-point format. An outline is an essential step in writing and planning a clearly organized paper.

Activity 1

Complete the partial outlines given for the supporting paragraphs that follow.

Paragraph A

The most important difference between the Chalet and McDonald's, though, is the price difference. Dinner for two at the Chalet, even one without appetizers or desserts, would easily cost $40. And the $40 doesn't include the cost of parking the car and tipping the waiter, which can come to an additional $10. At McDonald's a filling meal for two will cost around $8. With the extra $42, my wife and I can eat at McDonald's five more times, or go to the movies five times, or buy play-off tickets to a football game.

The most important difference between the Chalet and McDonald's is the price difference.

1. Chalet

   a. _____

   b. Additional costs of parking and tipping

2. _____ _____

   a. $8 for dinner for two

   b. _____

Complete the following statement: Paragraph A uses a _____

_____ method of development.

Paragraph B

In addition to learning how to cope with daily work, I've also learned to handle study sessions for big tests. My all-night study sessions in high school were experiments in self-torture. Around 2:00 A.M., my mind, like a soaked sponge, simply stopped absorbing things. Now, I space out exam study sessions over several days. That way, the night before can be devoted to an overall review rather than raw memorizing. Most important, though, I've changed my attitude toward tests. In high school, I thought tests were mysterious things with completely unpredictable questions. Now, I ask teachers about the kinds of questions that will be on the exam, and I try to "psych out" which areas or facts teachers are likely to ask about. These practices really work, and for me they've taken much of the fear and mystery out of tests.

In addition to learning how to cope with daily work, I've also learned to handle study sessions for big tests.

1. Planning study time

    a. _____ (all-night study sessions)
    b. College (spread out over several days)

2. _____

    a. High school (tests were mysterious)

    b. _____ (_____)

Complete the following statement: Paragraph B uses a _____
_____ method of development.

Paragraph C

    I learned not only to be apart sometimes but also to work together when it's time to make decisions. When Ray and I were married, I left all the important decisions to him. He decided how we would spend money, whether we should sell the car or fix it, and where to take a vacation. I know now that I went along with this so that I wouldn't have to take the responsibility when things went wrong. I could always end an argument by saying, "It was your fault!" With my second marriage, I am really trying to be a full partner. We ask each other's opinions on major decisions and try to compromise if we disagree. If we make the wrong choice, we're equally guilty. When we recently rented an apartment, for example, we both had to take the blame for not noticing the drafty windows and the "no pets" clause in our lease.

I learned not only to be apart sometimes but also to work together when it's time to make decisions.

1. First marriage
    a. Husband made decisions.
    b. Husband took responsibility and blame.

2. _____

    a. _____

    b. Share responsibility and blame.

Complete the following statement: Paragraph C uses a _____
_____ method of development.

Activity 2

Following is a contrast essay about two sisters. The sentences in each supporting paragraph of the essay are scrambled. For each supporting paragraph, put a number 1 beside the point that all the other scrambled sentences support. Then number the rest of the sentences in a logical order. To do this, you will have to decide whether the sentences should be arranged according to the order of one side at a time or the order of point by point.

Introduction

When my sister and I were growing up, we shared the same bedroom. It wasn't hard to tell which half of the room was mine and which was Kathy's. My side was always as tidy as if a Holiday Inn chambermaid had just left. Kathy's side always looked like the aftermath of an all-night party. Back then, we argued a lot. Kathy said that I was a neatness nut, and I called her a slob. Today we get along just fine, since we have our own homes and don't have to share a room anymore. But Kathy's approach to housekeeping is still much different from mine.

First supporting paragraph

_____ Kathy, on the other hand, believes that a kitchen should look lived-in and not like a hospital operating room.

_____ I treat my kitchen as if a health inspector were waiting to close it down at the least sign of dirt.

_____ I wipe counters with Fantastik while I wait for bread to toast.

_____ She scrambles eggs and leaves the dirty pan on the stove until the nightly cleanup.

_____ She forgets to put the bread away.

_____ When I leave the kitchen, it's usually cleaner than it was before I started to cook.

_____ The kitchen is one room that points up the contrasts between us.

_____ I wrap leftovers in neat packages of aluminum foil or seal them tightly in Tupperware.

_____ Kathy doesn't mind leaving a messy kitchen behind if she has more interesting things to do.

_____ Leftovers go naked into the refrigerator, without covers or foil.

_____ Even as I'm scrambling a couple of eggs, I begin to wash the bowl I used to mix them.

*Second
supporting
paragraph*

_____ The clothes in my closet are carefully arranged.

_____ My bedroom is a place of rest, and I can rest only when everything is in order.

_____ A peek into Kathy's bedroom in midmorning might reveal last night's cheese and crackers growing stale on the night table and several magazines hiding under the rumpled bedcovers.

_____ Some clothes are hung haphazardly in the closet, but many more are under the bed, behind the drapes, or on the deck.

_____ When I leave my bedroom in the morning, the bed is made and there are no clothes lying on the floor or over the chairs.

_____ Plastic bags cover out-of-season items, and shoes are lined up on racks.

_____ We still treat our bedrooms differently.

_____ In contrast, Kathy feels that her bedroom is a private place where she can do as she pleases.

*Third
supporting
paragraph*

_____ After I brush my hair, I check the sink for stray hairs.

_____ The spot that shows our differences the most, though, is the bathroom.

_____ My bathroom must be sanitized and germ-free.

_____ She cleans her mirror only when she gets tired of the polka-dot effect of hardened toothpaste.

_____ I clean the tub with Ajax before and after taking a bath.

_____ Needless to say, her makeup and toiletries litter every available surface.

_____ Once in a while, she points her hair dryer at the sink to blow away the accumulation of hairs in it.

_____ She cleans the tub, but only after a clearly defined brown ring has formed around it.

_____ I wipe off any spots of toothpaste or soap from the mirror and put all my cosmetics and cleaners in their proper places.

_____ Kathy, however, thinks that Americans worry too much about germs.

Conclusion

> As adults, Kathy and I can joke about the habits that caused us so much trouble as adolescents. We can, at times, even see the other's point of view when it comes to housecleaning. But I'm afraid the patterns are pretty much set. It's too late for this "odd couple" to change.

Complete the following statement: The sentences in each supporting paragraph can be organized using a _____ _____ method of development.

WRITING THE ESSAY

■ Writing Assignment 1

Write an essay of comparison or contrast on one of the topics below:

Two courses	Two singers
Two teachers	Two dates
Two jobs	Two popular magazines
Two bosses	Two games
Two family members	Two vacations
Two friends	Two hobbies
Two pets	Two leisure activities
Two vacations	Two stores
Two sports	Two public figures

How to Proceed

a You must begin by making two decisions: (1) what your topic will be and (2) whether you are going to do a comparison or a contrast. Many times, students choose to do essays centered on the differences between two things. For example, you might write about how a math teacher you have in college differs from one you had in high school. You might discuss important differences between your mother and your father, or between two of your friends. You might contrast a factory job you had packing vegetables with a white-collar job you had as a salesperson in a shoe store.

b After you choose a tentative topic, write a simple thesis statement expressing that topic. Then see what kind of support you can generate for that topic. For instance, if you plan to contrast two restaurants, see if you can think of and jot down three distinct ways they differ. *In other words, prepare a brief outline.* An outline is an excellent prewriting technique to use when doing any essay; it is almost indispensable when planning a comparison or contrast essay. Here is a brief outline prepared by the author of the essay titled "A Vote for McDonald's":

Thesis: The advantages of McDonald's over the Chalet are clear.
1. Going to the restaurants
2. Eating at the restaurants
3. Prices at the restaurants

Keep in mind that this planning stage is probably the most important single phase of work you will do on your paper. Without clear planning, you are not likely to write an effective essay.

c After you have decided on a topic and the main lines of support, you must decide whether to use a one-side-at-a-time or a point-by-point method of development. Both methods are explained and illustrated in this chapter.

d Now, freewrite for ten minutes on the topic you have chosen. Do not worry about punctuation, spelling, or other matters relating to correct form. Just get as many details as you can onto the page. You want a base of raw material that you can add to and select from as you now work on the first draft of your paper.

After you do a first draft, try to put it aside for a day or at least several hours. You will then be ready to return with a fresh perspective on the material and build upon what you have already done.

e As you work on a second draft, be sure that each of your supporting paragraphs has a clear topic sentence.

f Use transition words like *first, in addition, also, in contrast, another difference, on the other hand, but, however,* and *most important* to link together points in your paper.

g As you continue working on your paper, refer to the checklist on page 119 and the inside front cover. Make sure that you can answer *Yes* to the questions about unity, support, and coherence.

h Finally, use the checklist on page 119 and the inside front cover to proofread the next-to-final draft of your paper for sentence-skills mistakes, including spelling.

■ Writing Assignment 2

Write a comparison or contrast essay on college versus high school life. Narrow the focus of your paper to a particular aspect of school—teachers, classes, sports, social life, or students' attitudes, for example. *Or,* you may write a paper on dormitory or apartment life versus living at home.

■ Writing Assignment 3

Write an essay that contrasts two attitudes on a controversial subject. The subject might be abortion, marijuana, capital punishment, homosexuality, euthanasia, prostitution, coed prisons, busing, school prayer, nuclear power plants, the social security system, or some other matter on which there are conflicting feelings and opinions. You may want to contrast your views with someone else's or to contrast the way you felt at some point in the past with the way you feel now.

■ Writing Assignment 4

In this essay, you will write with a specific purpose and for a specific audience.

Option 1: Your boyfriend or girlfriend wants to get married this year, but you think you'd rather just live together for a while. To help both of you think through the issue, write him or her a letter in which you compare and contrast the advantages and disadvantages of each approach. Use a one-side-at-a-time method in making your analysis.

Option 2: Write a letter to your boss in which you compare your abilities with those of the ideal candidate for a position to which you'd like to be promoted. Use a point-by-point method in which you discuss each ideal requirement and then describe how well you measure up to it. Use the requirements of a job you're relatively familiar with, perhaps even a job you would really like to apply for one day.

■ Writing Assignment 5

Write an essay that contrasts two characters or two points of view in one or more poems, stories, plays, or novels. The work you choose may be assigned by your instructor, or it may require your instructor's approval. For this assignment, your essay may have two supporting paragraphs, with each paragraph representing one side of the contrast. A student model is given on the following page.

Warren and Mary

In "Death of the Hired Man," Robert Frost uses a brief incident--the   1
return of Silas, an aging farmhand--to dramatize the differences between a
husband and wife. As Warren and Mary talk about Silas and reveal his story,
the reader learns their story, too. By the end of the poem, Warren and Mary
emerge as contrasting personalities; one is wary and reserved, while the
other is open and giving.

Warren is a kindly man but one whose basic decency is tempered by a   2
sense of practicality and emotional reserve. Warren is upset with Mary for
sheltering Silas, who is barely useful and sometimes unreliable: "What use he
is there's no depending on." Warren feels that he has already done his duty
toward Silas by hiring him the previous summer and that he is under no
obligation to care for him now. "Home," says Warren, "is the place where,
when you have to go there/They have to take you in." Warren's home is not
Silas' home, so Warren does not have a legal or moral duty to keep the
shiftless old man. Warren's temperament, in turn, influences his attitude
toward Silas' arrival. Warren hints to Mary--through a condescending
smile--that Silas is somehow playing on her emotions or faking his illness.
Warren considers Silas' supposed purpose in coming to the farm--to ditch the
meadow--nothing but a flimsy excuse for a free meal. The best that Warren
can find to say about Silas is that he does have one practical skill: the ability
to build a good load of hay.

Mary, in contrast, is distinguished by her giving nature and her   3
concentration on the workings of human emotion. In caring for Silas, Mary
sees not his lack of ability or his laziness but the fact that he is "worn out"
and needs help. To Mary, home represents not obligation ("They have to
take you in") but unconditional love: "I should have called it/Something you
somehow haven't to deserve." Mary is observant, not only of outer
appearance but also of the inner person; this is why she thinks not that Silas
is trying to trick them but that he is a desperate man trying to salvage a
little self-respect. She realizes, too, that he will never ditch the meadow, and
she knows that Silas' insecurity prompted his arguments with the college boy
who helped with the haying. Mary is also perceptive enough to see that Silas
could never humble himself before his estranged brother. Mary's attitude is
more sympathetic than Warren's; whereas Warren wonders why Silas and
his brother don't get along, Mary thinks about how Silas "hurt my heart the
way he lay/And rolled his old head on that sharp-edged chairback."

In describing Silas, Warren and Mary describe themselves. We see a   4
basically good man, one whose spirit has been toughened by a hard life.
Warren, we learn, would have liked to pay Silas a fixed wage but simply
couldn't afford to. Life has taught Warren to be practical and to rein in his
emotions. In contrast, we see a nurturing woman, alert to human feelings,
who could never refuse to care for a lonely, dying man. Warren and Mary
are both decent people. This is the reason why, as Mary instinctively feels,
Silas chooses their home for his final refuge.

DEFINITION

In talking with other people, we at times offer informal definitions to explain just what we mean by a particular term. Suppose, for example, we say to a friend, "Bob is really an inconsiderate person." We might then explain what we mean by "inconsiderate" by saying, "He borrowed my accounting book 'overnight,' but didn't return it for a week. And when I got it back, it was covered with coffee stains." In a written definition, we make clear in a more complete and formal way our own personal understanding of a term. Such a definition typically starts with one meaning of a term. The meaning is then illustrated with a series of details.

You will be asked in this section to write an essay in which you define a term. The three student essays below are all examples of definition essays. Read them and then answer the questions that follow.

ESSAYS TO CONSIDER

Definition of a Baseball Fan

What is a baseball fan? The word <u>fan</u> is an abbreviation of <u>fanatic</u>,   1
meaning "insane." In the case of baseball fans, the term is appropriate.
They behave insanely, they are insane about trivia, and they are insanely
loyal.

Baseball fans wear their official team T shirts and warm-up jackets to   2
the mall, the supermarket, the classroom, and even--if they can get away
with it--to work. Then, whenever the team offers a giveaway item, the fans
rush to the ball park to get the roll-up hat or tote bag that is being offered
that day. Baseball fans behave insanely, especially between April and
October. In addition, baseball fans cover the walls with items of every kind.
When they go to a game, which they do as often as possible, the true baseball
fans put on their team colors, grab their pennants, pin on their team buttons,
and even bring along hand-lettered bedsheet signs proudly proclaiming "Go
Dodgers" or "Braves Are Number One." At the game, these fans form a
rooting section, constantly encouraging their favorite players and obediently
echoing every cheer flashed on the electronic scoreboard.

Baseball fans, in addition to behaving insanely, are also insanely   3
fascinated by trivia. Every day, they turn to the sports page and study last
night's statistics. They simply have to see who has extended his hitting
streak and how many strikeouts the winning pitcher recorded. Their
bookshelves are crammed with record books, team yearbooks, and baseball
almanacs. They delight in remembering such significant facts as who was
the last left-handed third baseman to hit into an inning-ending double play in
the fifth game of the play-offs. And if you do not show equal interest or
enthusiasm, they look at you as if they were doubting your sanity.

Last of all, baseball fans are insanely loyal to the team of their choice.   4
Should the home team lose eight in a row, their fans may begin to call them
"bums." They may even suggest, vocally, that the slumping cleanup hitter be
sent to the minors or the manager be fired. But these reactions only hide
their broken hearts. They still check the sports pages and tune in to get the
score. Furthermore, this intense loyalty makes fans dangerous, for anyone
who dares to say to a loyal fan that some other team has sharper fielding or
a better attitude could be risking permanent physical damage. Incidents of
violence on the baseball field have increased in recent years and are a matter
of growing concern.

From mid-October through March, baseball fans are like any other   5
human beings. They pay their taxes, take out the garbage, and complain
about the high cost of living or the latest home repair. But when April
comes, the colors and radios go on, the record books come off the shelves, and
the devotion returns. For the true baseball fan, another season of insanity
has begun.

Stupidity

Although <u>stupidity</u> is commonly defined as "lack of normal intelligence," stupid behavior is not the behavior of a person lacking intelligence but the behavior of a person not using good judgment or sense. In fact, <u>stupidity</u> comes from a Latin word that means "senseless." Therefore, <u>stupidity</u> can be defined as the behavior of a person of normal intelligence who is acting in a particular situation as if he or she weren't very bright. Stupidity exists on three levels of seriousness.

1

First is the simple, relatively harmless level. Behavior on this level is often amusing. It is humorous when someone places the food from a fast-food restaurant on the roof of the car while unlocking the door and then drives away with the food still on the roof. We call this absentminded. The person's good sense or intelligence was temporarily absent. On this level, other than passing inconvenience or embarrassment, no one is injured by the stupid behavior.

2

More dangerous than simple stupidity is the next type--potentially serious stupidity. Practical jokes such as putting sugar in the restaurant salt shakers are on this level. The intent is humorous, but there is a potential for harm. Irresponsible advice given to others is also serious stupidity. An example is the person who plays psychiatrist on the basis of an introductory psychology course or a TV program on psychiatry. The intent may be to help, but if the victims really need psychiatric help, an amateur telling them that they "have no ego" or characterizing them as "neurotic" will only worsen the situation.

3

Even worse is the third kind of stupidity, which is always harmful. Otherwise kind persons, who would never directly injure another living thing, stupidly dump off a box of six-week-old kittens along a country road. Lacking the heart to have "the poor things put to sleep," they sentence them to almost certain death from parasites, upper respiratory infections, exposure, other animals, or the wheels of a passing vehicle. Yet they are able to tell themselves that "they will find nice homes" or "animals can get along in the wild." Another example of this kind of stupidity is the successful local businessman who tries to have as many office affairs as he can get away with. He risks the loss of his job, his home, his wife and children, and the goodwill of his parents and friends. He fails to see, though, that there is anything wrong with what he is doing. His is the true moral stupidity of a person not willing to think about the results of his actions or to take responsibility for them.

4

The common defense of the person guilty of stupidity is, "But I didn't think...." This, however, is an inadequate excuse, especially when serious or harmful stupidity is involved. We are all liable when we do not think about the consequences of our actions.

5

Student Zombies

Schools divide people up into categories. From first grade on up, students   1
are labeled "advanced" or "deprived" or "remedial" or "antisocial." Students
pigeonhole their fellow students, too. We've all known the "brain," the "jock,"
the "dummy," and the "teacher's pet." In most cases, these narrow labels are
misleading and inaccurate. But there is one label for a certain type of college
student that says it all. That is, of course, "zombie."

Most of us haven't known many real zombies personally, but we do know   2
how they act. Horror movies have given us portraits of zombies, the living
dead, for years. They stalk around graveyards, their eyes glued open by
Hollywood makeup artists, bumping like cheap toy robots into living people.
The special effects in horror movies are much better now. Zombie students
in college do just about the same thing. They stalk around campus, eyes
glazed, staring off into space. They wander into classrooms, sit down
mechanically, and contemplate the ceiling. Zombie students rarely eat, play
sports, or toss Frisbees on campus lawns. Instead, they mysteriously
disappear when classes are over and return only when they next feel the
urge to drift into a classroom. The urge may not return, however, for weeks.

Where student zombies come from is as weird as the origin of the   3
original zombies of the voodoo cults. According to voodoo legend, zombies
are corpses that have come alive again. They have been reanimated by
supernatural spells. Student zombies, too, are directed by a strange power.
They continue to attend school although they have no apparent motivation to
do so. They are completely uninterested in college-related activities like tests,
grades, papers, and projects. They seem to be propelled by some inner force
that compels them to wander forever through the halls of higher education.

All zombies, unfortunately, have a similar fate. In the movies, they are   4
usually shot, stabbed, or electrocuted, all to no avail. Then the hero or
heroine finally realizes that a counterspell is needed. Once the counterspell
is cast, with the appropriate props of chicken legs, human hair, and bats'
eyeballs, the zombie-corpse can return peacefully to its coffin. Student
zombies, if they are to change at all, must undergo a similar traumatic
experience. Sometimes the evil spell can be broken by a grade transcript
decorated with "F" grades. Sometimes a professor will hold a private,
intensive exorcism session. Sometimes, though, the zombies blunder around
for years until they are gently persuaded by the college administration to
head for another institution that accepts zombies. Then, they enroll in a new
college or get a job in the family business.

Every college student knows that it's not necessary to see Night of the   5
Living Dead or Voodoo Island in order to see zombies in action. Forget the
campus movie theater or the late late show. Just sit in a classroom and wait
for the students who walk in without books or papers of any kind and sit in
the farthest seats in the rear. Day of the Living Dead is showing every day at
a college near you.

■ Questions

About Unity

1. Which essay places the topic sentence for its first supporting paragraph within the paragraph rather than, more appropriately, at the beginning?

   _____

2. Which sentence in paragraph 2 of "Student Zombies" should be omitted in the interest of paragraph unity? (*Write the first two or three words.*)

   _____

3. Which sentence in paragraph 4 of "Definition of a Baseball Fan" should

   be omitted in the interest of unity? _____

About Support

4. Which supporting paragraph in the essay on stupidity needs more supporting

   details? (*Write the paragraph number.*) _____

5. Which essay develops its definition through a series of comparisons?

   _____

6. Which sentence in paragraph 2 of the essay on baseball needs supporting

   details? _____

About Coherence

7. Which essay uses emphatic order, saving its most important idea for last?

   _____

8. Which two essays use linking sentences between their first and second supporting paragraphs?

   _____   _____

9. What are five major transition words that appear in the three supporting paragraphs of "Definition of a Baseball Fan"?

   a. _____   b. _____   c. _____

   d. _____   e. _____

About the Introduction

10. Circle below the kind of introduction used for "Student Zombies."

    a. Broad, general statement narrowing to thesis

    b. Idea that is the opposite of the one to be developed

    c. Quotation

    d. Anecdote

    e. Questions

WRITING THE ESSAY

■ Writing Assignment 1

Shown below are an introduction, a thesis, and supporting points for an essay that defines the word *maturity*. Using separate paper, plan out and write the supporting paragraphs and a conclusion for the essay. Refer to the suggestions on "How to Proceed" that follow.

The Meaning of Maturity

Being a mature student does not mean being an old-timer. Maturity is not measured by the number of years a person has lived. Instead, the yardstick of maturity is marked by the qualities of self-denial, determination, and dependability.

Self-denial is an important quality in the mature student. . . .

Determination is another characteristic of a mature student. . . .

Although self-denial and determination are both vital, probably the most important measure of maturity is dependability. . . .

How to Proceed

a Prepare examples for each of the three qualities of maturity. For each quality, you should have one extended example that takes up an entire paragraph or two or three shorter examples that together form enough material for a paragraph.

b To generate these details, ask yourself the following questions:

What could I do, or have I done, that would be an example of self-denial?

What has someone I know ever done that could be described as self-denial?

What kind of behavior on the part of a student could be considered self-denial?

Write down quickly whatever answers occur to you for the questions. Don't worry about writing correct sentences; just concentrate on getting down as many details relating to self-denial as you can think of. Then repeat the questioning and writing process with the qualities of determination and dependability as well.

c Draw from and add to this material as you work on the drafts of your essay. Also, refer to the checklist on page 119 and the inside front cover to make sure you can answer *Yes* to the questions about unity, support, and coherence.

d Write a conclusion for the essay by adding a summarizing sentence or two and a final thought about the subject. See page 75 for an example.

e Finally, use the checklist on page 119 and the inside front cover to proofread the next-to-final draft for sentence-skills mistakes, including spelling.

■ Writing Assignment 2

Write an essay that defines one of the terms below. Each term refers to a certain kind of person.

Snob	Optimist	Slob
Cheapskate	Pessimist	Tease
Loser	Team player	Practical joker
Good neighbor	Scapegoat	Black sheep of a family
Busybody	Bully	Procrastinator
Complainer	Religious person	Loner
Con artist	Hypocrite	Straight arrow

Refer to ''How to Proceed'' on the following page.

How to Proceed

a   If you start with a dictionary definition, be sure to choose just one meaning of a term. (A dictionary often provides several different meanings associated with a word.) Also, don't begin your paper with the overused line, "According to Webster, . . .''

b   Remember that the thesis of a definition essay is actually some version of "What _____ means to me." The thesis presents what *you* think the term actually means.

c   You may want to organize the body of your paper around three different parts or qualities of your term. Here are the three-part divisions of the four essays considered in this chapter:

Maturity "is marked by qualities of self-denial, determination, and dependability."

"Stupidity exists on three levels of seriousness."

Baseball fans are fanatics in terms of "their behavior, their fascination with trivia, and their loyalty."

Student zombies usually have the same kind of behavior, origin, and fate.

Each division in a three-part breakdown should be supported by either a series of examples or a single extended example.

d   Be sure to outline the essay before you begin to write. As a guide, put your thesis and three supporting points in the spaces below.

Thesis: _____

_____

Support: 1. _____

         2. _____

         3. _____

e   While writing your paper, use as a guide the checklist of the four bases on page 119 and the inside front cover. Make sure you can answer *Yes* to the questions about unity, support, coherence, and sentence skills.

■ **Writing Assignment 3**

Write an essay that defines one of the terms below.

Persistence	Responsibility	Fear
Rebellion	Insecurity	Arrogance
Sense of humor	Assertiveness	Conscience
Escape	Jealousy	Class
Laziness	Practicality	Innocence
Danger	Nostalgia	Freedom
Curiosity	Gentleness	Violence
Common sense	Depression	Shyness
Soul	Obsession	Idealism
Family	Self-control	Christianity

As a guide in writing your paper, use the suggestions in "How to Proceed."

■ **Writing Assignment 4**

In this essay, you will write with a specific purpose and for a specific audience.

Option 1:   You work in a doctor's office and have been asked to write a brochure that will be placed in the patients' waiting room. The brochure is intended to tell patients what a healthy lifestyle is. Write a definition of a *healthy lifestyle* for your readers, using examples wherever appropriate. Your definition might focus on both mental and physical health and might include eating, sleeping, exercise, and recreational habits.

Alternatively, you might decide to take a playful point of view and write a brochure defining an *unhealthy lifestyle*.

Option 2:   Your Spanish class will be hosts to some students from Mexico. The class is preparing a mini-dictionary of slang for the visitors. Your job is to write a paragraph in which you define the phrase *to gross out*. In your paper, include a general definition as well as several examples showing how the phrase is used and the circumstances in which it would be appropriate. By way of providing background, you may also want to include the nonslang meaning of *gross* which led to the slang usage. To find the information, consult a dictionary.

Alternatively, you may write about any other slang term. If necessary, first get the approval of your instructor.

DIVISION
AND
CLASSIFICATION

When you return home from your weekly trip to the supermarket with five brown bags packed with your purchases, how do you sort them out? You might separate the food items from the nonfood items (like toothpaste, paper towels, and detergent). Or you might divide and classify the items into groups intended for the freezer compartment, the refrigerator, and the kitchen cupboards. You might even put the items into groups like "to be used tonight," "to be used soon," and "to be used last." Sorting supermarket items in such ways is just one small example of how we spend a great deal of our time organizing our environment in one manner or another.

In this section, you will be asked to write an essay in which you divide or classify a subject according to a single principle. To prepare for this assignment, first read the division and classification essays below and then work through the questions and the activity that follow.

ESSAYS TO CONSIDER

Mall People

1   Having fun can exhaust one's bank account. By the time a person drives to the city and pays the tired-looking parking attendant the hourly fee to park, there is little money left to buy movie tickets, let alone popcorn and soft drinks to snack on. As a result, people have turned from wining, dining, and moviegoing to the nearby free-parking, free-admission shopping malls. Teenagers, couples on dates, and the nuclear family can all be observed having a good time at this alternative recreation spot.

2   Teenagers are the largest group of mallgoers. The guys saunter by in sneakers, T shirts, and blue jeans, complete with a package of cigarettes sticking out of their pockets. The girls stumble along in high-heeled shoes and daring tank tops, with hairbrushes tucked snugly in the rear pockets of their tight-fitting designer jeans. Traveling in a gang that resembles a wolf pack, the teenagers make the shopping mall their hunting ground. Their raised voices, loud laughter, and occasional shouted obscenities can be heard from as far as half a mall away. They come to "pick up chicks," to "meet guys," and basically just to "hang out."

3   Couples are now spending their dates at shopping malls. The young lovers are easy to spot because they walk hand in hand, stopping to sneak a quick kiss after every few steps. They first pause at jewelry store windows so they can gaze at diamond engagement rings and gold wedding bands. Then, they wander into furniture departments in the large mall stores. Whispering happily to each other, they imagine how that five-piece living room set or brass headboard would look in their future home. Finally, they drift away, their arms wrapped around each other's waists.

4   Mom, Dad, little Jenny, and Fred, Jr., visit the mall on Friday and Saturday evenings. Jenny wants to see some of the special mall exhibits geared toward little children. Fred, Jr., wants to head for the places that young boys find appealing. Mom walks around looking at various things until she discovers that Jenny is no longer attached to her hand. She finally finds her in a favorite hiding place. Meanwhile, Dad has arrived at a large store and is admiring the products he would love to buy. Indeed, the mall provides something special for every member of the family.

5   The teenagers, the couples on dates, and the nuclear family make up the vast majority of mallgoers. These folks need not purchase anything to find pleasure at the mall. They are shopping for inexpensive recreation, and the mall provides it.

Movie Monsters

Dracula rises from the grave--again. Mutant insects, the product of
underground nuclear testing, grow to the size of boxcars and attack our
nation's cities. Weird-looking aliens from beyond the stars decide to invade
our planet. None of these events, if they ever happened, would surprise
horror-movie fans. For years, such moviegoers have enjoyed being
frightened by every type of monster Hollywood has managed to dream up,
whether it be natural, artificial, or extraterrestrial.

One kind of movie monster is a product of nature. These monsters may
be exaggerated versions of real creatures, like the single-minded shark in
Jaws or the skyscraper-climbing gorilla in King Kong. They may be extinct
animals, like the dinosaurs that terrorize cave dwellers and explorers in
movies. Actually, cave dwellers and dinosaurs would never have met, for
some unexplained event caused the dinosaurs to become extinct before the
cave dwellers existed. "Natural" monsters sometimes combine human and
animal features. Cat people, werewolves, and vampires fit into this category;
so do Bigfoot and the Abominable Snowman. All these monsters seem to
frighten us because they represent nature at its most threatening. We may
have come a long way since the Stone Age, but we're still scared of what's out
there beyond the campfire.

The second type of movie monster is a product of humans. Every giant
lobster or house-sized spider that attacks Tokyo or Cleveland is the result of a
mad scientist's meddling or a dose of radiation. In these cases, humans
interfere with nature, and the results are deadly. Frankenstein's monster,
for example, is put together out of spare parts stolen from graveyards. His
creator, an insane scientist in love with his own power, uses a jolt of
electricity to bring the monster to life. The scientist, along with lots of
innocent villagers, dies as a result of his pride. In dozens of other monster
movies, creatures grow to enormous proportions after wandering too close to
atomic bomb sites. Our real fears about the terrors of technology are given
the shape of giant scorpions and cockroaches that devour people.

The third type of movie monster comes from outer space. Since the
movies began, odd things have been crawling or sliding down the ramps of
spaceships. To modern movie fans, the early space monsters look
suspiciously like actors dressed in rubber suits and metal antennas. Now,
thanks to special effects, these creatures can horrify the bravest moviegoer.
The monster in Alien, for example, invades a spaceship piloted by humans.
The monster, which resembles a ten-pound raw clam with arms, clamps onto
a crew member's face. Later, it grows into a slimy six-footer with a double
jaw and long, toothed tongue. Movies like Alien reflect our fear of the
unfamiliar and the unknown. We don't know what's out there in space, and
we're afraid it might not be very nice.

Movie monsters, no matter what kind they are, sneak around the edges of
our imaginations long after the movies are over. They probably play on fears
that were there already. The movies merely give us the monsters that
embody those fears.

Selling Beer

The other night, my six-year-old son turned to me and asked for a light   1
beer. My husband and I sat there for a moment, stunned, and then explained
to him that beer was only for grown-ups. I suddenly realized how many, and
how often, beer ads appear on television. To my little boy, it must seem that
every American drinks beer after work, or after playing softball, or while
watching a football game. Beer makers have pounded audiences with all
kinds of campaigns to sell beer. Each type of ad, however, seems to be
targeted toward a different economic level of the TV viewing audience.

The first type of ad appeals to working-class people. There is the "this   2
Bud's for you" approach, which shows the "boys" headed down to the
neighborhood tavern after a tough day on the job at the auto plant or the
construction site. The Budweiser jingle congratulates them on a job well
done and encourages them to reward themselves--with a Bud. Miller beer
uses a slightly different approach to appeal to workers. Men are shown
completing a tough and unusual job and then relaxing during "Miller time."
"Miller time" jobs might be called fantasy blue-collar jobs. Some Miller men,
for example, fly helicopters to round up cattle or manage to cap blazing oil
well fires.

The second kind of ad aims not at working-class people but at an upper-   3
middle-class audience. The actors in these ads are shown in glamorous or
adventurous settings. Some ads show a group of friends in their thirties and
forties getting together to play a fancy sport, like tennis or rugby. One
Lowenbrau ad, featuring a group of compatible couples at a clambake, is
aimed at those rich enough to have a costly beach house.

The third type of ad appeals to people with a weight problem. These are   4
the ads for the light beers, and they use sports celebrities and indirect
language to make their points. For example, they never use the phrase "diet
beer." Instead, they use phrases like "tastes great, and is less filling." In the
macho world of beer commercials, men don't admit that they're dieting--
that's too sissy. But if former football coaches and baseball greats can order
a Lite without being laughed out of the bar, why can't the ordinary guy?

To a little boy, it may well seem that beer is necessary to every adult's   5
life. After all, we need it to recover from a hard day at work, to celebrate our
pleasurable moments, and to get rid of the beer bellies we got by drinking it
in the first place. At least, that's what advertisers tell him--and us.

■ Questions

About Unity

1. Which paragraph in ''Mall People'' lacks a topic sentence? _____
   Write a topic sentence for the paragraph:

   _____

2. Which sentence in paragraph 2 of ''Movie Monsters'' should be omitted
   in the interest of paragraph unity? _____

3. Which paragraph in ''Selling Beer'' does not logically support the thesis
   statement? _____

About Support

4. Which supporting paragraph in ''Movie Monsters'' uses a single extended
   example? _____

5. After which sentence in paragraph 3 of ''Selling Beer'' are more supporting
   details needed? _____

6. Which paragraph in ''Mall People'' lacks specific details? _____

About Coherence

7. What are the transition words used in the second supporting paragraph of
   ''Mall People''?

   a. _____   b. _____   c. _____

8. Which topic sentence in ''Selling Beer'' functions as a linking sentence
   between paragraphs? _____

About the Introduction and Conclusion

9. Circle the kind of introduction used in ''Selling Beer.''
   a. Broad, general statement narrowing to thesis
   b. Idea that is the opposite of the one to be developed
   c. Quotation
   d. Anecdote
   e. Questions

10. Which two essays have conclusions that include brief summaries of the
    essay's supporting points?
    a. ''Movie Monsters''
    b. ''Mall People''
    c. ''Selling Beer''

Activity

This activity will sharpen your sense of the classifying process. In each of the following groups, cross out the one item that has not been classified on the same basis as the other four. Also, indicate in the space provided the single principle of classification used for the four items. Note the examples.

Examples Shirts
  a. Flannel
  b. Cotton
  c. ~~Tuxedo~~
  d. Denim
  e. Silk

(Unifying principle: _material_)

Sports
  a. Swimming
  b. Sailing
  c. ~~Basketball~~
  d. Water polo
  e. Scuba diving

(Unifying principle: _water sports_)

1. School subjects
  a. Algebra
  b. History
  c. Geometry
  d. Trigonometry
  e. Calculus

(Unifying principle: _____)

2. Movies
  a. *The Sound of Music*
  b. *My Fair Lady*
  c. *Dracula*
  d. *Cabaret*
  e. *The Wizard of Oz*

(Unifying principle: _____)

3. Clothing
  a. Sweat shirt
  b. Shorts
  c. T shirt
  d. Evening gown
  e. Sweat pants

(Unifying principle: _____)

4. Fasteners
  a. Staples
  b. Buttons
  c. Zippers
  d. Snaps
  e. Velcro

(Unifying principle: _____)

5. Sources of information
    a. *Newsweek*
    b. *The New York Times*
    c. *People*
    d. *TV Guide*
    e. *Life*

    (Unifying principle: _____)

6. Fibers
    a. Wool
    b. Acrylic
    c. Cotton
    d. Silk
    e. Linen

    (Unifying principle: _____)

7. Tapes
    a. Cellophane
    b. Recording
    c. Masking
    d. Duct
    e. Electrical

    (Unifying principle: _____)

8. Fairy-tale characters
    a. Witch
    b. King
    c. Fairy godmother
    d. Wicked queen
    e. Princess

    (Unifying principle: _____)

9. Immigrants
    a. Haitian
    b. Irish
    c. Mexican
    d. Illegal
    e. 'German

    (Unifying principle: _____)

10. Famous buildings
    a. Lincoln Memorial
    b. Empire State Building
    c. White House
    d. Capitol Building
    e. Washington Monument

    (Unifying principle: _____)

11. Emotions
    a. Depression
    b. Anger
    c. Jealousy
    d. Despair
    e. Affection

    (Unifying principle: _____)

12. Crimes
    a. Rape
    b. Murder
    c. Robbery
    d. Prostitution
    e. Mugging

    (Unifying principle: _____)

WRITING THE ESSAY

■ Writing Assignment 1

Shown below are an introduction, a thesis, and supporting points for a classification essay on college stress. Using separate paper, plan out and write the supporting paragraphs and a conclusion for the essay. Refer to the suggestions on "How to Proceed" that follow.

College Stress

Jack's heart pounds as he casts panicked looks around the classroom. He doesn't recognize the professor, he doesn't know any of the students, and he can't even figure out what the subject is. In front of him is a test. At the last minute his roommate awakens him. It's only another anxiety dream. The very fact that dreams like Jack's are common suggests that college is a stressful situation for young people. The causes of this stress can be academic, financial, and personal.

Academic stress is common. . . .

In addition to academic stress, the student often feels financial pressure. . . .

Along with academic and financial worries, the student faces personal pressures. . . .

How to Proceed

a   To develop some ideas for the essay, freewrite for five minutes apiece on (1) *academic,* (2) *financial,* and (3) *personal* problems of college students.

b   Add to the material you have written by asking yourself these questions:

What are some examples of academic problems that are stressful for students?

What are some examples of financial problems that students must contend with?

What are some examples of personal problems that create stress in students?

Write down quickly whatever answers occur to you for the questions. As with the freewriting, do not worry at this stage about writing correct sentences. Instead, concentrate on getting down as much information as you can think of that supports each of the three points.

c   Now go through all the material you have accumulated. Perhaps some of the details you have written down may help you think of even better details that would fit. If so, write them down. Then make decisions about the exact information that you will use in each supporting paragraph. List the details (1, 2, 3, and so on) in the order in which you will present them.

d   As you work on the drafts of your paper, refer to the checklist on page 119 and the inside front cover to make sure you can answer *Yes* to the questions about unity, support, and coherence.

e   Write a conclusion for the essay by adding a summarizing sentence or two and a final thought about the subject. See page 75 for an example.

f   Finally, use the checklist on page 119 and the inside front cover to proofread the next-to-final draft of your paper for sentence-skills mistakes, including spelling.

■ Writing Assignment 2

Write a division and classification essay on one of the following subjects:

Crimes	Advertisements	Clothes
Dates	Churchgoers	Attitudes toward life
Teachers	Junk food	Eating places
Bosses	Jobs	Marriages
Friends	Shoppers	TV watchers
Sports fans	Soap operas	College courses
Parties	Bars	

How to Proceed

a The first step in writing a division and classification essay is to divide your tentative topic into three reasonably complete parts. *Always use a single principle of division when you form your three parts.* For example, if your topic was "Automobile Drivers" and you divided them into slow, moderate, and fast drivers, your single basis for division would be "rate of speed." It would be illogical, then, to have as a fourth type "teenage drivers" (the basis of such a division would be "age") or "female drivers" (the basis of such a division would be "sex"). You probably could classify automobile drivers on the basis of age or sex or another division, for almost any subject can be analyzed in more than one way. What is important, however, is that in any single paper, you choose only one basis for division and stick to it. Be consistent.

In "Movie Monsters," the single basis for dividing monsters into natural, artificial, and extraterrestrial is *origin*. It would have been illogical, then, to have a fourth category dealing with vampires. In "Selling Beer," the intended basis for the types of beer ads was *economic level*. The writer's first group was working-class people; his second group was upper-middle-class people. To be consistent, his third group should have been, perhaps, lower-middle-class people. Instead, the writer confusingly shifted to ads that appeal to people with a weight problem.

b To avoid such confusion in your own essay, fill in the outline below before starting your paper and make sure you can answer *Yes* to the questions that follow. You should expect to do a fair amount of thinking before coming up with a logical plan for your paper.

Topic: _____

Three-part division of the topic:

1. _____

2. _____

3. _____

Is there a single basis of division for the three parts? _____

Is the division reasonably complete? _____

c Refer to the checklist of the four bases on page 119 and the inside front cover while writing the drafts of your paper. Make sure you can answer *Yes* to the questions about unity, support, organization, and sentence skills. Also, use the checklist when you proofread the next-to-final draft of your paper for sentence-skills mistakes, including spelling.

■ Writing Assignment 3

In this essay, you will write with a specific purpose and for a specific audience.

Option 1:   Your younger sister or brother has moved to another city and is about to choose a roommate. Write her or him a letter about what to expect from different types of roommates. Label each type of roommate in your letter ("The Messy Type," "The Neatnik," "The Loud-Music Lover," etc.) and explain what it would be like to live with each.

Option 2:   Unsure about your career direction, you have gone to a vocational counseling service. To help you select the type of work you are best suited for, a counselor has asked you to write a detailed description of your "ideal job." You will present this description to three other people who are also seeking to make a career choice.

To describe your ideal job, divide work life into three or more elements, such as:

Activities done on the job

Skills used on the job

Physical environment

People you work with and under

How the job affects society

In your paper, explain your ideals for each element. Use specific examples where possible to illustrate your points.

DESCRIPTION

When you describe someone or something, you give a picture in words to your readers. To make the word picture as vivid and real as possible, you must observe and record specific details that appeal to your readers' senses (sight, hearing, taste, smell, and touch). More than any other type of essay, a descriptive paper needs sharp, colorful details.

Here is a sentence in which almost none of the senses is used: "In the window was a fan." In contrast, here is a description rich in sense impressions: "The blades of the rusty window fan clattered and whirled as they blew out a stream of warm, soggy air." Sense impressions here include sight (*rusty window fan, whirled*), hearing (*clattered*), and touch (*warm, soggy air*). The vividness and sharpness provided by the sensory details give us a clear picture of the fan and enable us to share in the writer's experience.

In this section, you will be asked to describe sharply a person, place, or thing for the readers through the use of words rich in sensory details. To help you prepare for the assignment, first read the three essays ahead and then answer the questions that follow.

ESSAYS TO CONSIDER

Family Portrait

My mother, who is seventy years old, recently sent me a photograph of herself that I had never seen before. While cleaning out the attic of her Florida home, she came across a studio portrait she had had taken about a year before she married my father. This picture of my mother as a twenty-year-old girl has fascinated me from the moment I began to study it closely.   1

The young woman in the picture has a face that resembles my own in many ways. Her face is a bit more oval than mine, but the softly waving brown hair around it is identical. The small, straight nose is the same model I was born with. My mother's mouth is closed, yet there is just the slightest hint of a smile on her full lips. I know that if she had smiled, she would have shown the same wide grin and downcurving "smile lines" that appear in my own snapshots. The most haunting features in the photo, however, are my mother's eyes. They are exact duplicates of my own large, dark brown ones. Her brows are plucked into thin lines, which are like two pencil strokes added to highlight those fine, luminous eyes.   2

I've also carefully studied the clothing and jewelry in the photograph. My mother is wearing a blouse and skirt that, although the photo was taken fifty years ago, could easily be worn today. The blouse is made of heavy eggshell-colored satin and reflects the light in its folds and hollows. It has a turned-down cowl collar and smocking on the shoulders and below the collar. The smocking (tiny rows of gathered material) looks hand-done. The skirt, which covers my mother's calves, is straight and made of light wool or flannel. My mother is wearing silver drop earrings. They are about two inches long and roughly shield-shaped. On her left wrist is a matching bracelet. My mother can't find this bracelet now, despite the fact that we spent hours searching through the attic for it. On the third finger of her left hand is a ring with a large, square-cut stone.   3

The story behind the picture is as interesting to me as the young woman it captures. Mom, who was earning twenty-five dollars a week as a file clerk, decided to give her boyfriend (my father) a picture of herself. She spent almost two weeks' salary on the skirt and blouse, which she bought at a fancy department store downtown. She borrowed the earrings and bracelet from her older sister, my aunt Dorothy. The ring she wore was a present from another young man she was dating at the time. Mom spent another chunk of her salary to pay the portrait photographer for the hand-tinted print in old-fashioned tones of brown and tan. Just before giving the picture to my father, she scrawled at the lower left, "Sincerely, Beatrice."   4

When I study this picture, I react in many ways. I think about the trouble that Mom went to in order to impress the young man who was to be my father. I laugh when I look at the ring that was probably worn to make my father jealous. I smile at the serious, formal inscription my mother used in this stage of the budding relationship. Sometimes, I am filled with a mixture of pleasure and sadness when I look at this frozen long-ago moment. It is a moment of beauty, of love, and--in a way--of my own past.   5

My Fantasy Room

Recently, the comic strip "Peanuts" had a story about Lucy's going to
camp for two weeks. At Camp Beanbag, Lucy tells Charlie Brown, there is no
flag raising or required activity. All the campers do is lie in a room in
beanbag chairs and eat junk food. This idea appealed to me, and I began to
think. If I could spend two weeks in just one place, what would that place be
like? I began to imagine the room of my dreams.

First of all, my fantasy room would be decorated in a way that would
make me feel totally at ease. The walls would be painted a tasteful shade of
pale green, the color supposed to be the most soothing. Psychologists have
conducted studies proving that color can affect a person's mood. Also, a deep
plush carpet in an intense blue would cover the floor from wall to wall--the
perfect foundation for padding silently around the room. In the entryway,
huge closets with sliding doors would contain my wardrobe of size-eight
designer originals. The closets I have now are always messy and crowded,
stuffed with old shoes and other kinds of junk. Lastly, on the walls, silver
frames would hold my memories: pictures of me with my sports star and
musician friends, news clippings reporting on my social life, a poster
advertising the movie version of my most recent best-selling novel.
Everything would be quiet and tasteful, of course.

I'd have a king-sized bed with a headboard full of buttons that would
allow me to turn on lights, start music playing, or run hot water for my
Jacuzzi bath without getting up. Tall bookcases with enough shelf space for
all the souvenirs from my world travels would line an entire wall. Against
the opposite wall would be a chrome and glass desk topped with lined pads
and a rainbow of felt-tipped pens. They would await the moment when I
became inspired enough to begin writing my next best-seller. And for my
purebred Persian cat, there would be a lavender satin pillow.

Finally, my fantasy room would have the latest technological advances.
The air-conditioning or heating, depending on the season, would function at a
whisper. A telephone, operated by a push button from my bed, would put me
in touch with the world. Or, if I were feeling antisocial, I could flick on my
quadraphonic stereo system and fill the room with music. I could select a
movie from my library of videocassette tapes to play on my giant-screen
projection TV. Or I could throw a switch, and the satellite dish on my roof
would bring me my choice of television programs from all over the world.

It's probably a good idea that my fantasy room exists only in my mind.
If it were a real place, I don't think two weeks would be long enough. I
might stay in it forever.

The Diner at Midnight

I've been in lots of diners, and they've always seemed to be warm, busy, friendly, happy places. That's why, on a recent Monday night, I stopped in a diner for a cup of coffee. I was returning home after an all-day car trip and needed something to help me make the last forty-five miles. A diner at midnight, however, was not the place I had expected. It was different--and lonely. 1

My Toyota pulled to a halt in front of the dreary gray aluminum building that looked like an old railroad car. A half-lit neon sign sputtered the message, "Fresh baked goods daily," on the surface of the rain-slick parking lot. Only a half dozen cars and a battered pickup were scattered around the lot. An empty paper coffee cup made a hollow scraping sound as it rolled in small circles on one cement step close to the diner entrance. I pulled hard at the balky glass door, and it banged shut behind me. 2

The diner was quiet when I entered. As there was no hostess on duty, only the faint odor of stale grease and the dull hum of an empty refrigerated pastry case greeted me. I looked around for a place to sit. The outside walls were lined with empty booths which squatted back to back in their orange vinyl upholstery. On each speckled beige-and-gold table were the usual accessories. The kitchen hid mysteriously behind two swinging metal doors with round windows. I glanced through these windows but could see only a part of the large, apparently deserted cooking area. Facing the kitchen doors was the counter. I approached the length of Formica and slid onto one of the cracked vinyl seats bolted in soldierlike straight lines in front of it. 3

The people in the diner seemed as lonely as the place itself. Two men in rumpled work shirts sat at the counter, on stools several feet apart, staring wearily into cups of coffee and smoking cigarettes. Their faces sprouted what looked like daylong stubbles of beard. I figured they were probably shift workers who, for some reason, didn't want to go home. Three stools down from the workers, I spotted a thin young man with a mop of black, curly hair. He was dressed in brown Levi cords with a checked western-style shirt unbuttoned at the neck. He wore a blank expression as he picked at a plate of limp french fries. I wondered if he had just returned from a disappointing date. At the one occupied booth was a middle-aged couple. They hadn't gotten any food yet. He was staring off into space, idly tapping his spoon against the table, while she drew aimless parallel lines on her paper napkin with a bent dinner fork. Neither said a word to the other. 4

Finally, a tired-looking waitress approached me with her thick order pad. I ordered the coffee, but I wanted to drink it fast and get out of there. My car, and the solitary miles ahead of me, would be lonely. But they wouldn't be as lonely as that diner at midnight. 5

■ Questions

About Unity

1. Which supporting paragraph in "My Fantasy Room" lacks a topic sentence?

   _____

2. Which two sentences in paragraph 2 of "My Fantasy Room" should be omitted in the interest of paragraph unity?

   _____   _____

3. Which sentence in paragraph 3 of "Family Portrait" should be omitted in the interest of paragraph unity?   _____

About Support

4. How many examples support the topic sentence, "The people in the diner seemed as lonely as the place itself," in "The Diner at Midnight"?
   a. One   b. Two   c. Three

5. Label as *sight, touch, hearing,* or *smell* all the sensory details in the following sentences taken from the three essays. The first one is done for you as an example.

   a. "As there was no hostess on duty, only the faint odor of stale grease
   sight   *smell*

   hearing   *sight*
   and the dull hum of an empty refrigerated pastry case greeted me."

   b. "He was staring off into space, idly tapping his spoon against the table, while she drew aimless parallel lines on her paper napkin with a bent dinner fork."

   c. "Also, a deep plush carpet in an intense blue would cover the floor from wall to wall—the perfect foundation for padding silently around the room."

   d. "The blouse is made of heavy eggshell-colored satin and reflects the light in its folds and hollows."

6. After which sentence in paragraph 3 of "The Diner at Midnight" are more details needed?   _____

About Coherence

7. Which method of organization (time order or emphatic order) does paragraph 2 of "Family Portrait" use?

   _____

8. Which sentence in this paragraph indicates the method of organization?

   _____

9. Which of the following topic sentences in "The Diner at Midnight" is a linking sentence?
   a. "My Toyota pulled to a halt in front of the dreary gray aluminum building that looked like an old railroad car."
   b. "The diner was quiet when I entered."
   c. "The people in the diner seemed as lonely as the place itself."

10. In paragraph 2 of "My Fantasy Room," what are the major transition words?

    a. _____   b. _____   c. _____

WRITING THE ESSAY

■ Writing Assignment 1

Write an essay about a particular place that you can observe carefully or that you already know well. The place might be one of the following or some other place:

Pet shop
Exam room
Laundromat
Bar or nightclub
Video arcade
Corner store
Library study area
Basement or garage
Hotel or motel lobby
Your bedroom or the bedroom of someone you know
Waiting room at a train station or bus terminal
Winning or losing locker room after an important game
Antique shop or other small shop

How to Proceed

a Remember that, like all essays, a descriptive paper must have a thesis. Your thesis should state a dominant impression about the place you are describing. State the place you want to describe and the dominant impression you want to make in a short single sentence. The sentence can be refined later. For now, you just want to find and express a workable topic. You might write, for example, a sentence like one of the following:

The study area was noisy.

The exam room was tense.

The pet shop was crowded.

The bar was cozy.

The video arcade was confusing.

The bus terminal was frightening.

The corner store was cheerful.

The antique shop was lonely.

The bedroom was very organized.

The motel lobby was restful.

The winners' locker room was chaotic.

b Now make a list of as many details as you can that support the general impression. For example, the writer of "A Diner at Midnight" made this list:

Tired workers at counter

Rainy parking lot

Empty booths

Quiet

Few cars in lot

Dreary gray building

Lonely young man

Silent middle-aged couple

Out-of-order neon sign

No hostess

Couldn't see anyone in kitchen

Tired-looking waitress

c Organize your paper according to one or a combination of the following:

Physical order—move from left to right, or far to near, or in some other consistent order

Size—begin with large features or objects and work down to smaller ones

A *special order*—use an order that is appropriate to the subject

For instance, the writer of "The Diner at Midnight" builds his essay around the dominant impression of loneliness. The paper is organized in terms of physical order (from the parking lot to the entrance to the interior); a secondary method of organization is size (large parking lot to smaller diner to still smaller people).

d Use as many senses as possible in describing a scene. Chiefly you will use sight, but to an extent you may be able to use touch, hearing, smell, and perhaps even taste as well. Remember that it is through the richness of your sense impressions that the reader will gain a picture of the scene.

e As you are working on the drafts of your paper, refer to the checklist on page 119 and the inside front cover. Make sure you can answer *Yes* to the questions about unity, support, and coherence.

■ Writing Assignment 2

Write an essay about a family photograph. You may want to use an order similar to the one in "A Family Portrait," where the first supporting paragraph deals with the subject's face, the second with clothing and jewelry, and the third with the story behind the picture. Another possible order might be (1) the people in the photo (and how they look), (2) the relationships among the people (and what they are doing in the picture), and (3) the story behind the picture (time, place, occasion, relationships, or feelings). Use whatever order seems appropriate.

■ Writing Assignment 3

Write an essay describing a person. First, decide on a dominant impression you have about the person, and then use only those details which will add to it. Here are some examples of interesting types of people you might want to write about:

Campus character	Enemy	TV or movie personality
Dentist	Clergyman	Street person
Bus driver	Teacher	Older person
Close friend	Child	Employer
Rival	Drunk	

■ Writing Assignment 4

In this essay, you will write with a specific purpose, for a specific audience.

Option 1:   You have just attended a richly satisfying event, such as a concert, a sports contest, a stage show, or even a family gathering. Now you want to share your experience with a good friend who lives in another city. Write a letter in which you enthusiastically describe the event. Include vivid details so that your friend will be able to see, hear, and feel the event as if he or she had been there in person.

Option 2:   You have subscribed to a video dating service. Clients of the service are asked to make a five-minute presentation which will be recorded on videotape. Prepare such a presentation in which you describe yourself in terms of your attitudes and beliefs, your interests, and your personal habits. Your purpose is to give interested members of the dating service a good sense of what you are like.

NARRATION

At times we make a statement clear by relating in detail something that has happened to us. In the story we tell, we present the details in the order in which they happened. A person might say, for example, "I was really embarrassed the day I took my driver's test," and then go on to develop that statement with an account of the experience. If the story is sharply detailed, we will be able to see and understand just why the speaker felt that way.

In this section, you'll be asked to tell a story that illustrates some point. The essays ahead all present narrative experiences that support a thesis. Read them and then answer the questions that follow.

ESSAYS TO CONSIDER

My First Professional Performance

I was nineteen, and the invitation to play my guitar and sing at the County Rescue Squad Carnival seemed the "big break" aspiring performers dream about. I would be sharing the program with well-known professionals. My spirits were not even dampened by the discovery that I would not be paid. I had no reason to suspect then that my first professional performance was to be the scene of the most embarrassing experience of my life.

I arrived at the carnival grounds early, which proved fortunate. The manager knew that, in addition to the amplifier and speakers, I needed an extra microphone for my guitar and a high stool. However, when I checked the stage, I found the amplifier and speakers but nothing else. I also couldn't find the manager. The drunks who would hassle me later, after I had gotten started, became another problem. Since I couldn't perform without all the equipment, I was ready to call the whole thing off. Only the large potential audience milling around the carnival grounds influenced me to go through with it. One eye on my watch, I drove to the music store, told the owner my story, borrowed the needed equipment, and got back just as the Stone Gravel Rock Band, which preceded me on the program, was finishing its set. The band plays bluegrass music in some local clubs, and the lead singer was recently offered a professional recording contract.   2

I had some attentive listeners for my first song, but then problems developed. A voice boomed, "Play 'Mister Bojangles.'" A group of noisy drunks, surrounded by empty beer cans, half-eaten hot dogs, and greasy paper plates, were sprawled on picnic tables to one side of the stage. "We want to hear 'Mister Bojangles,'" roared the others, laughing. "Not today," I answered pleasantly, "but if you like 'Bojangles,' you'll like this tune." I quickly slid into my next number. Unfortunately, my comment only encouraged the drunks to act in an even more outrageous manner. As they kept up the disturbance, my audience began drifting away to escape them.   3

I was falsely cheered by the arrival of a uniformed policeman and several older men in work clothes. "Fans," I thought hopefully. Then I gave a start as a large engine roared very close to me, filling the air with choking diesel fumes. Only then did I realize that my "stage" was really a huge flatbed truck and that the older men in work clothes were in the cab warming up the engine. As I played a song, the policeman approached me. "Hey, lady," he said, "you're going to have to get down from there with all that stuff. They've got to take this rig away now." "I can't do that," I said. "I'm a professional musician in the middle of a performance. Tell him to turn that engine off." (In my confusion, I left the mike open, transmitting this exchange to the entire carnival grounds.) "Sorry, lady, he has to take it now," insisted the policeman. The drunks happily entered into the spirit of the thing, yelling, "Take her away. We don't want her. Yeah, haul her away." To save a small amount of self-respect, I played one more chorus before I began packing up my gear.   4

Fortunately, in conversations I eventually had with other performers, I heard similar stories of experiences they had when starting out. Then I would tell them about the stage that nearly rolled away with me on it, and we would laugh. Now I see that it's all part of becoming a professional.   5

Adopting a Handicap

My church recently staged a "Sensitivity Sunday" to make our 1
congregation aware of the problems faced by people with physical
handicaps. We were asked to "adopt a handicap" for several hours one
Sunday morning. Some members chose to be confined to wheelchairs; others
stuffed cotton in their ears, hobbled around on crutches, or wore blindfolds.

Wheelchairs had never seemed like scary objects to me before I had to sit 2
in one. A tight knot grabbed hold in my stomach when I first took a close
look at what was to be my only means of getting around for several hours. I
was struck by the irrational thought, "Once I am in this wheelchair, the
handicap might become real, and I might never walk again." This thought,
as ridiculous as it was, frightened me so much that I needed a large dose of
courage just to sit down.

After I overcame my fear of the wheelchair, I had to learn how to cope 3
with it. I wiggled around to find a comfortable position and thought I might
even enjoy being pampered and wheeled around. I glanced over my shoulder
to see who would be pushing me. It was only then that I realized I would
have to navigate the contraption all by myself! My palms reddened and
started to sting as I tugged at the heavy metal wheels. I could not seem to
keep the chair on an even course or point the wheels in the direction I
wanted to go. I kept bumping into doors, pews, and other people. I felt as
though everyone was staring at me and commenting on my clumsiness.

When the service started, more problems cropped up to frustrate me even 4
further. Every time the congregation stood up, my view was blocked. I could
not see the minister, the choir, or the altar. Also, as the church's aisles were
narrow, I seemed to be in the way no matter where I parked myself. For
instance, the ushers had to step around me in order to pass the collection
plate. This made me feel like a nuisance. Thanks to a new building program,
however, our church will soon have the wide aisles and well-spaced pews
that will make life easier for the handicapped. Finally, if people stopped to
talk to me, I had to strain my neck to look up at them. This made me feel
like a little child being talked down to and added to my sense of helplessness.

My few hours as a disabled person left a deep impression on me. Now, I 5
no longer feel resentment at large tax expenditures for ramp-equipped buses,
and I wouldn't dream of parking my car in a space marked "Handicapped
Only." Although my close encounter with a handicap was short-lived, I can
now understand the challenges, both physical and emotional, that wheelchair-bound people must overcome.

A Night of Violence

According to my history teacher, Adolf Hitler once said that he wanted to sign up "brutal youths" to help him achieve his goals. If Hitler were still alive, he wouldn't have any trouble recruiting the brutal youths he wanted; he could get them right here in the United States. I know, because I was one of them. As a teenager, I ran with a gang. And it took a terrible incident to make me see how violent I had become. 1

One Thursday night, I was out with my friends. I was still going to school once in a while, but most of my friends weren't. We spent our days on the streets, talking, showing off, sometimes shoplifting a little or shaking people down for a few dollars. My friends and I were close, maybe because life hadn't been very good to any of us. On this night, we were drinking wine and vodka on the corner. For some reason, we all felt tense and restless. One of us came up with the idea of robbing one of the old people who lived in the high rise close by. We would just knock him or her over, grab the money, and party with it. 2

After about an hour, and after more wine and vodka, we spotted an old man. He came out of the glass door of the building and started up the street. Stuffing our bottles in our jacket pockets, we closed in behind him. Victor, the biggest of us, said, "We want your money, old man. Hand it over." Suddenly, the old man whipped out a homemade wooden club from under his coat and began swinging. The club thudded against the side of Victor's head, making bright-red blood spurt out of his nose. When we saw this, we went crazy. We smashed our bottles over the old man's head. Then Victor ground the jagged edges of a broken bottle into the old man's skull. As we ran, I kept seeing the bottom of that bottle sticking up out of the man's head. It looked like a weird glass crown. 3

Later, at home, I threw up. I wasn't afraid of getting caught; in fact, we never did get caught. I just knew I had gone over some kind of line. I didn't know if I could step back, now that I had gone so far. But I knew I had to. I had seen plenty of people in my neighborhood turn into the kind who hated their lives, people who didn't care about anything, people who wound up penned in jail or ruled by drugs. I didn't want to become one of them. 4

That night, I realize now, I decided not to become one of Hitler's "brutal youths." I'm proud of myself for that, even though life didn't get any easier and no one came along to pin a medal on me. I just decided, quietly, to step off the path I was on. I hope my parents and I will get along better now, too. Maybe the old man's pain, in some terrible way, had a purpose. 5

■ Questions

About Unity

1. Which sentence in paragraph 4 of "Adopting a Handicap" should be omitted in the interest of paragraph unity? _____

2. Which sentence in paragraph 2 of "My First Professional Performance" should be omitted in the interest of paragraph unity? _____

3. Which essay lacks a thesis statement?

    _____

About Support

4. Label as *sight, touch, hearing,* or *smell* all the sensory details in the following sentences taken from the three essays.

    a. "Then I gave a start as a large engine roared very close to me, filling the air with choking diesel fumes."

    b. "The club thudded against the side of Victor's head, making bright-red blood spurt out of his nose."

    c. "My palms reddened and started to sting as I tugged at the heavy metal wheels."

    d. "A group of noisy drunks, surrounded by empty beer cans, half-eaten hot dogs, and greasy paper plates, were sprawled on picnic tables to one side of the stage."

5. In "Adopting a Handicap," how many examples support the topic sentence "When the service started, more problems cropped up to frustrate me even further"? _____

6. After which sentence in paragraph 3 of "My First Professional Performance" are more specific details needed? _____

7. Which supporting paragraphs in "My First Professional Performance" use dialog to help recreate the event?

    _____

About Coherence

8. The first stage of the writer's experience in ''Adopting a Handicap'' might be called *sitting down in the wheelchair*. What are the other two stages of the experience?

    a. _____

    b. _____

9. In paragraph 2 of ''My First Professional Performance,'' which detail is out of chronological (time) order?

    _____

About the Conclusion

10. Which sentence in the conclusion of ''A Night of Violence'' makes the mistake of introducing a completely new idea? _____

WRITING THE ESSAY

■ Writing Assignment 1

Write an essay telling about an experience in which a certain emotion was predominant. The emotion might be disappointment, embarrassment, happiness, frustration, or any of the following:

Fear	Anger	Silliness
Pride	Nostalgia	Disgust
Jealousy	Relief	Loss
Sadness	Greed	Sympathy
Terror	Nervousness	Violence
Regret	Hate	Bitterness
Shock	Surprise	Envy
Love	Shyness	Loneliness

The experience should be limited in time. Note that the three essays presented in this chapter all describe experiences that occurred within relatively short periods. One writer described her embarrassing musical debut; another described her frustration in acting as a handicapped person at a morning church service; the third described the terror of a minute's mugging that had lifelong consequences. See ''How to Proceed'' on the following page.

How to Proceed

a Think of an experience or event in your life in which you felt a certain emotion strongly. Then spend at least ten minutes freewriting about that experience. Do not worry at this point about such matters as spelling or grammar or putting things in the right order; instead, just try to get down as many details as you can think of that seem related to the experience.

b This preliminary writing will help you decide whether your topic is promising enough to continue work on. If it is not, choose another emotion. If it is, do two things:

First, write out your thesis in a single sentence, underlining the emotion you will focus on. For example, "My first day in kindergarten was one of the scariest days of my life."

Second, make up a list of all the details involved in the experience. Then arrange those details in chronological (time) order.

c Using the list as a guide, prepare a rough draft of your paper. Use time signals such as *first, then, next, after, while, during,* and *finally* to help connect details as you move from the beginning to the middle to the end of your narrative.

d See if you can divide your story into separate stages (what happened first, what happened next, what finally happened). Put each stage into a separate paragraph. In narratives, it is sometimes difficult to write a topic sentence for each supporting paragraph. You may, therefore, want to start new paragraphs at points where natural shifts or logical breaks in the story seem to occur.

e One good way to recreate an event is to include some dialog, as does the writer of "My First Professional Performance." Repeating what you have said or what you have heard someone else say helps make the situation come alive. And, in general, try to provide as many vivid, exact details as you can to help your readers experience the event as it actually happened.

f As you work on the drafts of your paper, refer to the checklist on page 119 and the inside front cover to make sure that you can answer *Yes* to the questions about unity, support, and coherence. Also use the checklist to proofread the next-to-final draft of your paper for sentence-skills mistakes, including spelling.

■ **Writing Assignment 2**

Think of an experience in your life that supports one of the statements below.

■ "Before I got married I had six theories about bringing up children; now I have six children and no theories."—John Wilmot, Earl of Rochester

■ "The chains of habit are too weak to be felt until they are too strong to be broken."—Samuel Johnson

■ "Peter's Law—The unexpected always happens."—Laurence J. Peter

■ "Haste makes waste."—popular saying

■ "Good people are good because they've come to wisdom through failure."—William Saroyan

■ "Lying is an indispensable part of making life tolerable."—Bergen Evans

■ "The key to everything is patience. You get the chicken by hatching the egg—not by smashing it."—Arnold Glasgow

■ "A good scare is worth more to a man than good advice."—Ed Howe

■ "A fool and his money are soon parted."—popular saying

■ "Like its politicians and its wars, society has the teenagers it deserves."—J. B. Priestley

■ "It's what you learn after you know it all that counts."—John Wooden

■ "Wise sayings often fall on barren ground; but a kind word is never thrown away."—Sir Arthur Helps

■ "What a tangled web we weave/When first we practice to deceive."—Walter Scott

■ "All marriages are happy. It's the living together afterward that causes all the trouble."—Raymond Hull

■ "We lie loudest when we lie to ourselves."—Eric Hoffer

■ "The worst country to be poor in is America."—Arnold Toynbee

■ "Criticism—a big bite out of someone's back."—Elia Kazan

■ "Work is what you do so that sometime you won't have to do it anymore."—Alfred Polgar

■ "Hoping and praying are easier but do not produce as good results as hard work."—Andy Rooney

■ "A little learning is a dangerous thing."—Alexander Pope

■ "Nothing is so good as it seems beforehand."—George Eliot

■ "Give a pig a finger, and he'll take the whole hand."—folk saying

Write a narrative essay using as a thesis one of the statements. Refer to the suggestions in "How to Proceed" on page 200. Remember that the point of your story is to *support* your thesis. Feel free to select from and even add to your experience so that your story truly supports the thesis.

■ Writing Assignment 3

In this essay, you will write with a specific purpose and for a specific audience.

Option 1: Imagine that you are in a town fifty miles from home, that your car has broken down several miles from a gas station, and that you are carrying no money. You thought you were going to have a terrible time, but the friendly people who helped you turned your experience into a positive one. It was such a good day, in fact, that you don't want to forget what happened.

Write a narrative of the day's events in your diary, so that you can read it ten years from now and remember exactly what happened. Begin with the moment you realized your car had broken down and continue until you're safely back at home. Include a thesis at either the beginning or the end of your narration.

Option 2: Imagine that a friend or sister or brother has to make a difficult decision of some kind. Perhaps he or she must decide how to deal with a troubled love affair, or a problem with living at home, or a conflict with a boss or coworker. Write a narrative from your own experience that will teach him or her something about the decision that must be made.

ARGUMENTATION AND PERSUASION

Most of us know someone who enjoys a good argument. Such a person usually challenges any sweeping statement we might make. "Why do you say that?" he or she will ask. "Give your reasons." Our questioner then listens carefully as we state our case, waiting to see if we really do have solid evidence to support our point of view. Such a questioner may make us feel uncomfortable, but we may also feel grateful to him or her for helping us clarify our opinions.

Your ability to advance sound and compelling arguments is an important skill in everyday life. You can use persuasion to make a point in a class discussion, persuade a friend to lend you money, and talk an employer into giving you a day off from work. Learning about persuasion based on clear, logical reasoning can also help you see through the sometimes faulty arguments in advertisements, newspaper articles, political speeches, and the other persuasive appeals you see and hear every day.

In this section, you will be asked to argue a position and defend it with a series of solid reasons. You are in a general way doing the same thing—making a point and then supporting it—with all the essays in the book. The difference here is that, in a more direct and formal manner, you will advance a point about which you feel strongly and seek to persuade your readers to agree with you.

ESSAYS TO CONSIDER

Teenagers and Jobs

"The pressure for a teenager to work is great, and not just because of the economic plight in the world today. Much of it is peer pressure to have a little bit of freedom and independence, and to have their own spending money. The concern we have is when the part-time work becomes the primary focus," says Roxanne Bradshaw, educator and officer of the National Education Association. Many people argue that working can be a valuable experience for the young. However, working more than about fifteen hours a week is harmful to adolescents because it reduces their involvement with school, encourages a materialistic and expensive lifestyle, and increases the chance of having problems with drugs and alcohol.   1

Schoolwork and the benefits of extracurricular activities tend to go by the wayside when adolescents work long hours. As more and more teens have filled the numerous part-time jobs offered by fast-food restaurants and mall stores, teachers have faced increasing difficulties. They must both keep the attention of tired pupils and give homework to students who simply don't have time to do it. In addition, educators have noticed less involvement in the extracurricular events many consider healthy influences on young people. School bands and athletic teams are losing players to work, and sports events are poorly attended by working students. Those teenagers who try to do it all--homework, extracurricular activities, and work--may find themselves exhausted and prone to illness. A recent newspaper story, for example, described a girl in Pennsylvania who came down with mononucleosis as a result of aiming for good grades, playing on two school athletic teams, and working thirty hours a week.   2

Another drawback of too much work is that it may promote materialism and an unrealistic lifestyle. Some parents say that work teaches adolescents the value of a dollar. Undoubtedly, it can, and it's true that some teenagers work to help out with the family budget or save for college. However, surveys have shown that the majority of working teens use their earnings to buy luxuries--stereos, tape decks, clothing, even cars. These young people, some of whom earn $300 and more a month, don't worry about spending wisely--they can just about have it all. In many cases, experts point out, they are becoming accustomed to a lifestyle they won't be able to afford several years down the road, when they'll no longer have parents to pay for car insurance, food and lodging, and so on. At that point, they'll be hard pressed to pay for necessities as well as luxuries.   3

Finally, teenagers who work a lot are more likely than others to get involved with alcohol and drugs. Teens who put in long hours may seek a quick release from stress, just like the adults who need to drink a couple of martinis after a hard day at work. Stress is probably greater in our society today than it has been at any time in the past. Also, teens who have money are more likely, for various obvious reasons, to get involved with drugs.   4

Teenagers can enjoy the benefits of work while avoiding its drawbacks simply by limiting their work hours during the school year. As is often the case, a moderate approach will be the most healthy and rewarding.   5

A Vote against Computers

I was excited when my English composition instructor announced that computers would be a major part of our writing course. "Half of the classes will be held in the computer lab," she said, "and all required work will be done on the computer." I was thrilled while touring the new computer lab to see all the magical-looking machines with their glowing green screens. The machines hummed as if they were alive. I thought to myself excitedly, "We're living in the middle of the computer revolution, and here's my chance to get on board." But three months later, I've had some second thoughts. I now believe that computers are a bad idea in the writing classroom. The computer does not help me plan a paper, it requires too much time and trouble to use, and it has changed my instructor from a teacher to a technician.

To begin with, the computer does not help me go about writing a paper. When I start an essay, I like to use a yellow pad and scribble out my ideas. I may write a couple of sentences, scratch them out, and then write a few more. I may make a couple of rough outlines, and then cross out parts of them, and then combine those leftover parts to make a third outline. I may go back to some idea I rejected at first and write another idea in the margin. I may circle something from one part of the page and join it with something on another part. At any one time, I want to see everything I'm doing in front of me. With a computer, I can't do that. If I delete something, I can't look back at it later. If I write too much, I have to scroll back and forth, since not everything can fit on the screen at once. There's no room in the margin for questions. And I can't circle things on the computer screen and connect them the way I can on a sheet of paper. I want a chance to see and change everything at once when planning a paper, and a computer does not let me do that.

Next, the mechanics involved in using a computer are complicated and time-consuming. Before I can get down to some honest-to-goodness writing, I have to show the computer lab technician my student ID card and sign out the appropriate software. Then I have to find an open terminal, turn on my computer and monitor, insert the proper disks, create or find a file, and set the required format. When I'm finished writing, I have to make sure that my work is properly saved, that there's paper in the printer, and that the printer is on-line. And at any point, when I have mechanical problems or questions about the computer, I have to wait five or ten minutes or more for the teacher or a student technician to come to help me. Worst of all, I'm not a good typist. I spend half of my time hunting and pecking for the proper letters on the keyboard. If I had wanted to get a lot of typing practice, I would have taken a typing course, but this is supposed to be a writing course.

Finally, when we meet in the computer lab, the teacher spends most of the class walking around and helping students log on and off the computer, handing out and collecting software, and trying to locate and retrieve lost documents. I sat here the other day watching the class trying to write on computers, and my impression was that 75 percent of what the teacher did involved computers rather than writing. I've had other writing courses, before computers, where the teacher spent a lot of time going over students' work on a one-on-one basis or in a class discussion. It was in this workshop setting that I believe my writing improved the most. Now, my professor has much less time to devote to individual help and feedback. She's too busy being a computer troubleshooter.

In conclusion, it may be wise to take another look at the use of the   5
computer in college writing courses. At first glance the computer offers excitement and a world of promise, but I think there's a serious question about whether it actually improves students' writing.

Once Over Lightly: Local TV News

Are local television newscasts a reliable source of news? Do they provide   1
in-depth coverage and analysis of important local issues? Unfortunately, all too often they do not. In their battle for high ratings, local television news shows provide more entertainment than news. News personalities are emphasized at the expense of stories; visual appeal has more priority than actual news; and stories and reports are too brief and shallow.

Local TV newscasters are as much the subject of the news as are the   2
stories they present. Nowhere is this more obvious than in weather reports. Weatherpersons spend valuable news time by joking, drawing cartoons, chatting about weather fronts as "good guys" and "bad guys," and dispensing weather trivia such as statistics about relative humidity and record highs and lows for the date. Reporters, too, draw attention to themselves. Rather than just getting the story, we are shown the reporters jumping into or getting out of helicopters to get the story. When reporters interview crime victims or the residents of poor neighborhoods, the camera angle typically includes them and their reaction as well as their subjects. When they report on a storm, they stand outside in the storm, their styled hair blowing, so we can admire how they "brave the elements." Then there are the anchorpersons, who are chosen as much for their looks as for their skills. They too dilute the news by putting their personalities on center stage.

Often the selection of stories and the way they are presented is based on   3
visual impact rather than news value. If a story is not accompanied by an

interesting film clip, it is unlikely to be shown on the local news. The result is an overemphasis on fires and car crashes and little attention to such important issues as the local employment situation. As much as possible, every story is presented with a reporter standing "live" in front of something. If City Hall has passed a resolution, for instance, then the reporter will be shown standing live in front of City Hall. Very often, cars are zooming by or neighborhood kids are waving at the camera or passersby are recognizing suddenly that they are being filmed. Most people are natural hams, and they love to discover that they are on stage. Such background happenings are so distracting that viewers may not even listen to what the reporter is saying. And even if a story is not live, the visuals that accompany a story are often distracting. A recent story on falling oil prices, for example, was accompanied by footage of a working oil well that drew away attention from the important economic information in the report.

Finally, the desire of the local stations to entertain viewers is demonstrated in short news stories and shallow treatment. On the average, about half a minute is devoted to a story. Clearly, stories that take less than half a minute are superficial. Even the longest stories, which can take up several minutes, are not accompanied by meaningful analysis. Instead, the camera jumps from one location to another and the newscaster simplifies and trivializes the issues. For instance, one recent "in-depth" story about the homeless consisted of a glamorous reporter talking to a homeless person and asking him what should be done about the problem. The poor man was in no condition to respond intelligently. The story then cut to an interview with a city bureaucrat who mechanically rambled on about the need for more government funding. There were also shots of homeless people sleeping in doorways and on top of heating vents, and there were interviews with people on the street, all of whom said something should be done about the terrible problem of the homeless. There was, in all of this, no real exploration of the issue and no proposed solutions. It was also apparent that the homeless were just the issue-for-the-week. After the week's coverage was over, the topic was not mentioned again.   4

Because of the emphasis on newscasters' personalities and on the visual impact of stories and the short time span for stories, local news shows provide little more than diversion. What viewers need instead is news that has real significance. Rather than being amused and entertained, we need to deal with complex issues and learn uncomfortable truths that will help us become more responsible consumers and citizens.   5

■ Questions

About Unity

1. Which sentence in paragraph 4 of "Teenagers and Jobs" should be omitted in the interest of paragraph unity? _____

2. Which supporting paragraph in "A Vote against Computers" lacks a topic sentence? _____
Write a topic sentence for the paragraph:

_____

_____

About Support

3. Which paragraph in "Teenagers and Jobs" develops its point by citing and then refuting an opposing point of view? _____

4. After which sentence in paragraph 4 of "Teenagers and Jobs" are specific details needed? _____

5. After which sentence in paragraph 2 of "Once Over Lightly: Local TV News" is support needed? _____

6. Which supporting paragraph of which essay uses the longest single supporting example?

_____

About Coherence

7. What three transition words are used to introduce the three supporting paragraphs in "A Vote against Computers"?

    a. _____

    b. _____

    c. _____

8. What are the two main transition words in paragraph 2 of "Once Over Lightly: Local TV News"?

    a. _____

    b. _____

About the Introduction and Conclusion

9. Which method of introduction is used in "Teenagers and Jobs" ____? "A Vote against Computers" ____? "Once Over Lightly: Local TV News" ____?
   a. Broad, general statement narrowing to thesis
   b. Idea that is the opposite of the one to be developed
   c. Quotation
   d. Anecdote
   e. Questions

10. Which essay has a conclusion that briefly summarizes the supporting points? _____

Activity

In scratch-outline form on separate paper, provide brief supporting reasons for at least five of the fifteen statements below. Note the example. Make sure that you have three *separate* and *distinct* reasons for each statement.

Example   Recycling of newspapers, cans, and bottles should be mandatory.
   a. Towns sell recycled items rather than pay for dumping.
   b. Natural resources are protected.
   c. Respect for the environment is encouraged.

1. Couples should be required to live together for six months before marriage.
2. Many Americans are too materialistic.
3. High schools should distribute birth control devices and information to students.
4. All teachers should be graded by their students.
5. TV commercials are often particularly insulting to women.
6. Professional boxing should be outlawed.
7. Attendance at college classes should be optional.
8. When technology makes it possible, government should control the weather.
9. People should begin planning for retirement when they are young.
10. Cigarette companies should not be allowed to advertise.
11. Television does more harm than good.
12. Killing animals for food is wrong.
13. School does not prepare you for life.
14. Governments should not pay ransom for terrorist kidnappings.
15. All companies should be required to have day-care centers.

WRITING THE ESSAY

■ Writing Assignment 1

Decide, perhaps through discussion with your instructor or classmates, which of the outlines prepared in the preceding activity would be the most promising to develop into an essay. Make sure that your supporting reasons are logical ones that actually back up your thesis statement. Ask yourself in each case, "Does this reason truly support my thesis idea?"

How to Proceed

a On separate paper, make a list of details that might go under each of the supporting points. Provide more details than you can possibly use. Here, for example, are the details generated by the writer of "Teenagers and Jobs" when she was working on her first supporting paragraph:

School problems:

Less time for sports and other activities
Lower attendance at games
Students leave right after school
Students sleep in class and skip homework
Teachers are angry and frustrated
More time buying things like clothing and compact disks
More stress for students and less concentration
Some students try to do it all and get sick
Students miss school to go to work
Some drop out of school

b Decide which reasons and details you will use to develop each of your supporting paragraphs. Also, number the items in the order in which you will present them. Here is how the writer of "Teenagers and Jobs" made decisions on what to develop:

School problems
2 Less time for sports and other activities
~~Lower attendance at games~~
~~Students leave right after school~~
1 Students sleep in class and skip homework
~~Teachers are angry and frustrated~~
~~More time buying things like clothing and compact disks~~
~~More stress for students and less concentration~~
3 Some students try to do it all and get sick
~~Students miss school to go to work~~
~~Some drop out of school~~

c As you are working on the drafts of your paper, refer to the checklist on page 119 and the inside front cover. Make sure that you can answer *Yes* to the questions about unity, support, and coherence.

d You may also want to refer to pages 72–77 for suggestions on writing an effective introduction and conclusion to your essay.

e Finally, use the checklist on page 119 and the inside front cover when you are proofreading the next-to-final draft of your paper for sentence-skills mistakes, including spelling.

■ Writing Assignment 2

Write a paper in which you argue *for* or *against* any *one* of the three comments below (options 1–3). Support and defend your argument by drawing upon your reasoning ability and general experience. Refer to ''How to Proceed'' on the following pages.

Option 1

In some ways, television has proved to be one of the worst inventions of recent times. All too often, television is harmful because of the shows it broadcasts and the way it is used in the home.

Option 2

College athletes devote a lot of time and energy to teams that sometimes make a great deal of money for their schools. Often athletes stress a sport at the expense of their education. And their efforts rarely give these young men and women experiences and skills that are useful after college. It is only fair, therefore, that college athletes be paid for their work.

Option 3

Many of society's worst problems with drugs result from the fact that they are illegal. During Prohibition, America discovered that making popular substances unlawful causes more problems than it solves. Like alcohol, drugs should be legal in this country.

How to Proceed

a Take several minutes to think about the comments. Which one in particular are you for or against—and *why*?

b On a sheet of paper, make up a brief outline of support for *your* position on one of the comments. Preparing the outline will give you a chance to think further about your position. And the outline will show whether you have enough support for your position. (If you don't, choose another position, and prepare another outline.)

This initial thinking and outlining that you do is the key to preparing a solid paper. Your goal should be to decide on a position for which you can provide the most convincing evidence.

The writer of the model essay on computers was originally asked to take a position for or against the use of computers in the classroom. After a good deal of thinking, he came up with the following brief outline:

I am against the use of computers.
1. Don't help me plan a paper.
2. Are complicated to use.
3. Take up teacher's time.

While he had not yet written his first draft, he had already done the most important work on the paper.

c Next, decide how you will develop each of your three supporting points. Make up brief outlines of the three points. Here, for example, is what the author of the computer essay did:

1. <u>Don't help me plan a paper</u>:
   Like to scribble.
   Use margins.
   Circle details on different parts of paper.
   See whole thing at once.
2. <u>Are complicated to use</u>:
   Sign out software.
   Get machine started.
   Wait for help.
   Type slowly.
3. <u>Take up teacher's time</u>:
   Helps students use computers.
   Has less time for writing feedback.

Such preliminary work is vital; to do a good paper, you must *think and plan and prewrite*. In addition to preparing brief outlines, you may also find that other prewriting techniques are useful. You may, variously, want to freewrite, brainstorm, and make up lists—all of which are described on pages 17–23 of this book.

d Decide in what order you want to present your paragraphs. Often, emphatic order (in which you end with the most important reason) is an effective way to organize an argument, for the final reason is the one your reader is most likely to remember.

e Provide as many convincing details as possible. For example, in the computer essay, the writer includes such supportive details as the following:

"If I write too much [on the computer], I have to scroll back and forth, since not everything can fit on the screen at once."

"I spend half of my time hunting and pecking for the proper letters on the keyboard."

"I sat here the other day watching the class trying to write on computers, and my impression was that 75 percent of what the teacher did involved computers rather than writing."

f As you write, imagine that your audience is a jury that will ultimately believe or disbelieve your argument. Have you presented a convincing case? Do you need more details? If *you* were on the jury, would you be favorably impressed with this argument?

g As you are working on the drafts of your paper, keep the four bases of unity, support, coherence, and sentence skills in mind.

h Finally, proofread the next-to-final draft of your paper for sentence-skills mistakes, including spelling.

■ Writing Assignment 3

Write a paper in which you argue *for* or *against* any *one* of the three comments that follow. Support and defend your argument by drawing upon your reasoning ability and general experience.

Option 1

While it is now well known that smoking is very unhealthy, it would be very difficult in our society to make it illegal. But that does not mean smoking should be encouraged. On the contrary, cigarette advertising should be banned.

Option 2

By the time many students reach high school, they have learned the basics in most subjects. Some still have much to gain from the education that high schools offer, but others might be better off spending the next four years in other ways. For their benefit, high school attendance should be voluntary, not compulsory.

Option 3

It is sad but true that some of the most miserable days in many people's lives are their last days. It is also true there is no way to avoid dying. But establishing centers where people can choose to end their lives in peace can eliminate the long suffering that many fatal illnesses cause. The government should take an active role in creating such centers.

Remember that the best way to get started is *to think, plan, and prewrite*. Which comment do you feel most strongly for or against? What are three solid reasons you can give to support your position? After you work out a satisfactory scratch outline, go on to follow the rest of the steps described in Writing Assignment 2.

■ Writing Assignment 4

Write a paper in which you argue *for* or *against* any *one* of the three comments below. Support and defend your argument by drawing upon your reasoning ability and general experience.

Option 1

Giving students grades does more harm than good. Schools should replace grades with evaluations, which would benefit both students and parents.

Option 2

Because our jails are overcrowded and expensive, the fewer people sentenced to jail the better. Of course, it is necessary to put violent criminals in jail in order to protect others. Society, however, would benefit if nonviolent criminals received punishments other than jail sentences.

Option 3

Physical punishment is often a successful way of disciplining children. After all, no child wants to experience pain. But adults who frequently spank and hit are also teaching the lesson that violence is a good method of accomplishing a goal. Nonviolent methods are a more effective way of training children.

■ Writing Assignment 5

Write a paper in which you argue *for* or *against* any *one* of the three comments below. Support and defend your argument by drawing upon your reasoning ability and general experience.

Option 1

Junk food is available in school cafeterias and school vending machines, and the cafeteria menus do not encourage the best of eating habits. But good education should include good examples as well as class work. Schools should practice what they preach about a healthy diet and stop providing junk food.

Option 2

The sale of handguns to private citizens should be banned throughout America. It is true that the Constitution guarantees the right to bear arms, but that does not necessarily mean any type of arms. Some weapons, including handguns, are simply too dangerous to be legal.

Option 3

Many of today's young people are mainly concerned with prestigious careers, making money, and owning things. It seems we no longer teach the benefits of spending time and money to help the community, the country, and the world. Our country can strengthen these human values and improve the world by requiring young people to spend a year working in some type of community service.

■ Writing Assignment 6

In this essay, you will write with a specific purpose, for a specific audience.

Option 1: Your town is one of the few in the state that hasn't developed a recycling program. Write a speech to give at a city council meeting in which you argue for establishing a local recycling program. Include in your speech the environmental benefits of recycling. And, since we are more likely to persuade others of something if they feel they will benefit, note also how the town will benefit economically and otherwise.

Option 2:   You'd like to live in a big city, but your spouse or parent refuses to budge from the suburbs. Write him or her a letter in which you argue the advantages of city life. Since the success of your argument will depend to some degree on how well you overcome the other person's objections to city life, be sure to address those as well. Use specific, colorful examples wherever possible.

Option 3:   Write a letter to the editor of your local newspaper, responding to an issue that was discussed in a recent editorial in that paper. Agree or disagree with the position taken by the paper, and provide several short paragraphs of supporting evidence for your position. Actually send your letter to the newspaper. Turn in a copy to your instructor, with the editorial you responded to.

Writing Assignment 7

Write a paper in which you use research findings to help support one of the statements on page 209. Research the topic in one or both of these ways:

- Look up the topic in the subject section of your library book file. (You may want to review pages 249–251 of "Using the Library.") Subject headings for some of the statements on page 209 include *Birth control, Materialism, Day care, Marriage contracts, Animal rights, Advertising, Smoking, Retirement*, and *Terrorism*. Select the books that seem likely to give you information about your topic. Then find the books in the library stacks.
- Look up the topic in recent issues of the *Magazine Index* or the *Readers' Guide to Periodical Literature*. (Again, you may want to review "Using the Library" first.) Try some of the same headings noted above. Select the articles that appear most likely to provide information on your topic. Then see if you can find some of these articles in your library's magazine storage area.

Reading about your topic will help you think about it. See if you can organize your paper in the form of three reasons that support the topic. Put these reasons into a scratch outline, and use it as a guide. Here is an example:

Prayer should not be allowed in the public schools:
a. Children who are not religious will feel excluded.
b. Children may still pray silently whenever they please.
c. Not all schools and teachers will keep prayer nondenominational.

Note that statistical information, the results of studies, and the advice of experts may all help develop the supporting reasons for your thesis. Do not hesitate to cite such information in a limited way; it helps make your argument more objective and compelling.

PART THREE

SPECIAL
SKILLS

TAKING
ESSAY
EXAMS

Essay exams are perhaps the most common type of writing you will do in school. They include one or more questions to which you must respond in detail, writing your answers in a clear, well-organized manner. Many students have trouble with essay exams because they do not realize there is a sequence to follow that will help them do well on such tests. This section describes five basic steps needed to prepare adequately for an essay test and to take the test. It is assumed, however, that you are already doing two essential things: first, attending class regularly and taking notes on what happens in class; second, reading your textbook and other assignments and taking notes on them. If you are *not* consistently going to class, reading your text, and taking notes in both cases, you are likely to have trouble with essay exams and other tests as well.

To write an effective exam essay, follow these five steps:

Step 1: Anticipate ten probable questions.

Step 2: Prepare and memorize an informal outline answer for each question.

Step 3: Look at the exam carefully and do several things.

Step 4: Prepare a brief, informal outline before writing your essay answer.

Step 5: Write a clear, well-organized essay.

The following pages explain and illustrate these steps.

STEP 1: ANTICIPATE TEN PROBABLE QUESTIONS

Because exam time is limited, the instructor can give you only several questions to answer. He or she will reasonably focus on questions dealing with the most important areas of the subject. You can probably guess most of them.

Go through your class notes with a colored pen and mark off those areas where your instructor has spent a good deal of time. The more time spent on any one area, the better the chance you will get an essay question on it. If the instructor spent a week talking about present-day changes in the traditional family structure, or the importance of the carbon molecule, or the advantages of capitalism, or key early figures in the development of psychology as a science, you can reasonably expect that you will get a question on the emphasized area.

In both your class notes and your textbooks, pay special attention to definitions and examples and to basic lists of items (enumerations). Enumerations in particular are often the key to essay questions. For instance, if your instructor spoke at length about the causes of the Great Depression, the effects of water pollution, or the advantages of capitalism, you should probably expect a question such as ''What were the causes of the Great Depression?'' or ''What are the effects of water pollution?'' or ''What are the advantages of capitalism?''

If your instructor has given you study guides, look for probable essay questions there. (Some teachers choose essay questions from those listed in a study guide.) Look for clues to essay questions on any short quizzes that you may have been given. Finally, consider very carefully any review that the instructor provides. Always write down such reviews—your instructor has often made up the test or is making it up at the time of the review and is likely to give you valuable hints about it. Take advantage of them! Note also that if the instructor does not offer to provide a review, do not hesitate to *ask* for one in a friendly way. Essay questions are likely to come from areas the instructor may mention.

An Illustration of Step 1

A psychology class was given a day to prepare for an essay exam on stress—a subject that had been covered in class and that comprised a chapter in the textbook for the course. One student, Mark, read carefully through his class notes and the textbook chapter. On the basis of the headings, major enumerations, and definitions he noted, he decided that there were five likely essay questions:

1. What are the common sources of stress?
2. What are the types of conflict?
3. What are the defense mechanisms that people use to cope with stress?
4. What effects can stress have on people?
5. What are the characteristics of the well-adjusted person?

STEP 2: PREPARE AND MEMORIZE AN INFORMAL OUTLINE ANSWER FOR EACH QUESTION

Write out each question you have made up and, under it, list the main points that need to be discussed. Put important supporting information in parentheses after each main point. You now have an informal outline that you can memorize.

Note: If you have spelling problems, make up a list of words you might have to spell in writing your answers. For example, if you are having a psychology test on the principles of learning, you might want to study such terms as *conditioning, reinforcement, Pavlov, reflex, stimulus,* and so on.

An Illustration of Step 2

After identifying the likely questions on the exam, Mark made up an outline answer for each of the questions. For example, here is the outline answer that he made up for the first question:

Common sources of stress:
1. (Pressure) (internal and external)
2. (Anxiety) (sign of internal conflict)
3. (Frustration) (can't reach desired goal)
4. (Conflict) (three types of approach-avoidance)

   P A F C (People are funny creatures.)

Activity

See whether you can complete the following explanation of what Mark has done in preparing for the essay question.

First, Mark wrote down the heading and then numbered the sources of stress under it. Also, in parentheses beside each point he added _____ _____. Then he circled the four key words, and he wrote down the first _____ of each word underneath his outline. Mark then used the first letter in each key word to make up a catchphrase that he could easily remember. Finally, he _____ himself over and over until he could recall all four of the sources of stress that the first letters stood for. He also made sure that he recalled the supporting material that went with each idea.

Direction Words

Term	Meaning
Compare	Show similarities between things.
Contrast	Show differences between things.
Criticize	Give the positive and negative points of a subject as well as evidence for these positions.
Define	Give the formal meaning of a term.
Describe	Tell in detail about something.
Diagram	Make a drawing and label it.
Discuss	Give details and, if relevant, the positive and negative points of a subject as well as evidence for these positions.
Enumerate	List points and number them 1, 2, 3, etc.
Evaluate	Give the positive and negative points of a subject as well as your judgment about which outweighs the other and why.
Illustrate	Explain by giving examples.
Interpret	Explain the meaning of something.
Justify	Give reasons for something.
List	Give a series of points and number them 1, 2, 3, etc.
Outline	Give the main points and important secondary points. Put main points at the margin and indent secondary points under the main points. Relationships may also be described with logical symbols, as follows:

    1. _____

        a. _____

        b. _____

    2. _____

Term	Meaning
Prove	Show to be true by giving facts or reasons.
Relate	Show connections among things.
State	Give the main points.
Summarize	Give a condensed account of the main points.
Trace	Describe the development or history of a subject.

STEP 3: LOOK AT THE EXAM CAREFULLY
AND DO SEVERAL THINGS

1 Get an overview of the exam by reading *all* the questions on the test.

2 Note the direction words (*compare, illustrate, list,* and so on) for each question. Be sure to write the kind of answer that each question requires. For example, if a question says "illustrate," do not "compare." The list on the opposite page will help clarify the distinctions among various direction words.

3 Budget your time. Write in the margin the number of minutes you should spend for each essay. For example, if you have three essays worth an equal number of points and a one-hour time limit, figure twenty minutes for each one. Make sure you are not left with only a couple of minutes to do a high-point essay.

4 Start with the easiest question. Getting a good answer down on paper will help build up your confidence and momentum. Number your answers plainly so your instructor knows what question you are answering first.

An Illustration of Step 3

When Mark received the exam, the question was, "Describe the four common sources of stress in our lives." Mark circled the direction word *describe*, which meant that he should explain in detail each of the four causes of stress. He also jotted a "30" in the margin when the teacher said that students would have a half hour to write their answer.

Activity

Complete the short matching quiz below. It will help you review the meanings of some of the direction words listed on the opposite page.

1. List _____
2. Contrast _____
3. Define _____
4. Summarize _____
5. Describe _____

a. Tell in detail about something.
b. Give a series of points and number them 1, 2, 3, etc.
c. Give a condensed account of the main points.
d. Show differences between two things.
e. Give the normal meaning of a term.

STEP 4: PREPARE A BRIEF, INFORMAL OUTLINE BEFORE WRITING YOUR ESSAY ANSWER

Use the margin of the exam or a separate piece of scratch paper to jot down quickly, as they occur to you, the main points you want to discuss in each answer. Then decide in what order you want to present these points in your response. Put 1 in front of the first item, 2 beside the second, and so on. You now have an informal outline to guide you as you answer your essay question.

If there is a question on the exam which is similar to the questions you anticipated and outlined at home, quickly write down the catchphrase that calls back the content of the outline. Below the catchphrase, write the key words represented by each letter in the catchphrase. The key words, in turn, will remind you of the concepts they represent. If you have prepared properly, this step will take only a minute or so, and you will have before you the guide you need to write a focused, supported, organized answer.

An Illustration of Step 4

Mark immediately wrote down his catchphrase, ''People are funny creatures.'' He next jotted down the first letters in his catchphrase and then the key words that went with each letter. He then filled in several key details and was ready to write his essay answer. Here is what his brief outline looked like:

People are funny creatures.

P   Pressure (internal and external)
A   Anxiety (internal conflict)
F   Frustration (prevented from reaching goal)
C   Conflict (approach-avoidance)

STEP 5: WRITE A CLEAR, WELL-ORGANIZED ESSAY

If you have followed the steps to this point, you have done all the preliminary work needed to write an effective essay. Be sure not to wreck your chances of getting a good grade by writing carelessly. Keep in mind the principles of good writing: unity, support, organization, and clear, error-free sentences.

First, start your essay with a sentence that clearly states what your answer will be about. Then make sure that everything in your paper relates to your opening statement.

Second, though you must obviously take time limitations into account, provide as much support as possible for each of your main points.

Third, use transitions to guide your reader through your answer. Words such as *first, next, then, however,* and *finally* make it easy to follow your thought.

Last, leave time to proofread your essay for sentence-skills mistakes you may have made while you concentrated on writing your answer. Look for words omitted, miswritten, or misspelled (if it is possible, bring a dictionary with you); for awkward phrasings or misplaced punctuation marks; and for whatever else may prevent the reader from understanding your thought. Cross out any mistakes and make your corrections neatly above the errors. If you want to change or add to some point, insert an asterisk at the appropriate spot, put another asterisk at the bottom of the page, and add the corrected or additional material there.

An Illustration of Step 5

Read Mark's answer, reproduced below, and then do the activity that follows.

> There are four common sources of stress in our lives. The first one is pressure, which can be internal or external. Internal pressure occurs when a person tries to live up to his or her own goals and standards. This kind of pressure can help (when a person strives to be a better musician, for instance) or hurt (as when someone tries to reach impossible standards of beauty). External pressure occurs when people must compete, deal with rapid change, or cope with outside demands. Another source of stress is anxiety. People who are ~~anxous~~ anxious often don't know why they feel this way. Some psychologists think anxiety comes from some internal conflict, like feeling angry and trying hard to repress this ~~angry feeling~~ anger. A third source of stress is frustration, which occurs when people are prevented from reaching goals or obtaining certain needs. For example, a woman may do poorly on an important exam because she has a bad cold. She feels angry and frustrated because she could not reach her goal of an A or B grade. The most common source of stress is conflict. Conflict results when a person is faced with two incompatible ~~goals.~~ desires. The person may want both goals (a demanding career and motherhood, for instance). This is called approach/approach. Or a person may want to avoid both choices (avoidance/avoidance.) Or a person may be both attracted to and repelled by a desire (as a woman who wants to marry a gambler). This is approach/avoidance.

Activity 1

The following sentences comment on Mark's essay. Fill in the missing word or words in each case.

1. Mark begins with a sentence that clearly states what his paper _____ _____. Always begin with such a clear statement!

2. Notice the _____ that Mark made when writing and proofreading his paper. He neatly crossed out miswritten or unwanted words, and he used insertion signs (∧) to add omitted words.

3. The four signal words that Mark used to guide his readers, and himself, through the main points of his answer are _____, _____, _____, and _____.

Activity 2

1. Make up five questions you might be expected to answer on an essay exam in a social or physical science course (sociology, psychology, biology, or other).

2. Then make up for each of the five questions an outline answer comparable to the one on anxiety.

3. Finally, write a full essay answer, in complete sentences, to one of the questions. Your outline will serve as your guide.

Be sure to begin your essay with a statement that makes clear the direction of your answer. An example might be, "The six major kinds of defense mechanisms are defined and illustrated below." If you are explaining in detail the different causes of, reasons for, or characteristics of something, you may want to develop each point in a separate paragraph. For example, if you were answering a question in sociology about the primary functions of the family unit, you could, after starting with a statement that "There are three primary functions of the family unit," go on to develop and describe each function in a separate paragraph.

You will turn in the essay answer to your English instructor, who will evaluate it using the standards for effective writing applied to your other written assignments.

PREPARING
A SUMMARY

At some point in a course, your instructor may ask you to write a summary of a book, article, TV show, or the like. In a *summary* (also referred to as a *précis* or an *abstract*), you reduce material in an original work to its main points and key supporting details. Unlike an outline, however, a summary does not use symbols such as I, A, 1, 2, etc., to indicate the relations among parts of the original material.

A summary may be a word, a phrase, several sentences, or one or more paragraphs in length. The length of the summary you prepare will depend on your instructor's expectations and the length of the original work. Most often, you will be asked to write a summary of one or more paragraphs.

Writing a summary brings together a number of important reading, study, and writing skills. To condense the original matter, you must preview, read, evaluate, organize, and perhaps outline the assigned material. Summarizing, then, can be a real aid to understanding; you must ''get inside'' the material and realize fully what is being said before you can reduce its meaning to a few words.

HOW TO SUMMARIZE AN ARTICLE

To write a summary of an article, follow the steps described below. If the assigned material is a TV show or film, adapt the suggestions accordingly.

1 Take a few minutes to preview the work. You can preview an article in a magazine by taking a quick look at the following:

    a **_Title._** The title often summarizes what the article is about. Think about the title for a minute and how it may condense the meaning of an article.

    b **_Subtitle._** A subtitle, if given, is a short summary appearing under or next to the title. For example, in a _Newsweek_ article entitled ''Growing Old, Feeling Young,'' the following caption appeared: ''Not only are Americans living longer, they are staying active longer—and their worst enemy is not nature, but the myths and prejudices about growing old.'' In short, the subtitle, the caption, or any other words in large print under or next to the title often provide a quick insight into the meaning of an article.

    c **_First and last several paragraphs._** In the first several paragraphs, the author may introduce you to the subject and state the purpose of the article. In the last several paragraphs, the writer may present conclusions or a summary. These previews or summaries can give you a quick overview of what the entire article is about.

    d **_Other items._** Note any heads or subheads that appear in the article. They often provide clues to the article's main points and give an immediate sense of what each section is about. Look carefully at any pictures, charts, or diagrams that accompany the article. Page space in a magazine or journal is limited, and such visual aids are generally used only when they help illustrate important points in the article. Note any words or phrases set off in _italic type_ or **boldface print;** such words have probably been emphasized because they deal with important points in the article.

2 Read the article for all you can understand the first time through. Do not slow down or turn back. Check or otherwise mark main points and key supporting details. Pay special attention to all the items noted in the preview. Also, look for definitions, examples, and enumerations (lists of items), as these often indicate key ideas. You can also identify important points by turning any heads into questions and reading to find the answers to the questions.

3 Go back and reread more carefully the areas you have identified as most important. Also, focus on other key points you may have missed in your first reading.

4 Take notes on the material. Concentrate on getting down the main ideas and the key supporting points.

5 Prepare the first draft of your summary, keeping these points in mind:

a Identify at the start of the summary the title and author of the work. Include in parentheses the date of publication. For example, ''In 'Answers at Last' (*Time,* December 17, 1990), Nancy Gibbs states . . .''

b Do not write an overly detailed summary. Remember that the purpose of a summary is to reduce the original work to its main points and essential supporting details.

c Express the main points and key supporting details in your own words. Do not imitate the style of the original work.

d Quote from the material only to illustrate key points. Also, limit your quotations. A one-paragraph summary should not contain more than one or two quoted sentences.

e Preserve the balance and proportion of the original work. If the original devoted 70 percent of its space to one idea and only 30 percent to another, your summary should reflect that emphasis.

f Revise the first draft, paying attention to the principles of effective writing (*unity, support, coherence,* and *clear, error-free sentences*) explained in Part One.

g Write the final draft of the paper.

A MODEL SUMMARY

Here is a model summary of a magazine article.

In "Drowsy America" (<u>Time</u>, December 17, 1990), Anastasia Toufexis asserts that America has a major sleep-deprivation problem. While the typical adult needs about eight hours of nightly sleep, many Americans usually sleep less. This has numerous harmful effects. Tiredness weakens performance and increases irritability. Mental fatigue is a leading cause of traffic deaths and industrial and medical accidents. Also, disasters are sometimes caused by exhausted pilots and train engineers. For workers on unusual shifts, the effects of sleep loss are worsened by working in opposition to the body's natural rhythms. Researchers have found that overnight workers make even more mistakes than others. Another notably sleep-deprived group are teens, who need about 9½ hours of sleep. Faced with the demands of school, socializing, and work, many teens get far less sleep, a loss that is interfering with their learning. The causes of sleep loss range from the light bulb, which provides light for nighttime activities, to busy families trying to fit everything into their lives. To solve this problem, Americans must change their attitude that cheating on sleep is necessary and even admirable.

Activity 1

Write an essay-length summary of the following article. Include a short introductory paragraph that states the thesis of the article. Then summarize in your three supporting paragraphs the three important areas in which study skills can be useful. Your conclusion might be a single sentence restating the thesis.

POWER LEARNING

Jill had not done as well in high school as she had hoped. Since college involved even more work, it was no surprise that she didn't do better there. 1

The reason for her so-so performance was not a lack of effort. She attended most of her classes and read her textbooks. And she never missed handing in any assignment, even though it often meant staying up late the night before homework was due. Still, she just got by in her classes. Before long, she came to the conclusion she simply couldn't do any better. 2

Then one day, one of her teachers said something to make her think otherwise. "You can probably build some sort of house by banging a few boards together," he said. "But if you want a sturdy home, you'll have to use the right techniques and tools. Building carefully takes work, but it gets better results. The same can be said of your education. There are no shortcuts, but there are some proven study skills that can really help. If you don't use them, you may end up with a pretty flimsy education." 3

Jill signed up for a study skills course and found out a crucial fact—that learning how to learn is the key to success in school. There are certain dependable skills that have made the difference between disappointment and success for generations of students. These techniques won't free you from work, but they will make your work far more productive. They include three important areas: time control, classroom note-taking, and textbook study. 4

TIME CONTROL

Success in college depends on time control. Time control means that you deliberately organize and plan your time, instead of letting it drift by. Planning means that you should never be faced with a night-before-the-test "cram" session or an overdue term paper. 5

There are three steps involved in time control. *First,* you should prepare a large monthly calendar. Buy a calendar with a large white block around each date, or make one yourself. At the beginning of the college semester, circle important dates on this calendar. Circle the days on which tests are scheduled; circle the days papers are due. This calendar can also be used to schedule study plans. You can jot down your plans for each day at the beginning of the week. An alternative method would be to make plans for each day the night before. On Tuesday night, for example, you might write down "Read Chapter 5 in psychology" in the Wednesday block. Hang this calendar where you will see it every day—your kitchen, your bedroom, even your bathroom! 6

The *second step* in time control is to have a weekly study schedule for the   7
semester—a chart that covers all the days of the week and all the waking hours in
each day.

Time	Mon.	Tues.	Wed.	Thurs.	Fri.	Sat.	Sun.
6:00 A.M.							
7:00	B	B	B	B	B		
8:00	Math	STUDY	Math	STUDY	Math		
9:00	STUDY	Biology	STUDY	Biology	STUDY	Job	
10:00	Psychology	↓	Psychology	↓	Psychology		
11:00	STUDY	English		English			
12:00	L		L	↓	L	↓	

Above is part of one student's schedule. On your own schedule, mark in all the
fixed hours in each day—hours for meals, classes, job (if any), and travel time.
Next, mark in time blocks that you can *realistically* use for study each day. Depending
on the number of courses you are taking and the demands of the courses, you may
want to block off five, ten, or even twenty or more hours of study time a week.
Keep in mind that you should not block off time for study that you do not truly
intend to use for study. Otherwise, your schedule will be a meaningless gimmick.
Also, remember that you should allow time for "rest and relaxation." You will be
happiest, and able to accomplish the most, when you have time for both work and
play.

The *third step* in time control is to make a daily or weekly "to do" list. This   8
may be the most valuable time control method you ever use. On this list, you write
down the things you need to do for the following day or the following week. If you
choose to write a weekly list, do it on Sunday night. If you choose to write a daily
list, do it the night before. Here is part of one student's daily list:

To Do   Tuesday
 *1. Review biology notes before class
 *2. Proofread English paper due today
  3. See Dick about game on Friday
 *4. Gas for car
  5. Read next chapter of psychology text

You may use a three- by five-inch note pad or a small spiral-bound notebook for this list. Carry the list around with you during the day. Always concentrate on doing first the most important items on your list. Mark high-priority items with an asterisk and give them precedence over low-priority items in order to make the best use of your time. For instance, you may find yourself wondering what to do after dinner on Thursday evening. Among the items on your list are ''Clean inside of car'' and ''Review chapter for math quiz.'' It is obviously more important for you to review your notes at this point; you can clean the car some other time. As you complete items on your ''to do'' list, cross them out. Do not worry about unfinished items. They can be rescheduled. You will still be accomplishing a great deal and making more effective use of your time.

CLASSROOM NOTE-TAKING

One of the most important single things you can do to perform well in a college course is to take effective class notes. The following hints should help you become a better note-taker. 9

First, attend class faithfully. Your alternatives—reading the text or someone else's notes, or both—cannot substitute for the experience of hearing ideas in person as someone presents them to you. Also, in class lectures and discussions, your instructor typically presents and develops the main ideas and facts of the course— the ones you will be expected to know on exams. 10

Another valuable hint is to make use of abbreviations while taking notes. Using abbreviations saves time when you are trying to get down a great deal of information. Abbreviate terms that recur frequently in a lecture and put a key to your abbreviations at the top of your notes. For example, in sociology class, *eth* could stand for *ethnocentrism;* in a psychology class, *s-t mem* could stand for *short-term memory.* (When a lecture is over, you may want to go back and write out the terms you have abbreviated.) In addition, abbreviate words that often recur in any lecture. For instance, use *e* for *example; def* for *definition; info* for *information;* + for *and,* and so on. If you use the same abbreviations all the time, you will soon develop a kind of personal shorthand that makes taking notes much easier. 11

A third hint when taking notes is to be on the lookout for signals of importance. Write down whatever your teacher puts on the board. If he or she takes the time to put material on the board, it is probably important, and the chances are good that it will come up later on exams. Always write down definitions and enumerations. Enumerations are lists of items. They are signaled in such ways as: ''The four steps in the process are . . .''; ''There were three reasons for . . .''; ''The two effects were . . .''; ''Five characteristics of . . . ''; and so on. Always number (1, 2, 3, etc.) such enumerations in your notes. They will help you understand relationships among ideas and organize the material of the lecture. Watch for emphasis words— words your instructor may use to indicate that something is important. Examples of such words are ''This is an important reason . . .''; ''A point that will keep coming up later . . .''; ''The chief cause was . . .''; ''The basic idea here is . . .''; and so on. Always write down the important statements announced by these and other 12 emphasis words. Finally, if your instructor repeats a point, you can assume it is important. You might put an R for *repeated* in the margin, so that later you will know that your teacher has stressed it.

Next, be sure to write down the teacher's examples and mark them with an X. The examples help you understand abstract points. If you do not write them down, you are likely to forget them later when they are needed to help make sense of an idea. 13

Also, be sure to write down the connections between ideas. Too many students merely copy the terms the teacher puts on the board. They forget that, as time passes, the details that serve as connecting bridges between ideas quickly fade. You should, then, write down the relationships and connections in class. That way you'll have them to help tie together your notes later on. 14

Review your notes as soon as possible after class. You must make them as clear as possible while they are fresh in your mind. A day later may be too late, because forgetting sets in very quickly. Make sure that punctuation is clear, that all words are readable and correctly spelled, and that unfinished sentences are completed (or at least marked off so that you can check your notes with another student's). Add clarifying or connecting comments wherever necessary. Make sure important ideas are clearly marked. Improve the organization if necessary, so that you can see at a glance main points and relationships among them. 15

Finally, try in general to get down a written record of each class. You must do this because forgetting begins almost immediately. Studies have shown that within two weeks you are likely to have forgotten 80 percent or more of what you have heard. And in four weeks you are lucky if 5 percent remains! The significance of this is so crucial that it bears repeating: To guard against the relentlessness of forgetting, it is absolutely essential that you write down what you hear in class. Later on you can concentrate on working to understand fully and to remember the ideas that have been presented in class. And the more complete your notes are at this time of study, the more you are likely to learn. 16

TEXTBOOK STUDY

In many college courses, success means being able to read and study a textbook skillfully. For many students, unfortunately, textbooks are heavy going. After an hour or two of study, the textbook material is as formless and as hard to understand as ever. But there is a way to attack even the most difficult textbook and make sense of it. Use a sequence in which you preview a chapter, mark it, take notes on it, and then study the notes. 17

Previewing

Previewing a selection is an important first step to understanding. Taking the time to preview a section or chapter can give you a bird's-eye view of the way the material is organized. You will have a sense of where you are beginning, what you will cover, and where you will end. 18

There are several steps in previewing a selection. First, study the title. The title is the shortest possible summary of a selection and will often tell you the limits of the material you will cover. For example, the title "FDR and the Supreme Court" tells you to expect a discussion of President Roosevelt's dealings with the Court. You know that you will probably not encounter any material dealing with FDR's foreign policies or personal life. Next, read over quickly the first and last paragraphs of the selection; these may contain important introductions to, and summaries of, the main ideas. Then examine briefly the headings and subheadings in the selection. Together, the headings and subheadings are a mini-outline of what you are reading. Headings are often main ideas or important concepts in capsule form; subheadings are breakdowns of ideas within main areas. Finally, read the first sentence of some paragraphs, look for words set off in **boldface** or *italics,* and look at pictures or diagrams. After you have previewed a selection in this way, you should have a good general sense of the material to be read.   19

Marking

You should mark a textbook selection at the same time that you read it through carefully. Use a felt-tip highlighter to shade material that seems important, or use a ballpoint pen and put symbols in the margin next to the material: stars, checks, or NB (*nota bene,* Latin for "note well"). What to mark is not as mysterious as some students believe. You should try to find main ideas by looking for clues: definitions and examples, enumerations, and emphasis words.   20

1   *Definitions and examples:* Definitions are often among the most important ideas in a selection. They are particularly significant in introductory courses in almost any subject area, where much of your learning involves mastering the specialized vocabulary of that subject. In a sense, you are learning the "language" of psychology or business or whatever the subject might be.   21

   Most definitions are abstract, and so they usually are followed by one or more examples to help clarify their meaning. Always mark off definitions and at least one example that makes a definition clear to you. In a psychology text, for example, we are told that "rationalization is an attempt to reduce anxiety by deciding that you have not really been frustrated." Several examples follow, among them: "A young man, frustrated because he was rejected when he asked for a date, convinces himself that the girl is not very attractive or interesting."   22

2   *Enumerations:* Enumerations are lists of items (causes, reasons, types, and so on) that are numbered 1, 2, 3, . . . or that could easily be numbered in an outline. They are often signaled by addition words. Many of the paragraphs in this book use words like *First of all, Another, In addition,* and *Finally* to signal items in a series. Textbooks use this very common and effective organizational method as well.   23

3   *Emphasis words:* Emphasis words tell you that an idea is important. Common emphasis words include phrases such as *a major event, a key feature, the chief factor, important to note, above all,* and *most of all.* Here is an example: "The most significant contemporary use of marketing is its application to nonbusiness areas, such as political parties."   24

Note-Taking

Next, you should take notes. Go through the chapter a second time, rereading the 25 most important parts. Try to write down the main ideas in a simple outline form. For example, in taking notes on a psychology selection, you might write down the heading "Kinds of Defense Mechanisms." Below the heading you would number and describe each kind and give an example of each.

Defense Mechanisms
a. Definition: unconscious attempts to reduce anxiety
b. Kinds:
    (1) Rationalization: An attempt to reduce anxiety by deciding that you have not really been frustrated
    Example: A man turned down for a date decides that the woman was not worth going out with anyway
    (2) Projection: Projecting onto other people motives or thoughts of one's own
    Example: A wife who wants to have an affair accuses her husband of having one

Studying Notes

To study your notes, use the method of repeated self-testing. For example, look at 26 the heading "Kinds of Defense Mechanisms" and say to yourself, "What are the kinds of defense mechanisms?" When you can recite them, then say to yourself, "What is rationalization?" "What is an example of rationalization?" Then ask yourself, "What is projection?" "What is an example of projection?" After you learn each section, review it, and then go on to the next section.

Do not simply read your notes; keep looking away and seeing if you can recite 27 them to yourself. This self-testing is the key to effective learning.

Summary: Textbook Study

In summary, remember this sequence in order to deal with a textbook: previewing, 28 marking, taking notes, studying the notes. Approaching a textbook in this methodical way will give you very positive results. You will no longer feel bogged down in a swamp of words, unable to figure out what you are supposed to know. Instead, you will understand exactly what you have to do, and how to go about doing it.

Take a minute now to evaluate your own study habits. Do you practice many of the 29 above skills in order to take effective classroom notes, control your time, and learn from your textbooks? If not, perhaps you should. The skills are not magic, but they are too valuable to ignore. Use them carefully and consistently, and they will make academic success possible for you. Try them, and you won't need convincing.

Activity 2

Write an essay-length summary of the CBS television show *Sixty Minutes*. In your first sentence, include the date of the show. For example, ''The December 8, 1991, broadcast of CBS's *Sixty Minutes* dealt with three subjects most people would find of interest. The first segment of the show centered on . . . ; the second segment examined . . . ; the final segment discussed . . . .'' Be sure to use parallel form in describing the three segments of the show. Then summarize each segment in the three supporting paragraphs that follow.

Activity 3

Write an essay-length summary of a cover story of interest to you in a recent issue of *Time, Newsweek,* or *U.S. News and World Report.*

HOW TO SUMMARIZE A BOOK

To write a summary of a book, first preview the book by briefly looking at:

1 ***Title.***   The title is often the shortest possible summary of what a book is about. Think about the title and how it may summarize the whole book.

2 ***Table of contents.***   The contents will tell you the number of chapters in the book and the subject of each chapter. Use the contents to get a general sense of how the book is organized. You should also note the number of pages in each chapter. If thirty pages are devoted to one episode or idea and an average of fifteen pages to other episodes or ideas, you should probably give more space to the contents of the longer chapter in your summary.

3 ***Preface.***   Here you will probably find out why the author wrote the book. Also, the preface may summarize the main ideas developed in the book and may describe briefly how the book is organized.

4 ***First and last chapters.***   In these chapters, the author may preview or review important ideas and themes developed in the book.

5 ***Other items.***   Note the way the author has used headings and subheadings to organize information in the book. Check the opening and closing paragraphs of each chapter to see if they contain introductions or summaries. Look quickly at charts, diagrams, and pictures in the book, since they are probably there to illustrate key points. Note any special features (index, glossary, appendixes) that may appear at the end of the book.

Next, adapt steps 2 through 5 for summarizing an article on pages 228–229.

Activity

Write an essay-length summary of a book you have read.

DOING
A REPORT

Each semester, you will probably be asked by at least one instructor to read a book or an article and to write a paper recording your response to the material. In these reports or reaction papers, your instructor will most likely expect you to do two things: *summarize the material* and *detail your reaction to it*. The following pages explain both parts of a report.

PART 1 OF A REPORT: A SUMMARY OF THE WORK

To develop the first part of a report, do the following:

1 Identify the author and title of the work and include in parentheses the publisher and publication date. An example follows on page 239. With magazines, give the date of publication.

2 Write an informative summary of the material. Condense the content of the work by highlighting its main points and key supporting points. (See pages 227–230 for a complete discussion of summarizing techniques.) Use direct quotations from the work to illustrate important ideas.

   Do not discuss in great detail any single aspect of the work and neglect to mention other equally important points. Summarize the material so that the reader gets a general sense of *all* key aspects of the original work. Also, keep the summary objective and factual. Do not include in the first part of the paper your personal reaction to the work; your subjective impression will form the basis of the second part of the paper.

PART 2 OF A REPORT: YOUR REACTION TO THE WORK

To develop the second part of a report, do the following:

1 Focus on any or all of the questions that follow. (Check with your instructors to see if they want you to emphasize specific points.)

   a How is the assigned work related to ideas and concerns discussed in the course? For example, what points made in the course textbook, class discussions, or lectures are treated more fully in the work?

   b How is the work related to problems in our present-day world?

   c How is the work related to your life, experiences, feelings, and ideas? For instance, what emotions did it arouse in you? Did it increase your understanding of an issue or change your perspective?

2 Evaluate the merit of the work: the importance of its points; its accuracy, completeness, and organization; and so on. You should also indicate here whether you would recommend the work to others, and why.

POINTS TO KEEP IN MIND WHEN WRITING A REPORT

Here are some important matters to consider as you prepare the report.

1 Apply the four basic standards of effective writing (unity, support, coherence, and clear, error-free sentences) when writing the report.

   a Make sure each major paragraph presents and then develops a single main point. For example, in the model report that follows, a paragraph summarizes the book, and the three paragraphs that follow detail three separate reactions that the student writer had to the book. The student then closes the report with a short concluding paragraph.

   b Support any general points or attitudes you express with specific reasons and details. Statements such as ''I agreed with many ideas in this article'' or ''I found the book very interesting'' are meaningless without specific evidence that shows why you feel as you do. Look at the model report to see how the main point or topic sentence of each paragraph is developed by specific supporting evidence.

   c Organize the material in the paper. Follow the basic *plan of organization* already described: an introduction, a summary of one or more paragraphs, a reaction of two or more paragraphs, and a conclusion. Use *transitions* to connect the parts of the paper.

   d Proofread the paper for grammar, mechanics, punctuation, and word use.

2 Document quotations from all works by placing the page number in parentheses after the quoted material (see the model report). You may use quotations in the summary and reaction parts of the paper, but do not overrely on them. Use them only to emphasize key ideas.

A MODEL REPORT

Here is a report written by a student in an introductory sociology course. Look at the paper closely to see how it follows the guidelines for report writing described in this chapter.

A Report on I Know Why the Caged Bird Sings

Introductory paragraph

In I Know Why the Caged Bird Sings (New York: Bantam Books, 1971), Maya Angelou tells the story of her earliest years. Ms. Angelou, a dancer, poet, and television producer as well as a writer, has continued her life story in three more volumes of autobiography. I Know Why the Caged Bird Sings is the start of Maya Angelou's story; in this book, she writes with crystal clarity about the pains and joys of being black in America.

PART 1: SUMMARY Topic sentence for summary paragraph

I Know Why the Caged Bird Sings covers Maya Angelou's life from age three to age sixteen. We first meet her as a gawky little girl in a white lady's cut-down lavender silk dress. She has forgotten the poem she had memorized for the Easter service, and all she can do is rush out of the church. At this point, Maya is living in Stamps, Arkansas, with her grandmother and uncle. The town is heavily segregated: "People in Stamps used to say that the whites in our town were so prejudiced that a Negro couldn't buy vanilla ice cream" (40). Yet Maya has some good things in her life: her adored older brother Bailey, her success in school, and her pride in her grandmother's quiet strength and importance in the black community. There is laughter, too, as when the preacher is interrupted in midsermon by an overly enthusiastic woman shouting, "Preach it, I say preach it!" The woman, in a frenzied rush of excitement, hits the preacher with her purse, making his false teeth fly out of his mouth and land at Maya's feet. Shortly after this incident, Maya and her brother are taken by her father to live in California with their mother. Here, at age eight, she is raped by her mother's boyfriend, who is mysteriously murdered after receiving only a suspended sentence for his crime. Maya returns, silent and withdrawn, to Stamps, where the gloom is broken when a friend of her mother introduces her to the magic of great books. Later, at age thirteen, Maya returns to California. She learns how to dance. She runs away after a violent family fight and lives for a month in a junkyard. She becomes the first black female to get a job on the San Francisco streetcars. She graduates from high school eight months pregnant. And she survives.

PART 2: REACTION Topic sentence for first reaction paragraph

I was impressed with the vividness of Maya Angelou's writing style. For example, she describes the lazy dullness of her life in Stamps: "Weekdays revolved in a sameness wheel. They turned into themselves so steadily and inevitably that each seemed to be the original of yesterday's rough draft" (93). She also knows how to bring a scene to life, as when she describes her eighth-grade graduation. For months, Maya has been looking forward to this event, knowing she will be honored for her academic successes. She is even happy with her appearance: her hair has become pretty, and her yellow dress is a miracle of hand-sewing. But the ceremony is spoiled when the speaker-- a white man--implies that the only success available to blacks is in athletics. Maya remembers: "The man's dead words fell like bricks around the auditorium and too many settled in my belly.... The proud graduating class of 1940 had dropped their heads" (152). Later, Maya uses a crystal- clear image to describe her father's mistress sewing: "She worked the thread through the flowered cloth as if she were sewing the torn ends of her life together" (208). With such vivid details and figures of speech, Maya Angelou recreates her life for her readers.

Topic ──────⟶ I also reacted strongly to the descriptions of injustices suffered by blacks
sentence two generations ago. I was as horrified as the seven-year-old Maya when
for second some "powhitetrash" girls torment her dignified grandmother, calling her
reaction "Annie" and mimicking her mannerisms. In another incident, Mrs. Cullinan,
paragraph Maya's white employer, decides that Marguerite (Maya's real name) is too difficult to pronounce and so renames her Mary. This loss of her name--a "hellish horror" (91) to Maya--is another humiliation suffered at white hands, and Maya leaves Mrs. Cullinan's employ soon afterward. Later, Maya encounters overt discrimination when a white dentist tells her grandmother, "Annie, my policy is I'd rather stick my hand in a dog's mouth than in a nigger's" (160)--and only slightly less obvious prejudice when the streetcar company refuses to accept her application for a streetcar conductor's job. We see Maya over and over as the victim of a white society.

Topic ──────⟶ Although I was saddened to read about the injustices, I rejoiced in Maya's
sentence triumphs. Maya is thrilled when she hears the radio broadcast of Joe Louis'
for third victory over Primo Carnera: "A Black boy. Some Black mother's son. He was
reaction the strongest man in the world" (114). She weeps with pride when the class
paragraph valedictorian leads her and her fellow eighth-graders in singing the Negro National Anthem. And there are personal victories, too. One of these comes after her father has gotten drunk in a small Mexican town. Though she has never driven before, she manages to get her father into the car and drives fifty miles through the night as he lies intoxicated in the back seat. Finally, she rejoices in the birth of her son: "He was beautiful and mine. Totally mine. No one had bought him for me" (245). Maya shows us, through these examples, that she is proud of her race--and of herself.

Concluding ──────⟶ I Know Why the Caged Bird Sings is a remarkable book. Maya could
paragraph have been just another casualty of race prejudice. Yet by using her intelligence, sensitivity, and determination, she succeeds in spite of the odds against her. And by writing with such power, she makes us share her defeats and joys. She also teaches us a vital lesson: with strength and persistence, we can all escape our cages--and sing our songs.

Activity 1

Read a magazine article that interests you. Then write a report on the article. Include an introduction, a one-paragraph summary, a reaction of one or more paragraphs, and a brief conclusion. You may, if you like, quote briefly from the article. Be sure to enclose the words that you take from the article in quotation marks and put the page number in parentheses at the end of the quoted material.

Activity 2

Read a book suggested by your instructor. Then write a report on the book. Include an introduction, a one-paragraph summary, a reaction of one or more paragraphs, and a brief conclusion. Also, make sure that each major paragraph in your report develops a single main point. You may quote some sentences from the book, but they should be only a small part of your report. Follow the directions in Activity 1 above when you quote material.

WRITING A RÉSUMÉ AND JOB APPLICATION LETTER

When applying for a job through the mail, you should ordinarily send (1) a résumé and (2) a letter of application.

RÉSUMÉ

A *résumé* is a summary of your personal background and your qualifications for a job. It helps your potential employer see at a glance whether you are suited for a job opening. A sample job résumé follows.

SARAH BECKETT
27 Hawkins Road
Clarksboro, New Jersey 08020
609-723-2166

Professional objective	A challenging position in the computer technology field.
Education	1989 to present: Glassboro State College, Glassboro, New Jersey 08028
	Degree: B.S. (in June)

Major courses:
Computer Programming I and II
Basic Computer Languages
Introduction to Microprocessors
Communications Circuits and Systems
Word Processing Systems
Advanced Computer Technologies

Related courses:
College Math I and II
Trigonometry
Calculus I and II
Small Business Management
Business Law
Organizational Systems Management

Special school project	As part of a class project, I chaired a study group which advised a local business about the advantages of installing a computerized payroll system. We projected comparative cost figures, developed a time-sharing purchase plan, and prepared a budget. The fifteen-page report received the highest grade in the class.
Work experience	1989 to present: As a salesperson at Radio Shack, I am involved in sales, inventory control, repairs, and customer relations. I have designed a computer program that our store uses to demonstrate the Radio Shack TRS-80 microcomputer. This program, written in BASIC, demonstrates ways the TRS-80 can be used in the home and small businesses.
	1987–1989: My temporary jobs included waitress, theater usher, and child care aide.
Skills	I am experienced in the following computer languages: PASCAL, BASIC, and COBOL. I have sales experience, am good with figures, relate easily to people, have initiative, and am dependable.
References	My references are available upon request from the Glassboro State College Placement Office, Glassboro, New Jersey 08028.

Points to Note about the Résumé

1   Your résumé, along with your letter of application, is your introduction to a potential employer. First impressions count, *so make the résumé neat!*

   a   If possible, type the résumé on good-quality letter (8½ by 11 inches) paper.

   b   Proofread *very carefully* for sentence-skills and spelling mistakes. A potential employer may regard such mistakes as signs of carelessness in your character. You might even want to get someone else to proofread the résumé for you.

   c   Be brief and to the point: use only one page if possible.

   d   Use a format like that of the model résumé (see also the variations described ahead). Balance your résumé on the page so that you have roughly the same margin on all sides.

   e   Note that you should start with your most recent education or employment and work backward in time.

2   Your résumé should point up strengths, not weaknesses. Don't include ''Special Training'' if you have had none. Don't refer to your grade point average if it's a low C.

   On the other hand, include a main heading like ''Extracurricular Activities'' if the activities or awards seem relevant. For example, if Sarah Beckett had been a member of the Management Club or vice president of the Science Club in high school or college, she should have mentioned these facts.

   If you have no work experience related to the job for which you're applying, then list the jobs you have had. Any job that shows a period of responsible employment may favorably impress a potential employer.

3   You can list the names of your references directly on the résumé. Be sure to get the permission of people you cite before listing their names.

   You can also give the address of a placement office file that holds references, as shown on the model résumé.

   Or you can simply say that you will provide references on request.

JOB APPLICATION LETTER

The purpose of the letter of application that goes with your résumé is to introduce yourself briefly and to try to make an employer interested in you. You should include only the high points of the information about yourself given in the résumé.

Following is the letter of application that Sarah Beckett sent with her résumé:

27 Hawkins Road
Clarksboro, New Jersey 08020
May 13, 1991

Mr. George C. Arline
Personnel Manager, Indesco Associates
301 Sharptown Road
White Plains, New York 10019

Dear Mr. Arline:

I would like to be considered as a candidate for the assistant computer programmer position advertised in the Philadelphia Inquirer on April 28, 1991.

I am currently finishing my degree in Computer Technology at Glassboro State College. I have taken every computer course offered at the college and have a solid background in the following computer languages: PASCAL, BASIC, and COBOL. In addition to my computer background, I have supplemented my education with business and mathematics courses.

My knowledge of computers and the business field goes beyond my formal classroom education. For the past two years I have worked part-time at Radio Shack, where I have gained experience in sales and inventory control. Also, on my own initiative, I designed a demonstration program for Radio Shack's TRS-80 microcomputer and developed promotional fliers about the program.

In short, I believe I have the up-to-date computer background and professional drive needed to contribute to your organization. I have enclosed a copy of my résumé to give you further details about my experience. Some time next week, I'll plan to give you a call to see whether I can come in for an interview at your convenience. I look forward to speaking with you then.

Sincerely,
Sarah Beckett
Sarah Beckett

Points to Note about
the Job Application Letter

1   Your letter should do the following:

a   In the first paragraph, state that you are an applicant for a job and tell the source through which you learned about the job.

Here is how Sarah's letter might have opened if her source had been the college placement office. "I learned through the placement office at Glassboro State College of the assistant computer programmer position at your company. I would like to be considered as a candidate for the job."

Sometimes an ad will list only a box number (Y 172) to reply to. Your inside address should then be:

Y 172
Philadelphia Inquirer
Philadelphia, Pennsylvania 19101

Dear Sir or Madam:

b   In the second paragraph, state briefly your qualifications for the job and refer the reader to your résumé.

c   In the last paragraph, state your willingness to come for an interview. If you can be available for an interview at only certain times, indicate this.

2   As with the résumé, neatness is crucial. Follow the same hints for the letter that you did for the résumé:

a   Type the letter on good paper.

b   Proofread *very carefully* for sentence-skills mistakes and spelling mistakes. Use the checklist of sentence skills on page 119 and the inside front cover.

c   Be brief and to the point: use no more than one page.

d   Use a format like the model letter. Keep roughly the same margin on all sides.

e   Use punctuation and spelling in the model letter as a guide. For example:

(1)   Skip two spaces between the inside address and the salutation ("Dear Mr. Arline").

(2)   Use a colon after the salutation.

(3)   Sign your name at the bottom, in addition to typing it.

Activity

Clip a job listing from a newspaper or copy a job description posted in your school placement office. The job should be one you feel you are qualified for or that you would one day like to have.

Write a résumé and a letter of application for the job. Use the models already considered as guides.

Use the checklist of the four bases on page 119 and the inside front cover as a guide in your writing.

USING THE LIBRARY

This chapter provides the basic information you need to use your college library with confidence. It also describes the basic steps you should follow in researching a topic.

Most students seem to know that libraries provide study space, typing facilities, and copying machines. They also seem aware that a library has a reading area, which contains recent copies of magazines and newspapers. But the true heart of a library consists of the following: a *main desk,* a *book file,* *book stacks,* a *magazine file,* and a *magazine storage area.* Each of these will be discussed on the pages that follow.

PARTS OF THE LIBRARY

Main Desk

The main desk is usually located in a central spot. Check at the main desk to see if there is a brochure that describes the layout and services of the library. You might also ask if the library staff provides tours of the library. If not, explore the library on your own to find each of the areas described below.

Activity

Make up a floor plan of your college library. Label the main desk, card file, book stacks, magazine file, and magazine storage area.

Book File

The book file will be your starting point for almost any research project. The book file is a list of all the books in the library. It may be an actual card catalog: a file of cards alphabetically arranged in drawers. Increasingly, however, the book file is computerized, and it appears on a number of computer terminals located at different spots in the library.

Finding a Book—Author, Title, and Subject: Whether you use an actual file of cards or a computer terminal, it is important for you to know that there are three ways to look up a book: according to *author, title,* or *subject.*

For example, suppose you wanted to see if the library had *Read with Me,* by Walter Anderson. You could check for the book in any of three ways:

1   You could go to the *title* section of the book file and look it up there under *R.* Note that you always look up a book under the first "significant" word in the title, excluding the words *A, An,* or *The.*

2   You could go to the *author* section of the book file and look it up there under *A.* An author is always listed under his or her last name. Here is the author entry in a card catalog for Anderson's book *Read with Me:*

LC151 A64	**Anderson, Walter** Read with me / by Walter Anderson — Boston: Houghton, Mifflin, 1990. vi, 320 p. Includes bibliographical references. 1. Literacy—United States. 2. Functional Literacy—United States—Case studies 3. Volunteer workers in education—United States—Case studies. 4. Reading (Adult education)—United States—Case studies.

3   Or, since you know the subject of the book—in this case, "literacy"—you could go to the *subject* section of the book file and look it up under L.

Generally, if you are looking for a particular book, it is easier to use the *author* or *title* section of the book file.

On the other hand, if you hope to find other books about literacy, then the *subject* section is where you should look. You will get a list of all the books in the library that deal with literacy. You'll also be given related subject headings under which you might find additional books about the subject.

■   In the catalog card shown above, how many subject headings are listed under which you might find books about literacy? _____

Using a Computerized Book File: Recently, I visited a local library that had just been computerized. The card catalog was gone, and in its place was a table with ten computer terminals. I approached a terminal and looked, a bit uneasily, at the instructions placed nearby. The instructions turned out to be very simple. They told me that if I wanted to look up the author of a book, I should type ''A = '' on the keyboard in front of the terminal and then the name of the author. I typed ''A = Anderson, Walter,'' and then (following the directions) I hit the Enter/Return key on the keyboard.

In seconds a new screen appeared, showing me a numbered list of several books by Walter Anderson, one of which was *Read with Me*. This title was numbered ''2'' on the list, and at the bottom of the screen was a direction to type the number of the title I wanted more information about. So I typed the number ''2'' and hit the Enter/Return key. I then got the following screen:

AUTHOR:	Anderson, Walter
TITLE:	Read with Me
PUBLISHER:	Houghton, Mifflin, 1990.
SUBJECTS:	1. Literacy—United States. 2. Functional Literacy—United States—Case studies. 3. Volunteer workers in education—United States—Case studies. 4. Reading (Adult education)—United States—Case studies.

Call Number	Material	Location	Status
374.012And	Book	Cherry Hill	Available

I was very impressed. The terminal was easier and quicker to use than a card catalog. The screen gave me the basic information I needed to know about the book, including where to find it. In addition, the screen told me that the book was ''Available'' on the shelves. (A display card nearby explained that if the book was not on the shelves, the message under ''Status'' would be ''Out on loan.'') I noticed other options. If the book was not on the shelves at the Cherry Hill location of the library, I would be told if it was available at other libraries nearby, by means of interlibrary loan.

The computer gave me two other choices. I could type ''T = '' plus a name to look up the title of a book. Or I could type ''S = '' plus the subject to get the names of any books that the library had dealing with the subject of literacy.

Using Subject Headings to Research a Topic: Whether your library has a card catalog or a computer terminal, it is the *subject section* that will be extremely valuable to you when you are researching a topic. If you have a general topic, the subject section will help you find books on that general topic and will also suggest more specialized topics.

For example, I typed "S = Literacy" to see how many book titles there were dealing with the subject of literacy. In seconds a screen came up showing me fifteen different titles. In addition, the screen informed me of related subject headings under which I could find other books about literacy. These related headings included the ones shown on the catalog card for *Read with Me* plus several others. With the help of the book titles and the subject headings in the book file (as well as the article titles and the subject headings suggested in the magazine file, which will be explained later in this chapter), a student could really begin to think about a limited research topic within the general subject of literacy.

There are three points to remember here: (1) Start researching a topic by using the subject section of the book file. (2) Look at the book titles as well; they sometimes suggest specific directions in which you might develop a paper. (3) Keep trying to narrow your topic. Chances are, you will be asked to do a paper of five to fifteen pages or so. You do not want to choose a topic so broad that covering it would require an entire book or more. Instead, you want to come up with a limited topic that can be dealt with adequately in a relatively short paper.

Activity

Part A: Answer the following questions about the card catalog.

1. Is your library's book file an actual file of cards in drawers, or is the book file on computer terminals?

    _____

2. What are the three ways of looking up a book in the library?

    a. _____

    b. _____

    c. _____

3. Which section of the book file will help you research and limit a topic?

    _____

Part B: Use your library book file to answer the following questions.

1. What is the title of one book by Maya Angelou?

   _____

2. What is the title of one book by Andy Rooney?

   _____

3. Who is the author of *The White House Years?* (Remember to look up the title under *White,* not *The.*)

   _____

4. Who is the author of *The Woman Warrior?* _____

5. List two books dealing with the subject of stress reduction, and note their authors.

   a. _____

   b. _____

6. List two books dealing with the subject of Martin Luther King, and note their authors.

   a. _____

   b. _____

7. Look up a book titled *The Immense Journey* or *Passages* or *The Lives of a Cell* and give the following information about it:

   a. Author _____

   b. Publisher _____

   c. Date of publication _____

   d. Call number _____

   e. Subject headings _____

8. Look up a book written by Carl Sagan or Ellen Goodman or Calvin Trillin and give the following information about it:

   a. Title _____

   b. Publisher _____

   c. Date of publication _____

   d. Call number _____

   e. Subject headings _____

Book Stacks

The book stacks are the library shelves where books are arranged according to their call numbers. The call number, as distinctive as a social security number, appears on a call file for any book and is printed on the spine of the book.

If your library has *open stacks* (ones that you are permitted to enter), follow these steps to find a book. Suppose you are looking for *Read with Me,* which has the call number LC151.A64 in the Library of Congress system. (Libraries using the Dewey decimal system have call letters made up entirely of numbers rather than letters and numbers. However, you use the same basic method to locate a book.) First you go to the section of the stacks that holds the L's. After you locate the L's, you look for the LC's. After that, you look for LC151. Finally, you look for LC151/A64, and you have the book.

If your library has *closed stacks* (ones you are not permitted to enter), you write down title, author, and call number on a slip of paper. (Such paper will be available near the card catalog or computer terminals.) You'll give the slip to a library staff person, who will locate the book and bring it to you.

Activity

Use the book stacks to answer one of the following sets of questions. Choose the questions related to the system of classifying books (Library of Congress or Dewey Decimal) used by your library.

Option 1:
Library of Congress System (Letters and Numbers)

1. Books in the E184.6-E185.9 area deal with
   a. Benjamin Franklin.
   b. American presidents.
   c. American Indians—history and writings.
   d. African Americans—history and writings.
2. Books in the HM-HN65 area deal with
   a. sociology.   b. economics.   c. history.   d. psychology.
3. Books in the M1-M220 area deal with
   a. painting.   b. music.   c. sculpture.   d. architecture.
4. Books in the PR4553-PR4595.H3 area deal with
   a. Thomas Hardy.
   b. George Eliot.
   c. Charles Dickens.
   d. Samuel Coleridge.

Option 2:
Dewey Decimal System (Numbers)

1. Books in the 200–299 area deal with
   a. language.   b. religion.   c. philosophy.   d. sports.
2. Books in the 370–372 area deal with
   a. education.   b. the military.   c. death.   d. waste disposal.
3. Books in the 613 area deal with
   a. wildflowers.   b. drugs.   c. health.   d. the solar system.
4. Books in the 916 area deal with
   a. Japan.   b. Israel.   c. China.   d. Africa.

Magazine File

The magazine file is also known as the *periodicals* file. *Periodicals* (from the word *periodic,* which means "at regular periods") are magazines, journals, and newspapers. In this chapter, the word *magazine* stands for any periodical.

The magazine file often contains recent or very specialized information about a subject, which may not be available in a book. It is important, then, to check magazines as well as books when you are doing research.

Just as you use the book file to find books on your subject, you use the magazine file to find articles on your subject in magazines and other publications. There are two files in particular that should help.

Readers' Guide to Periodical Literature: The familiar green volumes of the *Readers' Guide,* found in just about every library, list articles published in almost two hundred popular magazines, such as *Newsweek, Health, People, Ebony, Redbook,* and *Popular Science.* Articles are listed alphabetically under both subject and author. For example, if you wanted to learn the titles of articles published on the subject of child abuse within a certain time span, you would look under the heading "Child abuse."

Here, for example, is a typical entry from the *Readers' Guide:*

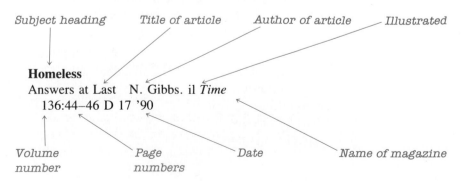

Note the sequence in which information is given about the article:

1 Subject heading.

2 Title of the article. In some cases, there will be bracketed words [like these] after the title that help make clear just what the article is about.

3 Author (if it is a signed article). The author's first name is always abbreviated.

4 Whether the article has a bibliography (*bibl*) or is illustrated with pictures (*il*). Other abbreviations sometimes used are shown in the front of the *Readers' Guide*.

5 Name of the magazine. A short title like *Time* is not abbreviated, but longer titles are. For example, the magazine *Popular Science* is abbreviated *Pop Sci*. Refer to the list of magazines in the front of the index to identify abbreviations.

6 Volume number of the magazine (preceding the colon).

7 Page numbers on which the article appears (after the colon).

8 Date when the article appeared. Dates are abbreviated: for example, *Mr* stands for *March, Ag* for *August, N* for *November*. Other abbreviations are shown in the front of the *Readers' Guide*.

The *Readers' Guide* is published in monthly supplements. At the end of a year, a volume is published covering the entire year. You will see in your library large green volumes that say, for instance, *Readers' Guide 1988* or *Readers' Guide 1990*. You will also see the small monthly supplements for the current year.

The *Readers' Guide* is also now available in a much more useful form, on a computer. I was amazed to see at my local library that I could now sit down at a terminal and quickly search for an article on almost any subject published in the last seven years. Searching on the computer was much easier than having to go through seven or so different paper volumes of the *Readers' Guide*.

Magazine Index: The *Magazine Index* is an automated system that lists articles in about four hundred general-interest magazines. Given a choice, you should always use this system rather than the *Readers' Guide*: it lists articles from twice as many sources as the *Guide* and is both fast and easy to use.

You sit in front of what looks like a large television screen that is already loaded with a microfilmed index. By pushing the first of two buttons, you quickly advance the film forward from A to B to C and so on. By pushing the other button, you move in the opposite direction. It really is as simple as that! The entries on the screen look just like the entries in the *Readers' Guide*. You'll note that the most recent articles on a topic are given first. This machine is an excellent research tool that is finding its way into more and more libraries.

Activity 1

At this point in the chapter, you know the two basic steps in researching a topic in the library. What are the steps?

1. _____

2. _____

Activity 2

Use the excerpt from the *Readers' Guide* on the opposite page to answer the following questions.

1. Who is the author of an article titled "The Next Big One"?

   _____

2. What is the title of an article by M. Ivey?

   _____

3. How many articles are listed that deal with the genetic aspects of alcoholism?

   _____

4. In what issue of *Science News* is there an article about alcoholism therapy?

   _____

5. On what pages of *People Weekly* is the article "Children in Peril"?

   _____

Activity 3

1. Look up a recent article on date rape in the *Readers' Guide* or the *Magazine Index* and fill in the following information:

   a. Article title _____

   b. Author (if given) _____

   c. Name of magazine _____

   d. Pages _____ e. Date _____

2. Look up a recent article on unemployment in the *Readers' Guide* or the *Magazine Index* and fill in the following information:

   a. Article title _____

   b. Author (if given) _____

   c. Name of magazine _____

   d. Pages _____ e. Date _____

Excerpt from *Readers' Guide*

ALCOHOL
> *See also*
> Prohibition
>> **Physiological effects**
>> *See also*
>> Fetal alcohol syndrome

Cheers? The sobering news about women and alcohol [diminished levels of alcohol dehydrogenase means women get drunk faster than men] D. Sobel. il *Mademoiselle* 96:138 My '90

ALCOHOL AND AIR PILOTS
Frank, open and humane [rehabilitation programs] *Aviation Week & Space Technology* 132:9 Ap 23 '90

ALCOHOL AND AUTOMOBILE DRIVERS
Kevin Tunell is paying $1 a week for a death he caused and finding the price unexpectedly high [death of S. Herzog in drunk driving accident] B. Hewitt. il pors *People Weekly* 33:118-19 Ap 16 '90

Motorists boil and civil libertarians burn as New Jersey police set a broad net to discourage drunk drivers [sobriety check point on Route 202] K. S. Schneider. il *People Weekly* 33:69-70+ Je 11 '90

The next big one. P. Bedard. il *Car and Driver* 35:14 My '90

Patty's legacy [school bus crash in Kentucky] K. Nunnallee. il por *Ladies' Home Journal* 107:28+ Ap '90

A war on drunk driving [Prince Edward Island] A. Prodanou. *Maclean's* 103:65 Ap 9 '90

ALCOHOL AND CELEBRITIES
In his most arresting performance, Cheers star Kelsey Grammer runs afoul of booze, coke and L.A. law. M. Neill. il pors *People Weekly* 33:101-2 Je 4 '90

ALCOHOL AND INDIANS (AMERICAN)
Children in peril [A. Kayitah, Apache child with fetal alcohol syndrome] M. Brower. il pors *People Weekly* 33:86-9 Ap 16 '90

ALCOHOL AND MUSICIANS
Still struggling to save her marriage [cover story; interview with V. Bertinelli] C. Dreifus. il pors *Redbook* 174:38+ Ap '90

ALCOHOL AND RELIGION
Demon rum on the run. H. A. Snyder. il *Christianity Today* 34:24-6 Je 18 '90

ALCOHOL AND WOMEN
> *See also*
> Fetal alcohol syndrome

Cheers? The sobering news about women and alcohol [diminished levels of alcohol dehydrogenase means women get drunk faster than men] D. Sobel. il *Mademoiselle* 96:138 My '90

Could you stop drinking for a month? S. Jacoby. il *Glamour* 88:288-9+ Ap '90

Drinking in America: portrait of a teenage alcoholic (I). A. N. LeBlanc. il *Seventeen* 49:179-83 Mr '90

Drinking in America: portrait of a teenage alcoholic (II). A. N. LeBlanc. il *Seventeen* 49:77-80 Ap '90

ALCOHOL AND YOUTH
Cosby on chemicals [mistreatment of youthful drinking on episode of The Cosby show] G. Vandal. *Phi Delta Kappan* 71:632-3 Ap '90

Drinking in America: portrait of a teenage alcoholic (I). A. N. LeBlanc. il *Seventeen* 49:179-83 Mr '90

Drinking in America: portrait of a teenage alcoholic (II). A. N. LeBlanc. il *Seventeen* 49:77-80 Ap '90

A nation under the influence. S. Nelson. *Seventeen* 49:183-4 Mr '90

ALCOHOL AS FUEL
The corn is green [Archer-Daniels-Midland's advertising neglects mentioning profits from price supports and gasohol program] M. Kinsley. *The New Republic* 202:4+ Je 18 '90

Fuel wars: big oil is running scared. M. Ivey. il *Business Week* p132+ Je 4 '90

Their battle cry: 'say yes to enthanol'. D. Ohrtman. il *Successful Farming* 88:34 Mr '90

ALCOHOL DEHYDROGENASE *See* Dehydrogenases

ALCOHOLIC BEVERAGES
> *See also*
> Beer
> Wine

Tropical tonics. E. Fried. il *Black Enterprise* 20:101-2 My '90

ALCOHOLICS AND ALCOHOLISM
> *See also*
> Alcohol—Physiological effects
> Temperance
>> **Genetic aspects**

DNA and the desire to drink [role of dopamine receptors] A. Purvis. il *Time* 135:88 Ap 30 '90

The drink link [questions concerning alcohol gene findings of Kenneth Blum and Ernest Nobel] R. Bazell. *The New Republic* 202:13-14 7 '90

The gene and the bottle [dopamine receptor gene] G. Cowley. il *Newsweek* 15:59 Ap 30 '90

Gene may be tied to 'virulent' alcoholism [dopamine D2 receptor gene; research by Kenneth Blum] B. Bower. *Science News* 137:246 Ap 21 '90

Genes with a don't-drink label [dopamine receptor may be linked to alcoholism; research by Ernest Noble and Kenneth Blum] *U.S. News & World Report* 108:15 Ap 30 '90

>> **Rehabilitation**
>> *See* Alcoholics and alcoholism—Therapy
>> **Therapy**

Alcoholism treatment under scrutiny [disulfiram; research by U. D. Register] R. Cowen. *Science News* 137:254 Ap 21 '90

Frank, open and humane [rehabilitation programs for pilots] *Aviation Week & Space Technology* 132:9 Ap 23 '90

Specialized Indexes: Once you know how to use the *Readers' Guide* and the *Magazine Index,* you will find it easy to use some of the more specialized indexes in most libraries. Here are some helpful ones:

- *New York Times Index.* This is an index to articles published in *The New York Times.* After you look up a subject, you'll get a list of articles published on that topic, with a short summary of each article.
- *Business Periodical Index.* The articles here are from over three hundred publications that generally treat a subject in more detail than it would receive in the popular magazines indexed in the *Readers' Guide.* At the same time, the articles are usually not *too* technical or hard to read.
- *Social Sciences Index.* This is an index to articles published by journals in the areas of anthropology, environmental science, psychology, and sociology. Your teachers in these areas may expect you to consult this index while doing a research project on any of these subjects.

Other specialized indexes that your library may have include the following:

Art Index
Applied Science and Technology Index
Biological and Agricultural Index
Book Review Digest
Education Index
General Science Index
Humanities Index
Nursing Index
Religious Periodical Literature Index

Depending on the subject area you are researching, you may want to consult the appropriate index above. Note that some libraries have most of these indexes on a computer, as well as the *Readers' Guide.*

Activity

1. Check the magazine area in your library. (It might be known as the *Periodicals* area.) Place a check by each of the indexes that it includes:

    _____ Readers' Guide Index

    _____ Business Periodicals Index

    _____ Magazine Index

    _____ Social Sciences Index

    _____ *New York Times* Index

2. Are any of these indexes available on a computer as well as in paperbound volumes? _____ If so, which ones? _____

    _____

3. What are two other indexes in this area of your library besides the five mentioned above?

    _____

    _____

A Note on Other Reference Materials: Every library has a reference area, often close to the place where the *Readers' Guide* is located, in which other reference materials can be found. Such general resource materials include dictionaries, encyclopedias, atlases, yearbooks, almanacs, a subject guide to books in print (this can help in locating books on a particular subject), anthologies of quotations, and other items.

You may also find in the reference area a series of filing cabinets called the *pamphlet file*. These cabinets are full of pamphlets, booklets, and newsletters on a multitude of topics. One file drawer for example, may include all the pamphlets and the like for subjects that start with A. I looked in the A drawer of the pamphlet file in my library and found lots of small pieces about subjects like abortion, adoption, and animal rights, along with many other topics starting with A. On top of these filing cabinets may be a booklet titled ''Pamphlet File Subject Headings''; it will quickly tell you if the file includes material on your subject of interest.

Activity

1. What is one encyclopedia that your library has?

    _____

2. What unabridged dictionary does your library have?

    _____

3. Where is your library's pamphlet file located?

    _____

4. Is there a booklet or small file that tells you what subject headings are included in the pamphlet file? _____

    Where is it? _____

Magazine Storage Area

Near your library's *Readers' Guide* or *Magazine Index,* you'll probably notice slips of paper. Here, for instance, is a copy of the slip used in my local library:

PERIODICAL REQUEST

Name of Magazine _____

Date of Magazine _____

(For your reference: Title and pages of article:)

_____

As you locate each magazine and journal article that you would like to look at, fill out a slip. Take the slips to a library staff person working nearby. Don't hesitate to do this: helping you obtain the articles you want is part of his or her job.

Here's what will probably happen next:

- If a magazine that you want is a very recent one, it may be on open shelves in the library. The staff member will tell you, and you can go find it yourself.

- If the magazine you want is up to a year or so old, it may be kept in a closed area. The staff person will go find it and bring it to you.

- Sometimes you'll ask to see a magazine that the library does not carry. You'll then have to plan to use other articles, or go to a larger library. However, most college libraries or large county libraries should have what you need.

- In many cases, especially with older issues, the magazine will be on microfilm or microfiche. (*Microfilm* is a roll of film on which articles have been reproduced in greatly reduced size; *microfiche* is the same thing but on easily handled sheets of film rather than on a roll.) The staff person will bring you the film or fiche and at your request will then show you how to load this material onto a microfiche or microfilm machine nearby.

Faced with learning how to use a new machine, many people are intimidated and nervous. I know I was. What is important is that you ask for as much help as you need. Have the staff person demonstrate the machine and then watch you as you do it. (Remember that this person is being paid by the library to help you learn how to use the resources in the library, including the machine.) While the machine may seem complex at first, in fact most of the time it turns out to be easy to use. Don't be afraid to insist that the person give you as much time as you need to learn the machine.

After you are sure you can use the machine to look up any article, check to see if the machine will make a copy of the article. Many will. Make sure you have some change to cover the copying fee, and then go back to the staff person and ask him or her to show you how to use the print option on the machine. You'll be amazed at how quickly and easily you can get a printed copy of almost any article you want.

Activity

1. Use the *Readers' Guide* or *Magazine Index* to find an article on divorce that was published in the last three months. Write the name of the magazine and the date on a slip of paper and give it to a library staff person. Is the article

   available in the actual magazine? _____ If so, is it on an open shelf or is

   it in a closed area where a staff person must bring it to you? _____

2. Use the *Readers' Guide* or *Magazine Index* to find an article on divorce that was published more than one year ago. Write down the name of the magazine and the date on a slip of paper and give it to a library staff person. Is the article available in the actual magazine, or is it on microfiche or microfilm?

   _____

3. Place a check if your library has:

   _____ Microfiche machine   _____ with a print option

   _____ Microfilm machine   _____ with a print option

A Summary of Library Areas

You now know the five areas of the library that will be most useful to you in doing research:

1. **Main desk.**
2. **Book file.** In particular, you can use the *subjects* section of the card file to get the names of books on your subject, as well as suggestions about other subject headings under which you might find books. It is by exploring your general subject in books and then in magazine articles that you will gradually be able to decide upon a subject limited enough to cover in your research paper.
3. **Book stacks.** Here you will get the books themselves.
4. **Magazine files and indexes.** Once again, you can use the *subjects* sections of these files to get the names of magazine and journal articles on your subject.
5. **Magazine storage area.** Here you will get the articles themselves.

PRACTICE IN USING THE LIBRARY

Activity

Use your library to research a subject that interests you. Select one of the following areas, or (with your teacher's permission) one of your own choice:

Date rape

Problems of retirement

Organ donation

Medical care for the aged

Pro-choice movement

Pro-life movement

Health insurance reform

Drinking water pollution

Food poisoning (salmonella)

Cremation

Fertility drugs

Acid rain

Drug treatment programs for adolescents

Air bags

Witchcraft in the 1990s

New treatments for AIDS

Changes in immigration policy

Euthanasia

Hazardous substances in the home

Day-care programs that work

Capital punishment

Prenatal care

Noise control

New aid for the handicapped

New remedies for allergies

Censorship in the 1990s

New prison reforms

Drug treatment programs

Sudden infant death syndrome

New treatments for insomnia

Greenhouse effect

Safe sex

Voucher system in schools

Self-help groups

Indoor air pollution

Gambling and youth

Nongraded schools

Earthquake forecasting

Ethical aspects of hunting

Video display terminals— health aspects

Recent consumer frauds

Stress reduction in the workplace

Sex in television

Everyday addictions

Toxic waste disposal

Sexual harassment in business

Telephone crimes

Heroes for the 1990s

New programs for the homeless

Marriage contracts

Research the topic first through the *subjects* section of the book file and then through the *subjects* section of one or more magazine files and indexes.

On a separate sheet of paper, provide the following information:

1. Topic.

2. Three books that cover the topic directly or at least touch on the topic in some way. Include these items:

   Author
   Title
   Place of publication
   Publisher
   Date of publication

3. Three articles on the topic published in 1990 or later from the *Readers' Guide* or the *Magazine Index*. Include these items:

   Title of article
   Author (if given)
   Title of magazine
   Date
   Page(s)

4. Three articles on the topic published in 1990 or later from other indexes (such as the *New York Times Index*, *Business Periodical Index*, *Social Sciences Index*, or *Humanities Index*). Include these items:

   Title of article
   Author (if given)
   Title of magazine
   Date
   Page(s)

5. Finally, include a photocopy of one of the three articles. Note whether the source of the copy was the article on paper, on microfiche, or on microfilm.

WRITING A RESEARCH PAPER

The process of writing a research paper can be divided into six steps:

1 Select a topic that you can readily research.
2 Limit your topic and make the purpose of your paper clear.
3 Gather information on your limited topic.
4 Plan your paper and take notes on your limited topic.
5 Write the paper.
6 Use an acceptable format and method of documentation.

This chapter explains and illustrates each of these steps and then provides a model research paper.

STEP 1: SELECT A TOPIC THAT YOU CAN READILY RESEARCH

First of all, go to the *Subjects* section of your library book file (as described on page 249) and see whether there are at least three books on your general topic. For example, if you initially choose the topic ''day care,'' see if you can find at least three books on day care. Make sure that the books are actually available on the library shelves.

Next, go to the *Magazine Index* or *Readers' Guide* (see pages 254–255), and try to find five or more articles on your subject.

If both books and articles are at hand, pursue your topic. Otherwise, you may have to choose another topic. You cannot write a paper on a topic for which research materials are not readily available.

STEP 2: LIMIT YOUR TOPIC AND MAKE THE PURPOSE OF YOUR PAPER CLEAR

A research paper should develop a *limited* topic. It should be narrow and deep rather than broad and shallow. Therefore, as you read through books and articles on your general topic, look for ways to limit the topic.

For instance, in reading through materials on the general topic "adoption," you might decide to limit your topic to the problems that single people have in adopting a child. The general topic "drug abuse" might be narrowed to successful drug treatment programs for adolescents. After doing some reading on the worldwide problem of overpopulation, you might decide to limit your paper to the birth-control policies of the Chinese government. The broad subject "death" could be reduced to unfair pricing practices in funeral homes; "divorce" might be limited to its most damaging effects on the children of divorced parents; "stress in everyday life" could be narrowed to methods of stress reduction in the workplace.

The subject headings in the book file and the magazine file will give you helpful ideas about how to limit your subject. For example, under the subject heading "Adoption" in the *book file* at one library were several related headings, such as "Intercountry adoption" and "Interracial adoption." In addition, there was a list of eighteen books, with several of the titles suggesting limited directions for research: the tendency toward adopting older children; problems faced by the adopted child; problems faced by foster parents. Under the subject heading "Adoption" in the *magazine file* at the same library were subheadings and titles of many articles which suggested additional limited directions that a research paper might explore: corrupt practices in adoption; the increase in mixed-race adoptions; ways to find a child for adoption. The point is that *subject headings and related headings, as well as book and article titles, may be of great help to you in narrowing your topic*. Take advantage of them.

Do not expect to limit your topic and make your purpose clear all at once. You may have to do quite a bit of reading as you work out the limited focus of your paper. Note that many research papers have one of two general purposes. Your purpose might be to *make and defend a point* of some kind. (For example, your purpose in a paper might be to provide evidence that gambling should be legalized.) Or, depending on the course and the instructor, your purpose might simply be to *present information* about a particular subject. (For instance, you might be asked to do a paper that describes the latest scientific findings about what happens when we dream.)

STEP 3: GATHER INFORMATION ON YOUR LIMITED TOPIC

After you have a good sense of your limited topic, you can begin gathering information that is relevant to it.

A helpful way to proceed is to sign out the books you need from your library—or to use the copier in your library to duplicate the pages you need from those books. In addition, make copies of all the articles you need from magazines, journals, or other reference materials. Remember that, as described in ''Using the Library'' on page 261, you should be able to make copies even of articles on microfiche or microfilm.

In other words, take the steps needed to get all your key source materials together in one place. You can then sit and work on these materials in a quiet, unhurried way in your home or some other place of study.

STEP 4: PLAN YOUR PAPER AND TAKE NOTES ON YOUR LIMITED TOPIC

Preparing a Scratch Outline

As you carefully read through the material you have gathered, think constantly about the specific content and organization of your paper. Begin making decisions about exactly what information you will present and how you will arrange it. Prepare a scratch outline of your paper that shows both its thesis and the areas of support for the thesis. It may help to try to plan at least three areas of support.

Thesis: _____

Support: (1) _____

(2) _____

(3) _____

Here, for example, is the brief outline that one student, Jodi Harris, prepared for her paper on a national family policy:

Thesis: *The United States should establish a national policy for the family.*

Support: *(1) A national parental leave policy*

(2) A national day-care policy

(3) A national policy for school-age children

Note-Taking

With a tentative outline in mind, you can begin taking notes on the information that you expect to include in your paper. Write your notes on four- by six-inch or five- by eight-inch cards or on sheets of loose-leaf paper. The notes you take should be in the form of *direct quotations, summaries in your own words,* or both. (At times you may also *paraphrase*—use an equal number of your own words in place of someone else's words. Since most research involves condensing information, you will summarize much more than you will paraphrase.)

A *direct quotation* must be written *exactly* as it appears in the original work. But as long as you don't change the meaning, you may omit words from a quotation if they are not relevant to your point. Show such an omission with three spaced periods known as *ellipses* in place of the deleted words:

Original passage

We cannot guarantee that bad things will happen, but we can argue that good things are not happening. It is the contention of this report that increasing numbers of young people are left to their own devices at a critical time in their development.

Direct quotation with ellipses

"We cannot guarantee that bad things will happen, but we can argue that good things are not happening.... Increasing numbers of young people are left to their own devices at a critical time in their development."

(Note that there are four dots in the above example, with the first dot indicating the period at the end of the sentence.)

In a *summary,* you condense the original material by expressing it in your own words. Summaries may be written as lists, as brief paragraphs, or both. Following is one of Jodi Harris' summary note cards:

Maternity leave

America is an undeveloped country when it comes to programs for working parents. Unlike over one hundred other countries, we do not grant mothers the right to a leave of absence after the birth of a child. In France, mothers receive sixteen weeks' maternity leave at 84 percent of their salary. In Sweden, mothers get twenty-six weeks' leave at 90 percent of their salary. In Russia, mothers get about four months' fully paid leave.

Wallis, 60

Keep in mind the following points about your research notes:

- Write on only one side of each card or sheet of paper.
- Write only one kind of information, from one source, on any one card or sheet. For example, the sample card above has information on only one idea (maternity leave) from one source (Wallis).
- Include at the top of each card or sheet a heading that summarizes its content. This will help you organize the different kinds of information you gather.
- Identify the source and page number at the bottom.

Whether you quote or summarize, be sure to record the exact source and page from which you take each piece of information. In a research paper, you must document all information that is not common knowledge or a matter of historical record. For example, the birth and death dates of Martin Luther King are established facts and do not need documenting. On the other hand, the number of adoptions granted to single people in 1991 is a specialized fact that should be documented. As you read several sources on a subject, you will develop a sense of what authors regard as generally shared or common information about a subject and what is more specialized information that must be documented.

If you do not document specialized information or ideas that are not your own, you will be stealing (the formal term is *plagiarizing*—using someone else's work as your own work). A good deal of the material in research writing, it can usually be assumed, will need to be documented.

STEP 5: WRITE THE PAPER

After you have finished your reading and note-taking, you should have a fairly clear idea of the plan of your paper. Make a *final outline* and use it as a guide to write your first full draft. If your instructor requires an outline as part of your paper, you should prepare either a *topic outline*, which contains your thesis plus words and phrases, or a *sentence outline*, which contains all complete sentences. A topic outline is shown in the model paper on page 274. You will note that roman numerals are used for first-level headings, capital letters for second-level headings, and numbers for third-level headings.

In your *introductory paragraph*, include a thesis statement expressing the purpose of your paper and indicate the plan of development that you will follow. The section on writing an introductory paragraph for the essay (pages 72–74) is appropriate for the introductory section of the research paper as well. Note also the opening paragraph in the model research paper on page 275.

As you move from introduction to *main body* to *summary, conclusion,* or *both,* strive for unity, support, and coherence so that your paper will be clear and effective. Repeatedly ask, "Does each of my supporting paragraphs develop the thesis of my paper?" Use the checklist on page 119 and the inside front cover to make sure that your paper touches all four bases of effective writing.

STEP 6: USE AN ACCEPTABLE FORMAT AND METHOD OF DOCUMENTATION

Format

The model paper on pages 273–283 shows an acceptable format for a research paper. Comments and directions are set in small print in the margins of each page; be sure to note these.

Documentation of Sources

You must tell the reader the sources (books, articles, and so on) of the borrowed material in your paper. Whether you quote directly or summarize ideas in your own words, you must acknowledge your sources. In the past, you may have used footnotes and a bibliography to cite your sources. Now, you will learn a simplified documentation style used by the Modern Language Association. This easy-to-learn style resembles the documentation used in the social sciences and natural sciences.

Citations within a Paper: When citing a source, you must mention the author's name and the relevant page number. The author's name may be given either in the sentence you are writing or in parentheses following the sentence. Here are two examples:

> "There is, at present, no centralized program to provide quality day care to all children in the United States," states Angela Browne Miller (4).

> One expert states, "There is, at present, no centralized program to provide quality day care to all children in the United States" (Miller 4).

There are several points to note about citations within the paper:

- When the author's name is provided within the parentheses, only his or her last name is given.
- There is no punctuation between the author's name and the page number.
- The parenthetical citation is placed after the borrowed material but before the period at the end of the sentence.
- If you are using more than one work by the same author, include a shortened version of the title within the parenthetical citation. For example, suppose you were using several books by Angela Browne Miller and you included the quotation above, which is from Miller's book *The Day Care Dilemma*. Your citation within the text would be:

> (Miller, Day Care, 4)

Citations at the End of a Paper: Your paper should end with a list of "Works Cited" which includes all the sources actually used in the paper. (Don't list any other sources, no matter how many you have read.) Look at "Works Cited" in the model research paper (pages 282–283) and note the following points:

- The list is organized alphabetically according to the authors' last names. Entries are not numbered.

- Entries without an author (such as "Child Care News") are listed alphabetically by the first word.

- When more than one work by the same author or authors is listed, three hyphens followed by a period should be substituted for the author's or authors' names after the first entry.

- Entries are double-spaced, with no extra space between entries.

- After the first line of each entry, there is an indentation for each additional line in the entry.

Model Entries for a List of "Works Cited":   Model entries for "Works Cited" are given below. Use these entries as a guide when you prepare your own list.

Book by One Author

Rhodes, Richard. A Hole in the World: An American Boyhood. New York: Simon & Schuster, 1990.

Always give the complete title, including any subtitle. Separate a subtitle from the title with a colon.

Two or More Entries by the Same Author

- - - . The Making of the Atomic Bomb. New York: Simon & Schuster, 1986.

If you cite two or more entries by the same author (in the example above, a second book by Richard Rhodes is cited), do not repeat the author's name. Instead, begin with a line made up of three hyphens followed by a period. Then give the remaining information as usual. Arrange the works by the same author alphabetically by title. Note in the examples above that the words *A, An,* and *The* are ignored when alphabetizing by title.

Book by Two or More Authors

Bassis, Michael A., Richard J. Gelles, and Ann Levine. Sociology: An
   Introduction. New York: Random House, 1991.

For a book with two or more authors, give all the authors' names but reverse
only the first name.

Magazine Article

Quinn, Jane Bryant. "The Middle-Class Melt." Newsweek 17 Dec. 1990:49.

Write the date of the issue as follows: day, month (abbreviated in most cases to
three letters), and year. The final number or numbers refer to the page or pages
of the issue on which the article appears.

Newspaper Article

Lopez, Steve. "Grandfather's Footsteps." The Philadelphia Inquirer 9 Dec.
   1990:B1.

The final letter and number refer to section B, page 1.

Editorial

"Better to Give Than to Retrieve." Editorial. The New York Times 21 Dec.
   1990, sec. A:22.

List an editorial as you would any signed or unsigned article, but indicate the
nature of the piece by adding *Editorial* or *Letter* after the article's title.

Encyclopedia Article

Foulkes, David, and Rosalind D. Cartwright. "Sleep and Dreams."
   Encyclopaedia Britannica. 1989 ed.

Selection in an Edited Collection

Moody, Harry R. "Education as a Lifelong Process." Our Aging Society. Eds.
   Alan Pifer and Lydia Bronte. New York: Norton, 1986.

Revised or Later Edition

Quinn, Virginia Nichols. Applying Psychology. 2d ed. New York: McGraw-
   Hill, 1990.

Note that the abbreviations *Rev. ed., 2d ed., 3d ed.,* and so on are placed right
after the title.

Chapter or Section in a Book by One Author

Chancellor, John. "How Do We Get Out of This Mess?" Peril and Promise: A Commentary on America. New York: Harper and Row, 1990. 127–163.

Pamphlet

1990 Heart and Stroke Facts. American Heart Association, 1990.

Television Program

"Is There Poison in Your Mouth?" Narr. Morley Safer. Prod. Patti Hassler. 60 Minutes. CBS. 16 Dec. 1990.

Film

Havana. Dir. Sidney Pollack. Universal, 1990.

Recording

Turner, Tina. "Paradise Is Here." Break Every Rule. Capitol Records CD 7463232.

Personal Interview

Thornton, Dr. Roger K. Personal interview. 19 Nov. 1991.

Activity

On a separate sheet of paper, convert the information in each of the following references into the correct form for a list of "Works Cited." Use the appropriate model on pages 269–272 as a guide.

1. A Book by Michael Fox called *Inhumane Society* and published in Boston by Houghton, Mifflin in 1990.
2. An article by Kenneth L. Woodward titled "A Time to Seek" on pages 50–56 of the December 17, 1990, issue of *Time*.
3. An article by Karen S. Peterson titled "Young Adults Are Leaning to the Right" on page 1D of the December 13, 1990, issue of *USA Today*.
4. A book by James F. Calhoun and Joan Ross Acocella titled *Psychology of Adjustment and Human Relations* and published in a third edition by McGraw-Hill in New York in 1990.
5. An article by Katherine Griffin titled "The Unbearable Darkness of Being" on pages 62–67 of the January/February 1991 issue of *In Health*.

AMERICA'S NEGLECTED CHILDREN:
HOW THE GOVERNMENT CAN HELP

by

Jodi Harris

English 101
Professor Lessig

20 December 1991

OUTLINE

Thesis: The United States should establish a national family policy that supports parental leaves, day care, and after-school care.

  I. Great need for child care
     A. Great numbers of children with working mothers
     B. Predicted increase of children with working mothers
 II. Comparison of our national commitment to child care with that of other countries
     A. Commitment of other countries
     B. Our own failure
III. Solution: Establishment of a three-part national family policy
     A. National parental leave program
        1. Problem: financial consequences to women who leave work to have a baby
        2. Solution:
           a. Two-part policy
              (1) Unpaid leave
              (2) Full restoration to job and benefits
           b. State programs as evidence such policies can work
     B. National day-care policy
        1. Problems
           a. Lack of facilities
           b. Low-quality facilities
           c. High cost of day care
           d. Government's hands-off policy and its effects
        2. Solutions for families and employers
           a. Tax breaks for companies with day-care centers
           b. Encouragement of day-care centers for government employees
           c. Denial of federal funding to states without stringent standards for child care facilities
     C. National policy for after-school child care
        1. Problems
           a. Great numbers of school-age children needing care
           b. Problems of latchkey children
        2. Solution
           a. Use of schools for before- and after-school care
           b. Model example in Independence, Missouri

*Your last name and the page number should
go in the upper-right-hand corner of each page.*

Harris 1

*Double
space
between
lines of
the text.
Leave
about a
1-inch
margin all
the way
around
the page.*

With both Mom and Dad at work in today's world, child care has become a wrenching personal problem for millions of America's families (Wallis 54). The overriding question for most expectant American mothers--rich, middle-class, or working poor--is how to take time off from work to have the baby. Soon after the birth, parents must cope with the problem of how to find care for their baby when they are both back at work. And later, parents must face the question of who will watch their older children when the school day is over. To help working families properly care for their children, the United States should establish a national family policy that supports parental leave, day care, and after-school care.

*Thesis,
with plan
of
development.*

The need for such a policy is great and continues to grow. Only a minority of families fit the traditional "Dick and Jane" mold, with a breadwinner father and homemaker mother. Today, more than two-thirds of all mothers with children under the age of eighteen work outside the home (Papalia and Olds 329). Twelve million children under age six have working mothers (Weber 65). In the 1900s, an estimated 75 percent of all mothers with children under six will be employed outside their homes (Miller 6). Elinor Guggenheimer, president of the Child Care Action Campaign, says, "We are in the midst of an explosion," and predicts that within ten years, the number of children under six needing daytime supervision will grow by more than 50 percent (qtd. in Wallis 55).

*Parenthetic
citations,
with
author
and page
number
but no
comma.*

*The
abbreviation
qtd. means
quoted.*

Compared with other industrialized nations, the United States is an underdeveloped country when it comes to policies and programs for working parents. Ours, for instance, is the only Western industrialized nation that does not guarantee a mother the right to a leave of absence after she has a child (Wallis 56). In France, Sweden, and Denmark, mothers and fathers are guaranteed the right to take time off to be with their newborns (Wallis 60).

We also rate poorly when it comes to day care. Many European nations with a high percentage of working women have invested in public nurseries and subsidize in-home care (Dreskin and Dreskin 138). In Germany, for example, parents can deduct the cost of child care from their taxes. In Japan, the government and most companies subsidize parents whose children require day care (Gibbs 45).

Clearly, our national commitment to child care lags notably. When Democratic Representative Pat Schroeder arrived in Washington from Colorado in 1973 with her two small children, she expected it would take only a year or so for Congress to pass an all-inclusive child care bill. Yet today, almost twenty years later, the United States is still without a national family policy (Mernit 65). "Under our laws," observes Congresswoman Schroeder, "a business woman can deduct a new Persian rug for her office but can't deduct most of her costs for child care" (qtd. in Gibbs 45).

Recent efforts to persuade Congress to pass a parental leave bill have been unsuccessful. The most recent failure occurred in the summer of 1990 when Congress did not override President Bush's veto of the Family and Medical Leave Act (Lewin A8).

The absence of a national policy to help working parents reflects our antiquated attitudes toward motherhood. For the most part, the workplace still operates as if workers had no families and women were not half of the entire labor force

Harris 3

(Kantrowitz 57). Jay Belsky, a professor of human development at Pennsylvania State University, reminds us, "We are as much a society dependent on female labor, and thus in need of a child-care system, as we are a society dependent on the automobile, and thus in need of roads" (qtd. in Wallis 55).

An important first step toward a strong child care system in the United States would be the development of a policy helping parents take leave for birth and for the care of newborns. At present, women lose one-fifth of their earning power when they leave a job to have a baby (Hewlett 194). Speaking for the Women's Legal Defense Fund at a hearing on family leave before the House Committee on Education and Labor, Donna Lenhoff said, "Children of course suffer whenever either of their parents is too pressured by work and financial considerations to spend time with them. . . . This problem becomes acute at certain times . . . such as birth." She continued, "[Family leave] would be an essential first step toward meeting the needs and realities of American families today" (Sweeney 146–148).

Because most women work out of economic necessity, we must create a parental leave policy with two requirements. First, employers would have to grant men and women as much as eighteen weeks of unpaid leave after the birth or adoption of a child. Second, employers would have to restore those persons to the same job or an equivalent job with continued benefits and seniority when they return. As John J. Sweeney, International President of the Service Employees International Union, AFL-CIO, said at a Congressional committee hearing on family leave, "No one should have to choose between being a breadwinner and being a caring family member" (Sweeney 140).

Brackets mark words inserted to clarify a quotation.

That such a program can work is evidenced by the fact that fifteen states have adopted some form of job protection for parents requesting leave, and thirty others have considered similar legislation in the past year (Lewin A8). The legislation permits mothers and fathers at least six weeks of leave with continued health benefits and a guarantee of employment at the end of the leave (Parents 38).

The second component of a national family policy should be day care. Our present day-care system is clearly inadequate. First of all, we do not have enough facilities to meet the demand. Long waiting lists at child care centers are routine. In addition, many day-care facilities have marginal standards of health and safety and are short of qualified help (Traver 17).

Moreover, finding an acceptable day-care arrangement is just the beginning of the problems parents face. With the average cost of day care at $3,000 a child, parents must struggle to pay for a suitable program once they have found it. The high price is a real financial strain for middle-class families and is beyond the reach of the working poor (Traver 17).

"There is, at present, no centralized program to provide quality day care to all children in the United States," Angela Browne Miller states in her book The Day Care Dilemma (4). Instead, the prevailing belief is that parents alone should finance the cost of day care. An editorial in Glamour (84) reports that, according to Yale professor Edwin Zigler and researcher Susan Muenchen, the result of this belief is that in this country the issue is seen as a problem for mothers. Therefore, the editorial continues, "the care of America's most precious resource--her children--is left to chance, luck, or geography." The editorial

Harris 5

concludes that, on the whole, the government, employers, and society have chosen the ostrich approach to the issue of day care: "Ignore the need and maybe it will go away" (Glamour 84).

This attitude has had profound effects. Most American employers expect parents to behave in the same way as childless workers (Dreskin and Dreskin 138). Yet both parents and employers would benefit from a more enlightened attitude. As the Glamour editorial states, "The overwhelming burdens on working mothers must be relieved, not only for the health of the American family but for the increased productivity in the workplace.... Parents miss an average of 7.2 work days per year because of child care difficulties (Glamour 84)." Businesses that have made an investment in child care say that it pays off handsomely in reduced turnover and absenteeism (Wallis 60). Thus a national policy encouraging more high-quality day-care centers would help both working families and employers.

The government could stimulate the development of more good child care centers by giving larger tax breaks for companies that establish day-care centers for their employees. Furthermore, since the government is the nation's largest employer (Glamour 84), all levels of government should be encouraged to establish day-care centers for their employees.

Finally, states without stringent health, safety, and teaching standards for child care facilities should lose whatever federal funding they have. This will encourage a day-care system that provides children with enriching programs, well-paid teachers, and a safe environment.

To be complete, a national family policy must also include comprehensive after-school care for children. A child's entry

into the school system is too often equated with the end of the
struggle for child care. But the battle is not over. It is just
different--the need is now for a few hours of care instead of a
full day (Quindlen E17).

Indeed, for working parents, those few hours can become the
trickiest of all child care problems. According to recent
estimates, there may be in the United States today as many as
twelve million latchkey children, those children regularly left
without direct adult supervision before or after school (Quindlen
E17). Their parents are trying to make ends meet while
worrying about where the children are after school hours
(Lipsitz 5). These parents would obviously prefer to have their
children participate in organized after-school activities, but that
kind of program is not always available or affordable.

No one denies that latchkey children are at risk--of
loneliness, negative behavior, mistreatment, and actual physical
harm. Recognition of these risks must be translated into
programs. In the words of educational researcher Joan Lipsitz:

> We cannot guarantee that bad things will happen, but we
> can argue that good things are not happening. ...
> Increasing numbers of young people are left to their own
> devices at a critical time in their development. They are
> losing opportunities to be culturally enriched, to interact
> positively with peers and adults, and to contribute to their
> communities. (qtd. in Landers 7)

Such opportunities could be provided at our nation's schools,
natural sites for before- and after-school care. The most obvious
benefits of school-based programs are the convenience and
security they offer. Also, schools provide a well-equipped
environment with excellent facilities for day care (Egan 27).

Direct quotations of four lines or more are indented ten spaces from the left margin. Quotation marks are not used. The spaced periods (ellipses) show that material has been omitted from the quotation.

Harris 7

Dr. Gwendolyn C. Baker, president of the New York City Board of Education, would like to see schools open from early in the morning until six o'clock at night "for enrichment activities, for sports, for all kinds of things we don't have time for during the school day" (qtd. in Quindlen E17).

Such a program works well in Independence, Missouri, where elementary schools now stay open twelve hours a day. Corporate and public subsidies help to keep costs low. School Superintendent Robert L. Henley says, "Most parents work today, and we feel that we are providing a good service" (qtd. in Garland 68).

His attitude reflects the fact that child care is no longer just a women's issue. Rather, it is a family issue and, as such, a national issue. The economic needs of parents and employers will certainly cause a change in the attitude of the business community (Wallis 60). Our government can make the struggle less painful by instituting a national family policy which will relieve the stresses on working parents and improve the lives of their children. If we are serious about our nation's future, we must demand no less.

Harris 8

Works Cited

"Child Care News." Parents Feb. 1990: 38.

"Day-Care Center Slots." Editorial. Glamour Apr. 1985: 84.

Dreskin, William, and Wendy Dreskin. "The Family Here and
    Abroad." The Day Care Decision. New York: Evans, 1983.
    126–154.

Egan, Leslie A., and Barbara A. Lowe. "Debate." NEA Today Dec.
    1984: 27.

Garland, Susan B. "America's Child-Care Crisis: The First Tiny
    Steps toward Solutions." Business Week 10 July 1989:
    64–66.

Gibbs, Nancy. "Shameful Bequests to the Next Generation."
    Time 8 Oct. 1990: 42–46.

Hewlett, Sylvia Ann. "Why We Need a National Policy to Help
    Working Mothers." Glamour Nov. 1986: 194.

Kantrowitz, Barbara, et al. "Changes in the Workplace."
    Newsweek 31 Mar. 1986: 57.

Landers, Susan. "Latchkey Kids." The Monitor Dec. 1986: 1,
    6–7.

Lewin, Tamar. "Battle for Family Leave Will Be Fought in
    States." The New York Times 27 July 1990: A8.

Lipsitz, Joan. "3:00 to 6:00 P.M.: Programs for Young
    Adolescents." Report on School Age Day Care. New Jersey:
    Cherry Hill Public Schools, 1987.

Mernit, Susan. "The Day-Care Deadline." Harper's Bazaar July
    1989: 65, 130.

Miller, Angela Browne. The Day Care Dilemma. New York:
    Plenum, 1990.

Harris 9

Papalia, Diane E., and Sally Wendkos Olds. "Intellectual
    Development in Early Childhood." A Child's World: Infancy
    through Adolescence. 5th ed. New York: McGraw-Hill,
    1990. 311–345.

Quindlen, Anne. "Latchkey Summer." The New York Times
    8 July 1990: E17.

Sweeney, John J., Donna Lenhoff, and Karen Nussbaum. "Should
    the Proposed 'Family and Medical Leave Act' Be Approved?"
    Congressional Digest May 1988: 136–152.

Traver, Nancy. "The ABCs of Child Care." Time 3 July 1989: 17.

Wallis, Claudia. Time 22 June 1987: 54–60.

Weber, Joseph. "Why Day Care Is Still Mostly Mom and Pop."
    Business Week 10 July 1989: 65.

PART FOUR

HANDBOOK OF SENTENCE SKILLS

MANUSCRIPT FORM

When you hand in a paper for any course, it will probably be judged first by its format. It is important, then, to make the paper look attractive, neat, and easy to read. Here is a checklist you should use when preparing a paper for an instructor:

_____ ■ Is the paper full-sized paper, 8½ by 11 inches?

_____ ■ Are there wide margins (1 to 1½ inches) all around the paper? In particular, have you been careful not to crowd the right-hand or bottom margin?

_____ ■ If the paper is handwritten, have you:

Used a blue or black pen?

Been careful not to overlap letters or to make decorative loops on letters?

Made all your letters distinct, with special attention to *a, e, i, o,* and *u*—five letters that people sometimes write illegibly?

Kept all your capital letters clearly distinct from small letters?

_____ ■ Have you centered the title of your paper on the first line of page 1? Have you been careful *not* to put quotation marks around the title or to underline it? Have you capitalized all the words in the title except for short connecting words like *of, for, the, and, in,* and *to*?

_____ ■ Have you skipped a line between the title and the first line of your paper?

_____ ■ Have you indented the first line of each paragraph about five spaces (half an inch) from the left-hand margin?

_____ ■ Have you made commas, periods, and other punctuation marks firm and clear? If typing, have you left a double space after a period?

_____ ■ If you have broken any words at the end of a line, have you been careful to break only between syllables?

_____ ■ Have you put your name, the date, and other information at the end of the paper (or wherever your instructor has specified)?

Also ask yourself these important questions about the title and the first sentence of your paper:

_____ ■ Is your title made up of several words that tell what the paper is about? (The title should be just several words, *not* a complete sentence.)

_____ ■ Does the first sentence of your paper stand independent of the title? (The reader should *not* have to use the words in the title to make sense of the opening sentence.)

Activity

Use the checklist to locate the seven mistakes in format in the following lines from a student paper. Explain the mistakes in the spaces provided. One mistake is described for you as an example.

	"Being alone"
	This is something that I simply cannot tolera-
	te, and I will go to great lengths to
	prevent it. For example, if I know that I need

1. Hyphenate only between syllables (*toler-ate, not tolera-te*).

2. _____

3. _____

4. _____

5. _____

6. _____

7. _____

SUBJECTS AND VERBS

The basic building blocks of English sentences are subjects and verbs. Understanding them is an important first step toward mastering a number of sentence skills.

Every sentence has a subject and a verb. Who or what the sentence speaks about is called the *subject;* what the sentence says about the subject is called the *verb*. In the following sentences, the subject is underlined once and the verb twice:

The boy cried.

That fish smells.

Many people applied for the job.

The show is a documentary.

A SIMPLE WAY TO FIND A SUBJECT

To find a subject, ask *who* or *what* the sentence is about. As shown below, your answer is the subject.

Who is the first sentence about?   The boy

What is the second sentence about?   That fish

Who is the third sentence about?   Many people

What is the fourth sentence about?   The show

A SIMPLE WAY TO FIND A VERB

To find a verb, ask what the sentence *says about* the subject. As shown below, your answer is the verb.

What does the first sentence *say about* the boy?   He cried.

What does the second sentence *say about* the fish?   It smells.

What does the third sentence *say about* the people?   They applied.

What does the fourth sentence *say about* the show?   It is a documentary.

A second way to find the verb is to put *I, you, he, she, it,* or *they* in front of the word you think is a verb. If the result makes sense, you have a verb. For example, you could put *he* in front of *cried* in the first sentence above, with the result, *he cried,* making sense. Therefore you know that *cried* is a verb. You could use the same test with the other three verbs as well.

Finally, it helps to remember that most verbs show action. In the sentences already considered, the three action verbs are *cried, smells,* and *applied.* Certain other verbs, known as *linking verbs,* do not show action. They do, however, give information about the subject. In "The show is a documentary," the linking verb *is* tells us that the show is a documentary. Other common linking verbs include *am, are, was, were, feel, appear, look, become,* and *seem.*

Activity

In each of the following sentences, draw one line under the subject and two lines under the verb.

1. The ripening tomatoes glistened on the sunny windowsill.
2. Biofeedback reduces the pain of my headaches.
3. Elena nervously twisted a strand of hair around her fingers.
4. My brother made our stereo cabinet from inexpensive particleboard.
5. A jackrabbit bounds up to fifteen feet in one leap.
6. The blind woman knits woolen caps for Christmas presents.
7. The amateur astronomer set his alarm for 3 A.M. to view the lunar eclipse.
8. On St. Patrick's Day, our neighborhood tavern serves green beer.
9. Children sometimes eat the dangerous lead-based paint found in old houses.
10. During my parents' divorce, I felt like a rag doll being torn between two people.

MORE ABOUT SUBJECTS AND VERBS

1   A sentence may have more than one verb, more than one subject, or several subjects and verbs.

The engine coughed and sputtered.

Broken glass and empty cans littered the parking lot.

Joyce, Brenda, and Robert met after class and headed downtown.

2   The subject of a sentence never appears within a prepositional phrase. A *prepositional phrase* is simply a group of words that begins with a preposition. Following is a list of common prepositions:

about	before	by	inside	over
above	behind	during	into	through
across	below	except	of	to
among	beneath	for	off	toward
around	beside	from	on	under
at	between	in	onto	with

Cross out prepositional phrases when looking for the subject of a sentence.

The weathered old house perched unsteadily on its rotted foundation.

The label on that mayonnaise jar can be easily removed with hot water.

The color picture on our TV set turns black and white during a storm.

The murky waters of the polluted lake spilled over the dam.

The amber lights on its sides outlined the tractor-trailer in the hazy dusk.

3   Many verbs consist of more than one word. Here, for example, are some of the many forms of the verb *work*:

work	worked	should work
works	were working	will be working
does work	have worked	can work
is working	had worked	could be working
are working	had been working	must have worked

Notes

a   Words like *not, just, never, only,* and *always* are not part of the verb although they may appear within the verb.

Rebecca has just finished filling out her tax form.

The intersection has not always been this dangerous.

b   No verb preceded by *to* is ever the verb of a sentence.

At night, my son likes to read under the covers.

Evelyn decided to separate from her husband.

c   No *-ing* word by itself is ever the verb of a sentence. (It may be part of the verb, but it must have a helping verb in front of it.)

They going on a trip this weekend.   (not a sentence, because the verb is not complete)

They are going on a trip this weekend.   (a sentence)

Activity

Draw a single line under subjects and a double line under verbs. Crossing out prepositional phrases may help you to find the subjects.

1.   The top of our refrigerator is covered with dusty pots and pans.
2.   A new muffler and tail pipe were just installed in my car.
3.   The people in the all-night coffee shop seemed weary and lost.
4.   Every plant in the dim room bent toward the small window.
5.   A glaring headline about the conviction of a local congressman attracted my attention.
6.   Two of the biggest stores on our main shopping street are going out of business.
7.   The glow of the stereo's tiny red light always reminds me to turn off the amplifier.
8.   Both private wells and public reservoirs in our area are contaminated with deadly chemicals.
9.   The jar of peppercorns tumbled from the spice shelf and shattered on the floor.
10.   The scar in the hollow of Brian's throat is the result of an emergency operation to clear his windpipe.

■ Review Test

Draw a single line under subjects and a double line under verbs. Crossing out prepositional phrases may help you to find the subjects.

1. With one graceful motion, the shortstop fielded the grounder and threw to first base.
2. Forty-seven czars are buried within the walls of Moscow's Kremlin.
3. Before class, Barbara and Aaron rushed to the coffee machine in the hall.
4. I punched and prodded my feather pillow before settling down to sleep.
5. Waiting in the long ticket line, Matt shifted his weight from one foot to the other.
6. Cattle branding was practiced by ancient Egyptians over four thousand years ago.
7. Lilacs and honeysuckle perfume our yard on summer nights.
8. The mail carrier abruptly halted her Jeep and backed up toward the mailbox.
9. During the American Revolution, some brides rejected white wedding gowns and wore red as a symbol of rebellion.
10. The little girl's frantic family called a psychic to help locate the child.

SENTENCE FRAGMENTS

Every sentence must have a subject and a verb and must express a complete thought. A word group that lacks a subject or a verb and that does not express a complete thought is a *fragment*. Following are the most common types of fragments that people write:

1 Dependent-word fragments
2 *-ing* and *to* fragments
3 Added-detail fragments
4 Missing-subject fragments

Once you understand the specific kind or kinds of fragments that you may write, you should be able to eliminate them from your writing. The following pages explain all four fragment types.

DEPENDENT-WORD FRAGMENTS

Some word groups that begin with a dependent word are fragments. At the top of the next page is a list of common dependent words. Whenever you start a sentence with one of these words, you must be careful that a fragment does not result.

> ### *Dependent Words*
>
> | | | |
> |---|---|---|
> | after | if, even if | when, whenever |
> | although, though | in order that | where, wherever |
> | as | since | whether |
> | because | that, so that | which, whichever |
> | before | unless | while |
> | even though | until | who |
> | how | what, whatever | whose |

The word group beginning with the dependent word *After* in the example below is a fragment.

After I cashed my paycheck. I treated myself to dinner.

A *dependent statement*—one starting with a dependent word like *After*—cannot stand alone. It depends on another statement to complete the thought. *After I cashed my paycheck* is a dependent statement. It leaves us hanging. We expect in the same sentence to find out *what happened after* the writer cashed the check. When a writer does not follow through and complete a thought, a fragment results.

To correct the fragment, simply follow through and complete the thought:

After I cashed my paycheck, I treated myself to dinner.

Remember, then, that *dependent statements by themselves are fragments*. They must be attached to a statement that makes sense standing alone.

Here are two other examples of dependent-word fragments.

I won't leave the house. Until I hear from you.

Rick finally picked up the socks. Which he had thrown on the floor days ago.

Until I hear from you is a fragment; it does not make sense standing by itself. We want to know in the same statement *what cannot happen* until I hear from you. The writer must complete the thought. Likewise, *Which he had thrown on the floor days ago* is not in itself a complete thought. We want to know in the same statement what *which* refers to.

How to Correct a Dependent-Word Fragment

In most cases you can correct a dependent-word fragment by attaching it to the sentence that comes after it or the sentence that comes before it:

After I cashed my paycheck, I treated myself to dinner.
(The fragment has been attached to the sentence that comes after it.)

I won't leave the house until I hear from you.
(The fragment has been attached to the sentence that comes before it.)

Rick finally picked up the socks which he had thrown on the floor days ago.
(The fragment has been attached to the sentence that comes before it.)

Another way of correcting a dependent-word fragment is simply to eliminate the dependent word by rewriting the sentence.

I cashed my paycheck and then treated myself to dinner.
I will wait to hear from you.
He had thrown them on the floor days ago.

Notes

a Use a comma if a dependent word group comes at the *beginning* of a sentence (see also page 397):

After I cashed my paycheck, I treated myself to dinner.

However, do not generally use a comma if the dependent word group comes at the *end* of a sentence:

I won't leave the house until I hear from you.

Rick finally picked up the socks which he had thrown on the floor days ago.

b Sometimes the dependent words *who, that, which,* or *where* appear not at the very start but *near* the start of a word group. A fragment often results:

I drove slowly past the old brick house. The place where I grew up.

The place where I grew up is not in itself a complete thought. We want to know in the same statement *where was the place* the writer grew up. The fragment can be corrected by attaching it to the sentence that comes before it:

I drove slowly past the old brick house, the place where I grew up.

Activity 1

Turn each of the dependent word groups into a sentence by adding a complete thought. Put a comma after the dependent word group if a dependent word starts the sentence.

Examples   Although I felt miserable
Although I felt miserable, I tried to smile for the photographer.

The man who found my wallet
The man who found my wallet returned it the next day.

1. If I have to work late

   _____

   _____

2. Because it was raining

   _____

   _____

3. When I heard the news

   _____

   _____

4. Because I couldn't find the car keys

   _____

   _____

5. The restaurant that we tried

   _____

   _____

Activity 2

Underline the dependent-word fragment in each selection. Then rewrite the selections, correcting each fragment by attaching it to the sentence that comes before or the sentence that comes after—whichever sounds more natural. Put a comma after the dependent word group if it starts the sentence.

1. Whenever I spray deodorant. My cat arches her back. She thinks she is hearing a hissing enemy.

   _____

   _____

2. My father, a salesman, was on the road all week. We had a great time playing football in the house. Until he came home for the weekend.

    _____

    _____

3. If Kim takes too long saying good-bye to her boyfriend. Her father will start flicking the porch light. Then he will come out with a flashlight.

    _____

    _____

4. I bought a calendar watch. Which is running fast. Last week had sixteen days.

    _____

    _____

5. Before I move, I scrub both my old and new apartments. After all the apartments I've left spick-and-span. I think it's my turn to move into a clean one.

    _____

    _____

-*ING* AND *TO* FRAGMENTS

When an -*ing* word appears at or near the start of a word group, a fragment may result. Such fragments often lack a subject and part of the verb. Underline the word groups in the selections below that contain -*ing* words. Each is a fragment.

1. Ellen walked all over the neighborhood yesterday. Trying to find her dog Bo. Several people claimed they had seen him only hours before.
2. We sat back to watch the movie. Not expecting anything special. To our surprise, we clapped, cheered, and cried for the next two hours.
3. I telephoned the balloon store. It being the day before our wedding anniversary. I knew my wife would be surprised to receive a dozen heart-shaped balloons.

People sometimes write -*ing* fragments because they think the subject in one sentence will work for the next word group as well. Thus, in the first selection, they think the subject *Ellen* in the opening sentence will also serve as the subject for *Trying to find her dog Bo*. But the subject must actually be *in* the sentence.

How to Correct *-ing* Fragments

1 Attach the fragment to the sentence that comes before or the sentence that comes after it, whichever makes sense. Selection 1 could read: "Ellen walked all over the neighborhood yesterday trying to find her dog Bo."

2 Add a subject and change the *-ing* verb part to the correct form of the verb. Selection 2 could read: "We didn't expect anything special."

3 Change *being* to the correct form of the verb *be* (*am, are, is, was, were*). Selection 3 could read: "It was the day before our wedding anniversary."

How to Correct *to* Fragments

When *to* appears at or near the start of a word group, a fragment sometimes results:

At the Chinese restaurant, Tim used chopsticks. To impress his date. He spent one hour eating a small bowl of rice.

The second word group is a fragment and can be corrected by adding it to the preceding sentence:

At the Chinese restaurant, Tim used chopsticks to impress his date.

Activity 1

Underline the *-ing* fragment in each of the selections that follow. Then make it a sentence by rewriting it, using the method described in parentheses.

Example Stepping hard on the accelerator. Stan tried to beat the truck to the intersection. He lost by a hood.
(Add the fragment to the sentence that comes after it.)
Stepping hard on the accelerator, Stan tried to beat the truck

to the intersection.

1. Marble-sized hailstones fell from the sky. Flattening the young plants in the cornfield. A year's work was lost in an hour.
(Add the fragment to the preceding sentence.)

_____

_____

2. My grandmother, who is seventy, delivers papers by car every morning. Then returning home to make breakfast for my grandfather. She has more energy than I do.
    (Correct the fragment by adding the subject *she* and changing *returning* to the proper form of the verb, *returns*.)

    _____

    _____

3. My phone doesn't ring. Instead, a light on it blinks. The reason for this being that I am partially deaf.
    (Correct the fragment by changing *being* to the proper form of the verb, *is*.)

    _____

    _____

Activity 2

Underline the *-ing* or *to* fragment in each selection. Then rewrite each selection, correcting the fragments by using one of the three methods described above.

1. Flora scratched her mosquito bites. Trying to stop the itching. Instead, they began to bleed.

    _____

    _____

2. I put a box of baking soda in the freezer. To get rid of the musty smell. However, my ice cubes still taste like old socks.

    _____

    _____

3. Staring at the clock on the far wall. I nervously began my speech. I was afraid to look at any of the people in the room.

    _____

    _____

4. Larry sat quietly at his desk. Fantasizing about the upcoming weekend. He might meet the girl of his dreams at Saturday night's party.

    _____

    _____

5. To get to the bus station from here. You have to walk two blocks out of your way. The sidewalk is torn up because of construction work.

    _____

    _____

ADDED-DETAIL FRAGMENTS

Added-detail fragments lack a subject and a verb. They often begin with one of the following words:

also	especially	except	for example	including	such as

Underline the one added-detail fragment in each of the selections that follow:

1. Before a race, I eat starchy food. Such as bread and spaghetti. The carbohydrates provide quick energy.
2. Bob is taking a night course in auto mechanics. Also, one in plumbing. He wants to save money on household repairs.
3. My son keeps several pets in his room. Among them, hamsters, mice, and gerbils.

People often write added-detail fragments for much the same reason they write *-ing* fragments. They think the subject and verb in one sentence will serve for the next word group. But the subject and verb must be in *each* word group.

How to Correct Added-Detail Fragments

1 Attach the fragment to the complete thought that precedes it. Selection 1 could read: ''Before a race, I eat starchy foods such as bread and spaghetti.''

2 Add a subject and a verb to the fragment to make it a complete sentence. Selection 2 could read: ''Bob is taking a night course in auto mechanics. Also, he is taking one in plumbing.''

3 Change words as necessary to make the fragment part of the preceding sentence. Selection 3 could read: ''My son keeps several pets, including hamsters, mice, and gerbils, in his room.''

Activity 1

Underline the fragment in each of the selections on the following page. Then make it a sentence by rewriting it, using the method described in parentheses.

Example My mother likes watching daytime television shows. Especially old movies and soap operas. She says that daytime television is less violent.
(Add the fragment to the preceding sentence.)
My mother likes watching daytime television shows, especially old movies and soap operas.

1. Luis works evenings in a video store. He enjoys the fringe benefits. For example, seeing the new movies first.
   (Correct the fragment by adding the subject and verb *he sees*.)

   _____

   _____

2. Bob's fingernails are ragged from years of working as a mechanic. And his fingertips are always black. Like ink pads.
   (Add the fragment to the preceding sentence.)

   _____

   _____

3. Schools are beginning to use advanced technology. For instance, computers and word processors. Tomorrow's students will be "computer literate."
   (Correct the fragment by adding the subject and verb *they are using*.)

   _____

   _____

Activity 2

Underline the added-detail fragment in each selection. Then rewrite to correct the fragment. Use one of the three methods described above.

1. Left-handed students face problems. For example, right-handed desks. Spiral notebooks can also be uncomfortable to use.

   _____

   _____

2. Mrs. Daly always wears her lucky clothes to bingo. Such as a blouse printed with four-leaf clovers. She also carries a rhinestone horseshoe.

   _____

   _____

3. With all the moths swarming around the stadium lights. I almost thought it was snowing. The eighty-degree weather, though, made this unlikely.

   _____

   _____

4. Jack buys and sells paper collectors' items. For instance, baseball cards and movie posters. He sets up a display at local flea markets and county fairs.

   _____

   _____

5. I wonder now why I had to learn certain subjects. Such as geometry. No one has ever asked me about the hypotenuse of a triangle.

_____

_____

MISSING-SUBJECT FRAGMENTS

Underline the word group in which the subject is missing in each selection below.

1. Alice loved getting wedding presents. But hated writing thank-you notes.
2. Mickey has orange soda and potato chips for breakfast. Then eats more junk food, like root beer and cookies, for lunch.

How to Correct Missing-Subject Fragments

1 Attach the fragment to the preceding sentence. Selection 1 could read: "Alice loved getting her wedding presents but hated writing the thank-you notes."
2 Add a subject (which can often be a pronoun standing for the subject in the preceding sentence). Selection 2 could read: "Then he eats more junk food, like root beer and cookies, for lunch."

Activity

Underline the missing-subject fragment in each selection. Then rewrite that part of the selection needed to correct the fragment. Use one of the two methods of correction described above.

1. Every other day, Karen runs two miles. Then does fifty sit-ups. She hasn't lost weight, but what she had has been redistributed.

_____

_____

_____

2. I like all kinds of fresh pizza. But refuse to eat frozen pies. The sauce on them is always dried out, and the crust tastes like leather.

_____

_____

_____

3. Scientists have invented a computerized doctor. It takes every Wednesday off. And plays video golf.

    _____

    _____

    _____

4. To be a defensive driver, you must assume the worst. Every other driver on the road is incompetent. And is out there trying to kill you.

    _____

    _____

    _____

5. Last semester, I took six courses. And worked part-time in a discount drug store. Now that the term is all over, I don't know how I did it.

    _____

    _____

    _____

A Review: How to Check for Sentence Fragments

1   Read your paper aloud from the *last* sentence to the *first*. You will be better able to see and hear whether each word group you read is a complete thought.

2   Ask yourself of any word group you think is a fragment: Does this contain a subject and a verb and express a complete thought?

3   More specifically, be on the lookout for the most common fragments:

-   Dependent-word fragments (starting with words like *after, because, since, when,* and *before*)

-   *-ing* and *to* fragments (*-ing* or *to* at or near the start of a word group)

-   Added-detail fragments (starting with words like *for example, such as, also,* and *especially*)

-   Missing-subject fragments (a verb is present but not the subject)

■ Review Test 1

Each word group in the following student paragraph is numbered. In the space provided, write C if a word group is a complete sentence; write F if it is a fragment. You will find eight fragments in the paragraph.

1. [1]I'm starting to think that there is no safe place left. [2]To ride a

2. bicycle. [3]When I try to ride on the highway, in order to go to school. [4]I

3. feel like a rabbit being pursued by predators. [5]Drivers whip past me at

4. high speeds. [6]And try to see how close they can get to my bike without

5. actually killing me. [7]When they pull onto the shoulder of the road or make

6. a right turn. [8]Drivers completely ignore my vehicle. [9]On city streets, I feel

7. more like a cockroach than a rabbit. [10]Drivers in the city despise bicycles.

8. [11]Regardless of an approaching bike rider. [12]Street-side car doors will

9. unexpectedly open. [13]Frustrated drivers who are stuck in traffic will make

10. nasty comments. [14]Or shout out obscene propositions. [15]Even pedestrians

11. in the city show their disregard for me. [16]While jaywalking across the

12. street. [17]The pedestrian will treat me, a law-abiding bicyclist, to a

13. withering look of disdain. [18]Pedestrians may even cross my path

14. deliberately. [19]As if to prove their higher position in the pecking order of

15. the city streets. [20]Today, bicycling can be hazardous to the rider's health.

16.

17.

18.

19.

20.

Now (on separate paper) correct the fragments you have found. Attach the fragments to sentences that come before or after them or make whatever other change is needed to turn each fragment into a sentence.

■ Review Test 2

Underline the two fragments in each selection below. Then make whatever changes are needed to turn the fragments into sentences.

Example   Sharon was going to charge her new suit. <u>But then decided to pay</u> <u>cash instead.</u> She remembered her New Year's resolution. <u>To cut</u> <u>down on her use of credit cards.</u>

1. We both began to tire. As we passed the halfway mark in the race. But whenever I'd hear Reggie's footsteps behind me. I pumped my legs faster.

2. I have a few phobias. Such as fear of heights and fear of dogs. My nightmare is to be trapped in a hot-air balloon. With three German shepherds.

3. My children joke that we celebrate ''Hanumas.'' With our Jewish neighbors. We share Hanukkah and Christmas activities. Including making potato pancakes at their house and decorating our tree.

4. Punching all the buttons on his radio in sequence. Phil kept looking for a good song. He was in the mood to cruise down the highway. And sing at the top of his voice.

5. I noticed two cartons of cigarettes. Sticking up out of my neighbor's trash bag. I realized he had made up his mind. To give up smoking for the fifth time this year.

6. I've decided to leave home. And rent an apartment. By being away from home and on my own. I will get along better with my parents.

7. The alley behind our house was flat. Except for a wide groove in the center. We used to sail paper boats down the groove. Whenever it rained hard enough to create a ''river'' there.

8. Don passed the computer school's aptitude test. Which qualifies him for nine months of training. Don kidded that anyone could be accepted. If he or she had four thousand dollars.

■ Review Test 3

Turn each of the following word groups into a complete sentence.

Examples With trembling hands

With trembling hands, I headed for the front of the classroom.

As the race wore on

Some runners dropped out as the race wore on.

1. After the storm passed

   _____

2. Such as fresh fruits and vegetables

   _____

3. During the mystery movie

   _____

4. But soon grew frustrated

   _____

5. Norma, who hates housework

   _____

6. To get to class on time

   _____

7. The ants swarming over the lollipop

   _____

8. Hurrying to get dressed

   _____

9. Up in the attic

   _____

10. Losing my temper

   _____

RUN-ONS

WHAT ARE RUN-ONS?

A *run-on* is two complete thoughts that are run together with no adequate sign given to mark the break between them.*

Some run-ons have no punctuation at all to mark the break between the thoughts. Such run-ons are known as *fused sentences*: they are fused or joined together as if they were only one thought.

Fused Sentence

Tim told everyone in the room to be quiet his favorite show was on.

Fused Sentence

My blow-drier shorted out I showed up for work with Harpo Marx hair.

In other run-ons, known as *comma splices,* a comma is used to connect or "splice" together the two complete thoughts. However, a comma alone is *not enough* to connect two complete thoughts. Some stronger connection than a comma alone is needed.

Comma Splice

Tim told everyone in the room to be quiet, his favorite show was on.

Comma Splice

My blow-drier shorted out, I showed up for work with Harpo Marx hair.

Comma splices are the most common kind of run-on mistake. Students sense that some kind of connection is needed between two thoughts, and so they often put a comma at the dividing point. But the comma alone is *not sufficient*. A stronger, clearer mark between the two thoughts is needed.

*Note: Some instructors refer to each complete thought in a run-on as an *independent clause.* A *clause* is simply a group of words having a subject and a verb. A clause may be *independent* (expressing a complete thought and able to stand alone) or *dependent* (not expressing a complete thought and not able to stand alone). Using this terminology, we'd say that a run-on is two independent clauses run together with no adequate sign given to mark the break between them.

HOW TO CORRECT RUN-ONS

Here are three common methods of correcting a run-on:

1   Use a period and a capital letter to break the two complete thoughts into separate sentences.

   Tim told everyone in the room to be quiet. His favorite show was on.
   My blow-drier shorted out. I showed up for work with Harpo Marx hair.

2   Use a comma plus a joining word (*and, but, for, or, nor, so, yet*) to connect the two complete thoughts:

   Tim told everyone in the room to be quiet, for his favorite show was on.
   My blow-drier shorted out, and I showed up for work with Harpo Marx hair.

3   Use a semicolon to connect the two complete thoughts:

   Tim told everyone in the room to be quiet; his favorite show was on.
   My blow-drier shorted out; I showed up for work with Harpo Marx hair.

A fourth method of correcting a run-on is to use *subordination*. The following activities will give you practice in the first three methods. Subordination will be described fully on page 449, in a section of the book that deals with sentence variety.

Method 1: Period and a Capital Letter

One way of correcting a run-on is to use a period and a capital letter at the break between the two complete thoughts. Use this method especially if the thoughts are not closely related or if another method would make the sentence too long.

Activity

Locate the split in each of the run-ons on the following page. Each is a *fused sentence*—that is, each consists of two sentences that are fused or joined together with no punctuation at all between them. Reading each sentence aloud will help you ''hear'' where a major break or split in the thought occurs. At such a point, your voice will probably drop and pause.

   Correct the run-on sentence by putting a period at the end of the first thought and a capital letter at the start of the next thought.

Example   Bev's clock radio doesn't work anymore. ~~s~~he spilled a glass of soda
on it.

1.   The telephone salesman offered a deal on vinyl siding he wanted to drop
by and give us a free estimate.

2.   Joyce, a paralegal, helps some people to write wills she assists others in
divorce and child custody proceedings.

3.   Vicky has her own unique style of dressing she wore a man's tuxedo with
a red bow tie to her cousin's wedding.

4.   Ants are attracted to water in the summer they will often enter a house
through the dishwasher.

5.   Humans have managed to adapt to any environment they can survive in
Arctic wastes, tropical jungles, and barren deserts.

6.   A five-year-old child knows over six thousand words he or she has also
learned more than one thousand rules of grammar.

7.   I rummaged around the crowded drawer looking for a pair of scissors then
it suddenly stabbed me in the finger.

8.   Squirrels like to jump from trees onto our roof their footsteps sound like
ghosts running around our attic.

9.   Today I didn't make good time driving to work every traffic light along
the way was red.

10.   As a result of a cable hookup, we now receive over forty stations on our
television I sometimes waste an entire evening just clicking from one
channel to the next.

A Warning—Words That Can Lead to Run-Ons: People often write
run-on sentences when the second complete thought begins with one of the
following words:

I	we	there	now
you	they	this	then
he, she, it	that	next	

Remember to be on the alert for run-on sentences whenever you use one of these
words in writing a paper.

Method 2: Comma and a Joining Word

Another way of correcting a run-on sentence is to use a comma plus a joining word to connect the two complete thoughts. Joining words (also called *conjunctions*) include *and, but, for, or, nor, so,* and *yet.* Here is what the four most common joining words mean:

and   in addition to, along with

Teresa works full-time for an accounting firm, and she takes evening classes.

(*And* means *in addition:* Teresa works full time for an accounting firm; *in addition,* she takes evening classes.)

but   however, except, on the other hand, just the opposite

I turned to the want ads, but I knew my dream job wouldn't be listed.

(*But* means *however:* I turned to the want ads; *however,* I knew my dream job wouldn't be listed.)

for   because, the reason why, the cause for something

Lizards become sluggish at night, for they need the sun's warmth to maintain an active body temperature.

(*For* means *because* or *the reason why:* Lizards become sluggish at night; *the reason why* is that they need the sun's warmth to maintain an active body temperature.)

so   as a result, therefore

The canoe touched bottom, so Dave pushed it toward deeper water.

(*So* means *as a result:* The canoe touched bottom; *as a result,* Dave pushed it toward deeper water.)

Activity 1

Insert the joining word (*and, but, for, so*) that logically connects the two thoughts in each sentence.

1.   Napoleon may have been a brave general, _____ he was afraid of cats.
2.   The large dog was growling at me, _____ there were white bubbles of foam around his mouth.
3.   The library had just closed, _____ I couldn't get any of the reserved books.

4. He checked on the new baby every five minutes, _____ he was afraid something would happen to her.

5. Kate thought the milk was fresh, _____ it broke up into little sour flakes in her coffee.

6. An infant elephant has no thumbs, _____ it sucks its trunk.

7. Lew heard a noise and looked out the window, _____ the only thing there was his reflection.

8. Have you noticed that one of our English teacher's eyes is green, _____ the other is brown?

9. My sister saves all her empty wine bottles, _____ she likes to make lamps out of them.

10. A young woman in our neighborhood recently tried to kill herself, _____ her friends are afraid that she will try it again.

Activity 2

Add a complete and closely related thought to go with each of the following statements. Use a comma plus the italicized joining word when you write the second thought.

Example *for* I decided to leave school an hour early, *for I had a pounding headache.*

but 1. The corner store is convenient _____

for 2. Leo attended night class _____

and 3. Brenda studied for an hour before dinner _____

so 4. Our field trip had been canceled _____

but 5. I needed a haircut _____

Activity 3

Correct each run-on with either (1) a period and a capital letter or (2) a comma and a logical joining word. Do not use the same method of correction for every sentence.

You will notice that some of the run-ons are fused sentences (there is no punctuation between the two complete thoughts) and some are comma splices (there is only a comma between the two complete thoughts). One sentence is correct.

Example   There was a strange odor in the house,*so*Burt called the gas company immediately.

1. Jackie smeared cream cheese on the bagel half, then she popped it into her mouth.

2. Cockroaches adapt to any environment they have even been found living inside nuclear reactors.

3. My dog was panting from the heat I decided to wet him down with the garden hose.

4. The college installed a dish antenna outside the science building it picks up satellite broadcasting from all over the world.

5. The best-selling items in the zoo gift shop are the stuffed pandas and the polar bear T-shirts the profits from these items help support the real animals in the zoo.

6. The bristles of the paintbrushes were very stiff, soaking them in turpentine made them soft again.

7. Tran bought cassettes to listen to on the way to work, some of them were recordings of best-selling books.

8. Last week, Rita's two boys chased the baby-sitter out of the house, now the girl won't come back.

9. We knew there had been a power failure, for all the clocks in the building were forty-seven minutes slow.

10. I volunteered to run the ''Meals on Wheels'' service in our city we deliver hot meals to sick or housebound people.

Method 3: Semicolon

A third method of correcting a run-on sentence is to use a semicolon to mark the break between two thoughts. A *semicolon* (;) looks like a period above a comma and is sometimes called a *strong comma*. A semicolon signals more of a pause than a comma alone but not quite the full pause of a period. When it is used to correct run-on sentences, the semicolon can be used alone or with a transitional word.

Semicolon Alone: Here are some earlier sentences that were connected with a comma plus a joining word. Now they are connected by a semicolon alone. Notice that the semicolon alone—unlike the comma alone—can be used to connect the two complete thoughts in each sentence:

> There had been a huge power failure; every house on the street was dark.
>
> Lew heard a noise and looked out the window; the only thing there was his reflection.
>
> He checked on the new baby every five minutes; he was afraid something would happen to her.
>
> Lizards become sluggish at night; they need the sun's warmth to maintain an active body temperature.
>
> The large dog was growling at me; there were white bubbles of foam around his mouth.

Using the semicolon can add to sentence variety. For some people, however, the semicolon is a confusing mark of punctuation. Keep in mind that if you are not comfortable using it, you can and should use one of the first two methods of correcting a run-on sentence.

Activity

Insert a semicolon where the break occurs between the two complete thoughts in each of the following sentences.

Example   The plumber gave me an estimate of sixty dollars; I decided to repair the faucet myself.

1.   The children stared at the artichokes on their plates they didn't know how to eat the strange vegetable.

2. I changed that light bulb just last week now it's blown again.

3. The "no-frills" supermarket doesn't sell perishables like milk or meat customers must bring their own bags or boxes to pack their bargains.

4. Elaine woke up at 3 A.M. to the smell of sizzling bacon her husband was having another insomnia attack.

5. Jamie curled up under the covers she tried to get warm by grasping her icy feet with her chilly hands.

6. Three single mothers rent one house they share bills and help each other out.

7. Ice had formed on the inside edge of our window Joey scratched a J in it with his finger.

8. Charles peered into the microscope he saw only his own eyelashes.

9. Guests were laughing and drinking at the party my uncle was doing his John Wayne imitation.

10. I angrily punched a hole in the wall with my fist later I covered the hole with a picture.

Semicolon with a Transitional Word   A semicolon is sometimes used with a transitional word and a comma to join two complete thoughts. Here are some examples:

Larry believes in being prepared for emergencies; therefore, he stockpiles canned goods in his basement.

I tried to cash my paycheck; however, I had forgotten to bring identification.

Athletic shoes must fit perfectly; otherwise, the wearer may injure the feet or ankles.

A short nap at the end of the day relaxes me; in addition, it gives me the energy to spend the evening on my homework.

Some zoo animals have not learned how to be good parents; as a result, baby animals are sometimes brought up in zoo nurseries and even in private homes.

People use seventeen muscles when they smile; on the other hand, they use forty-three muscles when they frown.

On the following page is a list of common transitional words (also known as *adverbial conjunctions*), with brief meanings.

Transitional Word	*Meaning*
however	but
nevertheless	however
on the other hand	however
instead	as a substitute
meanwhile	in the intervening time
otherwise	under other conditions
indeed	in fact
in addition	also, and
also	in addition
moreover	in addition
furthermore	in addition
as a result	thus, therefore
thus	as a result
consequently	as a result
therefore	as a result

Activity

For each sentence, choose a logical transitional word from the group in the box above and write it in the space provided. Put a semicolon *before* the connector and a comma *after* it.

Example   I dread going to parties; *however*, my husband loves meeting new people.

1. Jackie suffers from migraine headaches _____ her doctor has advised her to avoid caffeine and alcohol.

2. Ray's apartment is always neat and clean _____ the interior of his car looks like the aftermath of a tornado.

3. I try to attend all my math classes _____ I'll get too far behind to pass the weekly quizzes.

4. Dan was singing Whitney Houston tunes in the shower _____ his toast was burning in the kitchen.

5. The reporter was tough and experienced _____ even he was stunned by the tragic events.

A Note on Subordination

A fourth method of joining related thoughts together is to use subordination. *Subordination* is a way of showing that one thought in a sentence is not as important as another thought. (Subordination is explained in full on page 449.) Here are three earlier sentences, recast so that one idea is subordinated to (made less important than) the other idea:

Because the library had just closed, I couldn't get any of the reserved books.

When the canoe touched bottom, Dave pushed the craft toward deeper water.

I didn't make good time driving to work today, because every traffic light was red.

A Review: How to Check for Run-On Sentences

1 To see if a sentence is a run-on, read it aloud and listen for a break marking two complete thoughts. Your voice will probably drop and pause at the break.

2 To check an entire paper, read it aloud from the *last* sentence to the *first*. Doing so will help you hear and see each complete thought.

3 Be on the lookout for words that can lead to run-on sentences:

I	he, she, it	they	this	then
you	we	there	that	next

4 Correct run-on sentences by using one of the following methods:

- A period and a capital letter
- A comma and a joining word (*and, but, for, or, nor, so, yet*)
- A semicolon
- Subordination (as explained on page 449)

■ Review Test 1

Correct each run-on with either (1) a period and a capital letter or (2) a comma (if needed) and the joining word *and, but, for,* or *so.* Do not use the same method of correction for every sentence.

Some of the run-ons are fused sentences (there is no punctuation between the two complete thoughts) and some are comma splices (there is only a comma between the two complete thoughts). One sentence is correct.

1. Our boss expects us to work four hours without a break, he wanders off to a vending machine at least once an hour.

2. By late afternoon the bank had closed its front doors for the day I moved my car into a long line waiting to use the bank's drive-in window.

3. Chuck bent over and lifted the heavy tray then he heard an ominous crack in his back.

4. The branches of the tree were bare they made a dark feathery pattern against the orange-pink sunset.

5. In the grimy bakery window, cobwebs were in every corner, a rat was crawling over a birthday cake.

6. Our class wanted to do something for the earthquake victims, we sent a donation to the Red Cross.

7. My ex-husband hit me just once in our marriage five minutes later I was packed and walking out the door.

8. The boys dared each other to enter the abandoned building then they heard a strange rustling noise coming from the murky interior.

9. The average American teenager spends thirty-eight hours a week on schoolwork the average Japanese teenager spends about sixty.

10. We stocked our backpacks with high-calorie candy bars, and we also brought bags of dried apricots and peaches.

■ Review Test 2

Correct each run-on by using either (1) a period and a capital letter, (2) a comma and a joining word, or (3) a semicolon. Do not use one method exclusively.

1. The magazine had lain in the damp mailbox for two days its pages were blurry and swollen.

2. With a groan, Margo pried off her high heels, then she plunged her swollen feet into a bucket of baking soda and hot water.

3. At 2 A.M. the last customer left the diner, a busboy began stacking chairs on the tables for the night.

4. Hypnosis has nothing to do with the occult it is merely a state of deep relaxation.

5. Many young adults today live at home with their parents this allows them to save money for the future.

6. I waited for the clanking train to clear the intersection rusty boxcars just kept rolling slowly along the rails.

7. Science will soon produce tomatoes that are more nutritious, they will also be square-shaped for easier packing.

8. Originally, horses were too small to carry riders very far larger horses had to be bred for use in warfare.

9. Suitcases circled on the conveyor belt at the airline baggage claim loose oranges from a broken carton tumbled along with them.

10. The broken soda machine dispensed either a cup or a soda, it would not provide both at the same time.

■ Review Test 3

Locate and correct the five run-ons in the passage that follows.

My worst experience of the week was going home for lunch, rather than eating at work. My children didn't know I was coming, they had used most of the bread on hand. All I had to make a sandwich with were two thin, crumpled pieces of crust. I sat there eating my tattered sandwich and trying to relax, then the telephone rang. It was for my daughter, who was in the bathroom, she called down to me that I should get the person's name and number. As soon as I sat down again, someone knocked on the door, it was a neatly dressed couple with bright eyes who wanted to talk with me about a higher power in life. I politely got rid of them and went back to finish lunch. I thought I would relax over my coffee I had to break up a fight between my two young sons about which television channel to watch. As a last bit of frustration, my daughter came downstairs and asked me to drive her over to a friend's house before I went back to work.

■ Review Test 4

Write quickly for five minutes about what you did this past weekend. Don't worry about spelling, punctuation, finding exact words, or organizing your thoughts. Just focus on writing as many words as you can without stopping.

After you have finished, go back and correct any run-ons in your writing.

REGULAR AND IRREGULAR VERBS

REGULAR VERBS

A Brief Review of Regular Verbs

Every verb has four principal parts: *present, past, past participle*, and *present participle*. These parts can be used to build all the verb tenses (the times shown by a verb).

Most verbs in English are regular. The past and past participles of a regular verb are formed by adding *-d* or *-ed* to the present. The *past participle* is the form of the verb used with the helping verbs *have, has,* or *had* (or some form of *be* with passive verbs). The *present participle* is formed by adding *-ing* to the present.

Here are the principal parts of some regular verbs:

Present	Past	Past Participle	Present Participle
shout	shouted	shouted	shouting
prepare	prepared	prepared	preparing
surprise	surprised	surprised	surprising
tease	teased	teased	teasing
frighten	frightened	frightened	frightening

Nonstandard Forms of Regular Verbs

Many people have grown up in communities where nonstandard forms of regular verbs are used in everyday speech. Instead of saying, for example, "That girl *looks* tired," a person using a community dialect might say, "That girl *look* tired." Instead of saying, "Yesterday I *fixed* the car," a person using a community dialect might say, "Yesterday I *fix* the car." Community dialects have richness and power but are a drawback in college and in the world of work, where regular English verb forms must be used.

The chart below compares the nonstandard and the regular verb forms of the verb *work*.

Nonstandard Verb Form (Do not use in your writing)		*Regular Verb Form* (Use for clear communication)	
Present tense			
I works	we works	I work	we work
you works	you works	you work	you work
he, she, it work	they work	he, she, it works	they work
Past tense			
I work	we work	I worked	we worked
you work	you work	you worked	you worked
he, she, it work	they work	he, she, it worked	they worked

To avoid nonstandard usage, memorize the forms shown above for the regular verb *work*. Then use the activities that follow to help make the inclusion of verb endings a writing habit.

Present Tense Endings: The verb ending *-s* or *-es* is needed with a regular verb in the present tense when the subject is *he, she, it,* or any *one person or thing*.

He read<u>s</u> every night.

She watch<u>es</u> television every night.

It appear<u>s</u> they have little in common.

Activity

Some verbs in the sentences that follow need -*s* or -*es* endings. Cross out each nonstandard verb form and write the standard form in the space provided.

_____ 1. My radio wake me up every morning with soft music.

_____ 2. Lyle always clown around at the start of the class.

_____ 3. My wife watch our baby in the morning, and I take over afternoons.

_____ 4. Brenda want to go to nursing school next year.

_____ 5. My brain work much better at night than it does in early morning.

Past Tense Endings: The verb ending -*d* or -*ed* is needed with a regular verb in the past tense.

This morning I completed my research paper.

The recovering hospital patient walked slowly down the corridor.

Some students hissed when the new assignment was given out.

Activity

Some verbs in the sentences that follow need -*d* or -*ed* endings. Cross out each nonstandard verb form and write the standard form in the space provided.

_____ 1. One of my teeth cave in when I bit on the hard pretzel.

_____ 2. The accident victim complain of dizziness right before passing out.

_____ 3. We realize a package was missing when we got back from shopping.

_____ 4. I burn a hole in my shirt while ironing it.

_____ 5. The impatient driver edge her car into the intersection while the light was still red.

IRREGULAR VERBS

Irregular verbs have irregular forms in the past tense and past participle. For example, the past tense of the irregular verb *choose* is *chose*; its past participle is *chosen*.

Almost everyone has some degree of trouble with irregular verbs. When you are unsure about the form of a verb, you can check the list of irregular verbs on the following pages. (The present participle is not shown on this list because it is formed simply by adding- *ing* to the base form of the verb.) Or you can check a dictionary, which gives the principal parts of irregular verbs.

A List of Irregular Verbs

Present	*Past*	*Past Participle*
arise	arose	arisen
awake	awoke *or* awaked	awoken *or* awaked
be (am, are, is)	was (were)	been
become	became	become
begin	began	begun
bend	bent	bent
bite	bit	bitten
blow	blew	blown
break	broke	broken
bring	brought	brought
build	built	built
burst	burst	burst
buy	bought	bought
catch	caught	caught
choose	chose	chosen
come	came	come
cost	cost	cost
cut	cut	cut
do (does)	did	done
draw	drew	drawn
drink	drank	drunk
drive	drove	driven
eat	ate	eaten
fall	fell	fallen
feed	fed	fed
feel	felt	felt
fight	fought	fought
find	found	found
fly	flew	flown
freeze	froze	frozen
get	got	got *or* gotten
give	gave	given
go (goes)	went	gone
grow	grew	grown
have (has)	had	had
hear	heard	heard
hide	hid	hidden
hold	held	held

Present	Past	Past Participle
hurt	hurt	hurt
keep	kept	kept
know	knew	known
lay	laid	laid
lead	led	led
leave	left	left
lend	lent	lent
let	let	let
lie	lay	lain
light	lit	lit
lose	lost	lost
make	made	made
meet	met	met
pay	paid	paid
ride	rode	ridden
ring	rang	rung
run	ran	run
say	said	said
see	saw	seen
sell	sold	sold
send	sent	sent
shake	shook	shaken
shrink	shrank	shrunk
shut	shut	shut
sing	sang	sung
sit	sat	sat
sleep	slept	slept
speak	spoke	spoken
spend	spent	spent
stand	stood	stood
steal	stole	stolen
stick	stuck	stuck
sting	stung	stung
swear	swore	sworn
swim	swam	swum
take	took	taken
teach	taught	taught
tear	tore	torn
tell	told	told
think	thought	thought
wake	woke *or* waked	woken *or* waked
wear	wore	worn
win	won	won
write	wrote	written

Activity

Cross out the incorrect verb form in each of the following sentences. Then write the correct form of the verb in the space provided.

flown

Example   After it had ~~flew~~ into the picture window, the dazed bird huddled on the ground.

1.   As graduation neared, Michelle worried about the practicality of the major she'd chose.

2.   Before we could find seats, the theater darkened and the opening credits begun to roll.

3.   To be polite, I drunk the slightly sour wine that my grandfather poured from his carefully hoarded supply.

4.   With a thunderous crack, the telephone pole breaked in half from the impact of the speeding car.

5.   The inexperienced nurse shrunk from touching the patient's raw, burned skin.

6.   After a day on the noisy construction site, Sam's ears rung for hours with a steady hum.

7.   Sheila had forgot to write her social security number on the test form, so the computer rejected her answer sheet.

8.   If I had went to work ten minutes earlier, I would have avoided being caught in the gigantic traffic snarl.

9.   After the bicycle hit a patch of soft sand, the rider was throwed into the thorny bushes by the roadside.

10. Prehistoric people blowed paint over their outstretched hands to stencil their handprints on cave walls.

Nonstandard Forms of Three Common Irregular Verbs

People who use nonstandard forms of regular verbs also tend to use nonstandard forms of three common irregular verbs: *be, have,* and *do.* Instead of saying, for example, ''My neighbors *are* nice people,'' a person using a nonstandard form might say, ''Our neighbors *be* nice people.'' Instead of saying, ''She doesn't agree,'' they might say, ''She *don't* agree.'' Instead of saying, ''We have tickets,'' they might say, ''We *has* tickets.''

The following charts compare the nonstandard and the standard forms of *be*, *have,* and *do*.

Be

Community Dialect (Do not use in your writing)		**Standard English** (Use for clear communication)	
Present tense			
I be (*or* is)	we be	I am	we are
you be	you be	you are	you are
he, she, it be	they be	he, she, it is	they are
Past tense			
I were	we was	I was	we were
you was	you was	you were	you were
he, she, it were	they was	he, she, it was	they were

Have

Community Dialect (Do not use in your writing)		**Standard English** (Use for clear communication)	
Present tense			
I has	we has	I have	we have
you has	you has	you have	you have
he, she, it have	they has	he, she, it has	they have
Past tense			
I has	we has	I had	we had
you has	you has	you had	you had
he, she, it have	they has	he, she, it had	they had

Do

<table>
<tr><td colspan="2">Community Dialect
(Do not use in your writing)</td><td colspan="2">Standard English
(Use for clear communication)</td></tr>
<tr><td colspan="4" align="center">Present tense</td></tr>
<tr><td>I does</td><td>we do</td><td>I do</td><td>we do</td></tr>
<tr><td>you does</td><td>you does</td><td>you do</td><td>you do</td></tr>
<tr><td>he, she, it do</td><td>they does</td><td>he, she, it does</td><td>they do</td></tr>
<tr><td colspan="4" align="center">Past tense</td></tr>
<tr><td>I done</td><td>we done</td><td>I did</td><td>we did</td></tr>
<tr><td>you done</td><td>you done</td><td>you did</td><td>you did</td></tr>
<tr><td>he, she, it done</td><td>they done</td><td>he, she, it did</td><td>they did</td></tr>
</table>

Note: Many people have trouble with one negative form of *do*. They will say, for example, "He don't agree" instead of "He doesn't agree," or they will say "The door don't work" instead of "The door doesn't work." Be careful to avoid the common mistake of using *don't* instead of *doesn't*.

Activity

Cross out the nonstandard verb form in each sentence. Then write the standard form of *be, have,* or *do* in the space provided.

_____ 1. My cat, Tugger, be the toughest animal I know.

_____ 2. He have survived many close calls.

_____ 3. Three years ago, he were caught inside a car's engine.

_____ 4. He have one ear torn off and lost the sight in one eye.

_____ 5. We was surprised that he lived through the accident.

_____ 6. Within weeks, though, he were back to normal.

_____ 7. Then, last year, we was worried that we would lose Tugger.

_____ 8. Lumps that was growing on his back turned out to be cancer.

_____ 9. But the vet done an operation that saved Tugger's life.

_____ 10. By now, we know that Tugger really do have nine lives.

■ Review Test 1

Cross out the incorrect verb form in each sentence. Then write the correct form in the space provided.

_____ 1. The health inspectors walk into the kitchen as the cook was picking up a hamburger off the floor.

_____ 2. The thieves would have stole my stereo, but I had had it engraved with a special identification number.

_____ 3. At the Chinese restaurant, Dave choose his food by the number.

_____ 4. He had tore his girl friend's picture into little pieces and tossed them out the window.

_____ 5. Because I has asthma, I carry an inhaler to use when I lose my breath.

_____ 6. Baked potatoes doesn't have as many calories as I thought.

_____ 7. The grizzly bear, with the dart dangling from its side, begun to feel the effects of the powerful tranquilizer.

_____ 8. Yesterday I check my bank balance and saw my money was getting low.

_____ 9. Many childhood diseases has almost vanished in the United States.

_____ 10. Nancy sticked notes on the refrigerator with fruit-shaped magnets.

■ Review Test 2

Write short sentences that use the form requested for the following verbs.

Example Past of _grow_ _I grew my own tomatoes last year._ _____

1. Past of _know_ _____

2. Present of _take_ _____

3. Past participle of _give_ _____

4. Past participle of _write_ _____

5. Past of _do_ _____

6. Past of _talk_ _____

7. Present of _begin_ _____

8. Past of _go_ _____

9. Past participle of _see_ _____

10. Present of _drive_ _____

SUBJECT-VERB AGREEMENT

A verb must agree with its subject in number. A *singular subject* (one person or thing) takes a singular verb. A *plural subject* (more than one person or thing) takes a plural verb. Mistakes in subject-verb agreement are sometimes made in the following situations:

1   When words come between the subject and the verb
2   When a verb comes before the subject
3   With compound subjects
4   With indefinite pronouns

Each of these situations is explained on the following pages.

WORDS BETWEEN SUBJECT AND VERB

Words that come between the subject and the verb do not change subject-verb agreement. In the sentence

The crinkly <u>lines</u> *around Joan's eyes* <u><u>give</u></u> her a friendly look.

the subject (*lines*) is plural and so the verb (*give*) is plural. The words *around Joan's eyes* that come between the subject and the verb do not affect subject-verb agreement.

To help find the subject of certain sentences, you should cross out prepositional phrases.

The lumpy <u>salt</u> ~~in the shakers~~ <u><u>needs</u></u> to be changed.

An old <u>television</u> ~~with a round screen~~ <u><u>has sat</u></u> in our basement for years.

Activity

Underline the subject and lightly cross out any words that come between the subject and the verb. Then double-underline the verb choice in parentheses that you believe is correct.

1. Some members of the parents' association (want, wants) to ban certain books from the school library.
2. The rising costs of necessities like food and shelter (force, forces) many elderly people to live in poverty.
3. Misconceptions about apes like the gorilla (has, have) turned a relatively peaceful animal into a terrifying monster.
4. Chuck's trench coat, with its big lapels and shoulder flaps, (make, makes) him feel like a tough private eye.
5. The high-pressure saleswomen in the designer dresses department (make, makes) me feel intimidated.

VERB BEFORE SUBJECT

A verb agrees with its subject even when the verb comes *before* the subject. Words that may precede the subject include *there, here,* and, in questions, *who, which, what,* and *where.*

Here are some examples of verb before subject:

There <u>are</u> wild <u>dogs</u> in our neighborhood.
In the distance <u>was</u> a <u>billow</u> of black smoke.
Here <u>is</u> the <u>newspaper</u>.
Where <u>are</u> the children's <u>coats</u>?

If you are unsure about the subject, ask *who* or *what* of the verb. With the first example above, you might ask, "*What* are in our neighborhood?" The answer, *wild dogs,* is the subject.

Activity

Write the correct form of the verb in the space provided.

(is, are) 1. There _____ dozens of frenzied shoppers waiting for the store to open.

(is, are) 2. Here _____ the notes from yesterday's anthropology lecture.

(do, does) 3. When _____ we take our break?

(was, were) 4. There _____ scraps of yellowing paper stuck between the pages of the book.

(was, were) 5. At the very bottom of the grocery list _____ an item that meant a trip all the way back to aisle 1.

COMPOUND SUBJECTS

Subjects joined by *and* generally take a plural verb.

A patchwork <u>quilt</u> and a sleeping <u>bag</u> <u>cover</u> my bed in the winter.
<u>Clark</u> and <u>Lois</u> <u>are</u> a contented couple.

When subjects are joined by *either . . . or, neither . . . nor, not only . . . but also,* the verb agrees with the subject closer to the verb.

Neither the government negotiator nor the union <u>leaders</u> <u>want</u> the strike to continue.

The nearer subject, *leaders,* is plural, and so the verb is plural.

Activity

Write the correct form of the verb in the space provided.

(sit, sits)   1. A crusty baking pan and a greasy plate _____ on the countertop.

(cover, covers) 2. Spidery cracks and a layer of dust _____ the ivory keys on the old piano.

(know, knows)   3. Not only the assistant manager but also the secretaries _____ that the company is folding.

(was, were)   4. In eighteenth-century France, makeup and high heels _____ worn by men.

(make, makes)   5. For women, a dark suit or dress and a pair of plain, closed shoes _____ the best impression at a job interview.

INDEFINITE PRONOUNS

The following words, known as *indefinite pronouns*, always take singular verbs:

(-*one* words)	(-*body* words)	(-*thing* words)	
one	nobody	nothing	each
anyone	anybody	anything	either
everyone	everybody	everything	neither
someone	somebody	something	

Note: *Both* always takes a plural verb.

Activity

Write the correct form of the verb in the space provided.

(suit, suits)   1. Neither of those hairstyles _____ the shape of your face.

(mention, mentions) 2. Somebody without much sensitivity always _____ my birthmark.

(give, gives)   3. Something in certain kinds of aged cheese _____ me a headache.

(enter, enters)   4. Everyone _____ the college kite-flying contest in the spring.

(fall, falls)   5. One of these earrings constantly _____ off my car.

■ Review Test 1

In the space provided, write the correct form of the verb shown in the margin.

(is, are)   1.   Some wheelchair-bound patients, as a result of a successful experiment, _____ using trained monkeys as helpers.

(was, were)   2.   Each of their children _____ given a name picked at random from a page of the Bible.

(seem, seems)   3.   Many of the headlines in the *National Enquirer* _____ hard to believe.

(is, are)   4.   Envelopes, file folders, and a telephone book _____ jammed into Karen's kitchen drawers.

(contains, contain)   5.   Neither of the textbooks _____ the answer to question 5 of the "open-book" exam.

(damage, damages)   6.   The use of metal chains and studded tires _____ roadways by chipping away at the paved surface.

(was, were)   7.   Next to the cash register _____ a can for donations to the animal protection society.

(makes, make)   8.   A metal grab bar bolted onto the tiles _____ it easier for elderly people to get in and out of the bathtub.

(cleans, clean)   9.   In exchange for a reduced rent, Karla and James _____ the dentist's office beneath their second-floor apartment.

(is, are)   10.   One of the hospital's delivery rooms _____ furnished with bright carpets and curtains to resemble a room at home.

■ Review Test 2

Cross out the incorrect verb form in each sentence. In addition, underline the subject or subjects that go with the verb. Then write the correct form of the verb in the space provided.

_____   1.   Why is Martha and her mother digging a hole in their garden so late at night?

_____   2.   Neither of my children look like me.

_____   3.   Several packages and a supermarket circular was lying on the porch mat.

_____   4.   The little balls all over my pink sweater looks like woolen goose bumps.

_____   5.   Here is the low-calorie cola and the double-chocolate cake you ordered.

——————   6. The odor of those perfumed ads interfere with my enjoyment of a magazine.

——————   7. One of my roommates are always leaving wet towels on the bathroom floor.

——————   8. A tiny piece of gum and some tape is holding my old glasses together.

——————   9. A man in his forties often begin to think about making a contribution to the world and not just about himself.

——————   10. Each of the players on the school's teams plan to give a uniform shirt to the charity auction.

■ Review Test 3

Complete each of the following sentences using *is, are, was, were, have,* or *has.* Then underline the subject.

Example   For me, popcorn at the movies _____*is like coffee at breakfast.*_____

1. Under my roommate's bed _____

2. The car with the purple fenders _____

3. My boss and her secretary _____

4. Neither of the football players _____

5. Here are _____

CONSISTENT VERB TENSE

Do not shift verb tenses unnecessarily. If you begin writing a paper in the present tense, do not shift suddenly to the past. If you begin in the past, do not shift without reason to the present. Notice the inconsistent verb tenses in the following selection:

Jean *punched* down the risen yeast dough in the bowl. Then she *dumps* it onto the floured worktable and *kneaded* it into a smooth, shiny ball.

The verbs must be consistently in the present tense:

Jean *punches* down the risen yeast dough in the bowl. Then she *dumps* it onto the floured worktable and *kneads* it into a smooth, shiny ball.

Or the verbs must be consistently in the past tense:

Jean *punched* down the risen yeast dough in the bowl. Then she *dumped* it onto the floured worktable and *kneaded* it into a smooth, shiny ball.

Activity

Make the verbs in each sentence consistent with the *first* verb used. Cross out the incorrect verb and write the correct form in the space at the left.

ran   **Example** Aunt Helen tried to kiss her little nephew, but he ~~runs~~ out of the room.

1. An aggressive news photographer knocked a reporter to the ground as the movie stars arrive for the Oscar awards.

2. As we leafed through the old high school yearbook, we laugh at our outdated clothes and hairstyles.

3. "My husband is so dumb," said Martha, "that when he went to Las Vegas he tries to play the stamp machines."

4. In a zero-gravity atmosphere, water breaks up into droplets and floated around in space.

5. Elliot lights the oven pilot and then stands back as the blue gas flames flared up.

■ Review Test 1

Make the verbs in each selection consistent with the *first* verb used. Cross out each incorrect verb and write the correct form in the space at the left.

recharge   **Example** Several times a year, I like to take a day off, go away by myself, and ~~recharged~~ my mental batteries.

1. Shampooing the plaid sofa upholstery, he was shocked as the colors fade before his eyes.

2. The jeep swerved around the corner, went up on two wheels, and tips over on its side.

3. On the TV commercial for mail-order kitchen knives, an actor cuts a tree branch in half and sliced an aluminum can into ribbons.

4. Ralph ripped open the bag of cheese puffs with his teeth and stuffs handfuls of the salty orange squiggles into his mouth.

5. The winning wheelchair racer in the marathon slumped back in exhaustion and asks for some ice to soothe his blistered hands.

6. From his perch high up on the rocky cliff, the eagle spots a white-tailed rabbit and swooped down toward his victim.

7. Earl wets his fingers and skimmed the rim of his water glass, producing an eerie whistling noise.

8. When the great earthquake struck San Francisco in 1906, the entire city burns to the ground in less than twenty-four hours.

9. Exploring the cloudy pond, the students collected a jar of tadpoles and gather some aquatic plants to grow in the school aquarium.

10. After the first Russian satellite was launched in 1957, American schools gear up their science programs to compete in the space race.

■ Review Test 2

Change verbs where needed in the following selection so that they are consistently in the past tense. Cross out each incorrect verb and write the correct form above it, as shown in the example. You will need to make ten corrections.

My uncle's shopping trip last Thursday was discouraging to him. First of all, he had to drive around for fifteen minutes until he ~~finds~~ *found* a parking space. There was a half-price special on paper products in the supermarket, and every spot is taken. Then, when he finally got inside, many of the items on his list were not where he expected. For example, the pickles he wanted are not on the same shelf as all the other pickles. Instead, they were in a refrigerated case next to the bacon. And the granola was not on the cereal shelves, but in the health food section. Shopping thus proceeds slowly. About halfway through his list, he knew there would not be time to cook dinner and decides to pick up a barbecued chicken. The chicken, he learned, was available at the end of the store he had already passed. So he parks his shopping cart in an aisle, gets the chicken, and came back. After adding half a dozen more items to his cart, he suddenly realizes it contained someone else's food. So he retraced his steps, found his own cart, transfers the groceries, and continued to shop. Later, when he began loading items onto the checkout counter, he notices that the barbecued chicken was missing. He must have left it in the other cart, certainly gone by now. Feeling totally defeated, he returned to the deli counter and says to the clerk, "Give me another chicken. I lost the first one." My uncle told me that when he saw the look on the clerk's face, he felt as if he'd flunked Shop-O-Rama.

ADDITIONAL INFORMATION ABOUT VERBS

The purpose of this special section is to provide additional information about verbs. Some people will find the grammar terms here a helpful reminder of earlier school learning about verbs. For them, the terms will increase their understanding of how verbs function in English. Other people may welcome more detailed information about terms used elsewhere in the text. In either case, remember that the most common mistakes that people make when writing verbs have been treated in earlier sections of the book.

VERB TENSE

Verbs tell us the time of an action. The time that a verb shows is usually called *tense*. The most common tenses are the simple present, past, and future. In addition, there are nine other tenses that enable us to express more specific ideas about time than we could with the simple tenses alone. Shown on the next page are the twelve verb tenses and examples of each tense. Read them over to increase your sense of the many different ways of expressing time in English.

Tenses	*Examples*
Present	I *work*.
	Tony *works*.
Past	Ellen *worked* on her car.
Future	You *will work* on a new project next week.
Present perfect	He *has worked* on his term paper for a month.
	They *have worked* out a compromise.
Past perfect	The nurse *had worked* two straight shifts.
Future perfect	Next Monday, I *will have worked* here exactly two years.
Present progressive	I *am working* on my speech for the debate.
	You *are working* too hard.
	The tape recorder *is* not *working* properly.
Past progressive	He *was working* in the basement.
	The contestants *were working* on their talent routines.
Future progressive	My son *will be working* in our store this summer.
Present perfect progressive	Sarah *has been working* late this week.
Past perfect progressive	Until recently, I *had been working* nights.
Future perfect progressive	My mother *will have been working* as a nurse for forty-five years by the time she retires.

Activity

On separate paper, write twelve sentences using the twelve verb tenses.

HELPING VERBS

There are three common verbs that can either stand alone or combine with (and "help") other verbs. Here are the verbs and their forms:

> be (am, are, is, was, were, being, been)
> have (has, having, had)
> do (does, did)

Here are examples of the verbs:

Used Alone	*Used as Helping Verbs*
I *was* angry.	I *was growing* angry.
Sue *has* the key.	Sue *has forgotten* the key.
He *did* well in the test.	He *did fail* the previous test.

There are nine helping verbs (traditionally known as *modals,* or *modal auxiliaries*) that are always used in combination with other verbs. Here are the nine verbs and sentence examples of each:

can	I *can see* the rainbow.
could	I *could* not *find* a seat.
may	The game *may be postponed.*
might	Cindy *might resent* your advice.
shall	I *shall see* you tomorrow.
should	He *should get* his car serviced.
will	Tony *will want* to see you.
would	They *would* not *understand.*
must	You *must visit* us again.

Note from the examples that these verbs have only one form. They do not, for instance, add an *-s* when used with *he, she, it,* or any one person or thing.

Activity

On separate paper, write nine sentences using the nine helping verbs.

VERBALS

Verbals are words formed from verbs. Verbals, like verbs, often express action. They can add variety to your sentences and vigor to your writing style. The three kinds of verbals are *infinitives, participles,* and *gerunds.*

Infinitive

An infinitive is *to* plus the base form of the verb.

I love *to dance.*
Lina hopes *to write* for a newspaper.
I asked the children *to clean* the kitchen.

Participle

A participle is a verb form used as an adjective (a descriptive word). The present participle ends in *-ing*. The past participle ends in *-ed* or has an irregular ending.

> *Peering* into the cracked mirror, the *crying* woman wiped her eyes.
> The *astounded* man stared at his *winning* lottery ticket.
> *Swinging* a sharp axe, Bob split the *rotted* beam.

Gerund

A gerund is the *-ing* form of a verb used as a noun.

> *Swimming* is the perfect exercise.
> *Eating* junk food is my diet downfall.
> Through *doodling,* people express their inner feelings.

Activity

On separate paper, write three sentences using infinitives, three sentences using participles, and three sentences using gerunds.

ACTIVE AND PASSIVE VERBS

When the subject of a sentence performs the action of a verb, the verb is in the *active voice*. When the subject of a sentence receives the action of a verb, the verb is in the *passive voice*.

The passive form of a verb consists of a form of the verb *be* plus the past participle of the main verb. Look at the active and passive forms of the verbs below and on the next page:

Active	*Passive*
Jan *sewed* the curtains. (The subject, *Jan,* is the doer of the action.)	The curtains *were sewn* by Jan. (The subject, *curtains,* does not act. Instead, something happens to them.)
The repairman *fixed* the air conditioner. (The subject, *repairman,* is the doer of the action.)	The air conditioner *was fixed* by the repairman. (The subject, *air conditioner,* does not act. Instead, something happens to it.)

In general, active verbs are more effective than passive ones. Active verbs give your writing a simpler and more vigorous style. At times, however, the passive form of verbs is appropriate when the performer of the action is unknown or is less important than the receiver of the action. For example:

The tests were graded yesterday.
(The performer of the action is unknown.)

Alan was very hurt by your thoughtless remark.
(The receiver of the action, Alan, is being emphasized.)

Activity

Change the following sentences from the passive to the active voice. Note that you may have to add a subject in some cases.

Examples   The dog was found by a police officer.
A police officer found the dog.

The baseball game was called off.
The officials called off the baseball game.
(Here a subject had to be added.)

1. Most of our furniture was damaged by the fire.

   _____

2. Marsha's new dress was singed by a careless smoker.

   _____

3. The problem was solved by the quiet student in the back of the room.

   _____

4. The supermarket shelves were restocked after the truckers' strike.

   _____

5. The children were mesmerized by the magician's sleight of hand.

   _____

MISPLACED MODIFIERS

Misplaced modifiers are words that, because of awkward placement, do not describe the words the writer intended them to describe. Misplaced modifiers often confuse the meaning of a sentence. To avoid them, place words as close as possible to what they describe.

Misplaced Words

George couldn't drive to work in his small sports car *with a broken leg*.
(The sports car had a broken leg?)

The toaster was sold to us by a charming salesman *with a money-back guarantee*.
(The salesman had a money-back guarantee?)

He *nearly* brushed his teeth for twenty minutes every night.
(He came close to brushing his teeth, but in fact did not brush them at all?)

Correctly Placed Words

With a broken leg, George couldn't drive to work in his small sports car.
(The words describing George are now placed next to "George.")

The toaster with a money-back guarantee was sold to us by a charming salesman.
(The words describing the toaster are now placed next to it.)

He brushed his teeth for nearly twenty minutes every night.
(The meaning—that he brushed his teeth for a long time—is now clear.)

Activity

Underline the misplaced word or words in each sentence. Then rewrite the sentence, placing related words together and thereby making the meaning clear.

Examples   Frozen shrimp lay in the steel pans <u>that were melting rapidly</u>.

Frozen shrimp that were melting rapidly lay in the steel pans.

The speaker discussed the problem of crowded prisons <u>at the college</u>.

At the college, the speaker discussed the problem of crowded prisons.

1. The patient talked about his childhood on the psychiatrist's couch.

2. The crowd watched the tennis players with swiveling heads.

3. Vonnie put four hamburger patties on the counter which she was cooking for dinner.

4. Steve carefully hung the new suit that he would wear to his first job interview in the bedroom closet.

5. Anne ripped the shirt on a car door that she made in sewing class.

6. The latest Arnold Schwarzenegger movie has almost opened in 2,200 theaters across the country.

7. The newscaster spoke softly into a microphone wearing a bulletproof vest.

8. The tenants left town in a dilapidated old car owing two months' rent.

9. The woman picked up a heavy frying pan with arthritis.

10. I discovered an unusual plant in the greenhouse that oozed a milky juice.

■ Review Test 1

Write MM for *misplaced modifier* or C for *correct* in the space provided for each sentence.

_____ 1. I nearly napped for twenty minutes during the biology lecture.

_____ 2. I napped for nearly twenty minutes during the biology lecture.

_____ 3. Ron paused as the girl he had been following stopped at a shop window.

_____ 4. Ron paused as the girl stopped at a shop window he had been following.

_____ 5. Marta dropped out of school after taking ten courses on Friday.

_____ 6. On Friday, Marta dropped out of school after taking ten courses.

_____ 7. Under his shirt, the player wore a good luck charm which resembled a tiny elephant.

_____ 8. The player wore a good luck charm under his shirt which resembled a tiny elephant.

_____ 9. I ordered a new telephone from the mail-order catalog shaped like a cartoon character.

_____ 10. I ordered from the mail-order catalog a new telephone shaped like a cartoon character.

■ Review Test 2

Make the changes needed to correct the misplaced modifier in each sentence.

1. Henry Wadsworth Longfellow wrote that rainbows are the flowers that have died and gone to heaven in a poem.

   _____

2. I almost filled an entire notebook with biology lab drawings.

   _____

3. The apprentice watched the master carpenter expertly fit the door with envious eyes.

   _____

4. The photographer pointed the camera at the shy deer equipped with a special night-vision scope.

   _____

5. The passengers on the bus stared at the ceiling or read newspapers with tired faces.

   _____

DANGLING
MODIFIERS

A modifier that opens a sentence must be followed immediately by the word it is meant to describe. Otherwise, the modifier is said to be dangling, and the sentence takes on an unintended meaning. For example, in the sentence

While reading the newspaper, my dog sat with me on the front steps.

the unintended meaning is that the *dog* was reading the paper. What the writer meant, of course, was that *he* (or *she*), the writer, was reading the paper. The writer should have said,

While reading the newspaper, *I* sat with my dog on the front steps.

The dangling modifier could also be corrected by placing the subject within the opening word group:

While *I* was reading the newspaper, my dog sat with me on the front steps.

Here are other sentences with dangling modifiers. Read the explanations of why they are dangling and look carefully at the ways they are corrected.

Dangling	*Correct*
Shaving in front of the steamy mirror, the razor nicked Ed's chin. (*Who* was shaving in front of the mirror? The answer is not *razor* but *Ed*. The subject *Ed* must be added.)	Shaving in front of the steamy mirror, *Ed* nicked his chin with the razor. *Or:* When *Ed* was shaving in front of the steamy mirror, he nicked his chin with the razor.
While turning over the bacon, hot grease splashed my arm. (*Who* is turning over the bacon? The answer is not *hot grease,* as it unintentionally seems to be, but *I*. The subject *I* must be added.)	While *I* was turning over the bacon, hot grease splashed my arm. *Or:* While turning over the bacon, *I* was splashed by hot grease.
Taking the exam, the room was so stuffy that Paula almost fainted. (*Who* took the exam? The answer is not the *room* but *Paula*. The subject *Paula* must be added.)	Taking the exam, *Paula* found the room so stuffy that she almost fainted. *Or:* When *Paula* took the exam, the room was so stuffy that she almost fainted.
To impress the interviewer, punctuality is essential. (*Who* is to impress the interviewer? The answer is not *punctuality* but *you*. The subject *you* must be added.)	To impress the interviewer, *you* must be punctual. *Or:* For *you* to impress the interviewer, punctuality is essential.

The preceding examples make clear two ways of correcting a dangling modifier. Decide on a logical subject and do one of the following:

1 Place the subject *within* the opening word group:

When *Ed* was shaving in front of the steamy mirror, he nicked his chin.

Note: In some cases an appropriate subordinating word such as *when* must be added, and the verb may have to be changed slightly as well.

2 Place the subject right *after* the opening word group:

Shaving in front of the steamy mirror, *Ed* nicked his chin.

Activity

Ask *Who?* of the opening words in each sentence. The subject that answers the question should be nearby in the sentence. If it is not, provide the logical subject by using either method of correction described above.

Example   While pitching his tent, a snake bit Tony on the ankle.

While Tony was pitching his tent, a snake bit him on the ankle.

Or: *While pitching his tent, Tony was bitten on the ankle by a snake.*

1. Dancing on their hind legs, the audience cheered wildly as the elephants paraded by.

   _____

   _____

2. Last seen wearing dark glasses and a blond wig, the police spokesperson said the suspect was still being sought.

   _____

   _____

3. Pouring out the cereal, a coupon fell into my bowl of milk.

   _____

   _____

4. Escorted by dozens of police motorcycles, I knew the limousine carried someone important.

   _____

   _____

5. Tired and exasperated, the fight we had was inevitable.

   _____

   _____

6. Packed tightly in a tiny can, Fran had difficulty removing the anchovies.

   _____

   _____

7. Kicked carelessly under the bed, Marion finally found her sneakers.

   _____

   _____

8. Working at the Xerox machine, the morning dragged on.

   _____

   _____

9. Sitting at a sidewalk café, all sorts of interesting people passed by.

   _____

   _____

10. Though somewhat warped, Uncle Zeke played his records from the forties.

   _____

   _____

■ Review Test 1

Write DM for *dangling modifier* or C for *correct* in the space provided for each sentence.

_____ 1. While riding the bicycle, a vicious-looking German shepherd snapped at Tim's ankles.

_____ 2. While Tim was riding the bicycle, a vicious-looking German shepherd snapped at his ankles.

_____ 3. Afraid to look at his father in the eye, Howard kept his head bowed.

_____ 4. Afraid to look his father in the eye, Howard's head remained bowed.

_____ 5. Boring and silly, I turned the TV show off.

_____ 6. I turned off the boring and silly TV show.

_____ 7. Munching leaves from a tall tree, the giraffe fascinated the children.

_____ 8. Munching leaves from a tall tree, the children were fascinated by the giraffe.

_____ 9. At the age of twelve, several colleges had already accepted the boy genius.

_____ 10. At the age of twelve, the boy genius had already been accepted by several colleges.

■ **Review Test 2**

Make the changes needed to correct the dangling modifier in each sentence.

1. Not having had much sleep, my concentration during class was weak.

   _____

2. Joined at the hip, a team of surgeons successfully separated the Siamese twins.

   _____

3. Wading in the shallow surf, a baby shark brushed past my leg.

   _____

4. While being restrained by federal marshals, the judge sentenced the kidnapper.

   _____

5. In a sentimental frame of mind, the music brought tears to Beth's eyes.

   _____

■ **Review Test 3**

Complete the following sentences. In each case, a logical subject should follow the opening words.

Example   Looking through the door's peephole, *I couldn't see who rang the doorbell.*

1. Noticing the light turn yellow, _____
2. Being fragile, _____
3. While washing the car, _____
4. Although very expensive, _____
5. Driving by the cemetery, _____

FAULTY PARALLELISM

Words in a pair or a series should have a parallel structure. By balancing the items in a pair or a series so that they have the same kind of structure, you will make the sentence clearer and easier to read. Notice how the parallel sentences that follow read more smoothly than the nonparallel ones.

Nonparallel (Not Balanced)	*Parallel (Balanced)*
My job includes checking the inventory, initiating the orders, and *to call* the suppliers.	My job includes checking the inventory, initiating the orders, and calling the suppliers. (A balanced series of *-ing* words: *checking, initialing, calling*)
The game-show contestant was told to be cheerful, charming, and *with enthusiasm.*	The game-show contestant was told to be cheerful, charming, and enthusiastic. (A balanced series of descriptive words: *cheerful, charming, enthusiastic*)
Lola likes to ride her moped, to do needlepoint, and *playing* games on her personal computer.	Lola likes to ride her moped, to do needlepoint, and to play games on her personal computer. (A balanced series of *to* verbs: *to ride, to do, to play*)
We painted the trim in the living room; *the wallpaper was put up by a professional.*	We painted the trim in the living room; a professional put up the wallpaper. (Balanced verbs and word order: *We painted . . . ; a professional put up . . .*)

Balanced sentences are not a skill you need worry about when writing first drafts. But when you rewrite, you should try to put matching words and ideas into matching structures. Such parallelism will improve your writing style.

Activity 1

The unbalanced part of each of the following sentences is italicized. Rewrite the unbalanced part so that it matches the rest of the sentence. The first one is done for you as an example.

1. Chocolate makes me gain weight, lose my appetite, and *breaking out in hives.*   *break out in hives* _____

2. Adam convinced most of the audience because he argued logically, calmly, and *was reasonable.* _____

3. If I didn't have to clean the garage and *an English paper that needed finishing,* I could really enjoy my weekend. _____

4. Ed's last job offered security; *a better chance for advancement is offered by his new job.* _____

5. A sale on electrical appliances, *furniture for the patio,* and stereo systems begins this Friday. _____

6. Steven prefers books that are short, scary, and *filled with suspense.*

   _____

7. The novelty shop sells hand buzzers, plastic fangs, and *insects that are fake.* _____

8. Because the dying woman was dignified and *with courage,* she won everyone's respect. _____

9. The politician trusted no one, rewarded loyalty, and *was dependent only on his own instincts.* _____

10. The chickens travel on a conveyor belt, where they are plucked, washed, rinsed, and *bags are put on them.* _____

Activity 2

Following are "plan of development" sentences that have been taken from student essays. Rewrite the sentences as needed so that the three points in each plan of development appear in parallel form.

1. To escape the stresses of everyday life, I rely upon watching television, reading books, and my kitchen.

   _____

   _____

2. If we're not careful, we'll leave the next generation polluted air, contaminated water, and forests that are dying.

_____

_____

3. Qualities that I look for in friends are a sense of humor, being kind, and dependability.

_____

_____

4. My three favorite jobs were veterinary assistant, gardener, and selling toys.

_____

_____

5. Many people have the same three great fears: being in high places, working with numbers, and speeches.

_____

_____

6. Housekeeping shortcuts will help you do a fast job of doing laundry, cleaning rooms, and food on the table.

_____

_____

7. The keys to improving grades are to take effective notes in class, to plan study time, and preparing carefully for exams.

_____

_____

8. To decide on a career, people should think closely about their interests, hobbies, and what they are skilled at.

_____

_____

9. The best programming on television includes news programs, shows on science, and children's series.

_____

_____

10. People in today's world often try to avoid silence, whether on the job, in school, or when relaxing at home.

_____

_____

■ **Review Test 1**

Draw a line under the unbalanced part of each sentence. Then rewrite the unbalanced part so that it matches the other item or items in the sentence. The first one is done for you as an example.

1. Curling overgrown vines, <u>porch furniture that was rotted</u>, and sagging steps were my first impressions of the neglected house.
    rotting porch furniture

2. In many ways, starting college at forty is harder than to start at eighteen.
    _____

3. The little girl came home from school with a tear-streaked face, a black eye, and her shirt was torn.
    _____

4. Studying a little every day is more effective than to cram.
    _____

5. At the body shop, the car was sanded down to the bare metal, painted with primer, and red enamel was sprayed on.
    _____

6. There are two ways to the top floor: climb the stairs or taking the elevator.
    _____

7. While waiting for the exam to start, small groups of nervous students glanced over their notes, drank coffee, and were whispering to each other.
    _____

8. In order to become a dancer, she is taking lessons, working in amateur shows, and auditioned for professional companies.
    _____

9. The "bag lady" shuffled along the street, bent over to pick something up, and was putting it in her shopping bag.
    _____

10. A teamsters' strike now would mean interruptions in food deliveries, a slowdown in the economy, and losing wages for workers.
    _____

■ **Review Test 2**

On separate paper, write five sentences of your own that use parallel structure.

PRONOUN AGREEMENT, REFERENCE, AND POINT OF VIEW

Pronouns are words that take the place of *nouns* (persons, places, or things). In fact, the word *pronoun* means "for a noun." Pronouns are shortcuts that keep you from unnecessarily repeating words in writing. Here are some examples of pronouns:

> Eddie left *his* camera on the bus. (*His* is a pronoun that takes the place of *Eddie's.*)
>
> Elena drank the coffee even though *it* was cold. (*It* replaces *coffee.*)
>
> As I turned the newspaper's damp pages, *they* disintegrated in my hands. (*They* is a pronoun that takes the place of *pages.*)

This section presents rules that will help you avoid three common mistakes people make with pronouns. The rules are:

1 A pronoun must agree in number with the word or words it replaces.
2 A pronoun must refer clearly to the word it replaces.
3 Pronouns should not shift unnecessarily in point of view.

PRONOUN AGREEMENT

A pronoun must agree in number with the word or words it replaces. If the word a pronoun refers to is singular, the pronoun must be singular; if that word is plural, the pronoun must be plural. (Note that the word a pronoun refers to is known as the *antecedent*.)

Marie showed me her antique wedding band.
Students enrolled in the art class must provide their own supplies.

In the first example, the pronoun *her* refers to the singular word *Marie;* in the second example, the pronoun *their* refers to the plural word *Students*.

Activity

Write the appropriate pronoun (*their, they, them, it*) in the blank space in each of the following sentences.

Example   I opened the wet umbrella and put _____*it*_____ in the bathtub to dry.

1. Kate and Bruce left for the movies earlier than usual, because _____ knew the theater would be packed.

2. The clothes were still damp, but I decided to fold _____ anyway.

3. Young adults often face a difficult transition period when _____ leave home for the first time.

4. Paul's grandparents renewed _____ marriage vows at a huge fiftieth wedding anniversary celebration.

5. The car's steering wheel began to pull to one side, and then _____ started to shimmy.

Indefinite Pronouns

The following words are always singular.

(*-one* words)	(*-body* words)	
one	nobody	each
anyone	anybody	either
everyone	everybody	neither
someone	somebody	

If a pronoun in a sentence refers to one of these singular words (also known as *indefinite pronouns*), the pronoun should be singular.

Somebody left (her) shoulder bag on the back of a chair.

One of the busboys just called and said (he) would be an hour late.

Everyone in the club must pay (his) dues next week.

Each circled pronoun is singular because it refers to an indefinite pronoun.

Note: There are two important points to remember about indefinite pronouns:

1   In the last example, if everyone in the club was a woman, the pronoun would be *her*. If the club had women and men, the pronoun would be *his or her:*

Everyone in the club must pay his or her dues next week.

Some writers follow the traditional practice of using *his* to refer to both women and men. Some now use *his or her* to avoid an implied sexual bias. To avoid using *his* or the somewhat awkward *his or her,* a sentence can often be rewritten in the plural:

Club members must pay their dues next week.

2   In informal spoken English, *plural* pronouns are often used with the indefinite pronouns. We would probably not say:

Everybody has his or her own opinion about the election.

Instead, we are likely to say:

Everybody has their own opinion about the election.

Here are other examples:

Everyone in the choir must buy their robes.
Everybody in the line has their ticket ready.
No one in the class remembered to bring their books.

In such cases, the indefinite pronouns are clearly plural in meaning. Also, the use of such plurals helps people to avoid the awkward *his or her.* In time, the plural pronoun may be accepted in formal speech or writing. Until that happens, however, you should use the grammatically correct singular form in your writing.

Activity

Underline the correct pronoun.

1. Neither of the potential buyers had really made up (her, their) mind.
2. Not one of the new cashiers knows what (he, they) should be doing.
3. Each of these computers has (its, their) drawbacks.
4. Anyone trying to reduce (his or her, their) salt intake should avoid canned and processed foods.
5. If anybody calls when I'm out, tell (him, them) I'll return in an hour.

PRONOUN REFERENCE

A sentence may be confusing and unclear if a pronoun appears to refer to more than one word or does not refer to any specific word. Look at this sentence:

Miriam was annoyed when they failed her car for a faulty turn signal.

Who failed her car? There is no specific word that *they* refers to. Be clear:

Miriam was annoyed when the inspectors failed her car for a faulty turn signal.

Here are sentences with other faulty pronoun references. Read the explanations of why they are faulty and look carefully at how they are corrected.

Faulty	*Clear*
Peter told Alan that his wife was unhappy. (Whose wife is unhappy: Peter's or Alan's? Be clear.)	Peter told Alan, "My wife is unhappy."
Sue is really a shy person, but she keeps it hidden. (There is no specific word that *it* refers to. It would not make sense to say, "Sue keeps shy hidden.")	Sue is really a shy person, but she keeps her shyness hidden.
Marsha attributed her success to her husband's support, which was generous. (Does *which* mean that Marsha's action was generous or that her husband's support was generous?)	Generously, Marsha attributed her success to her husband's support. *Or:* Marsha attributed her success to her husband's generous support.

Activity

Rewrite each of the following sentences to make clear the vague pronoun reference. Add, change, or omit words as necessary.

Example Susan and her mother wondered if she was tall enough to be a model.

Susan's mother wondered if Susan was tall enough to be a model.

1. Dad spent all morning bird-watching but didn't see a single one.

_____

2. At that fast-food restaurant, they give you free glasses with your soft drinks.

_____

3. Ruth told Annette that her bouts of depression were becoming serious.

_____

4. Dipping her spoon into the pot of simmering spaghetti sauce, Helen felt it slip out of her hand.

_____

5. Pete visited the tutoring center because they can help him with his economics course.

_____

PRONOUN POINT OF VIEW

Pronouns should not shift their point of view unnecessarily. When writing a paper, be consistent in your use of first-, second-, or third-person pronouns.

	Singular	*Plural*
First-person pronouns	I (my, mine, me)	we (our, us)
Second-person pronouns	you (your)	you (your)
Third-person pronouns	he (his, him)	they (their, them)
	she (her)	
	it (its)	

Note: Any person, place, or thing, as well as any indefinite pronoun like *one, anyone, someone,* and so on (page 356), is a third-person word.

For instance, if you start writing in the first person, *I*, do not jump suddenly to the second person, *you*. Or if you are writing in the third person, *they*, do not shift unexpectedly to *you*. Look at the examples.

Inconsistent	*Consistent*
One of the fringe benefits of my job is that *you* can use a company credit card for gasoline.	One of the fringe benefits of my job is that *I* can use a company credit card for gasoline.
(The most common mistake people make is to let a *you* slip into their writing after they start with another pronoun.)	
In this course, a person can be in class for weeks before the professor calls on *you*.	In this course, a person can be in class for weeks before the professor calls on *him*.
(Again, the *you* is a shift in point of view.)	(See also the note on *his or her* references on page 357.)

Activity

Cross out inconsistent pronouns in the following sentences and write the correct form of the pronoun above each crossed-out word.

Example   When I examined the used car, ~~you~~ *I* could see where a dent in the door panel had been repaired.

1. Ron refuses to eat pepperoni pizza because he says it gives you indigestion.

2. When I buy lipstick or nail polish, you never know how the color will actually look.

3. All you could hear was the maddening rattle of the heating registers, even though I buried my face in the pillow.

4. Hank searched the roadside mailboxes for the right name, but you couldn't see much in the pouring rain.

5. As we pulled on the heavy door, you could tell it wasn't going to budge.

■ Review Test

Cross out the pronoun error in each sentence on the opposite page and write the correction in the space provided at the left. Then circle the letter that correctly describes the type of error that was made.

Examples

his or her

Anyone without a ticket will lose their place in the line.
Mistake in: a. pronoun reference   (b.) pronoun agreement

Ellen
(or Cara)

When Ellen takes her daughter Cara to the park, she enjoys herself.
Mistake in: (a.) pronoun reference   b. pronoun point of view

we

From where we stood on the mountain, you could see three states.
Mistake in: a. pronoun agreement   (b.) pronoun point of view

1. Many people are ignorant of side effects that diets can have on your health.
   Mistake in: a. pronoun reference   b. pronoun point of view

2. Could someone volunteer their services to clean up after the party?
   Mistake in: a. pronoun reference   b. pronoun agreement

3. At the city council meeting, we asked them to provide better police protection for our neighborhood.
   Mistake in: a. pronoun reference   b. pronoun agreement

4. During the border crisis, each country refused to change their aggressive stand.
   Mistake in: a. pronoun reference   b. pronoun agreement

5. Darlene tried to take notes during class, but she didn't really understand it.
   Mistake in: a. pronoun reference   b. pronoun agreement

6. If people don't like what the government is doing, you should let Congress know.
   Mistake in: a. pronoun reference   b. pronoun point of view

7. Neither of those girls appreciates their parents' sacrifices.
   Mistake in: a. pronoun reference   b. pronoun agreement

8. There wasn't much to do on Friday nights after they closed the only movie theater in town.
   Mistake in: a. pronoun reference   b. pronoun agreement

9. Rita never buys a dress with horizontal stripes because she knows they make you look fat.
   Mistake in: a. pronoun reference   b. pronoun point of view

10. Any student who is working full-time and going to school knows that you need at least a twenty-five hour day.
    Mistake in: a. pronoun agreement   b. pronoun point of view

PRONOUN TYPES

This section describes some common types of pronouns: subject and object pronouns, possessive pronouns, and demonstrative pronouns.

SUBJECT AND OBJECT PRONOUNS

Pronouns change their form depending upon the place that they occupy in a sentence. In the box that follows is a list of subject and object pronouns.

Subject Pronouns	Object Pronouns
I	me
you	you (no change)
he	him
she	her
it	it (no change)
we	us
they	them

Subject Pronouns

The subject pronouns are subjects of verbs.

> *He* is wearing an artificial arm. (*He* is the subject of the verb *is wearing*.)
>
> *They* are moving into our old apartment. (*They* is the subject of the verb *are moving*.)
>
> *We* students should have a say in the decision. (*We* is the subject of the verb *should have*.)

Several kinds of mistakes that people sometimes make with subject pronouns are explained starting below.

1 Use a subject pronoun in spots where you have a compound (more than one) subject.

Incorrect	*Correct*
My brother and *me* are Bruce Springsteen fanatics.	My brother and *I* are Bruce Springsteen fanatics.
Him and *me* know the lyrics to all of Bruce's songs.	*He* and *I* know the lyrics to all of Bruce's songs.

Hint: If you are not sure what pronoun to use, try each pronoun by itself in the sentence. The correct pronoun will be the one that sounds right. For example, ''Him knows the lyrics to all of Bruce's songs'' does not sound right; ''He knows the lyrics to all of Bruce's songs'' does.

2 Use a subject pronoun after forms of the verb *be*. Forms of *be* include *am, are, is, was, were, has been, have been,* and others.

> It was *I* who left the light on.
> It may be *they* in that car.
> It is *he*.

The sentences above may sound strange and stilted to you because they are seldom used in conversation. When we speak with one another, forms such as ''It was me,'' ''It may be them,'' and ''It is him'' are widely accepted. In formal writing, however, the grammatically correct forms are still preferred.

Hint: Avoid having to use the pronoun form after *be* by simply rewording a sentence. Here is how the preceding examples could be reworded:

> I was the one who left the light on.
> They may be in that car.
> He is here.

3   Use subject pronouns after *than* or *as*. The subject pronoun is used because a verb is understood after the pronoun.

> You play better than I (play).   (The verb *play* is understood after *I*.)
>
> Jenny is as bored as I (am).   (The verb *am* is understood after *I*.)
>
> We don't need the money as much as they (do).   (The verb *do* is understood after *they*.)

Hint: Avoid mistakes by mentally adding the "missing" verb at the end of the sentence.

Object Pronouns

The object pronouns (*me, him, her, us, them*) are the objects of verbs or prepositions. (*Prepositions* are connecting words like *for, at, about, to, before, by, with,* and *of*. See also page 291.)

> Tony helped me.   (*Me* is the object of the verb *helped*.)
>
> We took *them* to the college.   (*Them* is the object of the verb *took*.)
>
> Leave the children with *us*.   (*Us* is the object of the preposition *with*.)
>
> I got in line behind *him*. (*Him* is the object of the preposition *behind*.)

People are sometimes uncertain about what pronoun to use when two objects follow the verb.

Incorrect	*Correct*
I gave a gift to Ray and *she*.	I gave a gift to Ray and *her*.
She came to the movie with Bobbie and *I*.	She came to the movie with Bobbie and *me*.

Hint: If you are not sure what pronoun to use, try each pronoun by itself in the sentence. The correct pronoun will be the one that sounds right. For example, "I gave a gift to she" does not sound right; "I gave a gift to her" does.

Activity

Underline the correct subject or object pronoun in each of the following sentences. Then show whether your answer is a subject or object pronoun by circling the S or O in the margin. The first one is done for you as an example.

S (*O*)   1.   The sweaters Mom knitted for Victor and (I, <u>me</u>) are too small.

S *O*   2.   The umpire and (he, him) started to argue.

S *O*   3.   No one has a quicker temper than (she, her).

S *O*   4.   Your grades prove that you worked harder than (they, them).

S *O*   5.   (We, Us) runners train indoors when the weather turns cold.

S *O*   6.   (She, Her) and Betty never put the cap back on the toothpaste.

S *O*   7.   Chris and (he, him) are the most energetic kids in the first grade.

S *O*   8.   Arguing over clothes is a favorite pastime for my sister and (I, me).

S *O*   9.   The rest of (they, them) will be arriving in about ten minutes.

S *O*   10.   The head of the ticket committee asked Linda and (I, me) to help with sales.

POSSESSIVE PRONOUNS

Here is a list of possessive pronouns:

my, mine	our, ours
your, yours	your, yours
his	their, theirs
her, hers	
its	

Possessive pronouns show ownership or possession.

Clyde revved up *his* motorcycle and blasted off.
The keys are *mine*.

Note: A possessive pronoun *never* uses an apostrophe. (See also page 385.)

Incorrect	*Correct*
That coat is *hers'*.	That coat is *hers*.
The card table is *theirs'*.	The card table is *theirs*.

Activity

Cross out the incorrect pronoun form in each of the sentences below. Write the correct form in the space at the right.

Example ___*hers*___ Those gloves are ~~hers'~~.

_____ 1. I discovered that my car had somehow lost its' rear license plate.

_____ 2. Are those seats theirs'?

_____ 3. I knew the sweater was hers' when I saw the monogram.

_____ 4. The dog in that cage is our's.

_____ 5. These books are yours' if you want them.

DEMONSTRATIVE PRONOUNS

Demonstrative pronouns point to or single out a person or thing. There are four demonstrative pronouns:

this	these
that	those

Generally speaking, *this* and *these* refer to things close at hand; *that* and *those* refer to things farther away. The four pronouns are commonly used in the role of demonstrative adjectives as well.

Is anyone using *this* spoon?
I am going to throw away *these* magazines.
I just bought *that* white Volvo at the curb.
Pick up *those* toys in the corner.

Note: Do not use *them, this here, that there, these here,* or *those there* to point out. Use only *this, that, these,* or *those.*

Activity

Cross out the incorrect form of the demonstrative pronoun and write the correct form in the space provided.

Example *Those* ~~Them~~ tires look worn.

_____ 1. This here map is out of date.

_____ 2. Leave them keys out on the coffee table.

_____ 3. I've seen them girls somewhere before.

_____ 4. Jack entered that there dog in an obedience contest.

_____ 5. Where are them new knives?

■ Review Test

Underline the correct word in the parentheses.

1. If the contract negotiations are left up to (they, them), we'll have to accept the results.
2. (Them, Those) student crafts projects have won several awards.
3. Our grandmother told David and (I, me) to leave our muddy shoes outside on the porch.
4. The judge decided that the fault was (theirs', theirs) and ordered them to pay the damages.
5. I gave the money to (she, her) and asked her to put it in the bank's night deposit slot.
6. The black-masked raccoon stared at Rudy and (I, me) for an instant and then ran quickly away.
7. When we saw the smashed window, Lynn and (I, me) didn't know whether to enter the house.
8. (This here, This) is my cousin Manuel.
9. This coat can't be (hers, her's); it's too small.
10. Because we weren't wearing shoes, Tara and (I, me) had a hard time walking on the sharp gravel.

ADJECTIVES
AND ADVERBS

ADJECTIVES

What Are Adjectives?

Adjectives describe nouns (names of persons, places, or things) or pronouns.

Polly is a *wise* woman. (The adjective *wise* describes the noun *woman*.)

She is also *funny*. (The adjective *funny* describes the pronoun *she*.)

I'll carry the *heavy* bag of groceries. (The adjective *heavy* describes the noun *bag*.)

It is *torn*. (The adjective *torn* describes the pronoun *it*.)

Adjectives usually come before the word they describe (as in *wise* woman and *heavy* bag). But they also come after forms of the verb *be* (*is, are, was, were,* and so on). They also follow verbs such as *look, appear, seem, become, sound, taste,* and *smell*.

That road is *slippery*. (The adjective *slippery* describes the road.)

The dogs are *noisy*. (The adjective *noisy* describes the dogs.)

Those customers were *impatient*. (The adjective *impatient* describes the customers.)

Your room looks *neat*. (The adjective *neat* describes the room.)

Using Adjectives to Compare

For all one-syllable adjectives and some two-syllable adjectives, add *-er* when comparing two things and *-est* when comparing three or more things.

> Phil's beard is *longer* than mine, but Lee's is the *longest.*
>
> Meg may be the *quieter* of the two sisters; but that's not saying much, since they're the *loudest* girls in school.

For some two-syllable adjectives and all longer adjectives, add *more* when comparing two things and *most* when comparing three or more things.

> Liza Minnelli is *more famous* than her sister; but their mother, Judy Garland, is still the *most famous* member of the family.
>
> The red letters on the sign are *more noticeable* than the black ones, but the Day-Glo letters are the *most noticeable.*

You can usually tell when to use *more* and *most* by the sound of a word. For example, you can probably tell by its sound that "carefuller" would be too awkward to say and that *more careful* is thus correct. In addition, there are many words for which both *-er* or *-est* and *more* or *most* are equally correct. For instance, either "a more fair rule" or "a fairer rule" is correct.

To form negative comparisons, use *less* and *least.*

> During my first dance class, I felt *less graceful* than an injured elephant.
>
> When the teacher came to our house to complain to my parents, I offered her the *least* comfortable chair in the house.

Points to Remember about Comparing

Point 1:   Use only one form of comparison at a time. In other words, do not use both an *-er* ending and *more* or both an *-est* ending and *most:*

Incorrect	*Correct*
My mother's suitcase is always *more heavier* than my father's.	My mother's suitcase is always *heavier* than my father's.
Rosemary's Baby is still the *most frighteningest* movie I've ever seen.	*Rosemary's Baby* is still the *most frightening* movie I've ever seen.

Point 2:   Learn the irregular forms of the words shown below.

	Comparative (for comparing two things)	Superlative (for comparing three or more things)
bad	worse	worst
good, well	better	best
little (in amount)	less	least
much, many	more	most

Do not use both *more* and an irregular comparative or *most* and an irregular superlative.

Incorrect	Correct
It is *more better* to give than to receive.	It is *better* to give than to receive.
Last night I got the *most worst* snack attack I ever had.	Last night I got the *worst* snack attack I ever had.

Activity

Add to each sentence the correct form of the word in the margin.

bad

Examples   The _____*worst*_____ job I ever had was baby-sitting for spoiled four-year-old twins.

wonderful

The __*most wonderful*__ day of my life was when my child was born.

good   1. The _____ chocolate cake I ever ate had bananas in it.

young   2. Aunt Sonja is the _____ of the three sisters.

bad   3. A rain that freezes is _____ than a snowstorm.

unusual   4. That's the _____ home I've ever seen—it's shaped like a teapot.

little   5. Being painfully shy has made Leon the _____ friendly person I know.

ADVERBS

What Are Adverbs?

Adverbs describe verbs, adjectives, or other adverbs. They usually end in *-ly*.

The father *gently* hugged the sick child. (The adverb *gently* describes the verb *hugged*.)

Newborns are *totally* innocent. (The adverb *totally* describes the adjective *innocent*.)

The lecturer spoke so *terribly* fast that I had trouble taking notes. (The adverb *terribly* describes the adverb *fast*.)

A Common Mistake with Adverbs and Adjectives

People often mistakenly use an adjective instead of an adverb after a verb.

Incorrect	*Correct*
Sam needs a haircut *bad*.	Sam needs a haircut *badly*.
I laugh too *loud* when I'm embarrassed.	I laugh too *loudly* when I'm embarrassed.
You might have won the race if you hadn't run so *slow* at the beginning.	You might have won the race if you hadn't run so *slowly* at the beginning.

Activity

Underline the adjective or adverb needed. (Remember that adjectives describe nouns, and adverbs describe verbs, or other adverbs.)

1. As Mac danced, his earring bounced (rapid, rapidly).
2. A drop of (thick, thickly) pea soup dripped down his chin.
3. I hiccupped (continuous, continuously) for fifteen minutes.
4. The detective opened the door (careful, carefully).
5. All she heard when she answered the phone was (heavy, heavily) breathing.

Well and *Good*

Two words that are often confused are *well* and *good*. *Good* is an adjective; it describes nouns. *Well* is usually an adverb; it describes verbs. *Well* (rather than *good*) is also used when referring to a person's health.

Activity

Write *well* or *good* in each of the sentences that follow.

1. If you girls do a _____ job of cleaning the garage, I'll take you for some ice cream.
2. If I organize the office records too _____, my bosses may not need me anymore.
3. After eating a pound of peanuts, I didn't feel too _____.
4. When Ernie got AIDS, he discovered who his _____ friends really were.
5. Just because brothers and sisters fight when they're young doesn't mean they won't get along _____ as adults.

■ Review Test 1

Underline the correct word in the parentheses.

1. The waitress poured (littler, less) coffee in my cup than in yours.
2. Humid air seems to make Sid's asthma (more worse, worse).
3. The movie is so interesting that the three hours pass (quick, quickly).
4. The talented boy sang as (confident, confidently) as a seasoned performer.
5. Our band played so (good, well) that a local firm hired us for its annual dinner.
6. Tri Lee is always (truthful, truthfully), even when it might be better to tell a white lie.
7. The driver stopped the bus (sudden, suddenly) and yelled, "Everybody out!"
8. Shirt and pants in one color make you look (more thin, thinner) than ones in contrasting colors.
9. Your intentions may have been (good, well), but I'd prefer that you ask before arranging a blind date for me.
10. Our cat likes to sit in the (warmest, most warm) spot of any room—by a fireplace, on a windowsill in the sunshine, or on my lap.

■ Review Test 2

Write a sentence that uses each of the following adjectives and adverbs correctly.

1. careless _____

2. angrily _____

3. well _____

4. most relaxing _____

5. best _____

CAPITAL LETTERS

MAIN USES OF CAPITAL LETTERS

Capital letters are used with:

1 The first word in a sentence or direct quotation
2 Names of persons and the word *I*
3 Names of particular places
4 Names of days of the week, months, and holidays
5 Names of commercial products
6 Titles of books, magazines, newspapers, articles, stories, poems, films, television shows, songs, papers that you write, and the like
7 Names of companies, associations, unions, clubs, religious and political groups, and other organizations

Each use is illustrated on the pages that follow.

First Word in a Sentence or Direct Quotation

The corner grocery was robbed last night.
The alien said, ''Take me to your leader.''
''If you feel lonely,'' said Carla, ''call me. I'll be over in no time.''

Note: In the third example, *If* and *I'll* are capitalized because they start new sentences. But *call* is not capitalized, because it is part of the first sentence.

Names of Persons and the Word *I*

Last night, I saw a hilarious movie starring Stan Laurel and Oliver Hardy.

Names of Particular Places

Although Bill dropped out of Port Charles High School, he eventually earned his degree and got a job with Atlas Realty Company.

But: Use small letters if the specific name of a place is not given.

Although Bill dropped out of high school, he eventually earned his degree and got a job with a real estate company.

Names of Days of the Week, Months, and Holidays

On the last Friday afternoon in May, the day before Memorial Day, my boss is having a barbecue for all the employees.

But: Use small letters for the seasons—summer, fall, winter, spring.

Most people feel more energetic in the spring and fall.

Names of Commercial Products

My little sister knows all the words to the jingles for Oscar Mayer hot dogs, Diet Pepsi, Meow Mix cat food, and McDonald's hamburgers.

But: Use small letters for the *type* of product (hot dogs, cat food, hamburgers, and so on.)

Titles of Books, Magazines, Newspapers, Articles, Stories, Poems, Films, Television Shows, Songs, Papers That You Write, and the Like

We read the book *Hiroshima,* by John Hersey, for our history class.

In the doctor's waiting room, I watched *All My Children,* read an article in *Reader's Digest,* and leafed through the *Miami Herald.*

Names of Companies, Associations, Unions, Clubs, Religious and Political Groups, and Other Organizations

Joe Naples is a Roman Catholic, but his wife is a Methodist.

The Hilldale Square Dancers' Club has won many competitions.

Brian, a member of Bricklayers Local 431 and the Knights of Columbus, works for Ace Construction.

Activity

Underline the words that need capitals in the following sentences. Then write the capitalized form of the words in the spaces provided. The number of spaces tells you how many corrections to make in each case.

Example In our biology class, each student must do a report on an article in the magazine *scientific american.*   *Scientific American*

1. Leon's collection of beatles souvenirs includes a pair of tickets from their last concert in candlestick park, San Francisco.

   _____   _____   _____

2. Yumi read in *psychology today* magazine that abraham lincoln suffered from severe depression.

   _____   _____   _____   _____

3. When i have a cold, I use vick's ointment and chew listerine lozenges.

   _____   _____   _____

4. This spring, the boy scouts and the jaycees will clean up madison Park.

   _____   _____   _____   _____

5. A nature trail for the blind in cape cod, massachusetts, has signs written in braille which encourage visitors to smell and touch the plants.

   _____   _____   _____

6. At a restaurant on Broad street called Joe's italian palace, the chefs use pasta machines to make fresh noodles right in the dining room.

   _____   _____   _____

7. My father is a confirmed Dallas cowboys fan, though he lives in boston.

   _____   _____

8. Martha bought a sugar-free tab to wash down her hostess twinkie.

   _____   _____   _____

9. Vince listened to a Billy Joel album called *The Stranger* while Donna read an article in *glamour* entitled ''What Do men Really want?''

   _____   _____   _____

10. After having her baby, joan received a card from one of her friends that read, ''congratulations, we all knew you had it in you.''

   _____   _____

OTHER USES OF CAPITAL LETTERS

Capital letters are also used with:

1 Names that show family relationships
2 Titles of persons when used with their names
3 Specific school courses
4 Languages
5 Geographic locations
6 Historical periods and events
7 Races, nations, and nationalities
8 Opening and closing of a letter

Each use is illustrated on the pages that follow.

Names That Show Family Relationships

All his life, Father has been addicted to gadgets.
I browsed through Grandmother's collection of old photographs.
Aunt Florence and Uncle Bill bought a mobile home.

But: Do not capitalize words like *mother, father, grandmother, grandfather, uncle, aunt,* and so on when they are preceded by a possessive word (*my, your, his, her, our, their*).

All his life, my father has been addicted to gadgets.
I browsed through my grandmother's collection of old photographs.
My aunt and uncle bought a mobile home.

Titles of Persons When Used with Their Names

I contributed to Congressman McGrath's campaign fund.
Is Dr. Gregory on vacation?
Professor Adams announced that there would be no tests in his course.

But: Use small letters when titles appear by themselves, without specific names.

I contributed to my congressman's campaign fund.
Is the doctor on vacation?
The professor announced that there would be no tests in his course.

Specific School Courses

The college offers evening sections of Introductory Psychology I, Abnormal Psychology, Psychology and Statistics, and Educational Psychology.

But: Use small letters for general subject areas.

The college offers evening sections of many psychology courses.

Languages

My grandfather's Polish accent makes his English difficult to understand.

Geographic Locations

He grew up in the Midwest but moved to the South to look for a better job.

But: Use small letters in directions.

Head west for five blocks and then turn south on State Street.

Historical Periods and Events

During the Middle Ages, the Black Death killed over one-quarter of Europe's population.

Races, Nations, Nationalities

The census questionnaire asked if the head of our household was Caucasian, Negro, Oriental, or Native American.

Linda has lived on army bases in Germany, Italy, and Spain.

Denise's beautiful features are the result of her Chinese and Mexican parentage.

Opening and Closing of a Letter

Dear Sir:	Sincerely yours,
Dear Ms. Henderson:	Truly yours,

Note: Capitalize only the first word in a closing.

Activity

Underline the words that need capitals in the following sentences. Then write the capitalized forms of the words in the spaces provided. The number of spaces tells you how many corrections to make in each case.

1. During world war II, many americans were afraid that the japanese would invade California.

   _____   _____   _____   _____

2. Many college students are studying spanish and french to help them in their business careers.

   _____   _____

3. When uncle harvey got the bill from his doctor, he called the American Medical Association to complain.

   _____   _____

4. Dr. Freeling of the business department is offering a new course called introduction to word processing.

   _____   _____   _____

5. A new restaurant featuring vietnamese cuisine has just opened on the south side of the city.

   _____

UNNECESSARY USE OF CAPITALS

Activity

Many errors in capitalization are caused by using capitals where they are not needed. Underline the incorrectly capitalized letters in the following sentences and write the correct forms in the spaces provided. The number of spaces tells you how many corrections to make in each sentence.

1. James Garfield—the last President to be born in a log cabin—was also the first to use a Telephone.

   _____ _____

2. While she cleans and cooks, my Mother wears a pair of Sony Stereo Headphones.

   _____ _____ _____

3. Americans were shocked when several members of the Chicago White Sox Baseball Team accepted bribes to ''fix'' the 1919 World Series.

   _____ _____

4. The Voyager spacecraft sent back pictures of Saturn's Rings which prove that they are made up of Millions of Small, icy Particles.

   _____ _____ _____ _____

5. Einstein's theory of relativity, which he developed when he was only twenty-six, led to the invention of the Electron Microscope, Television, and the Atomic bomb.

   _____ _____ _____ _____

■ Review Test 1

Add capitals where needed in the following sentences.

Example In an injured tone, Mary demanded, ''<ins>W</ins>hy wasn't <ins>U</ins>ncle Lou invited to the party?''

1. To keep warm, a homeless old man sits on a steam vent near the sears building on tenth street.

2. Silent movie stars of the twenties, like charlie chaplin and gloria swanson, earned more than a million tax-free dollars a year.

3. Insects living in mammoth cave, in kentucky, include blind crickets, spiders, and flies.

4. Fidel Castro, the cuban leader, once tried out for the washington senators, a professional baseball team.

5. In the marx brothers movie, an attractive young lady invited groucho to join her.

6. "why?" asked groucho. "are you coming apart?"

7. I was halfway to the wash & dry laundromat on elm street when i realized that my box of tide was still home on the kitchen counter.

8. Every november, I make another vow that I will not gain weight between thanksgiving and new year's day.

9. *Rolling stone* magazine features an article about the making of the latest *star trek* sequel and a review of a new paul mccartney album.

10. Celebrities earn big money for endorsing items like polaroid cameras, trident gum, and jell-O pudding.

■ **Review Test 2**

On separate paper, write:

1. Seven sentences demonstrating the seven main uses of capital letters
2. Eight sentences demonstrating the eight other uses of capital letters

APOSTROPHE

The two main uses of the apostrophe are:

1 To show the omission of one or more letters in a contraction
2 To show ownership or possession

Each use is explained on the pages that follow.

APOSTROPHE IN CONTRACTIONS

A contraction is formed when two words are combined to make one word. An apostrophe is used to show where letters are omitted in forming the contraction. Here are two contractions:

have + not = haven't (the *o* in *not* has been omitted)
I + will = I'll (the *wi* in *will* has been omitted)

Following are some other common contractions:

I + am = I'm	it + is = it's
I + have = I've	it + has = it's
I + had = I'd	is + not = isn't
who + is = who's	could + not = couldn't
do + not = don't	I + would = I'd
did + not = didn't	they + are = they're

Note: Will + not has an unusual contraction: won't.

Activity

Write the contractions for the words in parentheses. One is done for you.

1. (Are not) _____ *Aren't* _____ the reserve books in the library kept at the circulation desk?

2. If (they are) _____ coming over, (I had) _____ better cook more hot dogs.

3. (I am) _____ the kind of student (who is) _____ extremely nervous before tests.

4. (We are) _____ hoping to find out (who is) _____ responsible for this error; (it is) _____ important to us to keep our customers happy.

5. I (can not) _____ remember if (there is) _____ gas in the car or not.

Note: Even though contractions are common in everyday speech and in written dialog, usually it is best to avoid them in formal writing.

APOSTROPHE TO SHOW OWNERSHIP OR POSSESSION

To show ownership or possession, we can use such words as *belongs to, possessed by, owned by,* or (most commonly) *of*.

> the umbrella that *belongs to* Mark
> the tape recorder *owned by* the school
> the gentleness *of* my father

But the apostrophe plus *s* (if the word does not end in *s*) is often the quickest and easiest way to show possession. Thus we can say:

> Mark's umbrella
> the school's tape recorder
> my father's gentleness

Points to Remember

1 The *'s* goes with the owner or possessor (in the examples given, *Mark, the school, my father*). What follows is the person or thing possessed (in the examples given, *the umbrella, the tape recorder, gentleness*).

2 There should always be a break between the word and the *'s*.

Mark' s   not   Mark's

Yes   No

Activity 1

Rewrite the *italicized* part of each of the sentences below, using the *'s* to show possession. Remember that the *'s* goes with the owner or possessor.

Example   *The wing of the bluejay* was broken.

            The bluejay's wing was broken.

1. *The baton owned by the twirler* bounced on the ground.

2. *The performance of the quarterback* is inconsistent.

3. *The thin hand belonging to the old lady* felt as dry as parchment.

4. In *the window of the truck stop* is a sign: "Five Hundred Mile Coffee."

5. A fly flew into *the mouth of the TV weatherperson*.

6. *The new denim shirt belonging to Lamont* was as scratchy as sandpaper.

7. *The granite steps of the post office* were covered with green plastic turf.

8. *The bowl of cereal belonging to Dan* refused to snap, crackle, or pop.

9. *The Honda owned by Donna* was crammed with boxes and furniture.

10. *The previous tenant of the apartment* had painted all the walls bright green.

Activity 2

Add *'s* to each of the following words to make them the possessors or owners of something. Then write sentences using the words. The first one is done for you.

1. rock star   _rock star's_
    The rock star's limousine pulled up to the curb.

2. Arnold   _____

    _____

3. pilot   _____

    _____

4. neighbor   _____

    _____

5. school   _____

    _____

6. gunslinger   _____

    _____

Apostrophe versus Possessive Pronouns

Do not use an apostrophe with possessive pronouns. They already show ownership. Possessive pronouns include *his, hers, its, yours, ours,* and *theirs.*

The sun warped his albums.	*not*	The sun warped his' albums.
The restored Model T is theirs.	*not*	The restored Model T is theirs'.
The decision is yours.	*not*	The decision is yours'.
The plaid suitcase is ours.	*not*	The plaid suitcase is ours'.
The lion charged its prey.	*not*	The lion charged its' prey.

Apostrophe versus Simple Plurals

When you want to make a word plural, just add an *s* at the end of the word. Do *not* add an apostrophe. For example, the plural of the word *movie* is *movies,* not *movie's* or *movies'*. Look at this sentence:

Tim coveted his roommate's collection of cassette tapes and compact disks.

The words *tapes* and *disks* are simple plurals, meaning more than one tape, more than one disk. The plural is shown by adding *s* only. On the other hand, the *'s* after *roommate* shows possession—that the roommate owns the tapes and disks.

Activity

Insert an apostrophe where needed to show possession in the following sentences. Write *plural* above words where the *s* ending simply means more than one thing.

Example Arlene's tinted contact lenses protect her eyes from glare.

(plural written above "lenses" and "eyes")

1. Harry grasped his wifes arm as she stood up on skates for the first time.

2. Vonettes decision to study computer science is based on predictions of good opportunities for women in that field.

3. The fires extreme heat had melted the telephones in the office and welded its metal chairs into a twisted heap.

4. Maria tried her sisters fad diet, which forbids eating any food that is white.

5. At the doctors request, Jim pulled up his shirt and revealed the zipperlike scars from his operation.

6. At the end of the day, Cals shirt and pants smelled like gasoline, and his fingernails were rimmed with grease.

7. Most peoples fear of flying is based on their fear of giving control over their destinies to someone else—in this case, the pilot.

8. Tinas camping handbook suggests that we bring water purification tablets and nylon ropes.

9. Carmens leaky pen had stained her fingers a deep blue.

10. The rattlesnakes head has a sensitive pit below the eyes, capable of detecting the body heat of warm-blooded prey.

Apostrophe with Words Ending in -s

If a word ends in *-s*, show possession by adding only an apostrophe. Most plurals end in *-s*, and so show possession simply by adding the apostrophe.

the Thompsons' porch
James' cowboy boots
the players' victory
her parents' motor home
the Rolling Stones' last album
the soldiers' hats

Activity

Add an apostrophe where needed.

1. Dennis sudden appearance startled his wife.
2. The Murrays phone bill is over $200 a month.
3. Many buildings steep steps make it difficult for wheelchair-bound people to negotiate them.
4. The twins habit of dressing alike was started by their mother when they were children.
5. All the neighbors lawns are as parched as straw.

■ Review Test

In each sentence underline the two words that need apostrophes. Then write the words correctly in the spaces provided.

1. Although I hadnt met him before, Donalds voice sounded familiar to me.

2. A shaky rope ladder led from the barns wooden floor to the haylofts dusty shadows.

3. The paperback books glaring purple and orange cover was designed to attract the hurrying customers eye.

4. Phils essay was due in a matter of hours, but he suffered a writers block that emptied his brain.

5. While he waited in his boss office, Charlies nervous fingers shredded a Styrofoam coffee cup into a pile of jagged white flakes.

6. Jacks son stepped cautiously along the top of the farmyards splintery wooden fence.

7. Members of the parents association constructed a maze made of old tires for the childrens playground.

8. Barrys greatest accomplishment was conquering his addiction to his mothers chocolate pecan pie.

9. The suns rays beat down until the streets blacktopped surface softened with the heat.

10. The rivers swirling floodwaters lapped against the Thompsons porch.

QUOTATION MARKS

The two main uses of quotation marks are:

1 To set off the exact words of a speaker or writer
2 To set off the titles of short works

Each use is explained on the pages that follow.

QUOTATION MARKS TO SET OFF THE WORDS OF A SPEAKER OR WRITER

Use quotation marks to show the exact words of a speaker or writer.

"I feel as though I've been here before," Angie murmured to her husband.
(Quotation marks set off the exact words that Angie spoke to her husband.)

Ben Franklin once wrote, "To lengthen thy life, lessen thy meals."
(Quotation marks set off the exact words that Ben Franklin wrote.)

"Did you know," said the nutrition expert, "that it's healthier to be ten pounds overweight?"
(Two pairs of quotation marks are used to enclose the nutrition expert's exact words.)

The biology professor said, "Ants are a lot like human beings. They farm their own food and raise smaller insects as livestock. And, like humans, ants send armies to war."
(Note that the end quotation marks do not come until the end of the biology professor's speech. Place quotation marks before the first quoted word and after the last quoted word. As long as no interruption occurs in the speech, do not use quotation marks for each new sentence.)

Punctuation Hint: In the four examples on the preceding page, notice that a comma sets off the quoted part from the rest of the sentence. Also observe that commas and periods at the end of a quotation always go *inside* quotation marks.

Complete the following statements that explain how capital letters, commas, and periods are used in quotations. Refer to the four examples as guides.

1. Every quotation begins with a _____ letter.
2. When a quotation is split (as in the sentence of the nutrition expert), the second part does not begin with a capital letter unless it is a _____ sentence.
3. _____ are used to separate the quoted part of a sentence from the rest of the sentence.
4. Commas and periods that come at the end of a quotation go _____ quotation marks.

The answers are *capital, new, Commas,* and *inside.*

Activity 1

Place quotation marks around the exact words of a speaker or writer in the sentences that follow.

1.   I'll worry about that tomorrow, Scarlett said to Rhett.
2.   Beatrice asked, Do you give a discount to senior citizens?
3.   This hamburger is raw! cried Leon.
4.   The bumper sticker on the rear of the battered old car read, Don't laugh—it's paid for.
5.   I know why Robin Hood robbed only the rich, said the comedian. The poor don't have any money.
6.   These records, proclaimed the television announcer, are not sold in any store.
7.   When chefs go to great lengths, the woman at the reducing center said, I go to great widths.
8.   Did you know, the counselor said to my husband and me, that it now costs $85,000 to raise a child to the age of eighteen?
9.   On a tombstone in a Maryland cemetery are the words, Here lies an atheist, all dressed up and no place to go.
10.   The advice columnist advised, Be nice to people on your way up because you'll meet them on your way down.

Activity 2

1. Write a sentence in which you quote a favorite expression of someone you know. Identify the relationship of the person to you.

    Example   *My grandfather's favorite expression is, "It can't be as bad as all that."*

    _____

    _____

2. Write a quotation that contains the words *Nick asked Fran*. Write a second quotation that includes the words *Fran replied*.

    _____

    _____

    _____

    _____

    _____

    _____

    _____

3. Write down a sentence or two that interests you from a book or magazine. Identify the title and author of the work.

    Example   *In And More by Andy Rooney, the author writes, "Any line you choose to stand in during your life will usually turn out to be the one that moves the slowest."*

    _____

    _____

    _____

    _____

    _____

    _____

Indirect Quotations

An indirect quotation is a rewording of someone else's comments rather than a word-for-word direct quotation. The word *that* often signals an indirect quotation.

Direct Quotation	*Indirect Quotation*
The nurse said, "Some babies cannot tolerate cows' milk."	The nurse said that some babies cannot tolerate cows' milk.
(The nurse's exact spoken words are given, so quotation marks are used.)	(We learn the nurse's words indirectly, so no quotation marks are used.)
Vicky's note to Dan read, "I'll be home by 7:30."	Vicky left a note for Dan that said she would be home by 7:30.
(The exact words that Vicky wrote in the note are given, so quotation marks are used.)	(We learn Vicky's words indirectly, so no quotation marks are used.)

Activity

Rewrite the following sentences, changing words as necessary to convert the sentences into direct quotations. The first one has been done for you as an example.

1. Teddy asked Margie if she wanted to see his spider collection.
   Teddy asked, "Margie, do you want to see my spider collection?"

2. Andy said that his uncle looks just like a large basset hound.

3. Nathan said that he wanted a box of the extra-crispy chicken.

4. My boss told me that I could make mistakes as long as I didn't repeat them.

5. The announcer said that tonight's regular TV programs have been canceled.

QUOTATION MARKS TO SET OFF THE TITLES OF SHORT WORKS

Titles of short works are usually set off by quotation marks, while titles of long works are underlined. Use quotation marks to set off the titles of such short works as articles in books, newspapers, or magazines; chapters in a book; short stories; poems; and songs. But you should underline the titles of books, newspapers, magazines, plays, movies, record albums, and television shows. Following are some examples.

Quotation Marks	*Underlines*
the essay "On Self-Respect"	in the book <u>Slouching towards Bethlehem</u>
the article "The Problem of Acid Rain"	in the newspaper <u>The New York Times</u>
the article "Living with Inflation"	in the magazine <u>Newsweek</u>
the chapter "Chinese Religion"	in the book <u>Paths of Faith</u>
the story "Hands"	in the book <u>Winesburg, Ohio</u>
the poem "When I Have Fears"	in the book <u>Complete Poems of John Keats</u>
the song "Ziggy Stardust"	in the album <u>Changes</u>
	the television show <u>Sixty Minutes</u>
	the movie <u>High Noon</u>

Note: In printed works, italic type—slanted type that looks *like this*—is used instead of underlining.

Activity

Use quotation marks or underlines as needed.

1. In his short story entitled A Mother's Tale, James Agee describes a slaughterhouse from the cow's point of view.
2. I bought the National Enquirer to read an article entitled How Video Games Are Hazardous to Your Mental Health.
3. We read the chapter Pulling Up Roots in Gail Sheehy's book Passages.
4. Jane used an article titled Ten Ways to Unplug Your Kid's TV Habit in her research paper for developmental psychology.

5. The movie Casablanca, which starred Humphrey Bogart, was originally cast with Ronald Reagan in the leading role.

6. My favorite old TV show was Thriller, a horror series hosted by Boris Karloff, the man who starred in the 1931 movie Frankenstein.

7. When the Beatles' movie A Hard Day's Night was first shown, fans screamed so much that no one could hear the songs or the dialog.

8. On my father's wall is a framed front page of The New York Times of February 25, 1911—the day he was born.

9. The sociology test will cover the first two chapters: Culture and Diversity and Social Stratification.

10. An article in Consumer Reports called Which Cereal for Breakfast? claims that children can learn to like low-sugar cereals like Cheerios and Wheaties.

OTHER USES OF QUOTATION MARKS

Quotation marks are also used as follows:

1 To set off special words or phrases from the rest of a sentence:

In grade school, we were taught a little jingle about the ''i before e'' spelling rule.

What is the difference between ''it's'' and ''its''?

(In this book, *italics* are often used instead of quotation marks to set off words.)

2 To mark off a quotation within a quotation:

The physics professor said, ''Do the problems at the end of Chapter Five, 'Work and Energy,' for class on Friday.''

Elliot remarked, ''Did you know that Humphrey Bogart never actually said, 'Play it again, Sam' in the movie *Casablanca*?''

Note: A quotation within a quotation is indicated by *single* quotation marks, as shown above.

■ Review Test 1

Insert quotation marks where needed in the sentences that follow.

1. The psychology class read a short story called Silent Snow, Secret Snow about a young boy who creates his own fantasy world.

2. When asked for advice on how to live a long life, the old man said, Don't look back; something may be gaining on you.

3. I'm against grade school students using pocket calculators, said Fred. I spent three years learning long division, and so should they.

4. One updated version of an old saying goes, Absence makes the heart grow fonder—of somebody else.

5. When I gagged while taking a foul-tasting medicine, my wife said, Put an ice cube on your tongue first, and then you won't taste it.

6. I looked twice at the newspaper headline that read, Man in River Had Drinking Problem.

7. Gene reported to his business class on an article in *Money* magazine entitled Cashing In on the Energy Boom.

8. When a guest at the wedding was asked what he was giving the couple, he replied, About six months.

9. Theodore Roosevelt, a pioneer in conservation, once said, When I hear of the destruction of a species, I feel as if all the works of some great writer had perished.

10. If you're ever in trouble, said the police officer, you'll have a better chance of attracting aid if you shout Fire instead of Help.

■ Review Test 2

Go through the comics section of a newspaper to find a comic strip that amuses you. Be sure to choose a strip where two or more characters are speaking to each other. Write a full description that will enable people who have not read the comic strip to visualize it clearly and appreciate its humor. Describe the setting and action in each panel and enclose the words of the speakers in quotation marks.

Comma

Commas are used mainly as follows:

1 To separate items in a series
2 To set off introductory material
3 On both sides of words that interrupt the flow of thought in a sentence
4 Between two complete thoughts connected by *and, but, for, or, nor, so, yet*
5 To set off a direct quotation from the rest of a sentence
6 For certain everyday material

You may find it helpful to remember that the comma often marks a slight pause or break in a sentence. Read aloud the sentence examples given for each rule, and listen for the minor pauses or breaks that are signaled by commas.

1   Comma between Items in a Series

Use commas to separate items in a series.

The street vendor sold watches, necklaces, and earrings.

The pitcher adjusted his cap, pawed the ground, and peered over his shoulder.

The exercise instructor told us to inhale, exhale, and relax.

Joe peered into the hot, still-smoking engine.

Notes

a   The final comma in a series is optional, but it is often used.

b   A comma is used between two descriptive words in a series only if *and* inserted between the words sounds natural. You could say:

Joe peered into the hot *and* still-smoking engine.

But notice in the following sentence that the descriptive words do not sound natural when *and* is inserted between them. In such cases, no comma is used.

Tony wore a pale green tuxedo. (A pale *and* green tuxedo does not sound right, so no comma is used.)

Activity

Place commas between items in a series.

1. The old kitchen cabinets were littered with dead insects crumbs and dust balls.
2. Rudy stretched out on the swaying hammock popped open a frosty can of soda and balanced it carefully on his stomach.
3. The children splashed through the warm deep swirling rainwater that flooded the street.
4. The freezer was crammed with mysterious foil-wrapped lumps boxes of frozen french fries and empty ice cube trays.
5. The musty shadowy cellar with the crumbling cement floor was our favorite playground.

2   Comma after Introductory Material

Use a comma to set off introductory material.

Just in time, Sherry slid a plastic tray under the overwatered philodendron.

Muttering under his breath, Ken reviewed the terms he had memorized.

In a wolf pack, the dominant male holds his tail higher than the other pack members.

Although he had been first in the checkout line, Dave let an elderly woman go ahead of him.

After the fire, we slogged through the ashes of the burned-out house.

Note: If the introductory material is brief, the comma is sometimes omitted. In the activities here, you should include the comma.

Activity

Place commas after introductory material.

1.   As Patty struggled with the stuck window gusts of cold rain blew in her face.
2.   Before taking a blood sample the nurse taped Jake's arm to make a large vein stand out.
3.   Along the once-pretty river people had dumped old tires and loads of household trash.
4.   When the movie still hadn't come on well after dusk the occupants of the cars parked at the drive-in began beeping their horns.
5.   Setting down a smudged glass of murky water the waitress tossed Dennis a greasy menu and asked if he'd care to order.

3   Comma around Words Interrupting the Flow of Thought

Use a comma on both sides of words or phrases that interrupt the flow of thought in a sentence.

The vinyl car seat, sticky from the heat, clung to my skin.

Marty's personal computer, which his wife got him as a birthday gift, occupies all of his spare time.

The hallway, dingy and dark, was illuminated by a bare bulb hanging from a wire.

Usually you can "hear" words that interrupt the flow of thought in a sentence by reading it aloud. In cases where you are not sure if certain words are interrupters, remove them from the sentence. If it still makes sense without the words, you know that the words are interrupters and that the information they give is nonessential. *Such nonessential or extra information is set off with commas.*

In the following sentence,

Sue Dodd, who goes to aerobics class with me, was in a serious car accident.

the words *who goes to aerobics class with me* are extra information not needed to identify the subject of the sentence, *Sue Dodd.* Commas go around such nonessential information. On the other hand, in the sentence

The woman who goes to aerobics class with me was in a serious accident.

the words *who goes to aerobics class with me* supply essential information—information needed for us to identify the woman being spoken of. If the words were removed from the sentence, we would no longer know who was in the accident. Here is another example:

Watership Down, a novel by Richard Adams, is the most thrilling adventure story I've ever read.

Here the words *a novel by Richard Adams* could be left out, and we would still know the basic meaning of the sentence. Commas are placed around such nonessential material. But in the sentence

Richard Adams' novel *Watership Down* is the most thrilling adventure story I've ever read.

the title of the novel is essential. Without it the sentence would read, "Richard Adams' novel is the most thrilling adventure story I've ever read." We would not know which of Richard Adams' novels was so thrilling. Commas are not used around the title, because it provides essential information.

Most of the time you will be able to "hear" words that interrupt the flow of thought in a sentence and will not have to think about whether the words are essential or nonessential.

Activity

Use commas to set off interrupting words.

1. A slight breeze muggy with heat ruffled the bedroom curtains.
2. The defrosting chickens loosely wrapped in plastic left a pool on the counter.
3. Lenny's wallet which he kept in his front pants pocket was linked to his belt with a metal chain.
4. Mr. Delgado who is an avid Yankees fan remembers the great days of Mickey Mantle and Yogi Berra.
5. The fleet of tall ships a majestic sight made its way into the harbor.

4 Comma between Complete Thoughts

Use a comma between two complete thoughts connected by *and, but, for, or, nor, so, yet.*

> Sam closed all the windows, but the predicted thunderstorms never arrived.
>
> I like wearing comfortable clothing, so I buy oversized shirts and sweaters.
>
> Peggy doesn't envy the skinny models in magazines, for she is happy with her own well-rounded body.

Notes

a The comma is optional when the complete thoughts are short ones.

> The ferris wheel started and Wilson closed his eyes.
> Irene left the lecture hall for her head was pounding.
> I made a wrong turn so I doubled back.

b Be careful not to use a comma in sentences having one subject and a double verb. The comma is used only in sentences made up of two complete thoughts (two subjects and two verbs). In this sentence,

> The doctor stared over his bifocals and lectured me about smoking.

there is only one subject (*doctor*) and a double verb (*stared* and *lectured*). No comma is needed. Likewise, the following sentence

> Frank switched the lamp on and off and then tapped it with his fingers.

has only one subject (*Frank*) and a double verb (*switched* and *tapped*); therefore, no comma is needed.

Activity

Place a comma before a joining word that connects two complete thoughts (two subjects and two verbs). Remember, do *not* place a comma within sentences that have only one subject and a double verb.

1. The television sitcom was interrupted for a special news bulletin and I poked my head out of the kitchen to listen to the announcement.
2. The puppy was beaten by its former owner and cringes at the sound of a loud voice.
3. The eccentric woman brought all her own clips and rollers to the hairdresser's for she was afraid to use the ones in the shop.
4. The tuna sandwich in my lunch is crushed and the cream-filled cupcake is plastered to the bottom of the bag.
5. Lynn unscrewed the front panel of the air conditioner and removed the plastic foam filter in order to clean it.
6. Ruth was tired of summer reruns so she visited the town library to pick up some interesting books.
7. Debbie tried to trap the jumbo bumblebee bumping along the ceiling but the angry insect stayed just out of reach.
8. Carl strolled among the exhibits at the comic book collectors' convention and stopped to look at a rare first edition of *Superman*.
9. Our neighborhood crime patrol escorts elderly people to the local bank and installs free dead-bolt locks on their apartment doors.
10. Brendan tapped the small geraniums out of their pots and carefully planted them on his grandfather's grave.

5   Comma with Direct Quotations

Use a comma to set off a direct quotation from the rest of a sentence.

The carnival barker cried, "Step right up and win a prize!"

"Now is the time to yield to temptation," my horoscope read.

"I'm sorry," said the restaurant hostess. "You'll have to wait."

"For my first writing assignment," said Scott, "I have to turn in a five-hundred-word description of a stone."

Note: Commas and periods at the end of a quotation go inside quotation marks. See also page 389.

Activity

Use commas to set off direct quotations from the rest of the sentence.

1. The coach announced "In order to measure your lung capacity, you're going to attempt to blow up a plastic bag with one breath."
2. "A grapefruit" said the comedian "is a lemon that had a chance and took advantage of it."
3. The psychology professor said "Dreams about feeling paralyzed in emergencies can represent a real-life inability to cope with stressful situations."
4. "Speak louder" a man in the back row said to the guest speaker. "I paid five dollars to hear you talk, not whisper."
5. The zookeeper explained to the visitors "We can't tell the sex of a giant tortoise for almost ten years after its birth."

6 Comma with Everyday Material

Use a comma with certain everyday material.

Persons Spoken to

If you're the last to leave, Paul, please switch off the lights.
Fred, I think we're on the wrong road.
Did you see the play-off game, Lisa?

Dates

June 30, 1995, is the day I make the last payment on my car.

Addresses

I buy discount children's clothing from Isaacs Baby Wear Factory, Box 900, Chicago, Illinois 60614.

Note: No comma is used to mark off the zip code.

Openings and Closings of Letters

Dear Santa,   Sincerely yours,
Dear Larry,   Truly yours,

Note: In formal letters, a colon is used after the opening: Dear Sir: *or* Dear Madam: *or* Dear Allan: *or* Dear Ms. Mohr:.

Numbers

The insurance agent sold me a $50,000 term life insurance policy.

Activity

Place commas where needed.

1. Would you mind George if we borrowed your picnic cooler this weekend?
2. The enchiladas served at Los Amigos 5607 Pacific Boulevard are the best in town.
3. On August 23 1963 over 200000 blacks and whites marched for civil rights in Washington D.C.
4. The mileage chart shows Elaine that we'll have to drive 1231 miles to get to Sarasota Florida.
5. The coupon refund address is 2120 Industrial Highway Great Plains Minnesota 55455.

■ Review Test 1

Insert commas where needed. In the space provided below each sentence, summarize briefly the rule that explains the comma or commas used.

1. "Kleenex tissues" said the history professor "were first used as gas mask filters in World War I."

   _____

2. Dee ordered a sundae with three scoops of rocky road ice cream miniature marshmallows and raspberry sauce.

   _____

3. While waiting to enter the movie theater we studied the faces of the people just leaving to see if they had liked the show.

   _____

4. I had left my wallet on the store counter but the clerk called me at home to say that it was safe.

   _____

5. The demonstrators protesting nuclear arms carried signs reading "Humans have never invented a weapon that they haven't used."

   _____

6. Large cactus plants which now sell for very high prices are being stolen from national parks and protected desert areas.

___

7. On March 3 1962 Wilt Chamberlain scored one hundred points in a game against the New York Knicks.

___

8. Tom watched nervously as the dentist assembled drills mirrors clamps picks and cylinders of cotton on a tray next to the reclining chair.

___

9. The talk show guest a former child star said that one director threatened to shoot her dog if she didn't cry on cue.

___

10. Cats and dogs like most animals love the taste of salt and will lick humans' hands to get it.

___

■ Review Test 2

Insert commas where needed. Mark the one sentence that is correct with a C.

1. Before leaving for the gym Ellen added extra socks and a tube of shampoo to the gear in her duffel bag.
2. My father said "Golf isn't for me. I can't afford to buy lots of expensive sticks so that I can lose lots of expensive white balls."
3. Clogged with soggy birds' nests the chimney had allowed dangerous gases to accumulate in our house.
4. Bill took a time-exposure photo of the busy highway and the cars' taillights appeared in the developed print as winding red ribbons.
5. The graduating students sweltering in their hot black gowns fanned their faces with commencement programs.
6. Puffing a cigarette twitching his lips and adjusting his hat Bogie sized up the dangerous situation.
7. On May 31 1889 a flood in Johnstown Pennsylvania killed 2200 people.
8. "When I was little" said Ernie "my brother told me it was illegal to kill praying mantises. I still don't know if that's true or not."
9. A huge side of beef its red flesh marbled with streaks of creamy fat hung from a razor-sharp steel hook.
10. A line of dancing numerals on *Sesame Street* kicked across the screen like a chorus line.

■ **Review Test 3**

In the following passage, there are ten missing commas. Add the commas where needed. The types of mistakes to look for are shown in the box below.

> 2 commas missing between items in a series
> 1 comma missing after introductory material
> 4 commas missing around interrupting words
> 2 commas missing between complete thoughts
> 1 comma missing with a direct quotation

When I was about ten years old I developed several schemes to avoid eating liver, a food I despise. My first scheme involved my little brother. Timmy too young to realize what a horrible food liver is always ate every bit of his portion. On liver nights, I used to sit next to Tim and slide my slab of meat onto his plate when my parents weren't paying attention. This strategy worked until older and wiser Tim decided to reject his liver along with the rest of us. Another liver-disposal method I used was hiding the meat right on the plate. I'd cut the liver into tiny squares half the size of postage stamps and then I would carefully hide the pieces. I'd put them inside the skin of my baked potato beneath some mashed peas, or under a crumpled paper napkin. This strategy worked perfectly only if my mother didn't look too closely as she scraped the dishes. Once she said to me "Do you know you left a lot of liver on your plate?" My best liver trick was to hide the disgusting stuff on a three-inch-wide wooden ledge that ran under our dining-room table. I'd put little pieces of liver on the ledge when Mom wasn't looking; I would sneak the dried-up scraps into the garbage early the next day. Our dog would sometimes smell the liver try to get at it, and bang his head noisily against the bottom of the table. These strategies seemed like a lot of work but I never hesitated to take whatever steps I could. Anything was better than eating a piece of meat that tasted like old socks soaked in mud.

■ **Review Test 4**

On separate paper, write six sentences, one illustrating each of the six main comma rules.

OTHER
PUNCTUATION
MARKS

COLON (:)

Use the colon at the end of a complete statement to introduce a list, a long quotation, or an explanation.

1   A list:

The store will close at noon on the following dates: November 26, December 24, and December 31.

2   A long quotation:

The scientist Stephen Jay Gould wrote: "I am, somehow, less interested in the weight and convolutions of Einstein's brain than in the near certainty that people of equal talent have lived and died in cotton fields and sweatshops."

3   An explanation:

Here's a temporary solution to a dripping faucet: tie a string to it and let the drops slide down the string to the sink.

Activity

Place colons where needed in the sentences below:

1. Bring these items to registration a ballpoint pen, your student ID card, and a check made out to the college.
2. In our veterinarian's office is a grisly item a real dog's heart removed from an animal infested with heartworms.
3. Willa Cather, the American author, once wrote ''There are only two or three human stories, and they go on repeating themselves as fiercely as if they had never happened before.''

SEMICOLON (;)

The main use of the semicolon is to mark the break between two complete thoughts, as explained on pages 314–315. Another use is to mark off items in a series when the items themselves contain commas. Here are some examples:

Sharon's children are named Melantha, which means ''black flower''; Yonina, which means ''dove''; and Cynthia, which means ''moon goddess.''

My favorite albums are *Rubber Soul,* by the Beatles; *Songs in the Key of Life,* by Stevie Wonder; and *Bridge over Troubled Water,* by Simon and Garfunkel.

Activity

Place semicolons where needed in the sentences below.

1. Strange things happen at very low temperatures a rose will shatter like glass.
2. My sister had a profitable summer: by mowing lawns, she earned $125 by washing cars, $85 and by walking the neighbors' dogs, $110.
3. The salad bar was well stocked it included fresh spinach and sliced almonds.

DASH (—)

A dash signals a degree of pause longer than a comma but not as complete as a period. Use a dash to set off words for dramatic effect:

I was so exhausted that I fell asleep within seconds—standing up.

He had many good qualities—sincerity, honesty, and thoughtfulness—yet he had few friends.

The pardon from the governor finally arrived—too late.

Notes

a The dash is formed on the typewriter by striking the hyphen twice (- -). In handwriting, the dash is as long as two letters would be.

b Be careful not to overuse dashes.

Activity

Place dashes where needed in the following sentences.

1. The victim's leg broken in three places lay twisted at an odd angle on the pavement.
2. With a shriek, Jeannette dropped the hot iron pan on her toe.
3. After I had seen every exhibit and ride at Disney World, there was only one other thing I wanted to see my motel room.

PARENTHESES ( )

Parentheses are used to set off extra or incidental information from the rest of a sentence:

> In 1913, the tax on an annual income of four thousand dollars (a comfortable wage at that time) was one penny.

> A small mirror (a double-faced one) is useful to a camper for flashing signals or starting fires.

Note: Do not use parentheses too often in your writing.

Activity

Add parentheses where needed.

1. Though the original *Star Trek* series originally ran for only three seasons 1965–1968, it can still be seen on many stations around the country.
2. Whenever Jack has too much to drink even one drink is sometimes too much, he gets loud and abusive.
3. When I opened the textbook, I discovered that many pages mostly ones in the first chapter were completely blank.

HYPHEN (-)

1 Use a hyphen with two or more words that act as a single unit describing a noun.

The light-footed burglar silently slipped open the sliding glass door.

While being interviewed on the late-night talk show, the quarterback announced his intention to retire.

With a needle, Rich punctured the fluid-filled blister on his toe.

2 Use a hyphen to divide a word at the end of a line of writing or typing. When you need to divide a word at the end of a line, divide it between syllables. Use your dictionary to be sure of correct syllable divisions (see also page 411).

Mark's first year at college was a time filled with numerous new pres-sures and responsibilities.

Notes

a Do not divide words of one syllable.

b Do not divide a word if you can avoid it.

Activity

Place hyphens where needed.

1. The record breaking summer temperatures coincided with an upsurge of assaults and murders in the city.
2. My father, who grew up in a poverty stricken household, remembers putting cardboard in his shoes when the soles wore out.
3. The well written article in *Newsweek* described the nerve wracking experiences of a company of men who had fought in Vietnam.

■ Review Test

At the appropriate spot, place the punctuation mark shown in the margin.

—
1. A bad case of flu, a burglary, the death of an uncle it was not what you would call a pleasant week.

( )
2. My grandfather who will be ninety in May says that hard work and a glass of wine every day are the secrets of a long life.

:
3. Mark Twain once wrote ''The difference between the right word and the nearly right word is the difference between lightning and the lightning bug.''

-
4. The passengers in the glass bottomed boat stared at the colorful fish in the water below.

( )
5. Ellen's birthday December 27 falls so close to Christmas that she gets only one set of presents.

;
6. The police officer had spotted our broken headlight consequently, he stopped us at the next corner.

—
7. I feel I have two chances of winning the lottery slim and none.

-
8. Well stocked shelves and friendly service are what Mrs. Dale demands of her staff.

;
9. Some people need absolute quiet in order to study they can't concentrate with the soft sounds of a radio, air conditioner, or television in the background.

:
10. There are three work habits my boss hates taking long coffee breaks, making personal phone calls, and missing staff meetings.

USING THE DICTIONARY

The dictionary is a valuable tool. To take advantage of it, you need to understand the main kinds of information that a dictionary gives about a word. Look at the information provided for the word *tattoo* in the following entry from *The Random House Dictionary,* paperback edition.*

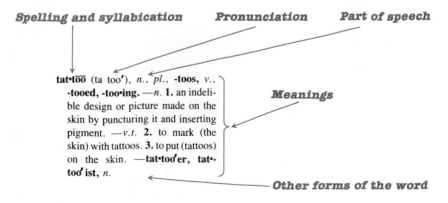

Spelling and syllabication   *Pronunciation*   *Part of speech*

tat•too (ta too′), *n., pl.,* **-toos,** *v.,* **-tooed, -too•ing.** —*n.* **1.** an indelible design or picture made on the skin by puncturing it and inserting pigment. —*v.t.* **2.** to mark (the skin) with tattoos. **3.** to put (tattoos) on the skin. —**tat•too′er, tat•too′ ist,** *n.*

Meanings

Other forms of the word

The Random House Dictionary (Ballantine Paperback edition). Copyright © 1978, 1980, by Random House, Inc.

SPELLING

The first bit of information, in the boldface (heavy type) entry itself, is the spelling of *tattoo*. Get into the habit of using the dictionary for spelling. When you write a paper, allow yourself time to look up the spelling of all those words you are unsure about.

Use your dictionary to correct the spelling of the following words:

accomodate	_____	intermitent	_____
crediter	_____	privlege	_____
decimel	_____	recesion	_____
unanamous	_____	propasition	_____
fulfil	_____	jepardy	_____
equivilent	_____	transmitt	_____
embarass	_____	adolesent	_____

SYLLABICATION

The second bit of information that the dictionary gives, also in the boldface entry, is the syllabication of *tattoo*. Note that a dot separates the syllables of the word.

Use your dictionary to mark the syllable divisions in the following words. Also indicate how many syllables are in each word.

f r u g a l   (_____ syllables)

t r a n s l u c e n t   (_____ syllables)

a n t i p a t h y   (_____ syllables)

s e m i a n n u a l   (_____ syllables)

i n f e r i o r i t y   (_____ syllables)

Noting syllable divisions will enable you to *hyphenate* a word, that is, divide it at the end of one line of writing and complete it at the beginning of the next line. You can correctly hyphenate a word only at a syllable division, and you may have to check your dictionary to make sure of a particular word's syllable divisions.

PRONUNCIATION

The third bit of information in the dictionary entry is the pronunciation of *tattoo* (*ta too'*). You already know how to pronounce *tattoo*, but if you did not, the information within the parentheses would serve as your guide. Use your dictionary to complete the following exercises that relate to pronunciation.

Vowel Sounds

You will probably use the pronunciation key in your dictionary mainly as a guide to pronouncing different vowel sounds (vowels are the letters *a, e, i, o,* and *u*). Here is part of the pronunciation key in *The Random House Dictionary:*

a bat / ā way / e ebb / ē equal / i if

The key tells you, for example, that the sound of the short *a* is pronounced like the *a* in *bat,* the sound of the long *a* is like the *a* in *way,* and the sound of the short *e* is like the *e* in *ebb.*

Look at the pronunciation key in your dictionary. It is probably located in the front of the dictionary or at the bottom of every page. What common word in the key tells you how to pronounce each of the following sounds?

ī _____   u _____

o _____   o͝o _____

ō _____   o͞o _____

Note: The long vowel always has the sound of its own name.

The Schwa (ə)

The symbol ə looks like an upside-down *e*. It is called a *schwa,* and it stands for the unaccented sound in such words as *ago, item, easily, gallop,* and *circus.* More approximately, it stands for the sound *uh*—like the *uh* that speakers sometimes make when they hesitate in their speech. Perhaps it would help to remember that *uh,* as well as ə, could be used to represent the schwa sound.

Here are some of the many words in which the sound appears: *credential* (kri-den' shəl); *horrify* (hôr'ə-fī); *signature* (sig'nə-choor). Open your dictionary to any page and you will almost surely be able to find three words that make use of the schwa in the pronunciation in parentheses after the main entry. Write three such words and their pronunciations in the spaces below.

1. _____   (_____)

2. _____   (_____)

3. _____   (_____)

Accent Marks

Some words contain both a primary accent, shown by a heavy stroke ('), and a secondary accent, shown by a lighter stroke ('). For example, in the word *individual* (in′də-vij′ o͞o əl) the stress, or accent, goes chiefly on the third syllable (vij′), and to a lesser extent on the first syllable (in′).

Use your dictionary to add accent marks to the following words:

prologue   (prō log)

tacit   (tas it)

corroborate   (kə rob ə rāt)

animosity   (an ə mos ə tē)

magnanimous   (mag nan ɔ mɔs)

Full Pronunciation

Use your dictionary to write out the full pronunciation (the information given in parentheses) for each of the following words.

binary _____

facsimile _____

vestige _____

antebellum _____

covert _____

euphemism _____

capitulate _____

derisive _____

tenacious _____

vociferous _____

satiate _____

aesthetic _____

anachronism _____

posthumous _____

millennium _____

Now practice pronouncing each word. Use the pronunciation key in your dictionary as an aid to sounding out each syllable. Do *not* try to pronounce a word all at once; instead, work on mastering *one syllable at a time*. When you can pronounce each of the syllables in a word successfully, then say them in sequence, add the accent, and pronounce the entire word.

PARTS OF SPEECH

The next bit of information that the dictionary gives about *tattoo* is *n*. This abbreviation means that the meanings of *tattoo* as a noun will follow.

Use your dictionary if necessary to fill in the meanings of the following abbreviations:

v. = _____   sing. = _____

adj. = _____   pl. = _____

PRINCIPAL PARTS OF IRREGULAR VERBS

Tattoo is a regular verb and forms its principal parts by adding *-ed, -ed,* and *-ing* to the stem of the verb. When a verb is irregular, the dictionary lists its principal parts. For example, with *give* the present tense comes first (the entry itself, *give*). Next comes the past tense (*gave*), and then the past participle (*given*)—the form of the verb used with such helping words as *have, had*, and *was*. Then comes the present participle (*giving*)—the *-ing* form of the verb.

Look up the parts of the following irregular verbs and write them in the spaces provided. The first one is done for you.

Present	Past	Past Participle	Present Participle
swim	*swam*	*swum*	*swimming*
lie			
drink			
freeze			

PLURAL FORMS OF IRREGULAR NOUNS

The dictionary supplies the plural forms of all irregular nouns (regular nouns like *tattoo* form the plural by adding *-s* or *-es*). Give the plurals of the following nouns. If two forms are shown, write down both.

crisis _____

phenomenon _____

library _____

cactus _____

shelf _____

MEANINGS

When there is more than one meaning to a word, the meanings are numbered in the dictionary, as with the word *tattoo*. In many dictionaries, the most common meanings of a word are presented first. The introductory pages of your dictionary will explain the order in which meanings are presented.

Use the sentence context to try to explain the meaning of the italicized word in each of the following sentences. Write your definition in the space provided. Then look up and record the dictionary meaning of the word. Be sure you pick out the meaning that fits the word as it is used in the sentence.

1. During the hiking trip, we had to *navigate* some difficult trails.

    Your definition _____

    Dictionary definition _____

2. I had a *yen* for ice cream, but I knew I should stick to my diet.

    Your definition _____

    Dictionary definition _____

3. I faced a *gauntlet* of questions from my parents after arriving home at 4 A.M.

    Your definition _____

    Dictionary definition _____

4. Mel tried to *cajole* me into going to the party, but I wasn't in the mood.

    Your definition _____

    Dictionary definition _____

ETYMOLOGY

Etymology refers to the origin and historical development of a word. Such information is usually enclosed in brackets and is more likely to be present in a hardbound dictionary than in a paperback one. Good desk dictionaries include:

The American Heritage Dictionary
The Random House Dictionary
Webster's New Collegiate Dictionary
Webster's New World Dictionary

See if your dictionary gives the origins of each of the following words:

guillotine _____

cereal _____

derrick _____

USAGE LABELS

As a general rule, use only standard English words in your writing. If a word is not standard English, your dictionary will probably give it a usage label like one of the following: *informal, nonstandard, slang, vulgar, obsolete, archaic, rare.*

Look up the following words and record how your dictionary labels them. Remember that a recent hardbound desk dictionary will always be the best source of information about usage.

brass (meaning ''rudeness'') _____

dope (meaning ''very stupid person'') _____

beat (meaning ''exhausted'') _____

croak (meaning ''die'') _____

snuck (meaning ''sneaked'') _____

SYNONYMS

A *synonym* is a word that is close in meaning to another word. Using synonyms helps you avoid unnecessary repetition of the same word in a paper. A paperback dictionary is not likely to give you synonyms for words, but a good desk dictionary will.

Consult a desk dictionary that gives you synonyms for the following words and write the synonyms in the space provided.

leave _____

difficult _____

important _____

You might also want to own a *thesaurus,* a book that lists synonyms and *antonyms*—words approximately opposite in meaning to another word. A thesaurus can improve your writing, helping you find the precise word needed to express your thoughts. A thesaurus works much like a dictionary. You look up a word, and instead of definitions provided by a dictionary, you get a list of synonyms for the word. Here are three good thesauruses:

The New American Roget's College Thesaurus in Dictionary Form,
    Paperback Edition
The Random House Thesaurus
Webster's Collegiate Thesaurus

IMPROVING
SPELLING

Poor spelling often results from bad habits developed in early school years. With work, such habits can be corrected. If you can write your name without misspelling it, there is no reason why you cannot do the same with almost any word in the English language. Following are steps you can take to improve your spelling.

STEP 1: USE THE DICTIONARY

Get into the habit of using the dictionary. When you write a paper, allow yourself time to look up the spelling of all those words you are unsure about. Do not overlook the value of this step just because it is such a simple one. By using the dictionary, you can probably make yourself a 95 percent better speller.

STEP 2: KEEP A PERSONAL SPELLING LIST

Keep a list of words you misspell and study the words regularly. Put the words on the back page of a frequently used notebook or on a separate sheet of paper titled "Personal Spelling List."

To master the words on your personal spelling list, do the following:

1   Write down any hint that will help you remember the spelling of a word. For example, you might want to note that *occasion* is spelled with two *c*'s, or that *all right* is two words, not one word.

2   Study a word by looking at it, saying it, and spelling it. You may also want to write out the word one or more times, or "air write" it with your finger in large, exaggerated motions.

3   When you have trouble spelling a long word, try to break the word into syllables and see whether you can spell the syllables. For example, *inadvertent* can be spelled easily if you can hear and spell in turn its four syllables: *in ad ver tent*. Or the word *consternation* can be spelled easily if you hear and spell in turn its four syllables: *con ster na tion*. Remember, then: Try to see, hear, and spell long words in terms of their syllable parts.

4   Keep in mind that review and repeated self-testing are the keys to effective learning. When you are learning a series of words, go back after studying each new word and review all the preceding ones.

STEP 3: MASTER COMMONLY CONFUSED WORDS

Master the meanings and spellings of the commonly confused words on pages 426–434. Your instructor may assign twenty words for you to study at a time and give you a series of quizzes until you have mastered the words.

STEP 4: LEARN KEY WORDS IN MAJOR SUBJECTS

Make up and master lists of words central to the vocabulary of your major subjects. For example, a list of key words in business might include: *economics, management, resources, scarcity, capitalism, decentralization, productivity, enterprise,* and so on; in psychology: *behavior, investigation, experimentation, frustration, cognition, stimulus, response, organism,* and so on. Set aside a specific portion of your various course notebooks to be used only for such lists, and study them using the methods for learning words that are described above.

STEP 5: STUDY A BASIC WORD LIST

Study the spellings of the words in the following list. They are 250 often-misspelled words in English. Your instructor may assign twenty-five or fifty words for you to study at a time and give you a series of quizzes until you have mastered the list.

250 Basic Words

absence
ache
achieve
acknowledge
advice
aisle
all right
already
amateur
answer
anxious
appearance
appetite
attempt
attendance
autumn
awful
bachelor
balance
bargain
basically
beautiful
believe
beneficial
25 bottom
breathe
brilliant
bureau
business
cafeteria
calendar
candidate
category
ceiling
cemetery
chief
choose
cigarette
citizen
college

column
comfortable
committed
completely
conceit
conscience
conscious
conversation
cruelty
50 daughter
deceit
definite
deposit
dictionary
disastrous
disease
distance
doctor
doubt
efficient
eighth
either
emphasize
entrance
environment
exaggerate
examine
existence
familiar
fascinate
February
financial
foreign
forty
75 friend
furniture
government
grammar
grieve
guidance

hammer
handkerchief
harass
height
hospital
hundred
husband
imitation
incredible
independent
instant
instead
intelligence
interest
interfere
interrupt
irresistible
January
kindergarten
100 leisure
library
lightning
likely
livelihood
loneliness
loose
magazine
making
maintain
marriage
material
mathematics
medicine
minute
mortgage
muscle
naturally
necessary
neither
nickel

niece
ninety
noise
obedience
125 obstacle
occasion
occur
occurrence
omission
opinion
opportunity
optimist
ounce
outrageous
pageant
pamphlet
people
perform
persistent
physically
picnic
plausible
pleasant
policeman
possible
precede
prefer
preference
prejudice
150 prescription
probably
psychology
pursue
quantity
quarter
quiet
quiz
raise
really
recede
receive
recognize
recommend

reference
region
reign
relieve
religion
representative
resistance
restaurant
rhythm
ridiculous
right
175 safety
said
salary
scarcely
scholastic
science
scissors
secretary
seize
separate
sergeant
several
severely
shriek
siege
similar
sincerely
sophomore
succeed
suppress
straight
telephone
temperature
tenant
tendency
200 tenth
than
theater
though
thousand
through
tomorrow

tongue
tonight
tournament
toward
transferred
trousers
truly
twelfth
unanimous
until
unusual
usage
used
usual
usually
vacuum
valuable
variety
225 vegetable
vengeance
view
villain
visitor
voice
Washington
wear
weather
Wednesday
weigh
weird
welcome
whether
which
woman
women
won't
writing
written
wrong
yesterday
yolk
your
250 you're

STEP 6: USE ELECTRONIC AIDS

There are three electronic aids that may help your spelling. First, many *electronic typewriters* on the market today will beep automatically when you misspell or mistype a word. They include built-in dictionaries that will then give you the correct spelling. Smith-Corona, for example, has a series of portable typewriters with an ''Auto-Spell'' feature that start at around $150 at discount stores.

Second, a *computer with a spell-checker* will identify incorrect words and suggest correct spellings. If you know how to write on a computer, you will have no trouble learning how to use the spell-check feature.

Third, *electronic spell-checkers* are pocket-size devices that look much like the pocket calculators you may carry to your math class. They are the latest example of how technology can help the learning process. Electronic spellers can be found in the typewriter or computer section of any discount store, at prices in the $100 range. The checker includes a tiny keyboard. You type out the word the way you think it is spelled, and the checker quickly provides you with the correct spelling of related words. Some of these checkers even *pronounce* the word aloud for you.

VOCABULARY DEVELOPMENT

A good vocabulary is a vital part of effective communication. A command of many words will make you a better writer, speaker, listener, and reader. Studies have shown that students with strong vocabularies, or students who work to improve a limited vocabulary, are more successful in school. And one research study found that *a good vocabulary, more than any other factor, was common to people enjoying successful careers in life*. This section will describe three ways of developing your word power: (1) regular reading, (2) vocabulary wordsheets, and (3) vocabulary study books. You should keep in mind from the start, however, that none of the approaches will help unless you truly decide to make vocabulary development an important goal. Only when you have this attitude can you begin doing the sustained work needed to improve your word power.

REGULAR READING

Through reading a good deal, you will learn words by experiencing them a number of times in a variety of sentences. Repeated exposures to a word in context will eventually make it a part of your working language.

You should develop the habit of reading a daily newspaper and one or more weekly magazines like *Time, Newsweek,* or even *People,* as well as monthly magazines suited to your interests. In addition, you should try to do some book reading for pleasure. This may be especially difficult at times when you also have textbook reading to do. Try, however, to redirect a regular one-half to one hour of your recreational time to book reading, rather than watching television, listening to music, or the like. By doing so, you may eventually reap the rewards of an improved vocabulary *and* the discovery that reading can be truly enjoyable. If you would like some book recommendations, ask your instructor for a copy of the "List of Interesting Books" that appears in the Instructor's Manual of *College Writing Skills.*

WORDSHEETS

Another means of vocabulary development is to use vocabulary wordsheets. You should first mark off words in your reading that you want to learn. After you have accumulated a number of words, sit down with a dictionary and look up basic information about each of them. Put this information on a wordsheet like the one shown on the next page. Be sure also to write down a sentence in which each word appears. A word is always best learned not in a vacuum but in the context of surrounding words.

Study each word as follows. First, make sure you can correctly pronounce the word and its derivations. (Page 412 explains the dictionary pronunciation key that will help you properly pronounce each word.) Second, study the main meanings of the word until you can say them without looking at them. Finally, spend a moment looking at the example of the word in context. You should then go on to follow the same process with the second word. Then, after testing yourself on the first and the second words, go on to the third word. Remember to continue going back and testing yourself on all the words you have studied after you learn each new word. Such repeated self-testing is the key to effective learning.

Activity

Locate four words in your reading that you would like to master. Enter them in the spaces on the vocabulary wordsheet that starts below and fill in all the needed information. Your instructor may then check your wordsheet and perhaps give you a quick oral quiz on selected words.

You may receive a standing assignment to add five words a week to a wordsheet and to study the words. Note that you can create your own wordsheets using loose-leaf paper, or your instructor may give you copies of the wordsheet that appears below.

Vocabulary Wordsheet

1. Word: _tenacious_   Pronunciation: _(tə nā' shəs)_

   Meanings: _1. Keeping a firm hold_

   2. Persistent; stubborn

   Other forms of the word: _tenaciously   tenacity_

   Use of the word in context: _I tried to loosen the tick's tenacious grip on my skin._

2. Word: _____   Pronunciation: _____

   Meanings: _____

   _____

   _____

   Other forms of the word: _____

   Use of the word in context: _____

   _____

3. Word: _____   Pronunciation: _____

   Meanings: _____

   _____

   _____

   Other forms of the word: _____

   Use of the word in context: _____

   _____

4. Word: _____   Pronunciation: _____

   Meanings: _____

   _____

   _____

   Other forms of the word: _____

   Use of the word in context: _____

   _____

5. Word: _____   Pronunciation: _____

   Meanings: _____

   _____

   _____

   Other forms of the word: _____

   Use of the word in context: _____

   _____

VOCABULARY STUDY BOOKS

A third means of increasing your word power is the use of vocabulary study books. One well-known series of books is the EDL *Word Clues,* which may be available in the learning skills center at your school. These books help you learn a word by asking you to look at the context, or the words around the unfamiliar word, to unlock its meaning. This method is called *using context clues,* or *using word clues.*

Here are some individual vocabulary study books you can find at most bookstores:

1100 Words You Need to Know (Barron's)—Bromberg and Gordon

30 Days to a More Powerful Vocabulary (Pocket Books)—Funk and Lewis

Instant Word Power (Signet Books)—Lewis

Vocabulary through Pleasurable Reading (Amsco School Publications)

Here is one book you can order:

Building Vocabulary for College, Second Edition, by R. Kent Smith. (For information on ordering this book, write to D.C. Heath and Company, 125 Spring Street, Lexington, MA 02173.)

Many other vocabulary books and programs are available. The best are those which present words in one or more contexts and then provide several reinforcement activities for each word. The books will help you increase your vocabulary *if* you have the determination required to work with them on a regular basis.

COMMONLY
CONFUSED
WORDS

HOMONYMS

The commonly confused words (also known as *homonyms*) on the following pages have the same sounds but different meanings and spellings. Complete the activity for each set of words, and check off and study the words that give you trouble.

all ready   completely prepared
already   previously; before

It was *already* four o'clock by the time I thought about lunch.
My report was *all ready*, but the class was canceled.

Fill in the blanks: David was _____ to sign up for the course

when he discovered that it had _____ closed.

brake   stop
break   come apart

The mechanic advised me to add *brake* fluid to my car.
During a commercial *break*, Marie lay on the floor and did fifty sit-ups.

Fill in the blanks: Tim, a poor driver, _____ *s* at the last minute

and usually _____ *s* the speed limit as well.

course   part of a meal; a school subject; direction
coarse   rough

At the movies, I tried to decide on a *course* of action that would put an end to the *coarse* language of the man behind me.

Fill in the blanks: Over the _____ of time, jagged, _____ rocks will be polished to smoothness by the pounding waves.

hear   perceive with the ear
here   in this place

I can *hear* the performers so well from *here* that I don't want to change my seat.

Fill in the blanks: The chairperson explained that the meeting was held _____ in the auditorium to enable everyone to _____ the debate.

hole   an empty spot
whole   entire

A *hole* in the crumbling brick mortar made a convenient home for the small bird and its *whole* family.

Fill in the blanks: The _____ in Dave's arguments wouldn't exist if he put his _____ concentration into his thinking.

its   belonging to it
it's   the shortened form for ''it is'' or ''it has''

The tall giraffe lowered *its* head (the head belonging to the giraffe) to the level of the car window and peered in at us.
It's (it is) too late to sign up for the theater trip to New York.

Fill in the blanks: I decided not to take the course because _____ too easy; _____ content offers no challenge whatever.

knew   past form of *know*
new   not old

No one *knew* our *new* phone number, but the obscene calls continued.

Fill in the blanks: Even people who _____ Charlie well didn't recognize him with his _____ beard.

know   to understand
no   a negative

By the time students complete that course, they *know* two computer languages and have *no* trouble writing their own programs.

Fill in the blanks: Dogs and cats usually _____ by the tone of the speaker's voice when they are being told "_____."

passed   went by; succeeded in; handed to
past   a time before the present; by, as in ''I drove past the house''

As Yvonne *passed* exit six on the interstate, she knew she had gone *past* the correct turnoff.

Fill in the blanks: Lewis asked for a meeting with his boss to learn why he had been _____ over for promotion twice in the _____ year.

peace   calm
piece   a part

The best *piece* of advice she ever received was to maintain her own inner *peace*.

Fill in the blanks: Upon hearing that _____ of music, my angry mood was gradually replaced by one of _____.

plain   simple
plane   aircraft

The *plain* box contained a very expensive model *plane* kit.

Fill in the blanks: After unsuccessfully trying to overcome her fear, Sally finally admitted the _____ truth: she was terrified of flying in _____*s*.

principal   main; a person in charge of a school
principle   a law or standard

If the *principal* ingredient in this stew is octopus, I'll abandon my *principle* of trying everything at least once.

Fill in the blanks: Our _____ insists that all students adhere to the school's _____*s* regarding dress, tardiness, and smoking.

right   correct; opposite of ''left''
write   what you do in English

Without the *right* amount of advance planning, it is difficult to *write* a good research paper.

Fill in the blanks: Connie wanted to send for the records offered on TV, but she could not _____ fast enough to get all the _____ information down before the commercial ended.

than (thăn)   used in comparisons
then (thĕn)   at that time

I made more money *then*, but I've never been happier *than* I am now.

Fill in the blanks: When I was in high school, I wanted a racy two-seater convertible more _____ anything else; but _____ my friends pointed out that only one person would be able to ride with me.

their   belonging to them

there   at that place; a neutral word used with verbs like *is, are, was, were, have,* and *had*

they're   the shortened form of "they are"

The tenants *there* are complaining because *they're* being cheated by *their* landlord.

Fill in the blanks: The tomatoes I planted _____ in the back of the garden are finally ripening, but _____ bright red color will attract hungry raccoons, and I fear _____ going to be eaten.

threw   past form of *throw*

through   from one side to the other; finished

As the inexperienced pizza maker *threw* the pie into the air, he punched a hole *through* its thin crust.

Fill in the blanks: As the President moved slowly _____ the cheering crowd, the Secret Service agent suddenly _____ himself at a man waving a small, metal object.

to   a verb part, as in *to smile;* toward, as in "I'm going *to* heaven"

too   overly, as in "The pizza was *too* hot"; also, as in "The coffee was hot, *too.*"

two   the number 2

I ran *to* the car *to* roll up the windows. (The first *to* means "toward"; the second *to* is a verb part that goes with *roll.*)

That amusement park is *too* far away; I hear that it's expensive, *too.* (The first *too* means "overly"; the second *too* means "also.")

The *two* players (2 players) jumped up to tap the basketball away.

Fill in the blanks: The _____ of them have been dating for a year, but lately they seem _____ be arguing _____ often to pretend nothing is wrong.

wear   to have on
where   in what place

> *Where* I will *wear* a purple feather boa is not the point; I just want to buy it.

Fill in the blanks: _____ were we going the night I refused to _____ a tie?

weather   atmospheric conditions
whether   if it happens that; in case; if

> Although meteorologists are *weather* specialists, even they can't predict *whether* a hurricane will change course.

Fill in the blanks: The gloomy _____ report in the paper this morning ended all discussion of _____ to pack a picnic lunch for later.

whose   belonging to whom
who's   the shortened form for "who is" and "who has"

> "*Who's* the patient *whose* filling fell out?" the dentist's assistant asked.

Fill in the blanks: _____ the salesperson _____ customers are always complaining about his high-pressure tactics?

your   belonging to you
you're   the shortened form of "you are"

> *You're* making a fool of yourself; *your* Elvis imitation isn't funny.

Fill in the blanks: If _____ having trouble filling out _____ tax return, why don't you call the IRS's toll-free hot line?

OTHER WORDS FREQUENTLY CONFUSED

Here is a list of other words that people frequently confuse. Complete the activities for each set of words, and check off and study the words that give you trouble.

a   Both *a* and *an* are used before other words to mean, approximately, "one."
an

Generally you should use *an* before words starting with a vowel (*a, e, i, o u*):

    an orange   an umbrella   an indication   an ape   an effort

Generally you should use *a* before words starting with a consonant (all other letters):

    a genius   a movie   a speech   a study   a typewriter

Fill in the blanks: The morning after the party, I had _____ pounding headache and _____ upset stomach.

accept (ăk sĕpt′)   receive; agree to
except (ĕk sĕpt′)   exclude; but

> It was easy to *accept* the book's plot, *except* for one unlikely coincidence at the very end.

Fill in the blanks: Nan would have _____ *ed* the position, _____ that it would add twenty minutes to her daily commute.

advice (ăd vīs′)   a noun meaning "an opinion"
advise (ăd vīz′)   a verb meaning "to counsel, to give advice"

> I have learned not to take my sister's *advice* on straightening out my life.
> A counselor can *advise* you about the courses you'll need next year.

Fill in the blanks: Karen seems so troubled about losing her job that I _____ *ed* her to seek the _____ of a professional counselor.

affect (uh fĕkt′)   a verb meaning "to influence"
effect (ĭ fĕkt′)   a verb meaning "to bring about something"; a noun meaning
                         "result"

    The bad weather will definitely *affect* the outcome of the election.
    If we can *effect* a change in George's attitude, he may do better in his courses.
    One *effect* of the strike will be dwindling supplies in the supermarkets.

Fill in the blanks: Scientists have studied the _____ of large
quantities of saccharine on lab animals but have yet to learn how similar
amounts _____ human beings.

among   implies three or more
between implies only two

    After the team of surgeons consulted *among* themselves, they decided that
    the bullet was lodged *between* two of the patient's ribs.

Fill in the blanks: _____ halves, one enthusiastic fan stood up
_____ his equally fanatic friends and took off his coat and shirt.

beside   along the side of
besides in addition to

    Besides doing daily inventories, I have to stand *beside* the cashier whenever
    the store gets crowded.

Fill in the blanks: _____ those books on the table, I plan to use
these magazines stacked _____ me while doing my research paper.

fewer   used with things that can be counted
less   refers to amount, value, or degree

    I've taken *fewer* classes this semester, so I hope to have *less* trouble finding
    time to study.

Fill in the blanks: This beer advertises that it has _____ calories
and is _____ filling.

former refers to the first of two items named
latter refers to the second of two items named

> Sue yelled at her sons, Greg and John, when she got home; the *former* had left the refrigerator open and the *latter* had left wet towels all over the bathroom.

Fill in the blanks: Eddy collects coupons and parking tickets: the ＿＿＿＿＿＿ save him money and the ＿＿＿＿＿＿ are going to cost him a great deal of money some day.

learn to gain knowledge
teach to give knowledge

> I can't *learn* a new skill unless someone with lots of patience *teaches* me.

Fill in the blanks: Because she is quick to ＿＿＿＿＿＿ new things, Mandy has offered to ＿＿＿＿＿＿ me how to play the latest video games.

loose (loos) not fastened; not tight-fitting
lose (looz) misplace; fail to win

> In this strong wind, the house may *lose* some of its *loose* roof shingles.

Fill in the blanks: A ＿＿＿＿＿＿ wire in the television set was causing us to ＿＿＿＿＿＿ the picture.

quiet (kwī′ĭt) peaceful
quite (kwīt) entirely; really; rather

> Jennifer seems *quiet* and demure, but she has *quite* a temper at times.

Fill in the blanks: Most people think the library is ＿＿＿＿＿＿ a good place to study, but I find the extreme ＿＿＿＿＿＿ distracting.

Activity

These sentences check your understanding of *its, it's; there, their, they're; to, too, two;* and *your, you're*. Underline the two incorrect spellings in each sentence. Then spell the words correctly in the spaces provided.

_____
_____

1. "Its not a very good idea," yelled Alexandra's boss, "to tell you're customer that the striped dress she plans to buy makes her look like a pregnant tiger."

_____

2. You're long skirt got stuck in the car door, and now its sweeping the highway.

_____
_____

3. When your young, their is a tendency to confuse a crush with true love.

_____
_____

4. After too hours of typing, Lin was to tired to type any longer.

_____
_____

5. It is unusual for a restaurant to lose it's license, but this one had more mice in its' kitchen than cooks.

_____
_____

6. The vampires bought a knife sharpener in order too sharpen there teeth.

_____
_____

7. Your sometimes surprised by who you're friends turn out to be in difficult times.

_____

8. When the children get to quiet, Clare knows their getting into trouble.

_____
_____

9. There friendship developed into love as the years passed, and now, in midlife, their newlyweds.

_____
_____

10. There is no reason to panic if you get a bad grade or too. Its well known that many successful people were not great students.

■ Review Test 1

Underline the correct word in the parentheses. Rather than guessing, look back at the explanations of the words when necessary.

1. I (know, no) that several of the tenants have decided (to, too, two) take (their, there, they're) case to court.
2. (Whose, Who's) the author of that book about the (affects, effects) of eating (to, too, two) much protein?
3. In our supermarket is a counter (where, wear) (your, you're) welcome to sit down and have free coffee and doughnuts.
4. (Its, It's) possible to (loose, lose) friends by constantly giving out unwanted (advice, advise).
5. For a long time, I couldn't (accept, except) the fact that my husband wanted a divorce; (then, than) I decided to stop being angry and get on with life.
6. I spent the (hole, whole) day browsing (threw, through) the chapters in my business textbook, but I didn't really study them.
7. The newly appointed (principal, principle) is (quite, quiet) familiar with the problems (hear, here) at our school.
8. I found that our cat had (all ready, already) had her kittens (among, between) the weeds (beside, besides) the porch.
9. I (advice, advise) you not to take children to that movie; the special (affects, effects) are (to, too, two) frightening.
10. It seems that nobody will ever be able to (learn, teach) Mario to take (fewer, less) chances in his car.

■ Review Test 2

On separate paper, write short sentences using the ten words shown below.

1. accept
2. its
3. you're
4. too
5. then
6. principal
7. their
8. passed
9. fewer
10. who's

EFFECTIVE WORD CHOICE

Choose your words carefully when you write. Always take the time to think about your word choices rather than simply use the first word that comes to mind. You want to develop the habit of selecting words that are appropriate and exact for your purposes. One way you can show your sensitivity to language is by avoiding slang, clichés, pretentious words, and wordiness.

SLANG

We often use slang expressions when we talk because they are so vivid and colorful. However, slang is usually out of place in formal writing. Here are some examples of slang expressions:

Someone *ripped off* Ken's new Adidas running shoes from his locker.
After the game, we *stuffed our faces* at the diner.
I finally told my parents to *get off my case*.
The movie really *grossed me out*.

Slang expressions have a number of drawbacks. They go out of date quickly, they become tiresome if used excessively in writing, and they may communicate clearly to some readers but not to others. Also, the use of slang can be an evasion of the specific details that are often needed to make one's meaning clear in writing. For example, in "The movie really grossed me out," the writer has not provided the specific details about the movie necessary for us to clearly understand the statement. Was it the acting, the special effects, or the violent scenes in the movie that the writer found so disgusting? In general, then, you should avoid the use of slang in your writing. If you are in doubt about whether an expression is slang, it may help to check a recently published hardbound dictionary.

Activity

Rewrite the following sentences, replacing the italicized slang words with more formal ones.

Example   When we told the neighbors to *can the noise,* they *freaked out.*
When we told the neighbors to be quiet, they got upset.

1. I didn't realize how *messed up* Joey was until he stole some money from his parents and *split* for a month.

     _____

     _____

     _____

2. After a hard day, I like to *veg out* in front of the *idiot box.*

     _____

     _____

     _____

3. Paul was so *wiped out* after his workout at the gym that he couldn't *get it together* to defrost a frozen dinner.

     _____

     _____

     _____

4. When Rick tried to *put the move on* Lola at the school party, she told him to *shove off.*

     _____

     _____

     _____

5. My father claims that most *grease monkeys* are *rip-off artists.*

     _____

     _____

     _____

CLICHÉS

A *cliché* is an expression that has been worn out through constant use. Some typical clichés are:

short but sweet	last but not least
drop in the bucket	work like a dog
had a hard time of it	all work and no play
word to the wise	it goes without saying
it dawned on me	at a loss for words
sigh of relief	taking a big chance
too little, too late	took a turn for the worse
singing the blues	easier said than done
in the nick of time	on top of the world
too close for comfort	time and time again
saw the light	make ends meet

Clichés are common in speech but make your writing seem tired and stale. Also, they are often an evasion of the specific details that you must work to provide in your writing. You should, then, avoid clichés and try to express your meaning in fresh, original ways.

Activity 1

Underline the cliché in each of the following sentences. Then substitute specific, fresh words for the trite expression.

> My boyfriend has stuck with me <u>through thick and thin.</u>
> *through good times and bad*

1. As the only girl in an otherwise all-boy family, I got away with murder.

_____

2. When I realized I'd lost my textbook, I knew I was up the creek without a paddle.

   _____

3. My suggestion is just a shot in the dark, but it's better than nothing.

   _____

4. Janice got more than she bargained for when she offered to help Larry with his math homework.

   _____

5. Bob is pushing his luck by driving a car with bald tires.

   _____

6. On a hot, sticky, midsummer day, iced tea or any frosty drink really hits the spot.

   _____

7. Melissa thanks her lucky stars that she was born with brains, beauty, and humility.

   _____

8. Anything that involves mathematical ability has always been right up my alley.

   _____

9. Your chances of buying a good used car from that dealer are one in a million.

   _____

10. Even when we are up to our eyeballs in work, our boss wonders if we have enough to do.

   _____

Activity 2

Write a short paragraph decribing the kind of day you had. Try to put as many clichés as possible into your writing. For example, ''I got up at the crack of dawn, ready to take on the world. I grabbed a bite to eat. . . .'' By making yourself aware of clichés in this way, you should lessen the chance that they will appear in your writing.

PRETENTIOUS WORDS

Some people feel that they can improve their writing by using fancy and elevated words rather than more simple and natural words. They use artificial and stilted language that more often obscures their meaning than communicates it clearly. Here are some unnatural-sounding sentences:

It was a splendid opportunity to get some slumber.
We relished the delicious repast.
The officer apprehended the intoxicated operator of the vehicle.
This establishment sells women's apparel and children's garments.

The same thoughts can be expressed more clearly and effectively by using plain, natural language, as below:

It was a good chance to get some sleep.
We enjoyed the delicious meal.
The officer arrested the car's drunken driver.
This store sells women's and children's clothes.

Here is a list of some other inflated words and the simpler words that could replace them.

Inflated Words	Simpler Words
subsequent to	after
finalize	finish
transmit	send
facilitate	help
component	part
initiate	begin
delineate	describe
manifested	shown
to endeavor	to try

Cross out the artificial words in each sentence. Then substitute clear, simple language for the artificial words.

Example   The ~~conflagration~~ was ~~initiated~~ by an arsonist.
                The fire was started by an arsonist.

1. Mark and his brother do not interrelate in a harmonious manner.

   _____

2. The meaning of the movie's conclusion eluded my comprehension.

   _____

3. The departmental conference will commence promptly at two o'clock.

   _____

4. A man dressed in odd attire accosted me on the street.

   _____

5. When my writing implement malfunctioned, I asked the professor for another.

   _____

WORDINESS

Wordiness—using more words than necessary to express a meaning—is often a sign of lazy or careless writing. Your readers may resent the extra time and energy they must spend when you have not done the work needed to make your writing direct and concise.

Here are examples of wordy sentences:

In this paper, I am planning to describe the hobby that I enjoy of collecting old comic books.
In Dan's opinion, he thinks that cable television will change and alter our lives in the future.

Omitting needless words improves the sentences:

I enjoy collecting old comic books.
Dan thinks that cable television will change our lives.

At the top of the next page is a list of some wordy expressions that could be reduced to single words.

Wordy Form	*Short Form*
at the present time	now
in the event that	if
in the near future	soon
due to the fact that	because
for the reason that	because
is able to	can
in every instance	always
in this day and age	today
during the time that	while
a large number of	many
big in size	big
red in color	red
five in number	five
return back	return
good benefit	benefit
commute back and forth	commute
postponed until later	postponed

Activity

Rewrite the following sentences, omitting needless words.

1. In conclusion, I would like to end my paper by summarizing each of the major points covered within my report.

   _____

   _____

2. Controlling the quality and level of the television shows that children watch is a continuing challenge to parents that they must meet on a daily basis.

   _____

   _____

3. In general, I am the sort of person who tends to be shy, especially in large crowds or with strangers I don't know well.

   _____

   _____

4. Someone who is analyzing magazine advertising can find hidden messages that, once uncovered, are seen to be clever and persuasive.

_____

_____

5. My greatest mistake that I made last week was to hurt my brother's feelings and then not to have the nerve to apologize and say how sorry I was.

_____

_____

■ Review Test 1

Certain words are italicized in the following sentences. In the space provided, identify the words as slang (S), a cliché (C), or pretentious words (PW). Then replace the words with more effective diction.

_____ 1. Losing weight is *easier said than done* for someone with a sweet tooth.

_____

_____ 2. After dinner, we washed the *culinary utensils* and wrapped the *excess* food.

_____

_____ 3. Bruce is so stubborn that talking to him is like *talking to a brick wall*.

_____

_____ 4. Michelle spent the summer *watching the tube* and *catching rays*.

_____

_____ 5. The fans, *all fired up* after the game, *peeled out* of the parking lot and honked their horns.

_____

_____ 6. The stew I made contained *everything but the kitchen sink*.

_____

_____ 7. That *guy* isn't really a criminal; he's just gotten a *bum rap*.

_____

_____ 8. My new *photographic equipment* is so complex that it *hinders my enjoyment* of taking pictures.

_____

_____ 9. I failed the test, and to *add insult to injury,* I got a low grade on my paper.

_____

_____ 10. I *perused* several *periodicals* while I waited for the doctor.

_____

■ Review Test 2

Rewrite the following sentences, omitting needless words.

1. In today's uncertain economic climate, it is clear that people, namely, average middle-class working people, have great difficulty saving much money or putting anything aside for emergencies.

    _____

    _____

2. He is of the opinion that children should be required by law to attend school until they reach the age of sixteen years old.

    _____

    _____

3. I reached the decision that I did not have quite enough native talent to try out to be one of the players on the basketball team.

    _____

    _____

4. We thought the television program that was on last night was enjoyable, whereas our parents reacted with dislike to the content of the show.

    _____

    _____

5. Because of the bad weather, the school district felt it would be safer to cancel classes and let everyone stay home than risk people having accidents on the way to school.

    _____

    _____

6. It seems to me that all the *Rocky* movies have been overrated, and that many people thought they were much better movies than they actually were.

    _____

    _____

7. I have a strong preference for candy over fruit, which, in my opinion, doesn't taste as good as candy does.

    _____

    _____

8.   Lynn is one of those people who rarely admit to being wrong, and it is
     very unusual to hear her acknowledge that she made a mistake.

     _____

     _____

9.   It seems obvious to me, and it should be to everyone else too, that people
     can be harmed as much by emotional abuse as by physical abuse, even if
     you don't lay a hand on them.

     _____

     _____

10. Out of all the regrets in my life so far, one of my greatest ones to the
     present time is that I did not take word-processing lessons when I was still
     in high school and had a chance to do so.

     _____

     _____

SENTENCE VARIETY

One part of effective writing is to vary the kinds of sentences that you write. If every sentence follows the same pattern, writing may become monotonous to read. This section of the book explains four ways you can create variety and interest in your writing style. It will also describe coordination and subordination—two important techniques for achieving different kinds of emphasis in writing.

The following are four methods you can use to make simple sentences more complex and sophisticated:

1 Add a second complete thought (coordination).
2 Add a dependent thought (subordination).
3 Begin with a special opening word or phrase.
4 Place adjectives or verbs in a series.

Each method will be discussed in turn.

ADD A SECOND COMPLETE THOUGHT

When you add a second complete thought to a simple sentence, the result is a compound (or double) sentence. The two complete statements in a compound sentence are usually connected by a comma plus a joining or coordinating word (*and, but, for, or, nor, so, yet*).

A compound sentence is used when you want to give equal weight to two closely related ideas. The technique of showing that ideas have equal importance is called *coordination*. Following are some compound sentences. In each case, the sentence contains two ideas that the writer regards as equal in importance.

Frank worked on the engine for three hours, but the car still wouldn't start.

Bananas were on sale this week, so I bought a bunch for the children's lunches.

We laced up our roller skates, and then we moved cautiously onto the rink.

Activity

Combine the following pairs of simple sentences into compound sentences. Use a comma and a logical joining word (*and*, *but*, *for*, *so*) to connect each pair of statements.

Note: If you are not sure what *and*, *but*, *for*, and *so* mean, review page 311.

Example
- The weather was cold and windy.
- Al brought a thick blanket to the football game.

The weather was cold and windy, so Al brought a thick

blanket to the football game.

1.
   - Stanley was starving.
   - He hadn't eaten a thing since breakfast.

   _____

   _____

2.
   - I tried to sleep.
   - The thought of tomorrow's math exam kept me awake.

   _____

   _____

3.
   - This diner has its own bakery.
   - It has takeout service as well.

   _____

   _____

4.
   - The cardboard storage boxes were soggy.
   - Rainwater had seeped into the basement during the storm.

   _____

   _____

5.
   - I didn't have enough money to buy my parents an anniversary present.
   - I offered to mow their lawn for the whole summer.

   _____

   _____

ADD A DEPENDENT THOUGHT

When you add a dependent thought to a simple sentence, the result is a complex sentence.* A dependent thought begins with one of the following subordinating words:

after	if, even if	when, whenever
although, though	in order that	where, wherever
as	since	whether
because	that, so that	which, whichever
before	unless	while
even though	until	who
how	what, whatever	whose

A complex sentence is used when you want to emphasize one idea over another in a sentence. Look at the following complex sentence:

Although the exam room was very quiet, I still couldn't concentrate.

The idea that the writer wishes to emphasize here—*I still couldn't concentrate*—is expressed as a complete thought. The less important idea—*Although the exam room was very quiet*—is subordinated to the complete thought. The technique of giving one idea less emphasis than another is called *subordination*.

Following are other examples of complex sentences. In each case, the part starting with the dependent word is the less emphasized part of the sentence.

Even though I was tired, I stayed up to watch the horror movie.
Before I take a bath, I check for spiders in the tub.
When Ivy feels nervous, she pulls on her earlobe.

---

* The two parts of a complex sentence are sometimes called an *independent clause* and a *dependent clause*. A *clause* is simply a word group that contains a subject and a verb. An independent clause expresses a complete thought and can stand alone. A dependent clause does not express a complete thought in itself and "depends on" the independent clause to complete its meaning. Dependent clauses always begin with a dependent or subordinating word.

Activity

Use logical subordinating words to combine the following pairs of simple sentences into sentences that contain a dependent thought. Place a comma after a dependent statement when it starts the sentence.

Example ■ Rita bit into the hard taffy.
 ■ She broke a filling.
 When Rita bit into the hard taffy, she broke a filling.

1. ■ I had forgotten to lock the front door.
 ■ I had to drive back to the house.

 _____

 _____

 _____

2. ■ The bear turned over the rotten log.
 ■ Fat white grubs crawled in every direction.

 _____

 _____

 _____

3. ■ Kevin had mailed away for a set of tools.
 ■ He changed his mind about spending the money.

 _____

 _____

 _____

4. ■ Lew is allergic to wool.
 ■ He buys only sweaters made from acrylic.

 _____

 _____

 _____

5. ■ Sara types one hundred words a minute.
 ■ She is having trouble landing a secretarial job.

 _____

 _____

 _____

BEGIN WITH A SPECIAL OPENING WORD OR PHRASE

Among the special openers that can be used to start sentences are *-ed* words, *-ing* words, *-ly* words, *to* word groups, and prepositional phrases. Here are examples of all five kinds of openers:

-ed *word*	Concerned about his son's fever, Paul called a doctor.
-ing *word*	Humming softly, the woman browsed through the rack of dresses.
-ly *word*	Hesitantly, Sue approached the instructor's desk.
to *word group*	To protect her hair, Eva uses the lowest setting on her blow dryer.
prepositional phrase	During the exam, drops of water fell from the ceiling.

Activity

Combine each of the following pairs of simple sentences into one sentence by using the opener shown at the left and omitting repeated words. Use a comma to set off the opener from the rest of the sentence.

Example   -ing *word*   ■ The pelican scooped small fish into its baggy bill.
■ It dipped into the waves.
Dipping into the waves, the pelican scooped small fish into its baggy bill.

-ed *word*   1. ■ The night sky glittered.
■ It was studded with thousands of stars.

_____

_____

-ing *word*   2. ■ She wondered how to break the news to the children.
■ She sat in the cold living room.

_____

_____

-ly *word*   3. ■ Shirley signed the repair contract.
           ■ She was reluctant.

_____

_____

to *word*   4. ■ Alan volunteered to work overtime.
group   ■ He wanted to improve his chances of promotion.

_____

_____

prepositional   5. ■ The accused murderer grinned at the witnesses.
phrase   ■ He did this during the trial.

_____

_____

-ed *word*   6. ■ The vet's office was noisy and confusing.
           ■ It was crowded with nervous pets.

_____

_____

-ing *word*   7. ■ Barry tried to find something worth watching.
           ■ He flipped from channel to channel.

_____

_____

-ly *word*   8. ■ My father asked me where I had been until 5 A.M.
           ■ He was casual.

_____

_____

to *word*   9. ■ Stan stood on the table with a carrot behind each ear.
group   ■ He did this to attract everyone's attention.

_____

_____

prepositional 10. ■ Doctors used leeches to draw blood from sick patients.
phrase   ■ They did this at one time.

_____

_____

PLACE ADJECTIVES OR VERBS IN A SERIES

Various parts of a sentence may be placed in a series. Among these parts are adjectives (descriptive words) and verbs. Here are examples of both in a series:

> **Adjectives**   I gently applied a *sticky new* Band-Aid to the *deep, ragged* cut on my finger.
>
> **Verbs**   The truck *bounced* off a guardrail, *sideswiped* a tree, and *plunged* down the embankment.

Activity

Combine the simple sentences into one sentence by using adjectives or verbs in a series and by omitting repeated words. In most cases, use a comma between the adjectives or verbs in a series.

Example
- Jesse spun the basketball on one finger.
- He rolled it along his arms.
- He dribbled it between his legs.

_____

_____

1.
- The baby toddled across the rug.
- He picked up a button.
- He put the button in his mouth.

_____

_____

2.
- Water dribbled out of the tap.
- The water was brown.
- The water was foul-tasting.
- The tap was rusty.
- The tap was metal.

_____

_____

3.
- In the dressing room, Pat tried on the swimsuit.
- She looked in the full-length mirror.
- She screamed.

_____

_____

4. ■ Art approached the wasps' nests hanging under the eaves.
   ■ The nests were large.
   ■ The nests were papery.
   ■ The eaves were old.
   ■ The eaves were wooden.

_____

_____

5. ■ Reeds bordered the pond.
   ■ The reeds were slim.
   ■ The reeds were brown.
   ■ The pond was green.
   ■ The pond was stagnant.

_____

_____

■ Review Test 1

On separate paper, use coordination or subordination to combine the groups of simple sentences on the opposite page into one or more longer sentences. Omit repeated words. Since various combinations are possible, you might want to jot down several combinations in each case. Then read them aloud to find the combination that sounds best.

Keep in mind that, very often, the relationship among ideas in a sentence will be clearer when subordinating rather than coordinating words are used.

Example ■ Lew arrived at the supermarket.
            ■ Lew had a painful thought.
            ■ He had clipped all the coupons from the paper.
            ■ He had forgotten to bring them.
            When Lew arrived at the supermarket, he had a painful
            thought. He had clipped all the coupons from the paper, but
            he had forgotten to bring them.

Comma Hints

a Use a comma at the end of a word group that starts with a subordinating word (as in "When Lew arrived at the supermarket, . . .").

b Use a comma between independent word groups connected by *and, but, for, or, nor, so, yet* (as in "He had clipped all the coupons from the paper, but . . .").

1. ■ Dan had repaired his broken watchband with a paper clip.
   ■ The clip snapped.
   ■ The watch slid off his wrist.

2. ■ The therapist watched.
   ■ Julie tried to stand on her weakened legs.
   ■ They crumpled under her.

3. ■ There were spaces on the street.
   ■ Richie pulled into an expensive parking garage.
   ■ He had just bought a new car.
   ■ He was afraid it would get dented.

4. ■ A sudden cold front hit the area.
   ■ Temperatures dropped thirty degrees in less than an hour.
   ■ My teeth began to chatter.
   ■ I was not wearing a warm jacket.

5. ■ The verdict was announced.
   ■ The spectators broke into applause.
   ■ The defendant looked stunned.
   ■ Then he let out a whoop of joy.

6. ■ The teacher watched closely.
   ■ The second-graders made candles.
   ■ Suddenly, one boy began to cry.
   ■ He had spilled hot wax on his arm.

7. ■ Vern works as a model.
   ■ He has to look his best.
   ■ He gained ten pounds recently.
   ■ He had to take off the extra weight.
   ■ He would have lost his job.

8. ■ The ball game was about to begin.
   ■ A dog ran onto the field.
   ■ The dog began nipping the infielders' ankles.
   ■ The game had to be delayed.
   ■ The dog was chased away.

9. ■ The lion was hungry.
   ■ It watched the herd of gazelle closely.
   ■ A young or sick animal wandered away from the group.
   ■ The lion would move in for the kill.

10. ■ I am a good mechanic.
    ■ My girl friend is a fast typist.
    ■ We decided to advertise our skills on the college bulletin board.
    ■ Unfortunately, we didn't get any calls at first.
    ■ We had forgotten to include our phone numbers on the notices.

■ Review Test 2

On separate paper, write:

1. Two sentences of your own that begin with *-ed* words
2. Two sentences that begin with *-ing* words
3. Two sentences that begin with *-ly* words
4. Two sentences that begin with *to* word groups
5. Two sentences that begin with prepositional phrases

Also write:

6. Two sentences of your own that contain a series of adjectives
7. Two sentences that contain a series of verbs

EDITING TESTS

PROOFREADING FOR SENTENCE-SKILLS MISTAKES

The ten editing tests in this section will give you practice in proofreading for sentence-skills mistakes. People often find it hard to proofread a paper carefully. They have put so much work into their writing, or so little, that it's almost painful for them to look at the paper one more time. You may simply have to *force* yourself to proofread. Remember that eliminating sentence-skills mistakes will improve an average paper and help ensure a strong grade on a good paper. Further, as you get into the habit of "proofing" your papers, you will get into the habit of using the sentence skills consistently. They are a basic part of clear and effective writing.

In the first five tests, the spots where errors occur have been underlined; your job is to identify each error. In the last five tests, you must locate as well as identify the errors.

■ Editing Test 1

Identify the sentence-skills mistakes at the underlined spots in the selection that follows. From the box below, choose the letter that describes each mistake and write it in the space provided. The same mistake may appear more than once. In one case, there is no mistake.

a. sentence fragment	d. dangling modifier
b. run-on	e. missing comma
c. inconsistent verb tense	f. no mistake

I had a strange experience last winter, I was shopping for Christmas presents when
<u>   </u>
                              1
I came to a small clothing shop. I was going to pass it by. <u>Until I saw a beautiful purple</u>
                                                                                        2
<u>robe on a mannequin in the window.</u> <u>Stopping to look at it, the mannequin seemed to</u>
                                                                  3
wink at me. I was really <u>startled, I looked</u> around to see if anyone else was watching.
                                    4
<u>Shaking my head I stepped</u> closer to the window. Then I really began to question my
            5
<u>sanity, it looked</u> like the mannequin <u>moved its</u> legs. My face must have shown alarm
     6   7
because the mannequin then <u>smiles.</u> <u>And even waved her arm.</u> I sighed with <u>relief, it</u>
                               8   9   10
was a human model after all.

1. _____   3. _____   5. _____   7. _____   9. _____

2. _____   4. _____   6. _____   8. _____   10. _____

Editing Test 2

Identify the sentence-skills mistakes at the underlined spots in the selection that
follows. From the box below, choose the letter that describes each mistake and
write it in the space provided. The same mistake may appear more than once.

a. run-on	d. missing quotation marks
b. mistake in subject- verb agreement	e. wordiness
	f. slang
c. faulty parallelism	g. missing comma

It is this writer's opinion that smokers should quit smoking for the sake of those
_____
                 1
who are around them. Perhaps the most helpless creatures that suffer from being near

a smoker is unborn babies, one study suggests that the risk of having an undersized baby
          ‾   ‾‾‾‾‾‾‾‾‾
          2   3
is doubled if pregnant women are exposed to cigarette smoke for about two hours a day.

Pregnant women both should refrain from smoking and to avoid smoke-filled rooms.
                                                            ‾‾‾‾‾‾‾‾‾‾
                                                                4
Spouses of smokers are also in big trouble. They are more likely than spouses of
                          ‾‾‾‾‾‾‾‾‾‾‾
                               5
nonsmokers to die of heart disease and the development of fatal cancers. Office workers
                                     ‾‾‾‾‾‾‾‾‾‾‾‾‾‾‾‾‾‾‾‾‾‾
                                              6
are a final group that can be harmed by a smoke-filled environment. The U.S. Surgeon

General has said "Workers who smoke are a health risk to their coworkers. While it is
         ‾‾‾‾‾‾‾‾‾‾‾‾‾‾‾‾‾‾   ‾‾‾‾‾‾‾‾‾‾‾‾‾‾
               7   8
undoubtedly true that one can argue that smokers have the right to hurt themselves they
          ‾‾‾‾‾‾‾‾‾‾‾‾   ‾‾‾‾‾‾‾‾‾‾‾
               9   10
do not have the right to hurt others. Smokers should abandon their deadly habits for

the health of others at home and at work.

1. _____ 3. _____ 5. _____ 7. _____ 9. _____

2. _____ 4. _____ 6. _____ 8. _____ 10. _____

■ Editing Test 3

Identify the sentence-skills mistakes at the underlined spots in the selection that follows. From the box below, choose the letter that describes each mistake and write it in the space provided. The same mistake may appear more than once.

a. sentence fragment	e. dangling modifier
b. run-on	f. missing comma
c. mistake in subject- verb agreement	g. wordiness
d. misplaced modifier	h. slang

America will never be a drug-free <u>society but</u> we could eliminate many of our drug-
                                        1
related problems by legalizing drugs. Drugs would be sold by companies and not criminals

if <u>they were legal.</u> The drug trade would then take place like any other <u>business freeing</u>
       2   3
the police and courts to devote their time to other problems. Lawful drugs would be sold

at a fair <u>price, no</u> one would need to steal in order to buy them. <u>By legalizing drugs,</u>
           4   5
organized crime would lose one of its major sources of revenue. <u>It goes without saying</u>
                                                                                      6
that we would, instead, create important tax revenues for the government. Finally, if

<u>drugs was</u> sold through legal outlets, we could reduce the drug problem among our young
      7
people. It would be illegal to sell drugs to people under a certain age. <u>Just as is the case</u>

<u>now with alcohol.</u> And because the profits on drugs would no longer <u>be out of sight,</u>
          8   9
there would be little incentive for drug pushers to sell to young people. Decriminalizing

drugs, in short, could be a solution. <u>To many of the problems that result from the illegal</u>
                                                                       10
drug trade.

1. ____	3. ____	5. ____	7. ____	9. ____
2. ____	4. ____	6. ____	8. ____	10. ____

■ Editing Test 4

Identify the sentence-skills mistakes at the underlined spots in the selection that follows. From the box below, choose the letter that describes each mistake and write it in the space provided. The same mistake may appear more than once. In one case, there is no mistake.

a. sentence fragment	e. mistake with quotation marks
b. run-on	f. mistake in pronoun point of view
c. mistake in subject-verb agreement	g. spelling error
d. mistake in verb tense	h. no mistake

One reason that I enjoy the commute to school is that the drive gives me <u>uninterupted</u>
₁
time to myself. The classes and socializing at college <u>is</u> great, and so is the time I spend
₂
with my family, but sometimes all this togetherness keeps <u>you</u> from being able to think.
₃
In fact, I look forward to the time I have <u>alone, it</u> gives me a chance to plan what I'll
₄
accomplish in the day ahead. For example, one Tuesday afternoon my history professor
<u>announces</u> that a rough outline for our semester report was due that Friday. <u>Fortunatly,</u>
₅ ₆
I had already done some <u>reading, and</u> I had checked my proposed topic with her the
₇
week before. <u>Therefore, on the way home in the car that evening.</u> I planned the entire
₈
history report in my mind. Then all I had to do when I got home was quickly jot it down
before I forgot it. <u>When I handed the professor the outline at 8:30 Wednesday morning.</u>
₉
She asked me <u>"if I had stayed up all night working on it."</u> She was amazed when I told
₁₀
her that I owed it all to commuting.

1. _____	3. _____	5. _____	7. _____	9. _____
2. _____	4. _____	6. _____	8. _____	10. _____

■ Editing Test 5

Identify the sentence-skills mistakes at the underlined spots in the selection that follows. From the box below, choose the letter that describes each mistake and write it in the space provided. The same mistake may appear more than once. In one case, there is no mistake.

a. sentence fragment	f. dangling modifier
b. run-on	g. homonym mistake
c. mistake in subject-verb agreement	h. missing apostrophe
d. missing comma	i. cliché
e. missing capital letter	j. no mistake

Cars can destroy your ego. First of all the kind of car you drive can make you feel
<u> </u>
1
like a second-class citizen. <u>If you can't afford a new, expensive car, and are forced to</u>
2
<u>drive an old clunker.</u> You'll be the object of pitying stares and nasty sneers. Drivers of
newer-model cars just <u>doesn't</u> appreciate it when a '68 <u>buick</u> with terminal body rust
3   4
lurches into the next parking slot. You may even find that drivers go out of <u>their</u> way
5
not to park near you. Breakdowns, too, can damage your self-respect. You may be an
assistant bank manager or a job <u>foreman,</u> you'll still feel <u>like two cents</u> when <u>your</u> sitting
6   7   8
on the side of the road. As the other cars whiz past, you'll stare helplessly at your <u>cars</u>
9
open hood or steaming radiator. In cases like this, you may even be turned into that
lowest of creatures, the pedestrian. <u>Shuffling humbly along the highway to the nearest</u>
10
<u>pay phone,</u> your car has delivered another staggering blow to your self-esteem.

1. _____   3. _____   5. _____   7. _____   9. _____

2. _____   4. _____   6. _____   8. _____   10. _____

■ Editing Test 6

See if you can locate and correct the ten sentence-skills mistakes in the following passage. The mistakes are listed in the box below. As you locate mistakes, put the sentence numbers in the spaces provided.

1 sentence fragment _____	1 missing comma after introductory material _____
1 run-on _____	2 missing quotation marks
1 mistake in verb tense _____	_____ _____
1 nonparallel structure _____	1 missing apostrophe _____
1 dangling modifier _____	
1 mistake in pronoun point of view _____	

¹The greatest of my everyday fears is technology. ²Beginning when I couldn't master bike riding and extending to the present day. ³Fear kept me from learning to operate a jigsaw, start an outboard motor, or even using a simple tape recorder. ⁴I almost didn't learn to drive a car. ⁵At age sixteen, Dad lifted the hood of our Chevy and said, All right, you're going to start learning to drive. ⁶Now, this is the distributor. . . When my eyes glazed over he shouted, "Well, I'm not going to bother if youre not interested!" ⁷Fortunately, the friend who later taught me to drive skipped what goes on under the hood. ⁸My most recent frustration is the 35 mm camera, I would love to take professional-quality pictures. ⁹But all the numbers and dials and meters confuse me. ¹⁰As a result, my unused camera is hidden away on a shelf in my closet. ¹¹Just last week, my sister gives me a beautiful digital watch for my birthday. ¹²I may have to put it on the shelf with the camera—the alarm keeps going off, and you can't figure out how to stop it.

■ Editing Test 7

See if you can locate and correct the ten sentence-skills mistakes in the following passage. The mistakes are listed in the box below. As you locate mistakes, put the sentence numbers in the spaces provided.

1 sentence fragment _____	1 mistake in subject-verb agreement _____
1 run-on _____	
1 missing comma around an interrupter _____	2 missing quotation marks _____ _____
2 apostrophe mistakes _____ _____	1 misplaced modifier _____
	1 nonparallel structure _____

¹I was six years old when, one day, my dog was struck by a car while getting ready for school. ²My mother and I heard the terrifying sound of squealing brake's. ³In a low voice, she said, Oh, my God—Blackie. ⁴I remember trailing her out the door and seeing a car filled with teenagers and a spreading pool of bright blood on our cobblestoned street. ⁵To me, it seemed only a matter of seconds until a police car pulled up. ⁶The officer glanced at the crumpled dog under the car. ⁷And drew his gun. ⁸My mother shouted, ''No!'' ⁹She crawled halfway under the car and took the dog, like a sack of flour, out from under the wheels. ¹⁰Her housedress was splashed with blood, she cradled the limp dog in her arms and ordered the officers to drive her to the vets office. ¹¹It was only then that she remembered me, I think. ¹²She patted my head, was telling me to walk up to school, and reassured me that Blackie would be all right. ¹³The rest of the story including Blackie's slow recovery and few more years of life, are fuzzy and vague now. ¹⁴But the sights and sounds of those few moments are as vivid to me now as they were twenty-five years ago.

Editing Test 8

See if you can locate and correct the ten sentence-skills mistakes in the following passage. The mistakes are listed in the box below. As you locate mistakes, put the sentence numbers in the spaces provided.

---

2 sentence fragments _____

_____

1 run-on _____

1 mistake in subject-verb agreement _____

1 nonparallel structure _____

2 apostrophe mistakes _____

_____

3 missing commas _____

_____ _____

---

[1] Most products have little or nothing to do with sex a person would never know that by looking at ads'. [2] A television ad for a headache remedy, for example shows the product being useful because it ends a womans throbbing head pain just in time for sex. [3] Now she will not say "Not tonight, Honey." [4] Another ad features a detergent that helps a single woman meet a man in a laundry room. [5] When it comes to products that do relate to sex appeal advertisers often present more obvious sexuality. [6] A recent magazine ad for women's clothing, for instance, make no reference to the quality of or how comfortable are the company's clothes. [7] Instead, the ad features a picture of a woman wearing a low-cut sleeveless T shirt and a very short skirt. [8] Her eyes are partially covered by semi-wild hair. [9] And stare seductively at the reader. [10] A recent television ad for perfume goes even further. [11] In this ad, a boy not older than twelve reaches out to a beautiful woman. [12] Sexily dressed in a dark room filled with sensuous music. [13] With such ads, it is no wonder that young people seem preoccupied with sex.

■ **Editing Test 9**

See if you can locate and correct the ten sentence-skills mistakes in the following passage. The mistakes are listed in the box below. As you locate mistakes, put the sentence numbers in the spaces provided.

1 sentence fragment _____	2 missing apostrophes _____
1 run-on _____	_____
1 mistake in subject-verb agreement _____	1 nonparallel structure _____
2 missing commas after introductory material	1 dangling modifier _____
_____ _____	1 mistake in pronoun point of view _____

₁Being a waitress is an often underrated job. ₂A waitress needs the tact of a diplomat, she must be as organized as a business executive, and the ability of an acrobat. ₃Serving as the link between customers and kitchen, the most demanding diners must be satisfied and the often-temperamental kitchen help must be kept tamed. ₄Both groups tend to blame the waitress whenever anything goes wrong. ₅Somehow, she is held responsible by the customer for any delay (even if it's the kitchens fault), for an overcooked steak, or for an unavailable dessert. ₆While the kitchen automatically blames her for the diners who change their orders or return those burned steaks. ₇In addition she must simultaneously keep straight who ordered what at each table, who is yelling for the check, and whether the new arrivals want cocktails or not. ₈She must be sure empty tables are cleared, everyone has refills of coffee, and no one is scowling because a request for more rolls are going unheard. ₉Finally the waitress must travel a hazardous route between the busy kitchen and the crowded dining room, she has to dodge a diners leg in the aisle or a swinging kitchen door. ₁₀And you must do this while balancing a tray heaped with steaming platters. ₁₁The hardest task of the waitress, though, is trying to maintain a decent imitation of a smile on her face—most of the time.

■ Editing Test 10

See if you can locate and correct the ten sentence-skills mistakes in the following passage. The mistakes are listed in the box below. As you locate mistakes, put the sentence numbers in the spaces provided.

2 sentence fragments _____	2 missing capital letters
_____	
1 run-on _____	_____ _____
2 irregular verbs _____	1 mistake in pronoun point of view _____
_____	1 subject pronoun mistake _____
1 misplaced modifier _____	

¹The thirtieth anniversary party of my uncle and aunt was the worst family gathering I've ever attended. ²On a hot saturday morning in july, Mom and I drove out into the country to Uncle Ted's house. ³It had already rained heavily, and the only place left to park was in a muddy field. ⁴Then, you would not believe the crowd. ⁵There must have been two hundred people in Uncle Ted's small yard, including his five daughters with their husbands and children, all the other relatives, all the neighbors, and the entire congregation of their church. ⁶Since the ground was soaked and light rain was falling. ⁷Mom and me went under the big rented canopy with everybody else. ⁸We couldn't move between the tables, and the humidity fogged my glasses. ⁹After wiping my glasses, I seen that there was a lot of food. ¹⁰It was mainly cold chicken and potato and macaroni salads, I ate a lot just because there was nothing else to do. ¹¹We were surprised that Uncle Ted and his wife were doing all the work themselves. ¹²They ran back and forth with trays of food and gathered trash into plastic bags staggering with exhaustion. ¹³It didn't seem like much of a way to celebrate. ¹⁴Mom was upset that she didn't get to speak with them. ¹⁵When we left, I was hot, sticky, and sick to my stomach from overeating. ¹⁶But quickly pushed our car out of the mud and got us on the road. ¹⁷I have never been happier to leave a party.

INDEX

CORRECTION SYMBOLS

Here is a list of symbols your instructor may use when marking papers. The numbers in parentheses refer to the pages that explain the skill involved.

Agr	Correct the mistake in agreement of subject and verb (329–337) or pronoun and the word the pronoun refers to (356–358).
Apos	Correct the apostrophe mistake (382–387).
Bal	Balance the parts of the sentence so they have the same (parallel) form (351–354).
Cap	Correct the mistake in capital letters (374–381).
Coh	Revise to improve coherence (62–71; 94–96).
Comma	Add a comma (395–404).
CS	Correct the comma splice (308–319).
DM	Correct the dangling modifier (346–350).
Det	Support or develop the topic more fully by adding details (40–44; 91–93).
Frag	Attach the fragment to a sentence or make it a sentence (294–307).
lc	Use a lowercase (small) letter rather than a capital (380).
MM	Correct the misplaced modifier (343–345).
¶	Indent for a new paragraph.
No ¶	Do not indent for a new paragraph.
Pro	Correct the pronoun mistake (355–367).
Quot	Correct the mistake in quotation marks (388–394).
R-O	Correct the run-on (308–319).
Sp	Correct the spelling error (417–436).
Trans	Supply or improve a transition (66–69).
Und	Underline (392).
Verb	Correct the verb or verb form (320–328; 335–342).
Wordy	Omit needless words (442–446).
WW	Replace the word marked with a more accurate one.
?	Write clearly the illegible word.
/	Eliminate the word, letter, or punctuation mark so slashed.
$\wedge$	Add the omitted word or words.
;/:/-/—/	Add the semicolon (406) or colon (405) or hyphen (408) or dash (406).
√	You have something fine or good here: an expression, a detail, an idea.